World Right Side Up

World Right Side Up

Investing Across Six Continents

CHRISTOPHER MAYER

WILEY
John Wiley & Sons, Inc.

Published by John Wiley & Sons, Inc., Hoboken, New Jersey.
Published simultaneously in Canada.

For general information on our other products and services or for technical support, please contact our Customer Care Department within the United States at (800) 762–2974, outside the United States at (317) 572–3993 or fax (317) 572–4002.

Wiley also publishes its books in a variety of electronic formats. Some content that appears in print may not be available in electronic books. For more information about Wiley products, visit our website at www.wiley.com.

Library of Congress Cataloging-in-Publication Data:

Mayer, Christopher W., 1972-
    World right side up : investing across six continents / Christopher W. Mayer.
        1 online resource.
    Includes index.
        Description based on print version record and CIP data provided by publisher; resource not viewed.
    ISBN 978-1-118-17140-0 (cloth); ISBN 978-1-118-22679-7 (ebk);
    ISBN 978-1-118-23978-0 (ebk); ISBN 978-1-118-26450-8 (ebk)
    1. Investments, Foreign. 2. Investments. 3. International finance. I. Title.
    HG4538
    332.67'3–dc23

                                                                    2012006627

Printed in the United States of America

10 9 8 7 6 5 4 3 2 1

Contents

Foreword

Sometimes It's Different

The material progress in the developed world over the past 300 years is undeniable. But the closer you examine it, the less it appears as a tribute to how clever the human race is, and the more it seems to be an illustration of how lucky Europeans have been.

Europeans embraced the Industrial Revolution. Others did not or could not. Thus, the world turned against the non-Western countries, relatively, at the beginning of the Industrial Revolution. But if the world turns long enough, it comes back to where it began. And such is the case today.

Over the past 10 years, the real, private-sector economies of the developed world have grown at medieval rates. Meanwhile, the emerging markets have enjoyed a growth spurt. They are catching up breathtakingly fast.

When I was a student in 1969, I visited Paris. I went back to live in Paris in 1999, 30 years later. Almost nothing had changed. Same buildings. Same people. Except for the automobiles people drove and the clothes they wore, you would barely know that it had changed at all.

In the early 1980s, I went to China. I was taken to a barren track of dirt and dust and told that a new city, Shenzhen, would be built there. It was hard to believe. The whole country seemed desolate, gritty, and poor. When I returned in 2010, it was not the same country. There are believed to be three times as many people living in Shenzhen as in the whole Paris metropolitan area, and it is only one of dozens of new cities. Beijing, which used to be such a gray, empty, and lifeless place, is a city of gleaming towers, luxury automobiles, and traffic jams that can stretch for a hundred miles.

There is a lesson in all of this.

Most people see material progress as a result of continual innovation, investment, and technical achievement. We have come to see it that way because that is how it has appeared for generations. Once the enlightenment was reached, we thought continued material progress was guaranteed. The scientific method made improvements routine, examing new ideas and re-examined old ones, systematically rejecting what was unsound and adding to the accumulated knowledge of the human race. Freed from the limitations of the past, we could look forward to more wealth and knowledge, forever.

But the world doesn't work that way. No one stays on top for long. Competitors are everywhere.

For example, agriculture seems to have begun in the fertile crescent of Mes-opotamia and the Valley of the Nile long before elsewhere. But the richness cre-ated by sedentary farming proved a lure for the steppe tribes, who seemed to have had an edge of their own. They had learned how to use the horse, to hunt, and to fight. Mounted warriors raided and later conquered the farmers.

Likewise, the tribes who invented the bow and arrow must have played hell with those who had not.

Technological progress did not bless all of the world's people evenly or at the same time. In the jungles of South America, Southeast Asia, and Africa, as recently as a few years ago, there were people who still lived as they had 10,000 or 20,000 years earlier.

In Europe, Asia, and America at the time of America's discovery, there were advanced civilizations of roughly similar standards of living. (I am probably being a little generous to the Americans of the fifteenth century.) Neither Inca nor Aztec civilizations could rival those of Europe or Asia. The Americans didn't even use the wheel. Still, in 1600, there was probably not much difference between the living standard of a serf in Europe, a slave in China, or a field hand in the Andes.

It is no surprise that those who took up the use of fossil fuels first and most aggressively, backed by institutions and customs that had evolved to suit the new technology, stole a march on their competitors.

Europe, and its colonies, raced ahead on coal-fired trains and oil-fired battleships until it had destroyed the civilizations of the New World and tamed those of Asia. India was host to the French and the Portuguese, before being taken over completely by the English. Japan was forced to open its doors to foreign trade and became a rapid, gifted imitator. China was be-sieged then battered by Western warships.

The world is different now. It's changing all the time, taking surprising twists and turns that create opportunities for venturesome investors. You'll read about many in this book.

Chris Mayer has traveled around the world looking for these opportuni-ties. Together, we've been to China, attended conferences in France, and dined in Nicaragua. He keeps his eyes and ears open. You'll enjoy reading about, and perhaps profiting from, what he has uncovered.

—Bill Bonner

Acknowledgments

Author Albert Jay Nock (1870–1945) once said, "You don't try to repay the help that is given you. You pass it along to others." This book is an effort in that direction, because I can never repay all the help given to me in putting it together.

I want to thank Addison Wiggin, my publisher at Agora Financial, friend and long-time booster of my work. We were bouncing around in a cab in Bogotá one day when he said to me, "I think you have another book in you." The result you hold in your hands would have been impossible without his support.

A special thanks to Samantha Buker, my associate editor at Agora, who was an enormous help in organizing and editing the mass of material into a coherent form. The book is much improved because of her efforts.

Thanks to Susi Clark for the wonderful cover and for all the charts, and to the unsung efforts of Erik Kestler, our diligent copyeditor. Thanks to all my friends at Agora Financial for their support and good cheer, especially Bill Bonner, Joe Schriefer, Eric Fry, Greg Grillot, Jack Forde, Joel Bowman, Bruce Robertson, and Mark O'Dell. Thanks to Deb Englander and Kimberly Bernard at John Wiley & Sons. And to Eric Winig, for all those conversations at HQ and the ideas they inspired. And thanks to all the people I met along the way who took time out of their busy lives to show me around. I must also thank my loyal readers who make it all possible.

Finally, thanks to my family, especially my wife Carol, who put up with my sometimes hectic travel schedule and late night and weekend writing as deadlines loomed.

Travel, its very motion, ought to suggest hope. Despair is the armchair; it is indifference and glazed, incurious eyes. I think travelers are essentially optimists, or else they would never go anywhere.
—Paul Theroux, *The Tao of Travel*

Preface

Notes before We Go

I want to say a few things about what you are about to read . . .
Please remember this book is written from the perspective of an investor—a great enthusiast of all the world's charms but still an investor searching for ideas. I'm not writing a piece of social commentary or proclaiming deep knowledge about the nature of a place or its people. My aim is to find investment opportunities and trends.

In my travels, I've met a lot of new people and gained valuable contacts. But the fact of the matter is that the spadework of successful investing is mostly done from afar. In fact, many of my most successful investments came from companies I never met in places I've never been. That is as it should be.

A great investment idea should be plain, clear, and nearly obvious. I say "should" because many times they are, but there are always exceptions. The idea of investors harboring secrets and holding insider knowledge is something drummed up by people as a way to explain something they don't understand. It's propagated by many people in the business to whom such ideas are self-serving.

Most investing insights come from unglamorous trolling of publicly available data, mixed with some creative foresight and a good stomach not afraid to stand against a crowd. Conviction, patience, diligence: These are more important than secrets (or travel, for that matter).

I'm a big believer in history as a teacher. Sometimes, the best history books don't come from the desks of historians. They come from the works of inquisitive and observant scribblers at the scene, suffused with the immediacy of the moment and of what they see and hear. The insights are fresh when recorded, unspoiled by the editing of long memory looking back over many years.

You'll see I often refer to the works of travelers. On a trip to China, I picked up a used copy of *Shark's Fins and Millet*, written by Ilona Ralf Sues, a journalist who traveled to China in the late 1930s. Sues' book is a personal look at China as she traveled it: Canton (now Guangzhou), Shanghai, Nanjing, Hankou, Shanxi, and Yan'an. In her words, the book:

> . . . *is neither a study, nor a travelogue, nor a political treatise. It is a medley of everything, as unorthodox as life itself—an unconventional set of stories and anecdotes—a series of big and small events, of great and little people observed, not through a high-powered microscope, but with the imperfect, naked, sympathetic, twinkling human eye.*

I write this book in that spirit.

What does all this have to do with the stock market and investing? A good investor is a worldly investor who has an understanding and appreciation of how the world works and how it came to be. Reading old (and new) travel books has given me a glimpse of such things. It teaches me how to ask better questions of my hosts: traders, fund managers, bartenders and cabbies alike.

I've been lucky to be able to see the world. They say travel broadens the mind. Maybe it does. Or maybe they have it backward. Maybe it's the broad-minded people who travel. When I think of all the wonderful, well-traveled people I've met out there on the road, I can't help but believe that's the right way to put it. It's a memorable experience to bump into another American in a bar in a small town somewhere in southern Brazil. Odds are he's worth chatting with, a curious mind with good stories to tell about his own small discoveries.

For me, a place is always about the people I've met and, especially, those who took some time from their own busy lives to show around a curious traveler. You'll meet more than a few of them in the pages that follow.

—Chris Mayer

CHAPTER 1

The World Right Side Up

O ne thought always strikes me in my travels. I'll be sitting in a comfortable bistro in Medellín with its doors open to the warm night air wafting in gently from a quiet street, in a restaurant on a man-made island gazing up at the tallest tower in the world twinkling on a starless night in Dubai, at a bar in Cape Town, in a noodle shop in Beijing, or countless other places around this ever-fascinating planet of ours. And the thought will hit me.

If I close my eyes, I could easily imagine myself in New York, Washington, D.C., or any number of American cities. Of course, each of these places is different from each other in many ways, and yet they are much the same.

People are people around the world. They like many of the same things. They want to have a better life. They want to have a safe home, wear clothes they like, and have friends. They want to have leisure time and eat well. They all want something.

They share all the same traits that make us human. People everywhere are humble and vain, generous and greedy, wise and foolish, and many other qualities besides. They've made mistakes. They have hopes and dreams.

Yet great disparities and differences exist, too. Since the Industrial Revolution, the Western world—mainly the United States and Western Europe—has vaulted well ahead of everyone else. Traditionally wealthy economies, such as China and India and parts of the Middle East, were left far behind. The Western world dominated—in manufacturing might and in military power, especially.

This gap probably reached its apex sometime in the 1950s. According to *Power and Plenty*, a good reference book on trade, the Western world (excluding Japan) represented 90 percent of the world's manufacturing output as late as 1953. The United States bestrode the globe as Tiger Woods once lorded it over golf's majors. America's economy alone was nearly half of the world's industrial output.

But things started to change in the late twentieth century. The gaps narrowed. And these trends continue to unfold in the present. My thesis is that such narrowing of the gaps will continue for decades. This will be the most important long-term investment theme of the twenty-first century.

I call it "the world right side up" because it is, in my mind, a more natural world, more the way the world ought to be. It's a Western conceit to think that the current technical, economic, and military superiority of the West is normal. When you look at the history of our planet over a longer time frame, the dominance of the West is a relatively recent affair.

The Polynesians had prosperous farming villages across a great swathe of the South Pacific while Europeans were still living in caves. In double canoes, using only the stars and their wits, Polynesians crossed distances as great as those of Columbus thousands of years before Christ was born. And of course, you surely already know the long list of inventions first made by people in China or Arabia.

The distinctions between "emerging markets" and "developed markets" are starting to disappear. Indeed, the term may already be obsolete. Such is the thesis of Everest Capital, which made the case in a white paper called "The End of Emerging Markets."

First, in terms of size, these emerging markets make up about half of the global economy. Take a look at Figure 1.1. GDP, or gross domestic product, is a flawed statistic, but it serves as a rough guess of economic size. "Purchasing power parity" (PPP) aims to take out the distorting effect of different currencies.

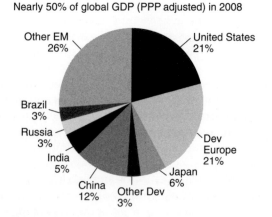

Nearly 50% of global GDP (PPP adjusted) in 2008

FIGURE 1.1 Let's Call It Even

Source: Everest Capital.

This is astonishing, but the comparisons get more interesting by country. Emerging markets make up 10 of the 20 largest economies in the world. India is bigger than Germany. Russia is bigger than the United Kingdom. Mexico is bigger than Canada. Turkey is bigger than Australia. These are things that I think would surprise the casual observer of markets, rooted in a Western view of the world as it was.

These trends will become more pronounced over time. The creation of new markets, the influx of hundreds of millions of people who will want cell phones and air conditioners and water filters, who will want to eat a more varied diet of meats and fruits and vegetables, among many other things, will have a tremendous impact on world markets. In fact, we've felt the impact in many areas, as we'll see.

In these pages, I'll focus on where these markets have been, where they are, and where they're headed. It is, necessarily, an eclectic and idiosyncratic look at the world. The world is still a big place. There are many patches of Earth and stretches of sea where I've never set foot. They are many places I don't write about here. This is not a comprehensive guide to global markets. It is one curious investor's sampling of that world.

That world is always changing. I first visited Dubai in 2007, when it was a boomtown. Buildings were going up everywhere. Trucks filled the highways. Cranes crowded the skyline. I learned later that two-thirds of the world's cranes were in Dubai back then. It had all the buzz and confidence of boomtowns I've seen in many other places.

My second trip was in October 2009, when everything was bust. It was a completely different place. There were still cranes, but they weren't moving. The many construction sites were still there, but there was no activity on most of them. The place was dead. The third palm island dredged out of the Arabian Gulf—it's never the Persian Gulf in that part of the world—wasted away in the waves and wind.

That's part of the business. Just when you think you've got a bead on a place, something happens that forces you to revisit all you thought you knew.

But the broader narrative never changes. The rest of world is catching up. That's the overwhelming tidal force in markets, and one that will continue to surge on its shores well into the twenty-first century. (Dubai is coming back, slowly, but surely. It's not going away; we'll take a look in Chapter 7).

The evidence is all around us, as you'll see in these pages. Every day, I find new snippets of it as I peruse the *Wall Street Journal* and the *Financial Times*. As I travel and meet people and research new investment ideas, I am confronted with this narrowing gap again and again. These experiences inspired this book.

The key idea is simply that the Industrial Revolution set off a yawning gap between the "West" and the "rest of the world." That gap is shrinking and will continue to shrink. Don't be afraid of this change. All is as it should be. The aberration was the last 200 years. The anomaly was that China, in 1970, had an economy smaller than that of Belgium. For hundreds of years before that, it was the world's largest economy.

It may already be on top again.

Arvind Subramanian, a senior fellow at the Peterson Institute, makes the case that China's economy is already the largest in the world, passing the United States in 2010. "On this basis," he writes, "the average American is 'only' four times as wealthy as the average Chinese, not 11 times as rich, as the conventional numbers suggest."

It might seem funny to you that we can't to seem agree on how big economies are. But it is not easy to estimate the size of something that doesn't sit still—so you can count it—and that consists of billions of transactions. All of these things are estimates, but the impact China's had on the global economy is real and not in doubt. We'll take a look at China in Chapter 5.

I stay away from statistical abstractions like GDP. What is GDP, or gross domestic product, exactly? What does it mean, and why should we care? The truth is there is an awful lot of guesswork in such figures, and they are not practical. You could lead a very successful and rich life as an investor and never know a thing about GDP figures.

In this book, I will stay away from such economic monstrosities as much as possible. This book is a boots-on-the-ground view, a first-hand look. It's more practical, and the aim is to stay close to what is happening and what we can understand in more tangible ways.

For instance, we may debate the size of China's economy—as many people spend an inordinate time doing—but don't doubt its impact. Take a look at Figure 1.2 to see the tangible impact of the growth of China on commodities.

So it is impossible to be an investor in iron ore, coal, or wheat without considering what's happening in China.

In any event, my view here is that we are headed back to a world more in line with a "normal" historical perspective. It is a world right side up.

The work of Angus Maddison, the late British economist, offers this helpful illustration. Again, I am skeptical of the ability to measure economic size in general—much less for, say, 1600—but I think Figure 1.3 makes intuitive sense.

During the Song Dynasty (960–1279), for instance, the capital city of Hangzhou had a population over a million people. It was one of the world's most advanced cities. Lars Tvede describes it in *Supertrends*:

Here you could find hundreds of restaurants, hotels, and theaters. There were tea houses with landscaped gardens, large colored lamps, fine porcelain, and calligraphy and paintings by famous artists. The night-life was rich and varied, and there were professional puppeteers, sword swallowers, theater actors, acrobats, musicians, snake charmers, storytellers, and whatnot. People with special interest could join exotic food clubs, antiquarian and art collector clubs, music clubs, horse-loving clubs, and poetry clubs. All of that about 1,000 years ago.

So, in some ways, the seemingly sudden and unprecedented boom in China is more a return to what was, when Chinese cities were among the largest and most advanced in the world. It's not there yet, but to anyone who's walked the Bund in Shanghai or seen the gleaming new airport terminal in Beijing or even visited the modern fashion shops in today's Hangzhou, you see the trend unfolding.

I mentioned Everest Capital's white paper earlier. It points to a few more ways in which you see how the gaps are closing.

One is to look at simple liquidity. Not that long ago, the value of IBM shares changing hands in a single day in New York were worth more than all the shares that traded hands in Shanghai or Bombay on a given day. No more.

China's consumption of select commodities,
as a percentage of world consumption

Commodity	China % of World
Cement	53.2%
Iron Ore	47.7%
Coal	46.9%
Pigs	46.4%
Steel	45.4%
Lead	44.6%
Zinc	41.3%
Aluminum	40.6%
Copper	38.9%
Eggs	37.2%
Nickel	36.3%
Rice	28.1%
Soybeans	24.6%
Wheat	16.6%
Chickens	15.6%
Oil	10.3%
Cattle	9.5%

FIGURE 1.2 China: Hungry Dragon

Source: Barclays Capital, Credit Suisse, Goldman Sachs, U.S. Geological Survey, BP Statistical Review of World Energy, Food and Agriculture Organization of the United Nations, IMF.

	Western Europe	Former Soviet Union	United States	Japan	China	India
1500	17.9%	3.4%	0.3%	3.1%	25.0%	24.5%
1600	20.0	3.5	0.2	2.9	29.1	22.5
1700	22.5	4.4	0.1	4.1	22.3	24.4
1820	23.6	5.4	1.8	3.0	32.9	16.0
1870	33.6	7.6	8.9	2.3	17.2	12.2
1913	33.5	8.6	19.1	2.6	8.9	7.6
1950	26.3	9.6	27.3	3.0	4.5	4.1
1973	25.7	9.4	22.0	7.7	4.6	3.1
1998	20.6	3.4	21.9	7.6	11.5	5.0
2008	17.1	4.4	18.6	5.7	17.5	6.7

FIGURE 1.3 Shifting Mix of Global GDP

Source: Morgan Stanley Research.

Today's emerging markets are large and liquid. As Everest Capital pointed out at the time of its report, "Chinese markets (granted, there is a lot of retail turnover there) traded more than the NYSE; Hong Kong and Korea traded more than Germany; India traded more than France; and Taiwan traded more than Italy, Australia, or Canada."

Others see shifting changes in the world's financial markets. My colleague and friend, Eric Fry, at *The Daily Reckoning*, pointed out a few in a piece titled "A Shrinking Distinction."

"The First might become last . . . and the Last, first" Fry wrote. "Generally speaking, the mature economies of the West are slipping, relative to many emerging economies around the globe. The First have not become last just yet, but they are working on it."

He pointed to the five-year credit default swap (CDS) on AAA-rated French government debt as compared to that of Chile's AA-rated debt. (A CDS is a kind of insurance against default. The higher the risk, the higher the price of the CDS.) Remarkably, Chile's CDS rate was lower.

This is not an isolated event; it is of a piece of what's going on all over. The CDS rate on French debt was higher than Brazilian, Peruvian, and Colombian debt. That would've been unimaginable 10 years ago! All three of the latter countries carry BBB-ratings, too, one notch above junk. But the market renders its own judgments, ahead of and more accurately than ratings agencies.

"Ten years ago," Fry continues, "Portugal, Ireland, and Greece were highly rated sovereign borrowers. Ireland was AAA. Meanwhile, Brazil, Peru, and Colombia were all 'junk credits.' Figure 1.4 below shows what has happened since. Today, Brazil, Peru, and Colombia are all investment grade, while Portugal, Ireland, and Greece are all junk credits."

And over this time frame, the stock markets of Brazil, Chile, and Colombia trounced the Europeans' as you can see in Figure 1.5.

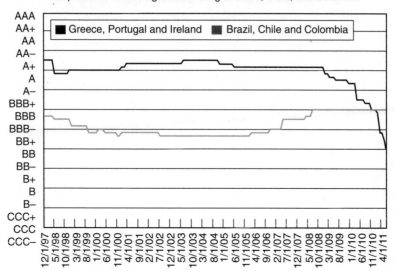

FIGURE 1.4 Submerging Markets

Source: AgoraFinancial.com.

FIGURE 1.5 World Markets Turn Right Side Up

Source: AgoraFinancial.com.

"This glimpse into the past," Fry offered, "will also be a glimpse into the future. Capital flees from abusive relationships and seeks out environments where it can be fruitful and multiply."

That is a core truth of wealth creation. That truth drives the world's financial markets to turn right side up.

Everest Capital's exhibits should shake off doubt from even the most moss-backed investor. The brontosaurus's lagoon is no longer his alone. His world has changed. He must compete with new furry and nimble animals.

Beyond this, Everest continues to clear away old attitudes as a man with a broom sweeps away cobwebs. For instance, "The belief that companies in the United States, Western Europe, or Japan are better managed than in emerging markets is also no longer valid. We meet a large number of managements in emerging market countries, and it is impressive to see how quickly they have adopted the best practices in terms of disclosure, governance, and creating shareholder value."

Supercycles: Where We Are Today?

I am not the only one who has picked up on this idea, which is broadly applicable to many areas of investing. For instance, in early 2011, I attended the 49 North Resources conference in Manhattan, meeting with mining companies and gathering intelligence. I heard mining strategist Christopher Ecclestone give a talk titled "A Mining Supercycle?"

I thought to myself: "Of course, he'll say we're in a mining supercycle and how wonderful mining is. I'm at a mining conference, for crying out loud, surrounded by mining companies and geologists. To expect otherwise is like walking into a Star Trek convention expecting to hear a guy talk about how dumb the whole show was."

Yet he surprised me. He said no, this isn't a mining supercycle. In fact, he turned the idea on its head. What he said folds neatly into our world right side up idea.

As you know, commodities have been going up in recent years, everything from copper to coal. It's getting harder to find big deposits of some of this stuff, and what we find is more expensive to dig out.

The Chinese get what's going on. They are securing supplies of those key resources of which they consume so much. So they're making deals with Brazil, all over Africa, and in a bunch of other places.

Ecclestone had a good line about the Chinese. He said they are more interested in natural resources than they are in intellectual property "because they know they can rip those off. It's harder to rip off a coal mine."

But Ecclestone's main point is that what we're seeing isn't anything new. It's not a new supercycle for mining. It's a return to normal. The aberration, he said, was the period from 1973 to 2003, when mining experienced its dark age.

The aberration was the kind of thinking that took natural resources for granted. "Metals and agricultural commodities were the epitome of cheap—regarded with some contempt as common and plentiful," he said. "The apogee of this disdain for minerals was during the tech boom."

Then, an immaterial service-oriented company like Pets.com could command a market cap of billions of dollars. You could've bought any number of mining companies for a fraction of that. "Today, Pets.com has evaporated into thin air," Ecclestone said, while the mines remain and are very valuable.

The 1973–2003 time frame "was a calamitous period for miners and commodity producers," he continued. "The only commodity for which the sun shone was oil, and even then the late 1990s were gruesome."

There was a brutal thinning of the herd of mining companies, particularly in the 1990s and particularly in the United States. During this time, we "lost" major mining companies—Anaconda, Kennecott Utah Corp., Magma Copper, Asarco, and many others. "And these were just the big ones," Ecclestone added. The mid-size and smaller miners were almost wiped out. We saw the "virtual annihilation of the U.S.-listed mining sector."

Metals became loss leaders. Capital spending fell. Exploration came to a near halt. Most of the mines in Africa closed. Miners also shut down many marginal or low-grade mines. Instead, they focused on the highest-grade ore, the low-hanging fruit of the mining world, just to stay alive.

Why did this happen?

Ecclestone cites a number of reasons that combined to create a kind of perfect storm. The postwar period created a proliferation of mega mines. China, too, became a low-cost producer of a number of metals. It has come to dominate certain sectors entirely (such as zinc and rare earths). Many mines in Africa and South America fell under state control. These states operated them without regard to economics. Later, the Soviet Union's industrial base collapsed, releasing a lot more commodities on the market. And Cold War stockpiling of metals stopped and reversed, releasing even more supply on the market.

But Ecclestone says, we are returning to something that more closely approximates what prevailed for a much larger slice of history.

The normal state is one that understands and recognizes the value of mineral commodities. The normal state is one in which the producers of these useful rocks and metals earn rewards for the risk and ownership of scarce resources.

Today, no new mega mines exist. The stockpiles are dwindling. That low-hanging fruit is gone. Today, for example, copper miners have to dig up 50 percent more rock than they did in 1994 to get the same amount of copper. And demand continues to grow apace.

An example of that demand is copper production going all the way back to 1900. Take a look at the nearby chart. Copper is not an exception. You can make the same point with any number of metals. "Where are the downturns in this?" Ecclestone asked showing a version of Figure 1.6. They are comparatively minor and short in a long climb upward. "There is no reason to think copper use shouldn't go onward and upward."

Far from being a special case or an outlier, the growing use of commodities looks normal against a long time series.

As commodities get more expensive, we'll have to change how we use and apply them. "If a lot of commodities get too expensive, then you have replacement and rationing," Ecclestone said. We could see this soon, as commodities price themselves out of some markets. Boeing opened a window into this future with its announcement that it is considering making the 737—the most widely flown commercial jet—out of plastic.

Ecclestone predicts that when it comes to some metals (lead, for example), recycling will largely replace the need for mining. "In rare earths," Ecclestone offered by way of example, "there is little recycling, but there will be more recycling soon."

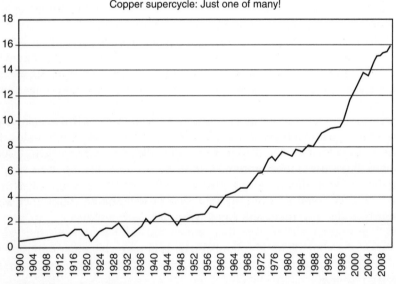

FIGURE 1.6 Find the Downturn

Source: Christopher Ecclestone.

Many interesting investment ideas spin off these last few paragraphs that are not necessarily mining related, but more about specialty materials and getting more out of what we have. A key investing theme for the next decade is how to make materials that make things more efficient, better, and/or longer lasting. There will be many such opportunities.

Even so, the business of mining will remain vital for many commodities. Ecclestone summed up: "[What we are seeing] is a reversal of the late 20th-century trend, which gave all the value to the service and intellectual property. . . . The whip hand is back with the owners of the inputs."

Our present age is not so much a new era as a return to a more historical norm. Another way to see this is to look at trade.

World's Economy Is Bigger—and More Open—Than Ever Before

In a little white-walled Spanish-style cottage overlooking a spectacular beach in Nicaragua, I presented to a small group of investors. I shocked them by saying this: The world's economy is twice the size it was a decade ago.

Think about that. Despite all the bad stuff that has gone down in recent years—including a big financial crisis and the ensuing recession—the global economy is nearly double what it was only 10 years ago!

Living in the United States (or Europe or Japan), one might wonder how that could be. Obviously, these economies didn't grow that much. Instead, most of the action is beyond the borders of these mature economies, which has a lot to do with why I was in Nicaragua in the first place.

We live during a time that future historians will cite as a hinge in the history of markets. For the first time since before the Industrial Revolution, the so-called emerging markets will be bigger than the Western countries (including Japan). This gap will widen as emerging markets continue to grow faster.

Global trade, too, is more important than ever. "The Super-Cycle Report" is a fascinating research piece put out by Standard Chartered. It shows us just how important global trade flows have become. In fact, global exports are nearly at their prerecession peaks.

Trade made the explosive growth in the world economy over the last 10 years possible. China goes nowhere without its ability to trade for commodities abroad, and Brazil goes nowhere without the ability to supply them.

Trade has been a fertilizing influence since time immemorial. Think of the camel trains laden with silk, indigo, and jewels, making their way across the land mass of Asia to the cities of the West in ancient times. Think of the old galleons under starry skies carrying spices and gold during the age of sail. What a different world it would be with closed borders.

Today, the world is more open than it has ever been. One way to see this is to look at exports as a percentage of the global economy. Today they are at all-time highs.

As an investor, it's been the right call to focus on companies that had exposure to rapidly growing markets overseas. This happy circumstance is something to keep an eye on because trade ebbs and flows. In 1945, for instance, trade was 40 percent below the level of 1913. How did that happen? Let us count the ways: two world wars, the fall of the Austro-Hungarian and Ottoman empires, hyperinflation in Germany, the Great Depression, and the demise of the gold standard. It was a tough 30 years.

The emerging markets still have a lot of catching up to do, which should power expanding trade for years to come. Standard Chartered points out that China's per capita income is still only 9 percent of the United States', or about where the United States was in 1878. If it were to get to half of the United States' total, China's economy would be twice the size of the United States'. Then consider Indonesia—the world's fourth most populous country. It has a per capita income only two-thirds that of China.

Don't underestimate the ability of a poor country to grow very rapidly for a long time under the power of open markets. The authors of the report note: "Since 1945, every country recognized for outstandingly rapid development has achieved 7 percent growth for twenty-five years or more, including China, Hong Kong, Indonesia, Japan, Korea, Malaysia, Singapore, and Thailand."

There are new contenders for the years ahead. Standard Chartered created a "Seven Percent Club." These are countries it estimates will grow 7 percent a year over the next 10 years—doubling in size. These happen to include almost half of the world's population. They are China, India, Indonesia, Bangladesh, Nigeria, Vietnam, Ethiopia, Tanzania, Uganda, and Mozambique. Others that ought to grow fast but will likely fall short of the 7 percent mark include Russia, Brazil, Pakistan, Mexico, the Philippines, Egypt, Turkey, and Korea.

Plenty of rich patches of Earth still exist where the pixie dust of the Industrial Revolution never fell or never really got to do its thing. China was, by far, the world's largest economy until the nineteenth century. It was left behind thereafter but is catching up again.

One of the effects of this second Industrial Revolution is that more and more people live in cities. By 2030, the authors of the report guess that 60 percent of the world's population will be urban dwellers, compared with only 29 percent in 1950.

"Historically, commodity consumption has significantly increased as annual per capita income approaches a level deemed 'middle class,'" the authors continue. "The next 20 years will bring an unprecedented increase in the number of people living in cities (close to 5 billion people will live in cities by 2030, compared with 3.4 billion). . . . [with] an equally significant increase in the size of the global middle class (from 1.8 billion in 2009 to about 5 billion in 2030)."

As an investor, your mouth should be watering. Think of what so many new consumers mean for businesses ranging from beer brewers to financial services companies. Consumers will use more stuff, eat more food, and use more water. They will buy more TVs, laptops, motorcycles, cars, and mobile phones.

The Old Silk Road and the New

> To follow the Silk Road is to follow a ghost. It flows through the heart of Asia, but it has officially vanished. . . .
> —Colin Thubron, *Shadow of the Silk Road*

A powerful metaphor that describes what is going on is the Silk Road. Its ghostly trade routes are reawakening.

The old Silk Road was not even a road in the normal sense of that term. It was, as travel writer Colin Thubron describes it, "a shifting fretwork of arteries and veins, laid to the Mediterranean." Thubron covered 7,000 miles in eight months following the old trails of this fabled trade route.

The Silk Road stretched from Antioch, Turkey, all the way to old Chang'an, or what is today known as Xi'an, in China. For a long time, it had no name. A German geographer coined the term "Silk Road" in 1877.

Yet traffic along the Silk Road goes way back into the slipstream of humanity's past. Thubron writes: "Chinese silk from 1500 B.C. has turned up in tombs in north Afghanistan, and strands were discovered twisted into the hair of a tenth-century B.C. Egyptian mummy." Archeologists found silk dating from 1100 B.C. lying in the grave of a prince in Germany. The stuff got around.

The Silk Road carried much more than just silk across its rugged landscape. From China, the West got jade, lacquer, ceramics, the first roses, azaleas, as well as oranges, peaches, mulberries, apricots, and rhubarb. Coming from the West to the East came glass, gold, silver, Indian spices, gems, and linen along with fig trees, flax, pomegranates, jasmine, dates, and olives.

Back and forth went vegetables, fruits, furniture, artifacts of all kinds, musical instruments, even slaves and weapons. The crossbow, a Chinese invention, made its way across the old Silk Road to arm the Norman and Capetian kings in their battle with the dreaded English longbow at Crécy (in which they were famously defeated).

The old Silk Road embraced almost every national and ethnic group from Arabia to Japan, including Persians, Turks, Sogdians, Syrians, Indians, and many others. (Often called the greatest Silk Road traders, the Sogdians were an Iranian people. The Chinese thought them born traders. Myth held that "their mothers fed them sugar to honey their voices, and their baby palms were daubed with paste to attract profitable things," writes Thubron.)

None of them made the journey the whole way through. No Roman ever walked the streets of Xi'an or visited the tomb of the Yellow Emperor. No Chinese trader ever gazed upon the pillars of imperial Rome or dipped his toes in the Mediterranean Sea.

Instead, the Silk Road was more like a long relay race. Only luxury items could generally make the whole journey—the jade and the silk, for example—or perhaps incidental items people carried with them, like a flute or an old trader's pipe. It was simply too expensive to ship most things the whole distance, except those things for which people were willing to pay a heavy price.

Still, the old Silk Road was the dominant trade route in human history for over a thousand years. Its importance diminished only sometime in the sixteenth century, when ships replaced the harrowing journey overland and transported goods much cheaper and faster.

There is a Silk Road revival, though, at least metaphorically. The old trading posts worked in storied cities such as Samarkand, Kashgar, and Meshed. The new Silk Road weaves through Dubai, Riyadh, through Mumbai and Chennai in India, to Kuala Lumpur, Singapore, Hong Kong—even as far as Tokyo.

Like the old Silk Road, the new one is not a road, either. But it's a great way to describe the surge in trade between the Middle East and Asia. From 1995 to 2005, trade between these two regions increased fourfold, according to McKinsey & Co. Projections call for trade between the six members of the Gulf Cooperation Council (GCC)—Bahrain, Kuwait, Oman, Qatar, Saudi Arabia, and the United Arab Emirates—and East Asia to explode from $59 billion to $300–500 billion by 2020.

Rapidly growing Asian economies have, at least in part, driven demand for oil. Higher oil prices in recent years mean overflowing GCC coffers. They need to put that treasure to work. More and more, it is winding up in Asia.

It's a feedback loop. More growth in Asia means more demand for oil—with more and more coming from the Middle East. By 2030, estimates put half of China's oil imports coming from the Middle East. Asia—including India—could account for half the increase in the world's demand for oil. That means more cash for the GCC and more investment in Asia—in real estate development, banking, communications, and infrastructure.

In the meantime, Chinese, Indian, and other Asian companies are active in the Middle East. They bring low-cost consumer goods (Dubai is already home to Chinamexmart, which McKinsey describes as a "mini-city of Chinese companies distributing their products throughout the region"). Asian companies also bid on major construction projects in the Middle East.

Travel traffic is a great barometer of economic activity. As late as 2000, there were only seven daily flights between the Gulf states and China. Today, there are over 50.

Thubron notes on his trip how the influence of the old Silk Road flowed into even remote hamlets. "The nervous system of the Silk Road radiated into the poorest extremities," he writes. "It traversed minor ecological divides, as well as empires."

One economist who has a lot of this figured out is Ben Simpfendorfer. His excellent study of this re-emergence of trade with the Arab world and China is *The New Silk Road: How a Rising Arab World Is Turning Away from the West and Rediscovering China.*

Simpfendorfer's Arabic and Mandarin served him well in his 15 years traveling the New Silk Road from Beirut to Beijing. He got stories straight from individual traders and actual people.

I met up with Ben one day when he was in Washington, D.C., and we talked about the changing world, appropriately, at a fusion restaurant. We've since struck up a correspondence. (You can follow Ben's adventures in his newsletter called *China Insider.*)

One of his most memorable meetings is with a wealthy Syrian trader in Damascus. They meet in a ramshackle 500-year-old office. "Wooden barrels filled with spices and sweets spill out into the streets," he writes. "The air is rich with the scent of olive soap and musky perfume." The stalls here have been hawking their wares for centuries, and today, more of these wares come from China.

He meets with other businesspeople in Yiwu, Cairo, Beijing, and many other cities, all offering human-level portraits of this New Silk Road. Change is happening at the grassroots level. "Who notices the activities of an Arab trader in Yiwu or a Chinese trader in Damascus?" he writes. "It isn't obvious how their activities have a meaningful impact on life in America and Europe." But this is how major changes begin, with smaller changes at the margin.

Dubai, for example, houses the Dragon Mart. It is the largest building to sell exclusively Chinese-made goods outside of China. It measures nearly 1.6 million square feet. And China seems to go out of its way to make Arabs feel at home in China, even using state money to build mosques. According to the book, the Chinese will issue visas for visiting Egyptians in 24 hours. It takes 18 days for an Egyptian to get one for America. This is just another among a string of many similar anecdotes.

In the bigger-picture sense, oil drives the strengthening of these ties. China needs lots of oil, and the Arab oil producers have it in spades. Arab oil producers and Iran produce 30 percent of the world's oil; the IEA projects that number will rise to 38 percent by 2030. Much of it will wind up in China.

China flipped to becoming a net oil importer in 1993 and has never looked back. It is the world's fifth-largest producer of oil, but its ability to produce oil lags its own demand by a long way. It is the second-largest consumer of oil, behind only the United States.

Thanks to higher oil prices, the Arab oil producers have staggering amounts of wealth. The task of investing all of that money falls on the Arab wealth funds. These pools of money are market movers.

The Arab wealth funds are very active in non-U.S. markets. Their big purchases reveal a pattern: Djibouti, Guinea, Kenya, Malaysia, and Pakistan, for instance. Arab wealth funds are also active buyers of Chinese stocks.

On Monsoon Seas: A Glimpse of the Future

There's a second way to look at the New Silk Road: its maritime aspect. Here again, we see a revival of an old trading pattern with consequences for today.

The Indian Ocean is one of the world's great trading seas. It was the seaway for the old windblown argosies laden in spices and silk and much more. Kuwaiti booms, double-ended dhows, little sambuks from the Red Sea, and many more vessels sailed these waters to trade along its rim.

If you ever want to learn more about this storied history, turn to Alan Villiers (1903–1982), a writer and adventurer from Melbourne, Australia, who traveled all around the Indian Ocean.

His dossier is extensive, with voyages up and down the Persian Gulf, the Red Sea, and along the coast of East Africa. A decorated officer in World War II, he oversaw landing craft in the Burma campaign, among other accomplishments. Over the years, he became quite a student of the Indian Ocean's history and geography. I have his 1952 book, *Monsoon Seas: The Story of the Indian Ocean*.

In it, he writes, "The Arab, the Indian, and the Chinese have been ubiquitous merchants and fearless wanderers far longer than it is possible to say." The monsoon seas were often cheaper and quicker and sometimes safer than overland, where you often had to pay tribute as you went. "The west winds could blow a square-rigged ship from Good Hope to Australia in three weeks and less" Villiers notes, "though the distance is 6,000 miles."

It was, in part, the rise of seaborne trade that doomed the old overland Silk Road.

Villiers also weaves in his own experiences with rich descriptions that stay with you. Zanzibar is where the "scent of cloves and . . . salted shark is heavy in the air." Mombasa is a "picturesque port, with the sweet smell of copra. . . . "

Maritime bottlenecks existed then, too. For example, the straits of Bab el-Mandeb, the so-called Gates of Affliction, narrow to only 15 miles. The straits were the key to controlling trade in the Red Sea and remain so today.

These waters remain as critically important a seaway as in Villier's account. But the key commodity traded is oil. About 40 percent of all the trade between China and the Arab world is oil, which makes the strategic importance of this ocean once again very great.

"Asia's is a largely maritime history, carried on the monsoon winds," *The Economist* has noted. "Asia's modern 'miracle'—economies plugged into globalized networks of supply and demand—is essentially a littoral story too, even when it falters, as now."

"Littoral" is an old word meaning "of, or pertaining to, the shore"—in this case, the rim of the Indian Ocean. Examine a map and let your fingers run around the edges of the Indian Ocean. This littoral territory stretches from East Africa, around the Saudi peninsula, to India, Southeast Asia, and Australia.

Robert Kaplan wrote about its importance in a *Foreign Affairs* piece, later expanded into a book. He pushes us to shift our focus from the Atlantic and Pacific oceans—leftover thinking from the World War II era—to the world's third largest body of water. "In what quarter of the Earth today can one best glimpse the future?" Kaplan asks. The answer is the Indian Ocean. He calls the monsoon seas a "vast web of energy trade."

Global energy needs are set to double by 2030—which is not all that far away—and India and China will make up about half of that. They will import most of it. That means the importance of the monsoon seas will only grow over time.

Nearly 80 percent of the world's crude oil that winds up in China crosses the vast Indian Ocean on its way through the narrow Strait of Malacca. China alone will import more than 7.3 million barrels a day over the next five years. That is half of Saudi Arabia's planned output.

India will soon be the fourth-largest consumer of energy in the world, behind the United States, China, and Japan. By 2030, it will have the world's largest population. It, too, depends on energy from faraway sources. India imports four-fifths of its oil, mostly from the Persian Gulf. India also ships coal from Mozambique, South Africa, Indonesia, and Australia. It imports liquefied natural gas (LNG) from Oman on the Arabian Peninsula and from Indonesia across the Bay of Bengal. All of this crosses the Indian Ocean.

The knitting between India and the six Arab states of the Gulf Cooperation Council (GCC) is tightening. Already, there are 3.5 million Indians working in the GCC. India has energy partners in the region, including Iran.

Iran recently began supplying India with LNG as part of a 25-year agreement signed in 2005.

China depends on Iran, too, which is currently its third-largest supplier of crude oil. Iran alone supplies 12 percent of total Chinese oil consumption. In exchange, China inked a deal to help Iran develop its massive South Pars natural gas field. As you can see, given the relations between the United States and Iran, the politics here can get complex.

Indeed, the importance of the monsoon seas extends beyond energy. It bleeds into the world of politics, as well. Tensions arise between China and India as they compete for mastery over the Indian Ocean. Kaplan writes: "As the competition between India and China suggests, the Indian Ocean is where global struggles will play out in the twenty-first century." These struggles will create dramatic changes, as they already have done.

There are parts of the littoral that Villiers would not recognize. When Villiers visited Kuwait in 1939, it had not yet discovered oil. "The oilmen were there," Villiers observes, "but they had as yet found nothing." He describes Kuwait as a "real Indian Ocean seaport of the old times." It was a city of some 70,000 people. It had no roads; the town was a sanded maze.

Today, there are 2.6 million people in Kuwait. Income per capita is over $60,000 annually. This puts it in the top 10 richest countries on Earth. It has one of the fastest economic growth rates in the world.

Dubai, which Villiers refers to as the mere "roadstead Dubai," is one of the world's largest ports, handling cargo from Asia. It is building what will be the world's largest airport.

Trade and oil have remade the map. But this trend is the continuation of an old idea. The monsoon winds have been blowing for centuries. The countries on the Indian Ocean have been trading with each other since ancient times, and they will continue to do so in the future.

The investment implications of the monsoon sea serve as a strong backdrop for energy investing. In particular, for the crude oil these growing regions need. It's a glimpse into the future. More and more, this part of the world is going to have a bigger say in what that world looks like.

BRICs . . . Meet MENA

Change is like a pin to the balloons of conventional wisdom. Just when people settle into their views, here comes the pin. For instance, it's become widely accepted when talking about emerging economies to focus on the BRIC countries: Brazil, Russia, India, and China. But there is a very important region that gets lost in that discussion.

In fact, this region collectively has a bigger economy than Brazil, Russia, or India. In terms of growth, it is growing faster than any of these countries.

In terms of population, it's bigger than the United States and nearly as populous as the European Union. It holds 60 percent of the world's proven oil reserves and nearly half of its natural gas.

That last clue probably gives it away. I'm talking about the Middle East and North Africa, or MENA. Among its largest economies are Saudi Arabia and the United Arab Emirates.

MENA is one of the fastest-growing regions in the world. Over the past 50 years, its population has gone up more than fourfold. Over the next 30 years, MENA's population will grow more than 60 percent to nearly 700 million people. And the population is still young. The majority of the population is under 25 years old. That means old practices are changing, too.

Syria, for instance, has been a mercantile crossroads between East and West since its days as a link on the old Silk Road. The ancient city of Aleppo was a key stop along the old Silk Road. Even today, it still has the longest covered market in the Middle East—a souk seven miles long. There, you can find goods that take you back in history—soap made from olive oil or silk scarves and keffiyehs of a variety of colors. Head down an alleyway and find gold jewelry and stands of fresh pistachios and sacks of spices and more. Then there are the backstreets of hawkers with lamb—always plenty of lamb—and you smell the scents of lime, garlic, and mint.

Much else has changed. Today, for the first time in more than two decades, banks in Syria can set their own interest rates on loans and deposits. Today, you can change money on the street without the threat of a ball and chain winding up around your ankles.

The largest investor in the country is Haier, a Chinese company, which makes 50,000 washing machines and 50,000 microwave ovens in Syria every year. Another Chinese company, Sichuan Machinery Import & Export, built a $180 million hydroelectric plant here. There are big real estate projects, including a $300 million resort on the Syrian Mediterranean coast. Some 40,000 new hotel beds came online in the past few years, up from 48,000. Tourism is already 13 percent of the economy. Syria is basically following the "China model" of maintaining a closed political order but carving out free zones and allowing trade.

Of course, this isn't some Big Rock Candy Mountain. There are all kinds of problems in Syria and elsewhere, but I find the changes taking place so far absolutely remarkable. (As this book goes to press, Syria is in crisis. It remains to be seen how that will impact the economic liberalization documented here.)

Again, we've seen this movie before. Roger Owen wrote the classic study on the Middle East and its economies. His book, *The Middle East in the World Economy,* covers the period 1800–1914, a time of growth and transformation. More than a few points are similar today. Then, as the region experienced a huge population explosion. The Middle East's population alone grew 300 percent. Then, as now, trade grew even faster under a more liberalized economic regime. The Middle East benefited from growing demand for agricultural goods from European markets. (Ironically, today, the Middle East is a key food importer.)

The takeaway here is that this other, non-BRIC growth engine creates new needs and new opportunities. We'll look at more at the GCC in the Dubai chapter, but for now, I want to leave you with this idea that old trade routes are once again reviving as the world turns right side up.

Snapshots on the Way to a World Right Side Up

In Tbilisi . . .

Travel writer Melik Kaylan wrote about visiting the Georgian capital of Tbilisi, on the eastern edge of Western Europe. He describes it as "improbably beautiful, a postcard-perfect lost kingdom set inside high hills surmounted by ancient forts and rock-steady 1,500-year-old Byzantine churches."

He meets a young Tbilisian who manages the Georgian investments of an oil-rich Kazakh corporation. He writes this is all "part of a flow of wealth that represents the ancient Silk Road common market coming back to life, Kazakhstan being the new oil powerhouse of Central Asia."

Kazakhstan is home to the Kashagan oil field, one of the largest discovered in the past 30 years. It will also be one of the most difficult to develop. Nonetheless, oil inspires booms and tickles the fortune-hunting bones. Prosperity in oil-rich Kazakhstan spills over and lends new life to old places in the region—like Tbilisi.

Not so long ago, nearby Azerbaijan, across the Caspian Sea from Kazakhstan, was a big oil producer. In 1901, more than half of the world's oil (about 11 million tons) came from relatively remote Azerbaijan, at the crossroads of Eastern Europe and western Asia. The Rothschilds and the Nobel brothers—including Alfred Nobel of Nobel Prize fame—made a fortune from the oil flowing out of Baku's fields in Azerbaijan.

On the road to Moscow . . .

"Now there are many roads, many cars. Supermarkets are coming. Electricity is coming. The Internet is coming. Credit cards are coming. Everything is becoming the same: Chinese goods and American freedom. Very cheap. Very easy."

In the quote above, Russian author and hitchhiking icon Anton Krotov was responding to a pair of American journalists. They were feeling rather proud after hitchhiking across Russia. When he did it in the 1990s, getting across Siberia was difficult and dangerous. That was a real adventure. And Krotov has backpacked all over the big landmass of Asia.

The Trans-Siberian Highway, arguably the longest highway in the world stretches from Saint Petersburg to Vladivostok, a distance of over 6,000 miles. For the first time, it connected one half of Russia with the other by road. It's also opened up a sort of curious east-west trade route in all sorts of things, including cars.

Used cars come over from Japan and land in Vladivostok. Some entrepreneurial Russians called peregonchiks (movers) drive the cars from Vladivostok to Russia's big cities in the west. It takes about a week. They sell the cars, make a profit, and head east to do it all over again. One writer called it "a revamped Russian dream: Go east, young man. Then go west. Then east again. Then west again."

McKenzie Funk recently made the 6,000-plus-mile trek and wrote about his experiences in *National Geographic Adventure*. It's a great glimpse at globalization on the frontiers of Russia.

The highway has upped the flow of trade across Russia. It helps Russia bring more timber, oil, and minerals to a hungry outside world. A 2,580-mile-long pipeline parallels the highway for stretches and carries Russian oil to Asian and American buyers. There are plans for a natural gas pipeline that will cut across the Ukok Plateau like a scythe across the plains. "There are plans for new roads to the north and west," Funk writes, "and new oil wells in every direction."

The car trade is also booming. Ships leave Vladivostok with timber and come back with cars. The new prosperity helps business in lots of ways. Funk reports that Vladivostok is so full of tourists and traders from South Korea, Japan, and China it can be hard to find a hotel room. The towns along the road also enjoy a new prosperity.

Lake Baikal, the world's largest freshwater lake, has a new 270-mile stretch specially zoned for tourism. There are plans for golf courses, spas, five-star hotels, and more.

Russia's new middle class also wants to buy cars. Ownership in Russia is still below that of other developing countries. In Russia, about 200 out of every 1,000 people own a car. The ratio is over 500 out of every 1,000 people in Europe and about 800 in the United States.

Some might mourn the passing of Russia's wild frontier. But these changes are like burning charcoal. They can't be undone. Russians, enjoying the taste of this life, would seem unlikely to knuckle under and go backward. Strange things happen all the time, of course, but I'm betting Russia will stay in the big leagues as a rising economic powerhouse.

On the roads, rails, and pipelines crisscrossing Asia . . .

In the early 1900s, Sun Yat-sen called for a countrywide "reconstruction" in China to spur modernization. He wanted bridges and roads and railways. This led one American to say at the time: "The engineering societies of the world should make Dr. Sun their patron saint, because if he ever got in a position where he could put his plans into effect, there would be work for engineers in China for the next 1,000 years."

Today, you could think the same kind of thing, except your attention would focus not just on China, but on the great landmass of Asia and the activity along the so-called New Silk Road.

The Economist reports that"[Asia] is no longer mainly a coastline with strong trade links to the rest of the world. Now links across Asia matter just as much. Trade within the region is growing at roughly twice the pace of trade with the outside world."

Hard to believe, but 20 years ago, China and India barely traded with each other. China is India's biggest partner. Central Asia's trade with China jumped from hardly anything in 1990 to grow more than 40-fold. And China is the biggest merchandise exporter to the Middle East.

Pipelines, roads, and railways are crisscrossing Asia, with more on the way. A new 4,400-mile pipeline carries gas from Turkmenistan to China. Russia and China have pipeline projects in the works. Iran and Pakistan are also building a pipeline, one that could, eventually, run all the way to China. There are many new road projects in the works throughout Central Asia and along the Mekong Delta. Railways push lines that may connect Singapore with south Germany.

Or in how the world spends its money . . .

Emerging market consumers are the dominant consumer group in the world, surpassing the United States. We've crossed an important threshold.

The next big consumer market to open up might be Indonesia. It has the world's fourth-largest population, behind China, India, and the United States, with 240 million people. Ford recently opened its first dealership there. Honda says it can't make motorcycles fast enough. And H.J. Heinz reports that Indonesia is a big part of why its Asia sales rose 40 percent one year.

Or from where the newest products will come . . .

These emerging markets are also becoming a source of innovative ideas. Fortune 500 companies are happy to set up brainy shops in emerging markets. They already have 98 R&D facilities in China and 63 in India. GE has a vast R&D facility in Bangalore, its biggest in the world. Cisco is spending a $1 billion on a second HQ, also in Bangalore. Accenture has a quarter of its workforce in India. Microsoft's biggest R&D center, outside of Redmond, is in Beijing.

They are enjoying tremendous success. For example, GE's Bangalore laboratory invented a new hand-held electrocardiogram that sells for $800, instead of the usual $2,000. The cost per test is only $1 per patient.

The Economist wrote that the emerging markets have become a "fizzing cocktail of creativity" and gave numerous examples. In Chennai, a Tata company created a water purifier that uses rice husks, a common waste product. A family can enjoy bacteria-free water for the grand price of $24. New filters every few months will cost $4. It's cheap and portable and will make a big impact for the poor the world over, most of whom lack access to clean water.

Another Indian manufacturer concocted a $70 fridge that runs on batteries! A Chinese company, Mindray, makes a lithium battery for $12, compared with $40 previously. Bharti Airtel, an Indian company, has the lowest cell phone fees in the world, two cents a minute and nationwide coverage.

One of the most astounding tales belongs to Devi Shetty. He is applying Henry Ford's assembly-line techniques to hospitals. Shetty's flagship hospital in Bangalore has 1,000 beds. (The average American hospital has only 160.) His team of 40-some cardiologists cranks out 600 operations a week. Open-heart surgery costs about $2,000, compared with $20,000–100,000 in an American hospital. Shetty and his team have performed tens of thousands of such operations with results as good as the best of American hospitals. Incredibly, these hospitals even make money. According to *The Economist*, "Dr Shetty's family-owned hospital group reports a 7.7 percent profit after taxes, compared with an average of 6.9 percent in American private hospitals."

The above is just a snippet of the mind-bending changes taking place. As Marco Polo once said, "I have not told the half of what I saw."

CHAPTER 2

Colombia: In Search of El Dorado

"Would you invest in Brazil 15 years ago if you had the chance?" my host asked one night, in an effort to frame the opportunity here.

"Of course, that would've been a home run," I said.

"Welcome to Colombia."

We were sitting in a comfortable restaurant in Medellín's downtown area. This pretty city spills out across a river valley and creeps up the walls of the surrounding mountains. Medellín's nickname is the City of Eternal Spring, thanks to its temperate weather.

If you have an image of Medellín (and Colombia) as a violent place, a visit here would change your opinion. I could have been in any number of cities around the world. I never felt unsafe. (As with any city, there are good and bad areas.) The bars and restaurants were full at night. The skyline was lit with tall buildings. The sidewalks busy with people. It was not always so, as Medellín was once a notoriously dangerous city.

Security issues have been a huge problem in Colombia's past, but it is much improved, and most of the remaining issues are deep in the jungles, near the porous borders with Venezuela or Ecuador. In fact, while I was there, rebels snatched 23 Talisman workers doing seismic work near the Venezuelan border. Even these occurrences, however, are now rare.

In the cities, all the buildings I visited had tight security. Almost all of them required me to put my bag through a scanner. If I had a laptop, they took the serial number down and checked it when I left, to make sure I took what I came in with. In addition, I handed over my ID, which I got back when I left. Almost all required an electronic fingerprint, a picture, or both.

Talking about security, I'll add that the security gauntlet to get out of Medellín was the most elaborate I have ever experienced, including travel in the Middle East. I received not one, but two full pat-downs along the way at the airport, once after checking in and again before I entered my gate. Moreover, there was no opting out. Security officials in blue latex gloves went through my carry-on, not once, but on two separate occasions. This was in addition to the usual scanners. I counted how many times people looked at my passport. I think I lost count after the eighth time.

In the past, security worries weighed down the economy in many ways. For example, during a meeting with Suramericana, a large financial services firm, the CFO pointed out that Colombia still ranks low in the global tourism derby. According to World Trade Organization figures for 2010, Colombia did not make the top fifty. More people visited Bosnia than Colombia, a country with less than 1/10th the population and about 1/20th the size.

It's starting to change, though, as the security issues recede. In 2010, Colombia received about 2.6 million visitors. Considering that in 2005, the official number was about 800,000, the country has already come a long way. I expect Colombia to be a top-50 country someday soon. It's too pretty not to be.

The fact that it is cheap also helps. It is one of the places in the world where the U.S. dollar still goes far. In Medellín, a men's haircut was $3. You could get a massage for $10 and a manicure or pedicure for $6. For $3.50, you could pick up a six-pack of beer. For 30 cents, you could get 30 eggs. A giant papaya would set you back about 60 cents.

Today, Colombia is a young and growing emerging market that is doing a lot of catching up, and that is the core phenomenon of the world right side up.

For example, I visited Cementos Argos, the largest cement company in Colombia, with a 51 percent market share. It is an asset-rich company. In addition to its cement operations, Argos owns a huge land bank of 5,000 hectares, a portfolio with stakes in three other listed Colombian companies worth $3.3 billion, and 600 million tons of coal reserves.

I met with Ricardo Andres Sierra, the CFO, who told us in the bad old days, plants could work only from 6:00 a.m. to 6:00 p.m. And there were parts of the country where the company simply did not go. But today, the plants run 24/7. "We can go wherever we want," he said.

Argos has a huge opportunity in Colombia. As is often the case when a boom arrives, the building of the infrastructure to support the boom comes later. Colombia is way behind in infrastructure, a familiar theme in many markets throughout this book. It needs miles and miles of roads. It needs bigger ports, expanded airports, and railroads.

Andres gave me an arresting statistic. He said Colombia consumes about half the cement per capita annually Vietnam does. The point being that Colombia is well below the consumption rates of comparable developing economies. There is tremendous room to grow.

We talked about new road projects, such as Ruta del Sol, which will connect Bogotá, the capital in the Andes, with Santa Marta, a port city on the Caribbean Sea. We talked about the Cartagena Refinery expansion. Both are huge projects, "as big as the Panama Canal expansion," Andres said. There is also a tunnel project that will connect Bogota to the Pacific port at Buenaventura. There are projects for hydropower plants, bus systems, pipelines and much more.

"Infrastructure is the key to growth in Colombia, that's for sure," Andres ventured. I had heard and read about the relative lack of good infrastructure in Colombia. But it is another thing to go down there and see it firsthand.

Traffic in Bogotá, for example, is impossible, or nearly so. The roads are choked with small cars that go nowhere fast. It seems to take forever to go even short distances. One of my contacts here told me that Colombia has only 186 miles of two-lane two-way roads.

The government knows this, and there is a lot of money slotted for infrastructure development in the coming years. Argos is in a great position to profit from the build-out of Colombia's infrastructure.

A People of the Mountains

What's funny is that lack of infrastructure seems to be part of the historical DNA of Colombia. Its cities have often been relatively inaccessible destinations in history, though aviation has conquered some of these challenges.

I arrived in Bogotá first, after a relatively short five-hour flight from Washington. Bogotá is 8,600 feet above sea level, a mountain fastness tucked in the Andes. The mountains are green with vegetation, not like the bare western flank of the Andes in Peru. The weather here is temperate, and the rainfall is plentiful. Colombians are primarily a mountain people. Only 15 percent of the country's land area is above 3,300 feet, but that is where the majority of the population lives. The lowlands, by contrast, cover 54 percent of the country, but hold only 3 percent of the population. (More on why below.)

It is nice to have a vibrant emerging market that is easy to get to. In fact, from Bogotá, you can be in New York or Rio de Janeiro in less than six hours. The city is in a convenient spot.

It's ironic that Bogotá should be so accessible today. It was notorious for being otherwise for most of its history, even late into the nineteenth century. Past travelers have left dramatic tales of ascending and descending the trails of the river valley of the Magdalena. The paths were steep, and there is a net gain in altitude of 7,800 feet occurring over a distance of less than 50 miles. The dangers were all the worse for the heavy rains that could wash out parts of the trail.

Further proof of the arduous nature of the journey lies in the market prices to ship goods to Bogotá. In the mid-nineteenth century, it cost 40–60 cents per ton-mile to carry freight overland—and this during the dry season. During the rainy season, freight rates would double, assuming you could find a mule train willing to make a go of it. By comparison, in the United States during this time, overland freight rates by canal or mule cost two–four cents per ton-mile.

So treacherous were the passes that some travelers crossed parts of the ridges in chairs mounted on the backs of human porters, thought more sure-footed than even the mules.

Historically, the relative difficulty of traversing these mountains helped to isolate Colombian communities from each other. There have been other theories advanced too, such as the fact that the mountains provided so well for the local communities that the need for trade was much diminished. Colombians could scale up and down the mountains, which provided enough climatic change for them to grow a wide range of crops close by. Higher up, grains such as wheat; further down corn; lower still, bananas, yucca, avocado, and much more. Local autonomy was easy to achieve.

Living up in the mountains had other compensations. Up in the mountains, you escaped the heat and tropical diseases of the lowlands. The weather is mild and doesn't vary much. Plentiful rainfall makes the mountains good for growing coffee, too.

Colombia is the world's third-largest coffee producer (after Brazil and Vietnam). While I was in Colombia, the price of coffee pushed past 34-year highs because of disappointing harvests in Colombia. Inventories fell to their lowest level in at least 40 years. The rains had been too heavy, and Colombia's harvests suffered.

Two years before, Colombia produced only 7.8 million bags of coffee (each bag is 60 kgs), the lowest total in 33 years. It was also facing another small crop of 8–9 million bags, while the market initially expected 10. Unusual weather had hit other coffee-growing regions as well, including Mexico and Brazil. The price of coffee was up over 145 percent over the last year.

Here Lies Oil

In recent years, though, the focus for many Colombians has not been in the mountains, but off them, down into the muggy eastern lowlands of the Llanos. Underneath these plains lies oil. Lots of oil.

Oil has come to dominate the market in Colombia. It's hard to talk about investing there without talking about oil. Besides the export figures, the two largest oil companies (Ecopetrol and Pacific Rubiales) make up nearly 45 percent of the trading volume on the Colombian exchange. Colombia is currently the world's twenty-fifth largest producer of oil, and oil companies continue to make big finds here, adding to Colombia's reserves.

Colombia's history as an oil producer goes back to 1918 with the discovery of "La Cira-Infantas," a giant oil field. Production peaked in the late 1990s, declined, and flattened out.

The reasons for the decline are complicated. The turmoil in the country certainly took its toll. Some of it had to do with the shifting nature of contracts and concessions. Some of it had to do with just neglect and poor management. And some of it was that the easy oil had already been found and pumped out.

But things have turned in the past several years. In 2009, production increased for the first time since the 1990s. Colombia's oil industry is thriving amid better security, a better investment climate, and the use of new technologies (Figure 2.1).

In addition, ex-Venezuelan oil hands, chased out by Hugo Chávez, headed to Colombia. In a classic case of brain drain for one country leading to a boom in another, these Venezuelans applied their knowledge of Venezuela's Orinoco fields, which produce heavy oil, to the same geology found over the border in Colombia. The rich source rocks that produce oil from Venezuela's massive oil fields share a history with those found in Colombia.

The results have been fantastic. As you can see in Figure 2.2, now Colombia is one of the few growing producers in South America. Colombia's oil production is up 50 percent from 2007.

The stocks of Colombia oil companies have exploded on the growth. Ecopetrol is the big partially state-owned oil company, and one of the key players in developing the tar-like oil in Colombia's eastern plains. Being the oldest of the oil companies, it holds some of the best assets and the majority of the unexplored land in the most prospective basins. Ecopetrol also controls key oil transport infrastructure (think pipelines, loading stations, and ports) as well as high-impact exploration licenses in Brazil, Peru, and the

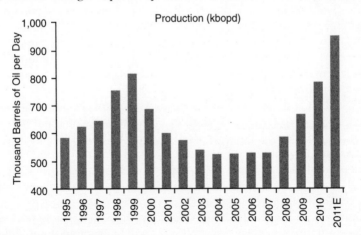

FIGURE 2.1 Colombia's Oil Revival
Source: Grupo InterBolsa.

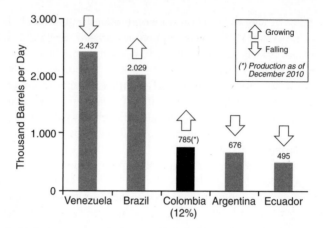

FIGURE 2.2 Colombia's Oil Production Set against South American Peers
Source: BP Statistical Review 2010 and ANH.

Gulf of Mexico. It jumped nearly threefold in two years. Pacific Rubiales is the star, though, and its stock was a 10-bagger in just two years.

Other companies exist, locking down acreage and exploring relatively untapped basins. I think it's still early enough in Colombia's oil boom to make a lot of hay, and I follow several Colombian oil stocks. In fact, I met with a bunch of them when I was there.

Oil is the easiest sector to invest in in Colombia, with many choices for U.S. or Canadian investors. Pacific Rubiales, Petrominerales, C&C Energia, Canacol, Gran Tierra, and Ecopetrol are all listed and easy to buy.

So overpowering is oil, I heard the phrase "Dutch disease" bandied about. *The Economist* coined the term in 1977 to describe the apparent decline of manufacturing in the Netherlands after a big natural gas discovery in 1959. The worry is that when the resource boom ends, nothing remains of a hollowed-out economy. I am unsure about the validity of this idea or how much it matters, but as resource-rich as Colombia is today, that day of reckoning must be far off.

What may surprise you is just how quickly this oil development has happened. Much of the acreage is already locked up. When new blocks come up for bid, they are heavily contested. I met with Charles Gamba, president and CEO of Canacol Energy. At the time, he told me there were 67 bidders on their latest block. Gamba also pointed out how quickly oil companies locked up acreage. In 2003, Colombia licensed only 4 percent of its available acreage. Today, 60 percent is licensed.

Still, several companies here have stocked up an enviable portfolio of prospects to explore. And oil and gas will be an important driver of Colombia's economy for years to come as it develops further.

As an aside to this, the onshore exploration of Brazil seems like a relative virginal opportunity, with only 5 percent licensed. So on this matter, at least, Brazil is more of a frontier market than Colombia, which we'll cover in the next chapter.

Beyond oil, investors can easily gain exposure to mining, particularly for gold, which brings me to the story of El Dorado.

The New El Dorado

About 35 miles northeast of Bogotá, up in the mountains, surrounded by wooded ridges, lies the blue-green lagoon called Laguna de Guatavita.

On the importance of this place, author Charles Nicholl writes:

> *In the mythic topography of South America, the Laguna de Guatavita is a nodal point. Beneath the secretive sheen of its waters lies the treasure of El Dorado. Though the legend of El Dorado sprouted and multiplied, and expeditions hacked through the jungles of Guiana and Peru in search of a fabulous city of gold, the reality behind it lay here in the highlands of Colombia.*

These ranges were once under the sway of the Chibcha kings that ruled before the Spaniards arrived. The Chibcha tribes were sun worshippers, farmers, and traders. They'd trade salts, emeralds, and woven blankets with the lowland tribes in exchange for cotton, seashells, and gold.

The latter was used in an elaborate ritual. El Dorado was not originally a place, but a man: El Dorado, the gilded man. More from Nicholl:

> *He was the central figure in a rite performed by the Chibchas here at this sacred lake. It was a kind of coronation ceremony, performed at the appointment of a new cacique, or chieftain. At the shores of the lagoon, he was stripped naked, anointed with a sticky resin and sprayed with gold dust. A raft of reeds was prepared, with braziers of moque incense and piles of gold jewels on it.*

Then he was floated out into the center of the lake, where he heaved all the gold and jewels into the water as a kind of spiritual offering. Finally, he jumped in the water, washing away the gold dust. It may sound fantastic, but it is grounded in historical fact.

Of course, as soon as the Spaniards got wind of this, they had visions of finding a great store of gold at the bottom of this lake. So began the long quest to find it and then drain it.

Find it they did. There were many attempts to drain the lake.

In 1545, Hernán Pérez de Quesada made the first attempt. He used a bucket chain of natives and lowered the level of the lagoon by 10 feet. Progress was slow, though, and soon rain refilled the lagoon. He did make off with some gold, though not enough to cover his losses.

Later, a Bogotáno merchant, Antonio Sepúlveda, tried a more ambitious project. He had a workforce of 8,000, which carved a great notch into the lake to channel the water away. (This notch is still visible today.) This method dropped the level of the lake by 60 feet, and the laborers found many golden ornaments and gems, including a large emerald ("the size of a hen's egg"). But the walls of the cut collapsed, many workers were killed, and that was the end of Sepúlveda's scheme. He tried again, but failed and supposedly died poor.

The attempts got more sophisticated and bigger. In 1899, a British company, Contractors Ltd., did finally drain the lake. The soft slimy bed of the lake was intractable, though, and the sun soon baked it into concrete. Then the lagoon filled with water again before drilling equipment could do any good.

"Many other attempts followed," Nicholl writes, "but always with the same teasing result—a few objects recovered, followed by mishap and abandonment, leaving the great mass of treasure still submerged."

In the 1960s, Colombia's government passed laws protecting the lake from exploitation, and thus, the treasures of El Dorado lie out of reach forever.

El Dorado is one of my favorite historical Colombian stories. But there is a modern gold boom that echoes these past desperate efforts. As the *New York Times* reported:

> *The gold rush here is just a part of a broader mining boom in Colombia, with gold production climbing more than 30 percent last year and attracting an array of fortune seekers, from multinational corporations to farmers who have left their fields and picked up shovels.*

Over 40 international mining companies were poking around Colombia's steamy basins looking for gold in 2011. By the end of 2012, Colombia could be at a run rate of 2 to 3 million ounces of gold annually—more than double what it produced in 2009. Miners are putting billions to work in Colombia to get its gold.

This is a nod to the world right side up, as Colombia was South America's largest gold producer until 1937. It has a long way to go before it catches Peru, the current leader. But Colombia could become a top-10 global gold producer in the next few years. As it is, Colombia ranks twenty-first in the world in gold production.

The turmoil in the country for the last half-century or so has preserved a lot of gold in place, relatively untapped and unexplored. But now with stability returning to the country, investment dollars are flowing back to Colombia.

Unfortunately, there is also a lot of illegal mining. FARC rebels and other groups that once grew coca leaves are turning to gold instead to finance their efforts. These illegal miners use mercury to separate the gold from river sediments. That's made Colombia the world's worst mercury polluter on a per capita basis, according to U.N. researchers. Now the Colombian government is cracking down on illegal gold miners, but it is slow, difficult work. In 2010, in a town called Caucasia, there were more than 60 grenade attacks as two rival groups fought for control over gold mines.

Still, such troubles shouldn't put investors off Colombia's modern gold story. Not all parts of the country are so lawless. In fact, murder and other violent crimes are in steep decline in Colombia overall. Investors have many good companies and projects to choose from. As Colombia climbs up the global gold producer rankings, some will make fortunes as a result.

One of my favorites is the largest Colombian gold miner, Gran Colombia (GCM:TSX). Gran Colombia merged with Medoro Resources in 2011. The new entity has kept the Gran Colombia name. Frank Holmes, who runs U.S. Global Investors Global Resources Fund, owned 15 percent of Medoro before the merger and shared with me his reasons for owning it. I know Frank through Agora Financial's Vancouver conference, where we are both regular speakers. His is one of the few presentations I make sure not to miss. I always enjoy his perspective, as he is a globe-trotting investor with a keen eye for value. Frank is also a fan of Colombia, having made several trips there. I reached Frank by phone, and we talked about our trips and what we liked about the country. We also talked about Gran Colombia.

Medoro sat on a mountain of 10 million ounces of gold and 60 million ounces of silver, which is why Gran Colombia was such an ardent suitor. "It's very difficult to find that around the world," Frank told me. Frank spoke highly of Serafino Iacono, the executive co-chairman and the new CEO, Maria Consuelo Araújo. As to the latter, she comes with a top-notch resume in cultural issues, which is critical to success in emerging markets. She is a former Colombian minister of foreign affairs and minister of culture. She is a diplomat and an economist with postgraduate degrees from Colombia and the United Kingdom.

As for Iacono, Frank also had many good things to say about this veteran mine builder. "He's built four mines and sold them. He's not afraid to sell." Thus, I also sought out Serafino Iacono. He gave me some history, perspective, and in particular, he opened my eyes to the potential of Gran Colombia's Frontino mine.

Serafino really stressed to me the importance of political and cultural factors in mine building in Latin America. "The mine is simple," he said. "The harder part is convincing the politicians and the local people that you aren't here to take away jobs and mess up the environment." That is why hiring CEO Araújo was so important. As mentioned, she has a star-studded resume. "She is a superstar over here," Serafino told me. Family members have held the posts of minister, governor, and senator. She is a great asset at this stage in the company's development. In addition to political connections, it is important to have size and clout.

When Gran Colombia merged with Medoro, it meant that the new entity employed some 7,000 workers, which represent about 70 percent of the employment in the region. That gives them some weight politically, as 7,000 jobs are not easily replaced in these poor mountain regions. Furthermore, the combination allows the two companies to streamline pieces of the operation to save money.

I also talked to Serafino about the Marmato project. It lies on the eastern slopes of Western Cordillera in the Colombian Andes. Marmato takes its name from an old Spanish word for "pyrite," a shiny mineral known also as fool's gold.

The name is ironic, because there is a lot of gold here and a long history of gold mining. The Quimbaya, a pre-Columbian society, lived in these mountains and mined gold. They were among the finest goldsmiths in Colombia. So rich in gold was Marmato that Simón Bolívar used the mines as collateral for loans from British banks to fund the fight for Colombia's independence from Spain in 1810–1819. In any event, on Marmato, Serafino said, "It's the easiest deposit that you can have." Medoro had the challenge of moving a town before it could mine the mountain, a move that the government fully supported.

As for the environment? "We're making it better," Serafino noted, as small miners have leaked cyanide down the mountain that eventually fed into Colombia's great Magdalena River. As to the site of the mine, there is good infrastructure, electricity, and water, and it is in a mining community. "I don't have to sell them on something they don't already know," he said of the community. "There's been mining here for 300 years."

As I say, my talk with Serafino made me appreciate much more the value of Gran Colombia's high-grade Frontino mine. (High grades mean that a given amount of rock yields comparatively high amounts of gold. The average production since 1995 has turned about 10 grams of gold per tonne or rock mined, an enviable deposit, indeed.) He called it "the best undeveloped mine in Colombia."

It's been producing for 50 years but has not been taken care of well or developed as it could have been. Serafino pointed out that the last time anybody drilled on the site was 1972. "And it hasn't been touched below 1,300 feet for over a hundred years," he added. Gran Colombia mines only three of the 29 known veins here. There is a lot of room to boost production and expand the resource. As Gran Colombia ramps up production here, it will impossible for the market to ignore it. If Gran Colombia comes anywhere close to its goals over the next year, ramping up from 100,000 ounces in 2011 to 600,000 ounces by 2016, the stock will soar.

I should mention the free option in silver. Gran Colombia has nearly 60 million ounces of silver at Marmato. "There's a billion dollars' worth of silver here," Serafino said.

Serafino was a co-founder of the Colombian oil giant Pacific Rubiales. It too was the product of a merger. Of course, the rest is history; the people who hung on made a fortune. Will history repeat with Medoro? As always, it is hard to say. But I wanted to share the Gran Colombia story, as it gives you a window into some of the opportunities and challenges of investing in Colombia as well as emerging markets generally.

Of course, there is more to Colombia than just commodities. I also met with a couple of banks, a communications firm, a cement company, a retailer, a construction contractor, and the stock exchange.

I have friends at Grupo InterBolsa, a leading asset manager and broker-dealer in Colombia. They opened up a lot of doors for me here. InterBolsa has access to seemingly everybody, from small exploration companies to the biggest banks, as well as government officials. The head of equity research at InterBolsa traveled with me and showed me around.

You always see things differently up close than from afar. There are investment opportunities invisible at 30,000 feet. These thoughts are what inspire many of my investment field trips abroad.

Let's take a quick cruise through some of the non-commodity opportunities.

More Opportunities in Colombia

One of the more interesting, if undercovered stories in Colombia is the growth of the middle class. I can show you all the charts you'd want to see. But maybe it's better to just tell you what I saw while I was in Bogotá and Medellín.

I saw lots of cars on the roads. "Car sales were up 40 percent last year and have been going up every month," one of my Colombian analyst friends told me. I saw restaurants that were full. I saw brightly lit grocery stores full of shoppers. I saw people wearing blue jeans and sunglasses and brand-name shoes. Surely, Medellín and Bogotá are not typical. There are many poor people in Colombia still. But something has changed, and the statistics back it up. Per capita income levels have doubled since 2003.

With Colombia's young and growing population, there is still plenty of room to grow. Colombia has the third-largest population in Latin America, after Brazil and Mexico. About 40 percent of that population is under 20 years old, and 80 percent is under 50.

Thus, one interesting investing angle that emerged on my trip was to invest in businesses that capitalize on that growing middle class. There are many ways to do that. I tend to favor the simpler businesses, the ones doing simple things like selling groceries or making wood.

Take Tablemac, which makes particleboards used in furniture, doors, and construction. Though it sounds like a pretty prosaic business, Tablemac has an interesting story on a lot of levels. I met with the CEO, Juan Vasquez Duque, and the CFO, Jhon Correa Sanchez, at their office in Medellín.

There is plenty of upside for furniture in Colombia. Vasquez showed us pictures of typical Colombian homes in which a crate might serve as a TV stand or makeshift shelving bends under the weight of books and other things. The market is still young and only just developing.

In fact, Tablemac was building the first medium-density fiber (MDF) plant in Colombia, a major venture that could double sales in three years. MDF is stronger than particleboard and you can use it more like plywood.

Colombia had no domestic MDF capacity, but Vasquez believes Tablemac's new facility will take a good chunk of the 145,000 cubic meters of MDF that Colombia currently imports. Tablemac's facility will also have a cost advantage over its distant competitors.

Tablemac is vertically integrated, with its own industrial forests for wood and its own resin plants. It owns 5,100 hectares of forest. Over the next six years, Tablemac plans to seed 10,000 hectares of forests.

Forestry is another great opportunity in Colombia. Thanks to warm weather and plentiful rains, growth rates are fast, 50 percent above those of Chile (which represents 23 percent of Colombian imports). Plus, the government supports forestry with tax benefits. You get $800 per year per hectare under one program, which cuts your net cost from $2,000 a hectare to $1,200.

So, that's one company I liked, but there were others.

One day, I drove to the town of Bello, a suburb of Medellín. I met with Felipe Hoyos Vieira, the vice president of Fabricato, a Colombian textile firm. Fabricato makes the fabrics used in clothing of all kinds, from Colombian army fatigues to Levi's jeans.

Fabricato creates 42 percent of its own energy from hydropower at a cost 1/10th of what it pays the utility. Since energy is perhaps 25 percent of total costs, this creates a useful advantage for Fabricato in a world of rising energy prices.

Then there is Exito, a grocery store chain that also has gas stations, travel agents, and real estate operations. Exito has 5 million customers. If you want to see what the middle class is buying, Exito gives you a window. It reports rising average ticket sales, increased buying of more expensive nonfood items, and more purchases on Exito's credit card.

Another company I met with was Davivienda, a strong banking franchise that began as a humble savings and loan. When you look at how banking has penetrated the Colombian economy, you see that it has a long way to go.

Just take a look at loans to GDP:

Colombia, 28 percent
Brazil, 37 percent
Chile, 86 percent

Of course, the United States is over 100 percent, but the point is that large chunks of the Colombian population have no loans and still use no banking products. That's changing, though, and you can see it in the growth rates of banks like Davivienda, which is now the third-largest in the country by assets.

These are some of the companies I met with in Colombia. As I tell you about these ideas, it occurs to me again why Colombia is an attractive investment destination. I hope these little vignettes open your eyes to the opportunities of these relatively young markets.

There is another company, though, that may be the best single play on Colombian markets overall. It's been up fourfold since 2005 but should be a top performer for years to come.

If I Had to Buy Only One

If I had to buy one Colombian stock and sit on it for five years, Grupo Inter-Bolsa would be my pick. InterBolsa is a leading asset manager and broker-dealer in Colombia. It handles something like 25 percent of the volume traded on the Colombian stock exchange.

As of this writing, Grupo InterBolsa has low leverage and pays a 3.5 percent dividend yield. The business is solidly profitable, with a 15 percent return on equity, even though it uses minimal leverage. I have many friends there now, so perhaps my view is no longer purely objective, but consider some of the accomplishments of the firm to date and the opportunities ahead of it.

Besides handling all those trades, Grupo InterBolsa was the lead underwriter in more than $1 billion in deals in just the last three years. It also created the first and only Colombian ETF (which trades on the NYSE under the ticker GXG). Moreover, an integration between the markets of Peru, Chile, and Colombia, called MILA is in the works. In the past, such regional integrations have been explosive. For example, the Nordic market alliance led to a tenfold increase in liquidity. Grupo InterBolsa would benefit from a similar alliance. (More on MILA a bit later.)

The company has nearly $6 billion assets under management and provides a whole suite of products: broker-dealer, asset management, investment banking, bond and equity issuances, private equity, insurance, and mortgages. It also has operations in Panama, Brazil, and the United States. Furthermore, it is in good position to expand its presence in Latin America.

Besides all of this, I've met a number of the people at InterBolsa, from officers to analysts. I am impressed with their team. I think they are trustworthy people trying to do the best for their clients. The head of research doesn't hesitate to put sells on stocks. In some cases, they are the only ones with sells on rather popular stocks.

Grupo InterBolsa was worth about $300 million in the market and could be worth over a billion dollars in the next five years.

Colombian *Keiretsu*

I found something else of interest in Colombia that surprised me: a *keiretsu*. The word comes from Japan and literally means "headless combine." It refers to a system of interlocking ownerships among companies. Most simply, it is when A owns shares in B, which in turn owns shares in A.

Finding a Colombian version of this Japanese creation made me feel like a biologist who stumbles on an unusual species of tree frog. The *keiretsu* in Colombia is more than just a hobby interest, though, as it could have a big influence on investor returns over time. Let's take a look.

In Medellín, I met with Andrés Bernal-Correa, the CFO of Grupo de Inversiones Suramericana, which is a large financial services company. Medellín, by the way, is a nice contrast to Bogotá. It was just under 5,000 feet above sea level; tropical; and prettier, with jagged mountains in the backdrop seemingly wherever you turned. There was certainly less traffic.

Bernal Correa presented a chart showing the ownership structure at the company. This is a *keiretsu*, Colombian-style in Figure 2.3.

This fascinated me, and I would run into it again and again in Colombia.

When looking over Colombian stocks, this was an additional wrinkle of value to consider the value of these stakes in other companies. I am tempted to show you a chart or two of some of the more complex interlocking ownership structures. They look like bowls of spaghetti.

I asked Bernal-Correa why these structures exist in Colombia. He explained that in the 1970s, stock prices got very low. In order to prevent takeovers, the families that controlled these companies got together and created the *keiretsu*. It would be impossible to take over, say, Suramericana with Argos and Chocolates owning half the company.

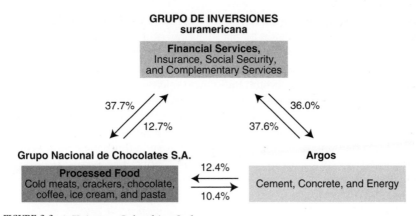

FIGURE 2.3 A *Keiretsu*, Colombian Style

One academic study I found ("Ownership and Control in Colombian Companies") shows the concentrated nature of ownership in Colombia. The authors point out that the largest stockholder in a Colombian company has, on average, a 35 percent stake. I don't know what the number in the United States is, but it's certainly not more than 10 percent and is probably less than 5 percent.

In my emerging market travels, I've found many of these conglomerate structures. In India, the most famous is the Tata Group, which has interests in everything from hotels to steel. But there are many others, such as Votorantim (Brazil), Alfa (Mexico), and Koç Holding (Turkey). In Hong Kong, 15 families control more than two-thirds of the stock market.

Mostly, these are just conglomerates, not true *keiretsus*. In the United States, we've had our own experiences with *keiretsus*, but they remain rare birds. Chrysler supposedly had one in the 1980s.

So, why does all this matter?

This issue of control is important. In fact, according to investing doyen Martin Whitman, "There is no more important topic in finance." Who runs the show and who has skin in the game seem like basic questions, but many investors never ask them.

This *keiretsu* is a relatively unstudied breed in public markets. I am not sure cross-ownership is good or bad for investors. Anecdotally, they seem successful. (As an aside, many also benefit from close ties to their governments. Joe Studwell has many examples in his book *Asian Godfathers*.) But I can see how problems emerge, as they have in Japan, where it is difficult to change things by way of management shake-ups, mergers, and so forth.

In any case, it's something to think about when looking at Colombian companies, or companies from any emerging market. Ownership and control are often more complicated than in the United States, where shareholders are usually a dispersed lot, but lines of authority are clear. It is something an investor should get a handle on before investing, no matter where in the world.

My overall conclusion on Colombia: I think Colombia, along with a handful of other places you'll read about in this book, is an attractive emerging market story. These are the next BRICs, you might say, after the famous quartet of Brazil, Russia, India, and China. Certainly, the BRICs will still have a lot to do with investing success, for good or ill, in the years ahead. But better opportunities may lie in the second-tier, less-explored markets, like Colombia.

This is the kind of thing that excites me as an investor. The world is like a big bandeja paisa, a Colombian dish overflowing with beans, rice, pork, and more. It seems with every bite you take, it just gets bigger!

The Colombia Canal

I'm fascinated by the ways in which geography plays a role in how a place develops. Many strategic sea lanes, mountain passes, and rivers in the world defined where cities grew up and how trade evolved.

One of the most famous of these key strategic trade lanes is the Panama Canal. Many countries have dreamed of ways to compete with the Panama Canal, including Nicaragua, but none of them had the backing of the Chinese. Colombia does.

Chinese officials agreed to invest nearly $8 billion in a project for a railway that will compete with the Panama Canal in bridging the Atlantic and Pacific oceans. Take a look at Figure 2.4. The railway would stretch 140 miles.

Why?

Because the Chinese want to ferry Colombian coal to China. Colombia has rich coal mines near its Caribbean coast. It is the world's fifth-largest producer of coal and has thermal coal (for electricity) and harder-to-find coking coal (for making steel). The idea is to load up coal in bulk on automated trains, which is much cheaper than loading and unloading containers.

It's not entirely clear that the Colombian dry canal would compete effectively with the Panama Canal, which is undergoing a $5 billion expansion. Plus, while safety is much more under control, I wonder how well Colombia could police the 140-mile track. The Beijing-Bogotá team thinks it's worth doing.

In reality, though, it won't directly compete with the Panama Canal, which handles all kinds of container ships. The Colombian Canal is a like a coal drip line directly into the veins of China's industrial machine.

It could be good for Colombia, a chance to develop its poor Caribbean coast, a traditional hideaway for drug lords and guerillas. For Colombia, too, it's a practical concession to a major trading partner. China is now Colombia's second-largest trading partner after the United States.

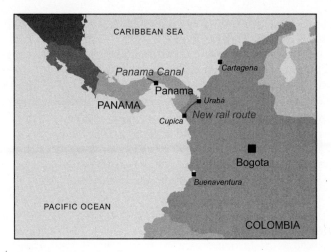

FIGURE 2.4 Colombia's Dry Canal
Source: The Guardian.

It also highlights China's push in South America. The plan mimics what China has done elsewhere, such as in Africa. (See Chapter 8.) And China is famous for feats of engineering. It laid out the Tibet railway, built on permafrost, and is also building the super port in Brazil.

I want to make note of the Colombian dry canal for another reason, though. It's a chance to highlight how important opening new trade lanes has been historically.

It has been so since ancient times. The Abbasid Empire had Baghdad as its capital, the center of its wealth and power. Trade flowed in from all directions. It would've been much less successful if not for the canal that connected it with the Euphrates. This allowed cargo to flow downstream from the Mediterranean and Syria and upstream from India and Southeast Asia from the Persian Gulf through Basra.

Throughout history, there have been canals that had dramatic effects on trade. The opening of the Suez Canal cut the distance between London and Bombay to 6,200 miles from 11,500. The Erie Canal in the United States cut travel time and shipping expenses by 90 percent on journeys from lake cities to New York. It also allowed grain from the Great Lakes to reach New York and helped make it the commercial hub of the union. Before this, Philadelphia had provided legitimate competition. There are many more examples.

A good place for an historical overview is Alasdair Nairn's *Engines That Move Markets*. Nairn was head of global equity research for Templeton, later moving on to be chief investment officer of the Scottish Widows Investment Fund, a $130-plus-billion fund. Nairn's book has a lot of lessons on how technologies develop from an investment point of view, which is rare. You may not think of canals and railways as technologies as such, but the opening chapter is a good discussion of both.

As Nairn puts it, stage one of the Industrial Revolution was to create the machinery that produced more and more goods at lower prices. Stage two was how to get these factory-made goods to markets near and far. Fortunately, the Industrial Revolution also pushed along the development of financial institutions capable of raising money to finance the big upfront capital requirements of railways and canals.

Canals offered a seductive carrot. Because shipping by canal often cost a third less than land-based transportation, it usually ate into the market share of the latter quickly and easily. Such efforts went boom and bust, of course, which is no surprise. Booms and busts seem part of the human condition. Whatever starts out as a good idea is almost a sure thing to be overdone eventually.

Nonetheless, the insight Nairn provides in his staging of the Industrial Revolution fits nicely with our thesis, part of which is the idea that the Industrial Revolution was late in doing its work on some of these markets. A kind of second Industrial Revolution has unfolded in China and India and Brazil, and so on; and stage two is railways and canals. It is transportation infrastructure, which we see being built out now, with much still to do.

The Colombian dry canal is part of that broader picture. As history makes plain, the building of such trade lanes can make fortunes and reshape the destiny of nations. My guess is that the dry canal will be more important for Colombia than most suspect. We'll see.

The Best Economy in Latin America?

There hasn't been much good in the way of travelogues through Colombia in recent times that don't have to do with its violent underworld. (If you have a recommendation, I'd be interested.) *The Fruit Palace: An Odyssey Through Colombia's Cocaine Underworld* was published in 1985. The aforementioned author, Charles Nicholl sets off, Hunter S. Thompson–style, in search of the Great Cocaine Story, "a one-eyed glimpse up the skirts of South America." The book takes its name from a little whitewashed café in the seaport of Santa Marta, where the author had his first encounter with drug trafficking.

Colombia is ideal for growing coca, which thrives in the lush, hot, semi-tropical slopes of its mountains. Nicholl writes, "Fiercely hot, plentifully watered, full of hidden cul-de-sac valleys and mostly impassable to any vehicle larger than a mule. . . . They call this the continent of fugitives, where a man can lose his own shadow."

This is the South America of imagination, shrouded in greenery and mist, full of steamy valleys and half-hidden villages and lost shrines. Slow-moving rivers, rice paddies, cane fields, coffee plantations. Nicholl's jaunt is a good read that gives you snippets of the country and its culture along the way.

Today, though, Colombia may be the best economic story in Latin America, which certainly wasn't true when Nicholl passed through. Bogotá, the capital, is now safer than Miami, Washington, or Atlanta. The economy is growing 5 percent per year and has a growing middle class, as we've discussed. In just the past six years, foreign investment in Colombia has gone up fourfold, and exports tripled.

Colombia has accumulated some trophies along the way. The famous IMD survey recently ranked Colombia second-best in Latin America in protecting private property, behind only Chile. The World Bank rated Colombia third in Latin America in the "business friendly" category, behind only Mexico and Peru. Business friendly it is; there are no capital gains taxes here on listed companies, and dividends are taxed only at the corporate level.

While in Colombia, I also stopped to visit the stock exchange—something I try to do in the markets I visit. The Colombian exchange, Bolsa de Valores de Colombia, began in 1920. By looking at the volume statistics of the exchange, you can see how it's grown 32 percent annually since 2003, an incredible pace.

Stock exchanges are less interesting than they used to be because computers do nearly everything. Still, you can sometimes pick up some useful nuggets visiting them. The main story in Colombia while I was there was the creation of the Integrated Latin American Market (MILA, in Spanish).

MILA will be Latin America's first combined trading platform, allowing electronic trading of stocks listed on Colombian, Chilean, and Peruvian exchanges. That way the average Colombian could buy Peruvian and Chilean stocks through an ordinary broker.

These kinds of regional exchanges tend to be very good for investors. It adds a lot of liquidity, making it easier for the big money to slosh around. MILA creates a significant regional market and counterweight in the region with Brazil. See Figure 2.5.

MILA is a great idea and should be good for investors in all three countries.

Bottom line: Colombia is a market worth paying attention to. It is the oldest democracy in Latin America (1819), and it has the third-largest population in Latin America, with 46 million people. With MILA, Colombia joins forces to create a large investment arena, something comparable to Mexico and Brazil in the region. It's also America's best friend in South America.

Remember, despite all the bad stuff most people know Colombia for—La Violencia, FARC, ELN, M-19, Pablo Escobar, and the drug trade—Colombia is different today. It's worked through the worst of the violence and is back on track to joining the global marketplace.

In 2011, Moody's, S&P, and Fitch upgraded Colombia to investment grade. It is the first time since 1999 that Colombia has held the coveted rating, which makes it easier for Colombian companies to raise money.

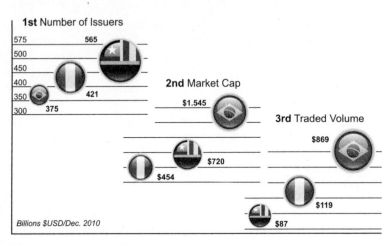

1st Number of Issuers

2nd Market Cap

3rd Traded Volume

FIGURE 2.5 MILA Is Comparable to Brazil and Mexico
Source: Bolsa de Valores de Colombia.

Finally, consider this: Colombia has never defaulted on its debt. That puts it ahead of some of the more "popular" South American countries that have been hot investment items of late.

Expect Colombia to be a leading player in the resurgence of South America's financial success.

Five Key Takeaways

- Check out Colombia's reawakened oil and gas sector: Pacific Rubiales, Petrominerales, Canacol, Gran Tierra, C&C Energia, and Ecopetrol.
- Look into adding some El Dorado gold to your portfolio with Gran Colombia (GCM:TSX). It's a risky development play in an ancient gold mining district and sits on more than 10 million ounces of gold and 60 million ounces of silver. Huge upside if it works.
- Consider the growing middle class investment angle with companies like Davivienda, Exito, Fabricato, and Tablemac. My favorite here is Grupo InterBolsa, which is also a great play on the growing financial market. If I could buy only one, it'd be Grupo InterBolsa.
- Keep your eye on MILA, the integration of the Peruvian, Chilean, and Colombian stock markets. A successful integration could be a real catalyst for all three markets, creating a counterweight to Brazil on the continent.
- Though the country has changed a lot in the meantime, Charles Nicholl's *The Fruit Palace* is an enjoyable, Hunter Thompson–esque romp through Colombia in the 1980s.

CHAPTER 3

Brazil: The Soil Superpower

A man in a hurry will be miserable in Brazil.
—Peter Fleming, *Brazilian Adventure*

The best place to start exploring this agricultural wonder is the western part of Brazil, in an interior state called Mato Grosso do Sul. Its capital, Campo Grande, is a good-sized city with a population close to a million people.

I arrived at a small airport with a band of readers along for the journey, walked off the plane onto the tarmac, and met with 95-degree heat. It was also very dry and dusty. Seasonally, it was the end of what passes for winter in these parts.

I packed a handful of books on Brazil to help give my some perspective. One of the oldies is Roy Nash's *The Conquest of Brazil*, first published in 1926. On Campo Grande, Nash writes "Mud to the knees during the rains from October to February, and dust for the rest of the year." Some things never change.

Nash is an interesting character, a former Army captain during World War I, he traveled widely in Brazil in the 1920s. He is good at putting together the pieces of Brazil's vast geography and history. We'll hear more from him in a bit.

The city has a slightly worn-down, yet energetic feel. People bustle about, and motorcycles are everywhere. There were the boxy, concrete buildings splashed with bright colors, a buttered-popcorn-yellow apartment building here, a melon-green body shop there. Our bus bounced along patchy roads to the hotel.

Campo Grande is nicknamed "the Brown City" (Cidade Morena) for the reddish-brown color of its soil. On the bus ride from the airport, we could see some new road construction and the rich turned-up earth, the color of red beans. Campo Grande has been growing smartly of late since opportunities abound here for investors in soil remediation, forestry, dairy, livestock, biofuels, and more.

The soil needs work before it can become productive farmland—that's the opportunity that attracted my small crew and me here in the first place. Investors can make a good return—doubling their capital in three years—by using a proven process that dates to the 1960s.

We endured the heat and some long bus rides to see farmland properties in the Cerrado, the vast grasslands of Brazil and the soil bank of the world.

The fly in the ointment is the political scene. Brazil has never been an easy place to do business, and it's tinkered with farm ownership rules, making it more difficult for foreigners. Nonetheless, over caipirinhas at the Bahamas Hotel, my contacts here told me there are a number of solutions to satisfy the new rules. Doing business in Brazil requires patience and a willingness to twist like a pretzel to meet the many rules in your way.

The Cerrado, full of scrub vegetation and grasses, covers some 22 percent of Brazil's land area. It's about eight times the size of the United Kingdom, and it has a good water supply. Water comes from nearby rivers and a huge underwater aquifer. There is a healthy amount of rain for about half of the year, and the land is also flat. Professionally managed, it becomes highly productive farmland.

It's also among the oldest soils in world and runs extremely deep, up to 65 feet in some places. Only here and in the plains of Africa do you find soil that has been undisturbed, in a geological sense, for so long. We're talking millions of years. The problem is that the soil is acidic, high in aluminum, and thus has low fertility. Luckily, this is where the opportunity comes in.

Turning this degraded pasture into good soil is an attractive investment proposition. It's a profitable arbitrage that takes place over three to four years and is largely self-funding. In the state of Mato Grosso do Sol, an investor could've bought scrubland for $3,000 per hectare. The next step is transforming this land into good productive soil by adding lime and fertilizer (chiefly phosphate), as well as planting restorative crops such as soy and crambe.

Soy helps fix the nitrogen deficiency, and crambe is a deep-rooted oilseed crop that brings nutrients closer to the soil. The cash earned from farming mostly pays for the transformation.

This is a proven strategy and quite straightforward. Over the years, much land has already been improved. In 1955, there were 200,000 hectares of land under cultivation in the Cerrado. Today, over 40 million hectares are under cultivation. That leaves over 80 million hectares still in play.

Once improved, the farmland is among the most productive in the world. Today, the Cerrado produces 54 percent of all the soybeans harvested in Brazil and 28 percent of the corn and 60 percent of the coffee.

It also supports 55 percent of Brazil's beef cattle. The Cerrado also produces rice, sugar, cassava, and cotton.

Not surprisingly, this improved land is worth a lot more. Farmland prices chiefly reflect the productivity of the land measured in sacks of soybeans. In Mato Grosso, land sold for around $22.50 per 60-kilogram sack. Thus, land that produces 50 sacks per hectare, which is a reasonable target, would be worth $6,750/ha.

That, in a nutshell, is the story here. Invest $3,000 to get the land, improve it, and then sell it for $6,750, a 100 percent-plus return for a low-risk process that takes three to four years. After allowing for management costs, the project ought to return at least 37 percent annually for investors.

You might wonder why, if the economics are so good, more people aren't doing it. The answer is that many people are trying to do this. "There is a bit of a Klondike going on now," one of my contacts told me, alluding to the Klondike gold rush of nineteenth century. "We've seen land in some places double in price, and it's still cheap," given the returns you can get for improving the land.

From 2001 to 2009, the return on this land just from appreciation alone has been 26 percent annually, beating the stuffing out of the stock market and just about every commodity I can think of offhand.

There is also an energy tie-in here, which I'll touch on only briefly. Brazil is a hot spot for ethanol made from sugar cane. Sugar cane is more profitable than soybeans, so the investment dollars are starting to flow toward ethanol production and the Cerrado.

Petrobras, the giant Brazilian oil firm, and the Brazilian government were building a pipeline in northern Mato Grosso, right through the farmland we were visiting. This pipeline would make it possible to produce ethanol in this northern region for the first time. In the larger Mato Grosso region, there were 21 plants in operation—12 of them opened in 2010 alone. There are 43 more on the drawing board, with signed tax concessions from the government. Most will be up and running by 2015. It's quite the boom.

In any event, it's another reason to own farmland. The biofuel mandates around the world will push farmers to produce more feedstock for years to come. It will also prop up prices for farmland and crops. What's more, emerging scarcity issues with arable land and clean water aren't going away anytime soon. Rising populations, especially in the less-developed world, mean we'll need to produce a lot more food. Farmland is also an investment not tied to the vagaries of the stock market.

This land will help feed the growing global population. Brazil is a great beneficiary of that need and has become an agricultural power. It also has a lot of room to grow, as it has more usable arable land than any other country in the world.

We drove through some small towns, and you can see what that prosperity brings. Neat little houses stick out from the older, tired structures that remain from when people were poorer.

Brazil's Meat King

> *The power of its soil always saves Brazil.*
> —Stefan Zweig, *Brazil: The Land of the Future*

Brazil's place as an agricultural superpower is secure given its vast amounts of land, ample rainfall, and bountiful sunshine, so it's no surprise that Brazil has come to dominate certain aisles of the world's grocery store. For example, of the top 10 meat producers in the world, 3 are Brazilian, and they control about 40 percent of the global protein trade. The largest is JBS-Friboi, owned by the Batista family and led by Joesley Batista, "The King of Meat." Batista's is a good story.

Joesley Batista started working at his father's butcher shop in the tropical highlands of Brazil before he was a teenager. His two brothers worked there, too. It was a small family-run affair. His father, who started the business in 1953, would carry slabs of meat on his back to walk them to the market. His was a typical working-class family, deep in the interior of Brazil.

The brothers stuck to the family business, through one crisis after another. Joesley Batista, in particular, showed a talent for business, and the family firm grew and grew and grew.

That family firm is JBS-Friboi, the largest meatpacking company in the world. JBS' sales have gone up nearly 2,000 percent from where it was in 2004. It is Brazil's second-largest privately-owned company, behind only Vale S.A., and most of its sales come from outside of Brazil.

The three brothers still run the show, and Joesley Batista, "the Meat King," is its chairman. He is a billionaire now, one of the most successful of Brazil's entrepreneurs.

Batista, though, had an assist from Brazil's development bank, BNDES, which has helped bankroll the company's acquisitions. BNDES exists to promote the international expansion of Brazilian companies. Taxes fund its efforts. In 2007, BNDES bought 13 percent of JBS to help it acquire Swift, which was America's third-largest pork and beef processor.

In September 2009, JBS bought a 64 percent stake in another American icon, Pilgrim's Pride, pulling it out of bankruptcy. *The Economist* commented on the deal:

> *This will be a big test for the Batista brothers and for Brazil's tropical brand of capitalism, which mixes family control with traded stock, and*

finance from state-run banks with foreign acquisitions. Brazilian companies in other industries are watching how JBS gets on and plotting similar moves themselves.

We see more of this cocktail these days, this mixture of government support and private enterprise, but that is a philosophical topic to explore another day.

With this deal, JBS became the largest meat processor in the world, surpassing Tyson Foods. Now, it's not just that Brazil is raising the animals and growing crops. More and more, Brazilians are getting into the processing business, which brings greater profits.

This too is an interesting commentary on Brazil and its evolving role in food production. Batista is the poster boy of these big ambitions. He wants JBS to become a global power in milk and dairy products, too. This is another area where Brazilian firms plan to expand rapidly in the next several years. The company is public now (only in Brazil, unfortunately) and has other shareholders, but the Batista family controls it.

The third-largest player is Brasil Foods, which trades on the NYSE under the ticker BRFS. It has grand ambitions to become a great branded food company like Kellogg's, General Mills, or Nestlé. Besides being huge in Brazil, it is also the largest poultry exporter in the world and the second-largest meat exporter. It has 9 percent of the global protein trade by itself.

If we know one thing for sure, it is that the new consumers in these emerging markets will eat more processed meats, Brazilians included. Just to get to a level of poorer European countries, consumption would more than double. This bodes well for Brasil Foods' business.

There is also a somewhat surprising opportunity in dairy. "Brazilians are eating yogurt for the first time," Renato Roscoe told us.

Renato is a soil expert and former Embrapa hand. (The latter is a government agribusiness research institute.) He holds a PhD in soil science and knows these lands well. He gave our group a good presentation before we embarked for our farmland tours. Sure enough, more than once on our trip, we heard people tell us that "Brazilians are eating yogurt!" Apparently, they didn't eat much before. Again, as part of this big bulging consumer class, some 30 million new consumers since 2005, people are starting to enjoy a more varied and complex diet. Brazilians consume only 2.5 liters of dairy per capita per year, versus nine in Argentina.

But the Brazilian dairy industry is gearing up for a lot more. It is forecast to grow by a third in the next decade. In the process, it will become a top exporter of milk and milk products. Why? Think Asia.

Per capita consumption of dairy is booming in Asia, too. For instance, in China, Vietnam, and Thailand, per capita consumption increased 206 percent, 91 percent, and 65 percent, respectively, since 2000. There is a lot of upside remaining. The typical Chinese citizen, for example, consumes less than a third of the dairy a typical EU citizen does. (I don't expect that gap will close completely, by the way, because the Chinese don't generally like cheese.)

Some of the fastest-growing importers are in markets where there are constraints to new production (such as a lack of available land). These include Thailand, the Philippines, Indonesia, and Malaysia, as well as North African states such as Algeria, Egypt, and the Middle East.

Brazil has no such constraints. There is plenty of pastureland and water. Production is low cost, so more and more of the world's dairy products will soon come from Brazil. Figure 3.1 shows you the opportunity unfolding in dairy.

When in Brazil, our crew visited a dairy project at Jaragua, a beautiful 3,000-hectare farm near Campo Grande. The farm is in a great location, right near a major road. It is also four kilometers from a new dairy factory under construction in a nearby township. We also drove by this site, which will produce 150,000 liters per day, expanding to 700,000 liters per day by 2014.

Vencedor, the firm building the plant, is an established dairy producer. "They are desperate for milk," one of our contacts told us. He had signed agreements at very attractive rates to provide them with milk.

And remember forestry. I would guess most investors have little patience for forestry investing, so I won't cover it here except to relate a funny story one of our contacts told us. He was giving a presentation in New York to a group of prospective investors. He told them it was a 20- to 25-year investment, to allow the trees sufficient time to mature. An elderly lady told him afterward that she couldn't wait that long. "Hell, I'm so old I don't buy green bananas!"

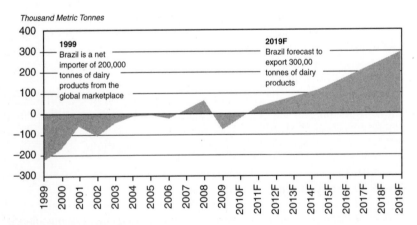

FIGURE 3.1 Brazil's Got Milk
Source: Fapri.

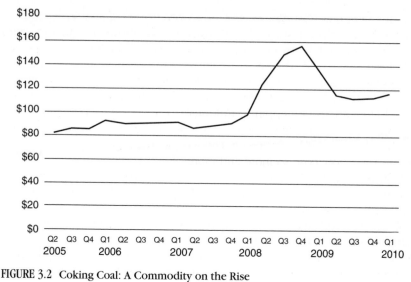

FIGURE 3.2 Coking Coal: A Commodity on the Rise

Source: Bloomberg.

Speaking of old, let's turn again to Roy Nash and his adventures in 1920s. Nash was a remarkable character who wrote a lot about these aspects of Brazil that interest us. He studied forestry at Yale and served in the Philippine Forest Service. He was a captain of artillery in World War I, then traveled far and wide in Brazil for three years and spent a summer in Portugal. During this time, Nash wrote *The Conquest of Brazil*. He continued his association with Brazil for the rest of his life. During World War II, he served in Brazil wearing various hats, including cultural attaché at the U.S. Embassy in Rio.

In his book, Nash talks about the great plains of Mato Grosso. The name "Mato Grosso," he points out, means "thick forest." Those forests are long gone. "When the world was young," Nash writes, "the forests were as luxuriant as the whiskers of the barbarians." After it was logged, beef farmers used great swaths of land as pasture.

Nash's book gave me a useful historical perspective on Brazil. It reminded me how some things never change. "Brazil is so predominantly an agricultural and pastoral country," Nash observed then, "that no other facts can have quite such importance as the facts of the productive occupation of her soil."

Brazil's Rising Affluence

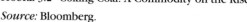

Everything is going to be all right in the end, and if everything is not yet all right, that's only because we haven't reached the end.

—Popular Brazilian saying

In one of our meetings, we met an economist who got everyone's attention when he started talking about Brazilian financial products and how he's averaged 25 percent a year in the past few years without doing any work (I'm suspicious). Asked how to get into these products, he said they are open only to Brazilian residents. Initially, he made his investments through his wife, who is Brazilian.

This led the reader to say, "I'm going to invest in a Brazilian wife."

While that may not be a bad investment for some, there are other Brazilian opportunities beyond agriculture.

As I remarked earlier, there is a rapidly expanding middle class here (a familiar theme in many of the markets we cover in this book). Over the past six years, Brazil has added some 30 million middle-class consumers. They are only starting to enjoy products we take for granted, like yogurt. "We're happy because we are getting richer," Renato said, unemployment being the lowest in his lifetime.

Not only is the middle class expanding, but Brazil is also minting millionaires. Only nine countries have more millionaires than Brazil, according to one study cited by Larry Rohter in his book *Brazil on the Rise*. "With about one-sixth the population of India, Brazil has more millionaires than India," he writes.

Rohter goes on:

> *In a matter of a few years, Brazil has seen a new surge in entrepreneurs who have built fortunes from activities as diverse as airlines, cosmetics, slaughterhouses, shoes, toys and computers. . . . This phenomenon, particularly notable in sectors such as agriculture and ranching and oil and mining, was accompanied by a burst of spending on luxury items ranging from jewelry and designer clothing to private airplanes and yachts.*

One such builder of fortune, Eike Batista happens to sit at number eight on Forbes's global rich list. He was worth about $30 billion at last count, on the back of Brazil's oil, gas, and mining assets (a field we'll explore later). He's also keen on the growing middle class: "China is putting more than 20 million new consumers into the world each year, add to that the two million we're adding in Brazil, and the 3 million from India . . . —it's clear we're living in a cycle," he told a BBC reporter from his office overlooking Rio's Sugarloaf Mountain.

In fact, Brazil's richest man believes that the outlook for Brazil is especially good. "We have our own oil, we've got natural resources—I believe we're living in a cycle of growth like the United States lived in the 1960s."

Given that context, you can understand some of the success companies are having in Brazil. Whirlpool is one example. According to the company, one in six Brazilians already has at least one of its appliances. In agriculture, AGCO, a maker of farm equipment, saw sales in South America surge, thanks mostly to Brazilian farmers. Owens-Illinois, the glass container company, finds its fastest-growing market in Brazil. And Brookfield Asset Management enjoys high growth rates in its Brazilian residential businesses.

Buy the One Thing Brazil Needs

Brazil is blessed with enormous reserves of the metals and minerals essential to modern manufacturing. . . . Coal may be the only substance vital to industrial production that is in short supply.
—Larry Rohter, *Brazil on the Rise:*
The Story of a Country Transformed

In São Paulo, I gave a short presentation to a group of readers about a few attractive Brazilian investment themes. My favorite was the case for hard coking coal, also known as met coal.

Steelmakers use hard coking coal for steel making. The big emerging markets are short of the stuff. China, India, and Brazil all import it.

The southern coast of Brazil bristles with steel expansion projects. Its need for coking coal will more than double over the next decade. The same kind of situation exists in China and India.

I made the case that Mozambique, Africa, is where the world will get a good chunk of the coking coal it needs. The play here was Riversdale Mining, which owned a heaping pile of it in the Moatize Basin.

The day after my presentation, the Brazilian mining giant Vale said it bought a 51 percent stake in a logistics firm in Mozambique. Vale has a coal project in the Moatize Basin, too. It had already invested approximately $1 billion there before this latest move. I look at it as further validation of the idea of investing in coking coal and also in the mining of the commodity in Mozambique. This firm Vale bought, SDCN, owns railway concessions that will carry Vale's coal to the port at Beira.

(About three months after I recommended Riversdale to my readers, it too, got a buyout offer for a 60 percent premium.)

Miner Vale, meanwhile, wants to become one of the world's largest fertilizer companies. It wants to boost potash output tenfold by 2017 and triple its output of phosphates. Acquisitions and investments in its own mines will make that happen. It sees the opportunity to serve farmers in its own backyard.

Vale has significant fertilizer assets in Vale Fertilizantes. This is a relatively new fertilizer company that will hold all of Vale's fertilizer assets. It was the second-biggest revenue generator for Vale after its more famous iron ore mines. Vale Fertilizantes has many of Brazil's best fertilizer assets, which is key, because Brazil also imports most of its fertilizer needs. See Figure 3.3.

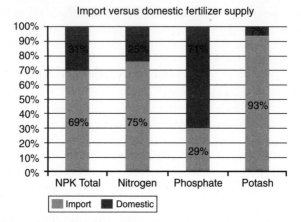

FIGURE 3.3 Brazil Lacks Fertilizer
Source: MBAC Fertilizer.

You can see that Brazil depends on the rest of the world for its fertilizer needs, which keep its mighty agricultural production humming. In particular, note the lack of domestic potash, with 93 percent of Brazil's needs coming from outside of the country.

In a bigger-picture sense, this adds to the broader theory that you will do well to invest in the commodities that the big emerging markets are short of. China, India, and Brazil import both hard coking coal and potash, and it looks likely they will import a lot more over the next decade.

São Paulo: The Economic Heart of Brazil

São Paulo, a mind-boggling immense sprawl of a city, sits at the economic heart of Brazil. The state of São Paulo has 45 million people and makes up nearly a third of Brazil's economic output. Half of the country's tax base is here. If it were its own economy, São Paulo state would be the second-largest in South America, behind only Brazil and ahead of Argentina and Colombia. It is also home to Brazil's stock market, the fourth-largest in the world by market cap.

The city of São Paulo is Brazil's New York City. Someone once said it was as if Los Angeles threw up on New York. It's a bustling, congested city of 11 million people, with another 9 million in the suburbs. Author Larry Rohter calls it, "Ground zero for [the] explosion of conspicuous consumption." São Paulo is the third-largest urban center in the world, behind only Tokyo and Mexico City as ranked by the United Nations.

For many, it's an ugly city, but I loved it right away. While gloom and doom hover over the economies of the United States and Europe, it is impossible to maintain a sense of pessimism in São Paulo—or Brazil, for that matter. It's a showcase for the kind of changes sweeping over the emerging markets.

São Paulo had a humble beginning. Jesuits founded it on the banks of the little Tietê River in the sixteenth century. For hundreds of years, it was an insignificant settlement. Even as late as the 1870s, only 26,000 inhabitants were cobbled around its narrow streets.

However, it would go on to make perhaps the greatest population growth curve of any major city in human experience (as the Fernand Braudel Institute maintains). A great coffee boom in the ninteenth century was the spark that kindled São Paulo's growth. A great deal of wealth jelled in São Paulo and expanded into other businesses. Thus, São Paulo quickly became Brazil's most industrious city.

Ambitious people of all kinds took root here over time, and today, São Paulo has an intriguing mix of people. It has more people of

- Japanese descent than any city outside of Japan.
- Syrian-Lebanese descent than any city outside of the Middle East.
- Italian descent than any city outside of Italy.

Each of these migrations happened at different times and for different reasons. For example, the big Japanese wave came in 1908 as the transition from feudalism caused much poverty in Japan, forcing many to look abroad for a better life. At the same time, Brazil desperately needed workers for its coffee plantations around São Paulo. Hence, the migration of Japanese to Brazil.

Those kinds of incidents fascinate me, as they bring together different, distant cultures. After all, I don't think most people realize there are so many people of Japanese, Syrian-Lebanese, or Italian descent, for that matter, in São Paulo.

São Paulo did not grow up slowly around a center, as did the cities of Europe. Rather, it grew hastily and in an improvised manner. You can see the consequences of that process today. Traffic is horrendous. It can take more than an hour to move only a handful of blocks. The subway system is not up to the task of serving the entire city, and record car sales overwhelm the construction of new roads.

Furthermore, an acute housing shortage provides an interesting investment opportunity. There are a lot of ways to show the data on housing. One common way to measure housing shortages is to look at how many families have three people per bedroom. This measure shows about 13 percent of families live in substandard housing. Expressed as a number of units, Brazil needs nearly 6 million new homes.

That's really not surprising when you think of the swelling ranks of the middle class. Millions of people have become consumers in the last decade, yet housing has not caught up with that demand. By some estimates, Brazil needs to build about 1.6 million homes every year just to keep up with new families entering the market.

In São Paulo, you can see the shortage in the price of homes. New construction often takes three years. People now taking delivery for housing units bought three years ago find that the value of their dwellings have doubled.

All this frothiness has some people worried about a housing bubble. Brazil's mortgage market, too, is in hyper-growth mode. Take a look at the total loans to homebuilders and buyers in Figure 3.4.

It looks impressive, but the starting base was very low. Brazil's home lending market is still only a fraction of that found in other Latin American countries, such as Mexico or Chile. Brazilians also have much more equity invested in their homes. Typically, loan-to-value ratio is 70 to 75 percent.

Eventually, supply will catch up with demand, and maybe even exceed it. Then you'll have a correction. For now, the easiest way to cash in on Brazil's housing boom is to buy Gafisa (GFA), the only Brazilian real estate company trading on the NYSE.

Gafisa has built and sold nearly 1,000 developments and more than 11 million square meters of housing in its 55-year run. Traditionally focused on the high-end market, Gafisa recently bought Tenda to tackle the low end of the housing market.

Gafisa has a good track record and nationally recognized brand names. It looks like a good speculation on the long-term demand for housing in Brazil.

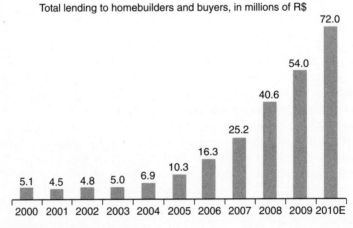

Total lending to homebuilders and buyers, in millions of R$

FIGURE 3.4 Home Lending Boom

Source: Gafisa.

Another surefire long-term demand is oil, and we met someone who knows perhaps more than anyone about that.

Meet Mr. Go-Deeper

What can one say about Rio, except that it's all true.
—Anthony Bourdain, *The Nasty Bits*

Rio de Janeiro is as great a city as everyone says it is. There are the pretty beaches, the verdant mountains, and the signature 130-foot-tall soapstone statue of Christ the Redeemer on a rocky crest 2,300 feet above the sea overlooking the city. There are the street-side cafes and the infectious, easygoing lifestyle of the Cariocas (which is what you call people from Rio).

One pleasant morning, a small crew of readers and I left our hotel at Ipanema beach to go on a short ride to nearby Copacabana. The main office for HRT Oil & Gas looks out over the storied beach. Here we visited with CEO Marcio Mello, which was one of the highlights of the trip.

Mello, aka "Mr. Go-Deeper" is full of energy. He had us mesmerized as he described the hunt for oil and gas in Brazil and off the coast of West Africa.

Petrobras, Brazil's giant oil firm, as you may know, found billions of barrels of oil in the deep waters of Brazil. Mello, an old Petrobras hand, wrote a book more than 20 years ago that predicted those discoveries. Today, he has another theory about oil off the coast of Namibia. Millions of years ago, Africa and South America were one big landmass. Following those clues, Mello found the geology of the coast of Namibia was similar to where the big oil finds were in Brazil. The idea is that the same kinds of discoveries exist in the waters off Namibia, where the continents once joined together.

I can't do justice to the whole story here, but suffice it to say Mello and his crew are on the cutting edge of oil exploration. We visited their lab in Botafogo and got a tour of the kind of work they do. It's incredibly high-tech and makes you appreciate just how difficult the oil business is.

Mello himself is a kind of magic man in the oil and gas industry. His company raised more than $1 billion by selling a third of the company in an IPO. His pre-IPO investors already made more than 10 times their money.

Interestingly, the IPO happened first on Brazil's stock exchange. I asked Mello why he didn't aim to list in the United States or London. His simple answer: "Speed." Mello doesn't like delays. "I was born in seven months," he says. "No joke. That is true. I couldn't wait." And so it has been his whole life. He says HRT will list in the United States, but the process takes longer. "And time is money," Mello said. "One day is a lot of money in the oil and gas business." The sooner HRT gets to production, the better.

So, the reason for the IPO was plain. "We know where the oil is," he said. "What we need is money." The money raised will go toward sinking wells and producing oil. It's an expensive proposition.

You might be curious as to where Mello is putting his money, beyond HRT. "I put all my money in oil and iron," he said. Mello is a shareholder of Petrobras and Vale, the giant mining outfit.

As to the government's rough treatment of these companies, which some call a "renationalization"? Mello is undeterred. "Just close your eyes and buy it," he says of Petrobras. "You'll never lose over the long term. It has so much value even government incompetence can't destroy it."

Mello may well be right. It makes me a bit nervous, though, having the government as such a big (and overbearing) partner. Plus, Petrobras has to spend hundreds of billions of dollars developing big offshore discoveries, which is risky. The final costs could be much higher than today's estimates. Still, Petrobras owns a huge amount of oil and is one of the largest producers in the world.

I'll end with one other anecdote about Mello. Over a fabulous lunch of melt-in-your-mouth pasta and fresh fish at a small Italian restaurant around the corner from his office, he shared some of his thoughts on life and business. Mello, as I've found with many successful businesspeople and investors, doesn't dwell on the negatives. As one of my readers put it, "You seldom find an Eeyore at the top of the heap," referring to the gloomy character of Winnie-the-Pooh fame.

Instead, Mello cheerfully makes the most of whatever cards life deals. He is passionate about his business and focused on opportunities and figuring out how to exploit them. "There are no problems," he says. "There are only opportunities." That could be the tag line of my own ceaseless combing of the globe for ideas. I've come to appreciate how an apparent (or potential) crisis, whether about food, water, or whatever, is the handmaiden of opportunity. Mello, for instance, turned the world's unquenchable thirst for oil into a fortune.

Florianopolis: Flip-Flops on the Ground

We were received with a hospitality hardly to be equaled . . . for [Brazil] asks neither who you are nor whence you come, but opens its doors to every wayfarer.
—Louis Agassiz and Elizabeth Cabot Cary Agassiz,
A Journey in Brazil (1879)

The southernmost part of our tour took in Florianopolis, the capital of the state of Santa Catarina, in southern Brazil. "Floripa," as it is known, is on the landward side of an island, where it can shelter ships from the brunt of the Atlantic Ocean's powers. (It boasts warmer water off its beaches, which pleases the growing number of local and international tourists.) The Portuguese colonists settled here in the seventeenth century, looking for gold.

They didn't find gold, but Floripa has become a favorite spot for wealthy Brazilians. I stayed at a resort on Jurerê Beach, which is one of 42 beaches on this 200-square-mile island. Jurerê is the best one, apparently, having won a number of awards. Jurerê is where the rich stay when they come, and I saw some monster houses that looked like beached cruise ships, one even had a helipad.

I came to Floripa to look at a new project by a group called Txai (pronounced "chai," like the tea). It is a spectacular piece of property. This project will be open to individuals to buy bungalows, lofts, and more.

I enjoy exploring these little nooks of the world unknown to most Americans, although on Sunday night, we took a break from the Brazilian cuisine and found an English pub that had the Dolphins-Jets game on TV. There we met an American who had lived on the island for 20 years. He is an old Mets and Jets fan from New York and had come to watch the game.

In my four-city tour of Brazil, what can I say about the experiences to sum up so far?

I can say the caipirinhas, Brazil's national drink, is a potent cocktail. Brazilian meats are very salty. Brazilian desserts are very sweet. This taste for the extremes of the flavor spectrum extends to Brazil's monetary brand, as well.

Brazil's Currency "Do-Overs"

The Brazilian currency is the real. The Brazilians pronounce "real" something like "hey-ALL." In plural form, it sounds like "hey-EYES." So we're all saying it wrong when we say "RAY-all".

The Brazilian real has been strong (and the dollar is weak). While I was there, it hit a 10–month high against the U.S. dollar. Since 2008, the Brazilian real gained 45 percent against the dollar, which means U.S. assets are cheap to Brazilians. This is why many are buying property in South Florida.

In the Miami area, Brazilians bought more homes and apartments than any other group of international buyers. According to International Sales Group, Brazilians bought about half of the Miami condos sold to foreigners for more than $500,000. Brazilians accounted for half the sales of condos bought for over $1 million.

Even so, the Brazilian finance minister frets and threatened to weaken the real. What he feared was that the strong real will hurt Brazil's export goods by making Brazilian goods more expensive, hence weakening the Brazilian economy. It is a tired line of reasoning. This idea that a country gets rich by destroying the value of its currency is a weed that won't go away no matter how many times you pull it from the soil.

What's curious about this is that you'd think a Brazilian would appreciate the dangers of weakening a currency more than most. Brazil has had a habit of blowing up its currency over the past 60 years.

From 1942 to the present, Brazil went through eight different currencies:

1. Mil Reis, 1833–1942
2. Cruzeiro, 1942–1967
3. Cruzeiro Novo, 1967–1986
4. Cruzado, 1986–1989
5. Cruzado Novo, 1989–1990
6. Cruzeiro, 1990–1993
7. Cruzeiro Real, 1993–1994
8. Real, 1994– ?

The present-day real is but a teenager, a mere youth sprung from a bad family. Yet it was among the world's strongest currencies in recent years, bolstered by the commodity wealth and strong growth rate of Brazil's economy.

Say what you will about the U.S. dollar, which has been a poor currency as far as retaining its purchasing power over time, but it's never gotten so bad that the United States had to start over, at least not yet. Brazil's experience makes the dollar look like a gold standard. It was not that long ago that Brazil's inflation rate hit 2,700 percent. It happened in one 12-month period from 1989 to 1990.

Even as late as 1999, Brazil was a financial basket case. In 1998 and 1999, its finances were such a mess that Brazil got the biggest IMF rescue package in history up to that point, $41.5 billion.

During the twentieth century as a whole, Brazil had a cumulative inflation rate of more than a quadrillion percent. If you were a net saver in Brazil and kept that money in Brazil's currency, you lost big. You might as well have set the money on fire.

Today, Brazil is in a different position. The currency is so strong, its politicians fret. American travelers find no bargains in the shops of São Paulo or Rio. Brazil, too, has huge currency reserves and is now a net creditor, not a debtor. Brazil is even accumulating gold, the real thing. An economist I met on my trip told me Brazil's central bank had 5 percent of its reserves in gold, and it's been buying more.

Today, U.S. investors go out of their way to buy products that give them exposure to Brazilian reals, instead of U.S. dollars. It's incredible when you think how much things have changed in just the past 10 years.

Brazil could screw it up again.

There are some worrisome signs. The new president is Dilma Rousseff. She is a former Marxist guerrilla. Hers is a quite a tale. Suffice to say, she has since mellowed out, supposedly. Most people see her as simply continuing the policies pursued under President Lula. But we'll see.

Some of her opening moves were not encouraging. She had been highly critical of foreigners buying Brazilian land during her campaign. "Brazilian land for Brazilians" was the chant. I mentioned how the Brazilian government restricted foreign ownership of Brazilian land. Worse, the legal rules were so unclear that all such acquisitions since 1988 could've been made null and void, in theory, with the land returned to nationals. Some political groups were saying this is exactly what should be done.

The mainstream papers seemed to treat this latter possibility as unlikely. I can tell you from talking to people down there that local businesspeople did not dismiss that possibility.

There have been a lot of foreigners buying. As I wrote above, the economics of turning the Cerrado to productive farmland is compelling. You get a 100 percent-plus return in three to four years without leverage using a proven 40-year-old process. Other folks started to figure this out, too. A group in Hong Kong, backed by Jacob Rothschild and a pair of Hong Kong tycoons, raised $179 million to do just what I described. Others are following suit, raising large piles of money in public markets to invest in Brazilian farmland.

In theory, the country could double the amount of land under cultivation—something no other large country could plausibly do. The land is also cheap and potentially very productive. Brazilians can harvest two crops a year, for instance. All these investors are doing the same math. Buy the land, improve the land, and boom: big returns only a few years later.

Many foreigners are already there. By some estimates, foreigners own or control about 20 percent of Brazil's cane production. Estimates for some other crops are even higher. Good estimates are tough to come by because many do business through a Brazilian company, even though foreigners own and control it. The government tried to close this loophole with its tinkering.

In any event, rule changes and uncertainty freeze agricultural investment in Brazil every time they strike. This is big news for global food markets because Brazil was such a key part of the equation. Brazil, as I've pointed out, is the world's arable-land bank. This is where we can get the added food supply the world needs.

As *Reuters* points out, "Brazil's essential role as a provider of food for the world's expanding population is at risk. . . . There are simply no large-scale alternatives to Brazil's unique agriculture potential."

However, Brazil can't do it alone. Getting the arable land to production is a process that takes significant investment and time. Foreigners brought the needed capital. Between 2002 and 2008, foreign investors poured nearly $2.5 billion into land alone.

Foreign money also brought the expertise of large-scale and modern farming techniques. Their investments create jobs for Brazilians. They pay taxes. They raise the value of Brazilian lands. A recent study said that farmland values had increased 54 to 70 percent over the last three years in frontier regions.

Of course, foreign money brought more food to the world. What did Brazilians do with Brazilian land before? Not much. It mostly sat there while the country was poor and backward.

Sometimes I think Brazilian politicians pine for the old days. Governments are "pathologically stupid," as my friend Doug Casey likes to say. So perhaps this shouldn't be a surprise. Nonetheless, I am always amazed at how readily politicians are so quick to kill the golden geese. (The U.S. government is, sadly, no different.)

We may not feel the effects immediately, but Brazil's hostile turn toward foreign investment helps plant the seed for a future food crisis. Brazil forgets there is a larger world out there. If Brazil is not careful, the money will just go elsewhere, and Brazil will be the poorer for it.

The Caipirinhas Crisis

In the four-month period beginning on December 20, 1994, the Mexican peso lost 50 percent of its value. Some wag dubbed it the Tequila Crisis. The name stuck. I don't think anything so severe will happen in Brazil, but there are warning signs that Brazil's boom needs a breather. A caipirinhas crisis, perhaps.

For all that there is to like about Brazil from an investment point of view, it has problems, too, some of which might surprise you.

For instance, Brazil's boom has been fueled in part by the free flow of credit, which is a warning sign all its own. Its major banks had all reported loan growth of more than 20 percent. As the *Financial Times* reports: "Brazil's economy has been riding a consumer credit boom as millions of new middle-class consumers borrow money at high interest rates to pay for everything from liposuction to cars."

Overall debt numbers as a percentage of the economy are still low, but the debt service burden on consumers is already very heavy. Brazilians pay high interest rates. And per capita incomes are still low, lower than in Mexico, Peru, and Venezuela. So, debt service as a percentage of disposable income is high at 24 percent, according to fund managers Paul Marshall and Amit Rajpal, who published their research in the *Financial Times*. The U.S. mortgage bubble blew up when that number hit 14 percent.

Prices were also rising. When I was there, I was surprised how expensive things were. The dollar did not go far there, that's for sure. At some point, the comparisons become a little absurd. You could stay at a Marriott Renaissance hotel in São Paulo, and it cost you 50 percent more than if you stayed at a Marriott Renaissance in Manhattan. As the *Wall Street Journal* pointed out, a Honda Civic EX-L cost $38,800 in São Paulo and $21,425 in New York City. A Starbuck's Grande café latte cost $5.40 in São Paul and $4.30 in NYC.

Brazilians are starting to feel the pinch, but Brazil's politicians made sure they won't get left behind. Brazil's Congress gave itself a 62 percent raise in December of 2010 to $210,000 per year. As is, Brazilian workers earn salaries more comparable to developed countries even though doing business in Brazil is more expensive as firms contend with bad roads, power outages, congested ports, high crime, and heavy taxes.

'People don't appreciate how difficult it is to do business in Brazil. In the "ease of doing business" World Bank survey, Brazil ranks 127 out of 183 countries. Rwanda and Belarus score better than Brazil. The survey points out, for instance, that it takes 120 days and the completion of 15 procedures to start a business in Brazil, compared to 56 days and 5 procedures in the rest of Latin America.

I have firsthand experience with this, given my involvement with a Brazilian farmland project. I can tell you it is a long process to get anything done in Brazil. Months rolled by as we waited for approvals of one kind or another as the rules changed or were applied differently in different offices. The place is thick with bureaucratic webbing.

Still, having said all that, the Brazilian market was among the cheapest of the big emerging markets in 2011. The price-to-earnings ratio based on earnings forecast for the next 12 months sank to only 9.5 times, and the Brazilian market has traded sideways for almost two years. A Caipirinhas Crisis would likely make them all cheaper still.

Brazil clearly offers numerous opportunities over the long haul. But one thing we have to realize is that none of these places will grow uninterrupted. There are always booms and busts.

So, while I am raising a caution flag on Brazil, I see the long-term as bright. The world right side up describes a multi-decade process that may halt for stretches, or even seem to go backwards, but over the long haul that gap between the emerging markets and the developed markets will continue to narrow.

Brazil has made tremendous leaps ahead in just the last decade. I don't think it's finished just yet.

Five Key Takeaways

- One of the best opportunities in Brazil is to invest in agriculture or the things Brazil's ag producers need. Potash is one. The big names are Potash Corp and Mosaic, but better values can be had among the smaller players and miners. MBAC Fertilizers is a small Brazilian player trying to become an integrated producer of potash and phosphate in Brazil.
- Meat: Brasil Foods (BRFS:NYSE) is the champion here. It's a good long-term play on Brazil continuing its dominance of the protein trade.
- Gafisa (GFA:NYSE) builds residential homes. Long-term this is another likely good play, though I expect short-term turbulence as Brazil works through what might be a credit crisis.
- Met coal: This brand of high-grade coal is being snapped up the world over. Riversdale, mentioned above, has a huge deposit. Quality met coal deposits are hard to find and hence valuable investment properties.
- Larry Rother's *Brazil on the Rise* is one of the better books on Brazil's recent renaissance. For the historically minded, you may enjoy Roy Nash's *Conquest of Brazil*.

CHAPTER 4

Nicaragua: This Side of Paradise

When my nine-year-old daughter Charlotte heard I was going to Nicaragua, she frowned and said, "No fair!"

Nicaragua used to be just another faraway place, an abstraction. But one time, my wife and kids got to come with me. We stayed at a house in Rancho Santana, a little slice of paradise on the Pacific Coast of Nicaragua. For the kids, the days consisted of playing on the beach or in the pool and having a good time.

Now Nicaragua means something entirely different to them.

The gaps between perception and reality make the investment world go round, too. The perception is that Nicaragua suffers from its past. *Nicaragua ha sufrido mucho,* as the saying goes ("Nicaragua has suffered a lot").

After 41 years of living under the oppressive Somoza dictatorship— supported by the United States—the Sandinistas came to power in 1979. (The Sandinistas named themselves after Augusto Sandino, a rebel who led the resistance movement against the U.S. occupation of Nicaragua in the 1920s and 1930s.)

The Sandinistas ran the country in the 1980s and Nicaragua devolved into the usual state of communist enterprises. It was a mess.

One of the books I read during a recent trip was *My Car in Managua*, a lighthearted look at living in post-revolutionary Nicaragua in the 1980s. Author Forrest Colburn, who was a frequent visitor and lived in Nicaragua for a year, tells many engaging vignettes about what it was like.

For example, the Sandinistas nationalized the country's largest grocery chain. Without market pricing and incentives driving it, the stores suffered. There were often shortages of basics like milk, eggs, rice, beans, and the like.

The stores fumbled around badly when it came to making choices about what to carry. Colburn writes how a store could routinely be out of cheese, but have an aisle's worth of cheese graters. Or how they might be out of toilet paper and toothpaste but carry plenty of imported fruit preserves and jams, in a country that produces an abundance of tropical fruit.

Other businesses struggled, too. McDonald's had a restaurant in Managua. The manager there had to improvise. When he couldn't get potatoes for fries, he sold fried cassava. When he ran out of lettuce, he used cabbage. When there was no American cheese, he'd use some other kind of cheese. This upset McDonald's, which prides itself on the uniformity of its product, no matter where in the world you find it.

Colburn says the phrase *"no hay"* became a kind of national refrain. It means, "There isn't any." Frequently, there wasn't much of anything.

Colburn tells a local joke. A poor Nicaraguan dies and goes before St. Peter, who tells the poor Nicaraguan that he will have to go to hell. But he gets to choose whether he wants to go to capitalist hell or communist hell.

"What's the difference?" the poor Nicaraguan asks.

"In both, they drop you in a vat, feed you manure, and bang you over the head with a shovel," St. Peter tells him.

"So which one should I choose?"

"I'd choose communist hell," St. Peter advises him. "Sometimes they lose the shovels or run out of manure."

Beyond these problems, the Sandinistas began to print a lot of money to finance their social agenda and money-losing enterprises. The córdoba traded at 10-to-1 against the U.S. dollar when the Sandinistas took over. However, it rapidly began to lose value. For McDonald's, it meant that every 1,000 córdobas (or $100) it earned at its Managua store in 1979 was worth $5 by 1985. Moreover, since the Sandinistas clamped down on foreign exchange, McDonald's couldn't even get its $5 out of the country.

The money printing continued. The value of the córdoba continued to plunge. Perhaps the best way to see the effects of this is to look at the cost of a single pineapple in Managua's markets. "Before the revolution," Colburn writes, "the going rate for a pineapple was half a córdoba." By the tenth anniversary of the Sandinista Revolution in 1989, the cost of a single pineapple was 10,000 córdobas, this for something that was readily grown locally.

These experiences repeat throughout history, yet we continue to ignore these lessons. It doesn't bode well for the U.S. dollar, given the free-spending ways of the U.S. government.

Eventually, the Sandinistas lost the election in 1990. Maybe this caused them to re-examine some of the ideals of the communist revolution. But today, back in power since 2006, the Sandinistas, while certainly not angels, have changed. They own hotels and businesses and aim to encourage tourism. They are about as communist as the Chinese.

I came to Nicaragua looking to buy property there. There are new projects and a growing number of tourists. Good food and drink are cheap and plentiful. It is another world from the one Colburn describes in *My Car in Managua*.

Latin America, in general, seems to be on the upswing. There are interesting stories and opportunities popping up in once-forlorn markets, such as in Colombia, which may be Latin America's most exciting comeback story (as we saw in Chapter 2).

I expect new opportunities to emerge from this resurgence.

All this is to say that markets work in cycles. Progress is often a labyrinth, as Scott Fitzgerald said. And the creation of wealth is a process driven by people with ideas and know-how and often a sprinkling of good luck. It happens where it is free to happen. Sometimes the most dramatic examples happen in places where it was not allowed to happen for a long time. As investors, it pays to look into these kinds of markets.

Central America's Rising Star

I love going to Nicaragua. I love the food, the culture, and the old Spanish colonial architecture. I love the pretty landscape of volcanoes, lakes, and unspoiled beaches. And I've found the people friendly and humble. I have many friends there. Recently, I've taken to learning Spanish, in part because I plan to make regular trips there.

Still, most people have a different opinion of Nicaragua. I remember when I first told friends of mine about going down there. I got many strange looks. "What's in Nicaragua?" "Isn't it dangerous?" Most people still have an image of Nicaragua from the 1980s.

But a lot has changed. Nicaragua has taken a number of steps to make it easier for foreigners to live and work there. It seems to be working. Nicaragua is a rising star in Central America. *Live and Invest Overseas* recently named Nicaragua its top retirement haven for 2011. "Nicaragua is more attractive than ever for one important reason," the magazine reports. "It's a super cheap place to live."

Then there is the World Bank's "ease of doing business" survey, ranking 183 countries. In the most recent survey, Nicaragua earned a ranking of 117. It's not a top ranking, but it's a lot higher than many countries that investors are falling all over themselves to invest in, such as Brazil or India. Nicaragua is ranked ahead of Costa Rica, which I think would surprise most people. It happens to be one of the safest countries in Central America.

Nicaragua has many other attributes that put it in a good spot. It is Central America's largest country, but the second–least densely populated. It has rich volcanic soils that support many crops. It has lots of water from its lakes, rivers, and rainfall. Plenty of potential is there for geothermal and wind power. Riches lie below the soil, including gold.

On one of my trips down, I read Thomas Belt's *The Naturalist in Nicaragua*, which first appeared in 1874. Belt was a mining engineer and traveled the world over. "I now write this brief preface and last chapter of my book," Belt begins, "on my way across the continent to the Urals, and beyond, to the country of the nomad Kirghizes and the far Altai Mountains on the borders of Tibet; and when readers receive my work, I shall probably have turned my face homewards again, and for weeks be speeding across the frozen Siberian steppes, wrapped in furs, listening to the sleigh bells and wondering how my book has sped."

Belt's book is mainly a work of natural history, and he observes all manner of plants and bugs and the like. However, Belt was in Nicaragua to check out the gold mines in Chontales, Nicaragua. Chontales had its own little gold rush in 1861. While checking out his story, I found a *New York Times* article with the dateline "Granada, Nicaragua, Tuesday, March 27, 1861." The story leads off: "Exceedingly rich gold mines have lately been discovered in the department of Chontales . . . and great numbers of persons have gone thither." I love the way that reads.

When Belt finally arrives at the mines, he reports on the quality of the deposits, noting thick veins laced with silver. At certain points, there is as much as 100 ounces of gold per ton of rock, a nice deposit, indeed. Belt describes the machinery and the working of the mine, which history buffs will enjoy. Belt's book inspired me to find out who is mining gold in Nicaragua today.

B2Gold is the largest exporter of gold in Nicaragua. In fact, it is the largest exporting company in the country, period. B2Gold is the fifth-largest employer. Its workers earn, on average, 45 percent more in salaries and benefits than the national average. In addition to Nicaragua, B2Gold has projects in Colombia, Uruguay, and Costa Rica. It has good production, cash costs of $550 an ounce, and loads of exploratory potential. Insiders own 16 percent of the stock, and AngloGold owns 10 percent of the company.

As of this writing, B2Gold has zero debt and no hedges. As gold goes wild topping $1,700, it's great to be hedgeless. That means way more upside for an outfit like B2Gold.

One of its big mines is La Libertad, 110 miles east of Managua. This mine has a seven-year life expectancy counting ahead from its 2010 opening and is expected to deliver 90,000 ounces of gold per year.

B2Gold trades on the Toronto exchange under the ticker BTO. I can only say I wish I'd come across its story sooner. The stock has gone up more than fivefold in the past two years.

B2Gold is an example of a Nicaraguan success story. More proof, too, of another opportunity in the rising star of Central America. It gives you an idea of what can be done there.

Granada: Oldest City in the Americas on Another Upswing

Granada is a city that feels like a village. Everyone knows everything about everyone, and what they don't know they invent.
—Tim Rodgers, *Living and Investing in the New Nicaragua*

In Granada, I woke up to church bells. Granada is the oldest city in the Americas that remains in the same place as where it was founded. It's been there since 1524, when Francisco Hernández de Córdoba, looking for gold, slaves, and whatever else he could get, set it up.

Its history tells an interesting tale, something to keep in mind when you think about what the world looks like today and what it might look like tomorrow. No one stays on the top, or the bottom, forever. Things often turn out dramatically different from what people expect. The wheels of fortune always turn, grinding away at existing piles of wealth and creating new ones in new places.

Granada was once one of the world's most prosperous cities. It sits on the shores of Lake Nicaragua, the nineteenth-largest lake in the world and the third-largest in Central and South America. The lake connects to the Atlantic Ocean by way of the San Juan River. So, there is plenty of water, and the soil is rich and fertile, as it is in most of Nicaragua.

Granada's early history was tumultuous. It was often a target of French, English, and Dutch pirates who would sail up the San Juan River and sack the city, setting churches on fire and making off with loot. In a six-year span (1665–1670), Granada was sacked three times.

By the nineteenth century, though, the pirate threat waned, and Granada looked to take its place among the world's more prominent cities. By the middle of the nineteenth century, it had trading houses dealing directly with New York, Paris, London, and Rome.

When the United States sought an easier way to get from the Atlantic to the Pacific Ocean, the first place it looked to build a canal wasn't in Panama, but in Nicaragua. There was a well-worn path there made by gold prospectors.

In 1848, gold prospectors looking for a way to get to California other than the treacherous overland route came through there. They floated up the river, across the lake to Granada, and took an overland coach to a waiting ship on the Pacific Coast. Thus, this was the natural place to put a canal.

In 1876, a U.S. commission chose this route over all others. It looked inevitable, and people took it for granted. Nicaragua was to be a great trading nation. Granada was going to be better than Constantinople, a linchpin in global commerce. Unfortunately, it was not to be. Instead, the canal wound up in Panama, and Nicaragua never reached the potential many people thought it would. The wheels of fortune never stop turning, though. Today, Granada is once again on the upswing.

I stayed at the Hotel Dario, a colonial mansion built in 1902. In 2006, it became a hotel, named after the famous Nicaraguan poet Rubén Darío. It's a nice hotel, either the best or second-best in the city, depending on whom you ask. There used to be only one hotel of comparable quality there, but that hotel runs third. Many more lodging options have opened up in the past five years.

Granada is popular with Americans and Europeans, both tourists and expats. Granada has more than 1,000 foreign residents in a city of about 150,000. Real estate prices have doubled and tripled in the past five years. In the mid-1990s, you could have picked up a colonial fixer-upper for $60,000, and for another $60,000 in renovations, you could've had a mansion for a small fraction of the price in the United States.

Around the city are plenty of bars and restaurants, and all the sights you'd expect to see in an old Spanish colonial city. There are central plazas, pretty cathedrals, and old-world brick roads.

We walked through an enormous open-air market covering several blocks. It was overflowing with fresh mangoes, bananas, papaya, and other fruits and vegetables, along with fish and meat markets. Plenty of people were shopping.

We took a boat ride around an area of Lake Nicaragua where there are 365 small islands, all privately owned, some with princely houses built on them. One empty island we saw had a "for sale" sign. You could have your own island for $265,000. (All the while, you see a big smoldering volcano in the distance. Hmm.)

In short, Granada looked like a bustling, healthy city to me. It's far from what most Americans probably think Nicaragua is like.

About an hour away from Granada is Rancho Santana, which is a spectacular 2,700-acre property on the Pacific Coast down near the city of Rivas. There are five different beaches. Pink sand, black sand, white sand, some with rocks, some without. There are several incredible ridges and points with breathtaking views of the beach. There's a comfortable clubhouse and bar. It's a great place to relax or have a vacation home. You don't hear anything but the crashing of the waves, and the howler monkeys in the wee morning hours.

All this is to say the differences between the emerging and developed markets continue to decrease. The United States and Europe slide slowly down a path toward bankruptcy while in other markets and other places, there are growth and opportunity, although there are risks, just as there are anywhere. Nicaragua is on the frontier of all of this.

León: How to Live Well in the Old Capital on $2,000 a Month

León is about an hour drive northwest of Managua. León is the second-largest city in the country. It was the capital for more than 200 years before

Managua became the capital in 1852. When I visit Nicaragua, I often stay with a friend of mine from college, who moved down there six years ago.

He lives well there for not much money. This house in which I stay is a comfortable 4,000 square feet with everything you could want in a house, including a big kitchen with granite countertops, beautiful ceramic tiles throughout, an open courtyard, balconies overflowing with pink flowers and vines, a red tile roof, all done in the Spanish-influenced style you find throughout South and Central America. It's bright, airy, and not at all humid. So, even though it is 90 degrees there, we have the windows open and feel fine.

It would cost you approximately $200,000 for this house. If you got the lot and built it yourself, it might cost you $150,000. This is a nice location, too, in a quiet neighborhood. I'm within walking distance of central León with its central park and the largest cathedral in Central America.

You could live extravagantly there for $2,000 a month and even have hired help like a maid, which would cost about $100 a month. One night, we went to dinner while walking the little narrow streets of León. We had nacatamales—meat, peppers, rice, and more mixed in with cornmeal and cooked in banana leaves—for $1.50 each. They were delicious. These were big tamales, a solid meal all by themselves. My friend added these were the high-end version. Cheaper versions existed in the city.

Labor is cheap there. Food is cheap. Some things are not so cheap. For example, gasoline costs more than in the United States Brand-name U.S. products are expensive there, too. If you want to buy a pair of jeans, it will cost at least 30 percent more.

Still, the overall cost of living is low. And there is a lot to like about Nicaragua besides that. There is plenty of fresh fruit, great beaches, and wonderful cultural experiences, all the things you'd want to enjoy as a tourist or expat.

Politics, as usual, is a risk in this otherwise idyllic setting. It is a situation to keep an eye on because Ortega seems to want to follow the model laid out by Hugo Chávez in Venezuela. Many billboards carry pictures of Ortega as well as murals and other pictures dedicated to revolutionary themes and heroes.

There are visible reminders everywhere of Nicaragua's troubled past. Walking around in the city of León, you see lots here and there where there might be a small park or an open space. There were once buildings in these places that were destroyed during the civil war and never rebuilt.

My friend's family is from León, and they left in 1983 as Nicaragua's civil war raged. My friend can still remember playing in the streets, hearing machine gun fire, and sprinting home. He can remember how his family slept in the center of the house where there were more walls between them and what might happen outside. He remembers people knocking on the door, begging for food or a place to hide. Only 11 at the time, he had nightmares for years afterward.

Even today, lots where buildings once stood are empty, and some buildings are still unoccupied and unclaimed, essentially in ruins. My friend's father told me, "This was a really nice town once. We had everything." He told me how there were once nine movie theaters in León, whereas there is only one today. There was once a nice park with tennis courts, right around the corner. Now it's weedy and unkempt, and on and on it goes.

Author Forrest Colburn's take on León was not charitable: "Unless you have family in León, there is nothing in the city of interest." But Nicaragua has changed a lot since the 1980s.

Beyond the politics, the region's geology contributed to the damage. A massive earthquake in 1972 destroyed most of Managua, from which it has yet to recover. In León, repeated earthquakes and eruptions from the Momotombo Volcano forced the city inland from the shores of Lake Managua in 1610. Nicaragua is full of volcanoes. In fact, there is one that is smoldering in Lake Nicaragua.

"We have it all here," my friend told me. "Earthquakes, tsunamis, hurricanes, volcanoes."

Riches from the Land of Lakes and Volcanoes

The sad thing is that Nicaragua ought to be a rich country. It is has acres of good land for agriculture. The soil supports a wide variety of crops and livestock. Coffee in the north. Bananas, papayas, mangoes, sugar cane, and more grow everywhere else.

It is a beautiful country with its volcanoes, lakes, and a lush tropical climate. The people are friendly, and Nicaragua is safe to travel through. It's a young country with more than half of the population under 25 years old. (Nicaragua makes one of the world's best rums, "Flor de Caña: flower of the [sugar] cane." I enjoyed it neat and in the national drink, *el macua*, made with guava juice.)

Nicaragua has another special resource: It is among the most water-rich countries in the world. Approximately one-third of the world's population lives in areas with only 8 percent of the world's renewable fresh water supply. The latter usually consists of surface streams, lakes, and fast-charging groundwater.

In a world where water scarcity is an issue, one part of the world stands out for its water wealth. Latin America has 28 percent of the world's renewable water and only 6 percent of its population. Steve Solomon writes in *Water* that the "super Water Have countries such as Brazil, Russia, Canada, Panama, and Nicaragua [have] far more water than their populations can ever use."

Lake Nicaragua, one of the largest lakes in the world, is the future water supply of Central America. There are many rivers and lakes, which make useful internal waterways. Nicaragua has access to both the Pacific and Atlantic oceans. Nicaraguan waters are great for fishing.

In addition, Nicaragua holds great potential for wind, geothermal—from volcanoes all along the western half of the country—and hydroelectric power. In fact, Rancho Santana is trying to become self-sufficient in energy. There are ridges there where the wind blows constantly. A wind feasibility study done there lately scored as high as it could. The conditions are ideal.

Finally, Nicaragua has great timber resources, in addition to those rich mineral resources like silver and gold.

Nicaragua has always been a place of intrigue, mostly because of geography. Thus, American involvement in Nicaragua goes way back, too. Militarily, the first Marines landed there in 1912 and occupied it until 1933. The Somoza regime, a dictatorship created and supported by the United States, ran the country until the Sandinistas took over in 1979.

Present-day Nicaragua folds in well with some of the investment themes we've been working out in these pages. For instance, when we get to Dubai in Chapter 7 we'll meet "penthouse gypsies," a term coined to describe people with money who go where they are treated best, wherever in the world that may be. Increasingly, they are no longer in the United States or Europe. It may be hard to believe, but there are plenty of penthouse gypsies down there in Rancho Santana.

Why not? They are able to diversify out of the United States, where tax rates are increasing. They get cheap, stunning real estate. Property taxes are hardly anything. You can live well down there on not much money. My good friend who moved to Nicaragua six years ago did so for this reason.

Most Americans worry about confiscation of property, but that risk seems remote after talking to people there. Tourism is the number one cash cow of what is still a poor country. Even Ortega doesn't want to do anything to upset that cash flow. (He owns several hotels.) Plus, there are many ways to hedge your bets, including insurance against confiscation.

As far as enforcement of contracts, the IMF and World Bank rank Nicaragua third among all Latin American and Caribbean countries. Foreign direct investment in Nicaragua is soaring, up fourfold since 2000.

It's world right side up in action, that closing of the gap between emerging and developed markets. I think back to what Bill Bonner said of India: "The world turned against them, relatively, at the beginning of the Industrial Revolution. But if the world turns long enough, it comes back to where it began."

I can't say my trip to Nicaragua yielded hot stock tips. But hopefully, my notes help you see the opportunities that are out there in this great big world if only we look at it with fresh eyes.

Five Key Takeaways

- Keep your eye on B2 Gold (BTO:TSX), the largest exporter of gold in Nicaragua.
- Consider visiting and perhaps investing in real estate in some place like León or Grenada. There is a fairly active rental market, and it's still early in the development curve.
- If beachfront property is your thing, check out Rancho Santana's Pacific Coast. For details, photographs and more, go here: http://www.ranchosantana.com/.
- Retire where property taxes are hardly anything. Housing could put you back only $200,000 or so, and you could live well, whether for a season or year-round.
- To learn more, read *Nicaragua: Living in the Shadow of the Eagle* by Thomas Walker. A good travelogue is Savage Shore by Edward Marriott called *Savage Shore*. Forrest Colburn's *My Car in Managua* is also a fun read, and I recommend it.

CHAPTER 5

China: Crisis and Opportunity in the Middle Kingdom

N o anecdote puts the China question in a nutshell better than this one I heard from one of my contacts there:

"I was in an antique store, negotiating for this antique knife," he told me. "I was about to make the deal when the guy looked at my Rolex watch and offered to exchange. I was ready to do it, but I knew my Rolex watch was a fake, and I didn't want to take advantage of this guy. So I told him that the watch was a fake. He said to me, 'That's okay, this knife is fake, too.'"

I think that is the one thing about China that is tough to untangle, figuring out what's real economic growth and what's fake. Walking around in Beijing, seeing all the new buildings, the traffic and the bustling stores, makes you wonder how much is due to natural demand and how much is artificial stimulus. If it's more of the latter, then much of what we see is unsustainable.

There are two important parts of the macro backdrop that are important to understand about China. First, there has been a tremendous increase in bank lending since the end of 2008; it's up fourfold. We know from experience that when banks grow that fast, bad things tend to happen later. What happens when banks grow too fast is that they slide down the credit-quality spectrum. In short, they make tomorrow's bad loans.

Second, we know that the Chinese government has put in place a huge stimulus plan. Again, we know from experience that when governments invest money, you inevitably wind up with "bridges to nowhere" and all kinds of boondoggles. The money doesn't flow to its best economic uses, but to political ends.

In Beijing, I saw some tangible evidence of this. I visited the largest mall in Asia. It was built six years ago by state-run enterprises. They put it on the western edge of the city, about 40 minutes from Tiananmen

Square. Real estate people thought it was a bad idea. It was too far away. It was too big.

Well, the pros were correct. Today, the place is empty, as it is most days. It was almost eerie walking through there. There were lines of bright shops with neatly dressed attendants and shelves full of the latest from the world's best brands, but there were no customers.

This place has over 10,000 free parking spaces. There is over 1.8 million square feet of retail space here, over 167,225 square meters. That's about three times the base of the Great Pyramid at Giza.

It makes you wonder. Why did this place ever get built? And, boy, are they losing their shirts. But then you wonder about the shops themselves. Why do they stay? How can they possibly make money here? It's all strange.

Then you go 30 minutes into town and visit another big mall packed with people. The parking lot is so full you have to wait to get in. When one car leaves, they let one in.

That's China.

Old Beijing's Last Days Make Way for New

In May 2010, my publisher, Addison Wiggin, and I checked into a fully booked Grand Hyatt on Chang'an Avenue, only a couple of blocks from Tiananmen Square and the Forbidden City. Soon, we met up with a couple of our Beijing contacts: Fred and Ginger. Fred is an entrepreneur who's been in China since 1990. Ginger is a born-and-raised Beijinger, former financial officer of a steel company and entrepreneur. Both have a great perspective on what's really happening in China.

They showed us around, and Beijing is a good place to start to get a sense of the changes.

It took a long time for Beijing to turn right side up. Kublai Khan moved the imperial capital here in the thirteenth century. It was probably the height of the city's grandeur, overshadowing anything that existed in Europe at the time. The Khan's Beijing was built for an emperor. His dining room sat 6,000 men. It had whitewashed walls and red gates, prized horses, exotic trees, parkland stocked with deer, and broad avenues and streets. It held the emperor's treasures, gold, silk, art, and concubines.

However, by the 1860s, it was a shadow of its former self. A Western journalist described the jumble of alleyways, called *hutongs*: "There is not a more squalid collection of houses in an Arab village or in the city of Limerick." Even as late as the 1920s, as New Yorkers had Grand Central Station, and the Empire State Building was under construction, Beijingers were getting water delivered to their homes by wheelbarrow.

Fast-forward to 2005. Michael Meyer, a Westerner who lived in the vanishing backstreets of a *hutong* in Beijing, tells its story in his book *The Last Days of Old Beijing*. In 2005, he paid $100 a month for two unheated rooms. Visiting the latrine required a few minutes' walk, during which he described "the vegetable seller arranging a pyramid of cabbages, the hairstylist massaging the temples of a customer, and the open doorways from which spills the clack of the gamblers' mahjongg tiles."

That's old Beijing, and probably closer to what many Americans have in mind when they think of what Beijing might be like. But that era is fading fast.

I think most Americans would be shocked to see Beijing today. A friend and reader of mine, well-traveled and well-read, told me he thought he'd find a city comparable to Mumbai or Managua. Instead, he found a city comparable New York or Chicago. I agree that a more bustling capitalistic city would be hard to imagine.

Beijing has a history of beating expectations. In 2001, consensus opinion had the population of Beijing hitting 14 million by 2040. It topped that by 2003. Today, it has about 22 million people. In 2001, experts thought that Beijing would have—gasp!—1 million cars on its roads by 2010. It topped that figure in 2003. Today, there are nearly 5 million cars on the road.

China is the world's largest car market and is quickly becoming the world's largest market for a number of consumer goods. It's the world's largest market for mobile phones. And we saw plenty of Beijingers chatting away at checkout counters and in their cars, just as people do in the United States.

The whole city isn't like this of course. We wandered about 40 minutes from downtown and visited a small village still technically in Beijing. We walked down dusty lanes, past modest dwellings and a small Buddhist temple. Villagers smiled as we passed. They don't see foreigners here much. Even here, though, you could stop and get a Coke and a Snickers bar.

We happened to meet the head of the village, who greeted us warmly and showed us inside his home, a small courtyard house. After snapping a group picture, he asked us to send a copy by email, and we dutifully wrote down his address. Some of these homes don't have a private bathroom, but you can still send email.

Somehow, the whole encounter captured much about China. It's been an uneven advance, and there is still a long way to go. That's where the main opportunity lies.

The Rise of the Asian Consumer

This takes us to one of the big stories in China: its growing middle class. By 2030, the consensus guess is that China will add some 370 million middle-class consumers. That's a huge number, about 38 percent of the world's estimated middle class in 2030. Whether this guess turns out right or not, there is no underestimating the transformation that has occurred within China. Back in the 1970s, the average income of a Chinese family was about the same as a Somali family in Africa. Today . . . well, there's no better way to see China's middle class in action then through the prisms of street-level economics. We walked into a Carrefour "hypermarket."

Carrefour, a French firm, is the world's second-largest retailer. It was one of the early birds to crack China, opening its first store in 1995. Today, it has over 150 stores and is a multibillion-dollar business.

The hypermarket was typical for China, but huge by U.S. standards. We visited one on a late Sunday afternoon. There were 54 checkout counters, and all but one were open. Every open checkout had a line five or six deep. It was amazing. You can see the burgeoning middle class in action here, as blue jeans–wearing shoppers in sneakers packed the aisles.

Carrefour's hypermarkets are a kind of Wal-Mart operation that sells everything from fresh meat and produce to deodorant and air conditioners. We saw Crest toothpaste, set off in its own display area as if it were designer perfume. I noted the price at 7.60 renminbi. That's just a bit more than a dollar.

The name "Carrefour" means "crossroads." And this store was certainly a crossroads of Western-style consumerism with Chinese tastes and sensibilities. All of the world's best-known brand names were on display in brightly lit, wide aisles. You almost have to see it to believe it. Even in the six years since I was there last, Beijing had changed a great deal.

Old China is visible there, too: We saw tanks of live fish and fresh-cut meat. There was a large area dedicated to butchering. We saw a couple of hogs suspended and butchers hacking away to cut whatever pieces you wanted right there for you.

I sent back video clips of some of the highlights to friends back home. One friend, after watching a few clips, wrote: "I suspect that what a lot of Americans are unsure about is the size and scope of what's really there in everyday life in China. In most memories, it's a nation of rice scroungers raking the good earth with fingers crossed. Yet here there's a butcher with piles of fresh, red meat out in the open (it MUST be selling fast to be out like that) and 30 kinds of toothpaste on the shelves, and 60-plus cash registers jammed with customers."

We visited an IKEA, which was similarly mammoth and packed. Our local contact there told us that on a Saturday, or in the middle of the day, these places are literally elbow-to-elbow jammed with people.

I see this as one of the great investment opportunities of the next decade: catering to the emerging middle class in China. Check out the shift in Figure 5.1.

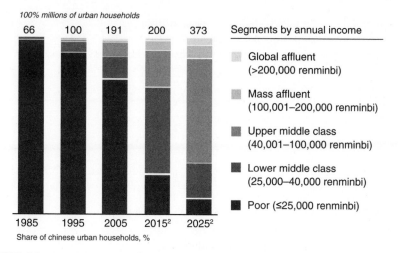

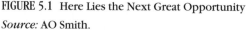

FIGURE 5.1 Here Lies the Next Great Opportunity
Source: AO Smith.

China is the main focal point of this story, but all of Asia is really experiencing similar transformations. Indonesia, for instance, is starting to contribute to the bottom lines of companies such as H.J. Heinz and others. Indonesia, with its population of 240 million, may be the next great consumer market to open up.

CLSA, an investment house with expertise in Asia, predicts the consumer markets in the big three of China, India, and Indonesia will enter a "hypergrowth" phase as disposable incomes rise. CLSA notes that the number of Asians (excluding Japan) with disposable income of $3,000 annually will rise from 570 million people to 945 million by 2015. About 85 percent of that increase comes from just China and India.

As CLSA notes, "The consumption spending of this middle class will rise from $2.9 trillion to $5.1 trillion by 2015, with China, India, and Indonesia contributing to 69 percent, 16 percent, and 4 percent of the increment." By 2014, about 44 percent of the population in China will top this $3,000 threshold, a 27 percent increase over 2009.

"The future of Asia is domestic," CLSA concludes. This marks an important shift. For a long time, China's economy (and Asia's generally) has been geared toward servicing the West—toward exports. Now begins a transformation, the rise of the Asian consumer.

Figure 5.2 shows you the dramatic increase in consumers this shift creates.

Focus in on the area under the line to the right of the dotted line, which nearly doubles. You can see the mass of consumers that will want all the things many of us take for granted, like Crest toothpaste and air

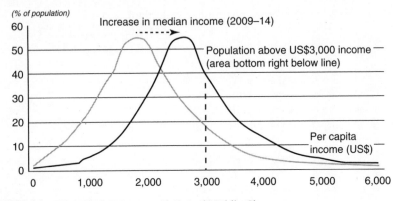

FIGURE 5.2 China Median-Income Shift And Middle Class

Source: CLSA Asia-Pacific Markets.

conditioners. That's a lot of money in the pool, and companies like Yum! Brands, McDonald's, Wal-Mart, Carrefour, Starbucks, and many others all want in. In many cases, they have substantial businesses there.

Take Starbucks, for example. In the United States, lattes may be losing their luster, but not in China, where Starbucks plans to triple its locations. As you might have guessed from the talk above, India is Starbucks' next target location. Vietnam will see Starbucks come in 2013.

High-end luxury will do well in China as new consumers clamor for status items. Luxury can mean different things in different markets. A tidbit from one consulting firm employee says it all: At the end of a successful project, his team gets a choice of meals out. They could pick the Four Seasons or the Ritz, but they always choose Pizza Hut instead.

Still, the investment consequences and opportunities are enormous. The Chinese are buying more cars and televisions than anyone else. They're number two when it comes to computer sales. I think some of the decade's best-performing ideas will come directly out of what's happening in Asian markets.

Let me give you an example of one of my favorite long-term plays.

Selling Clean Water to the Chinese

Beijing is typical of China's dry northern plains. Water wells sometimes reach half a mile to tap deep aquifers below. Over the past 50 years, about half of the nonrenewable water in northern China's huge aquifer has been used up. Perhaps more pressing is the fact that so much of the water China has left is unfit for human use.

The city declared its reservoirs unfit for drinking in 1997. It's only gotten worse since then. Early in 2010, China's government said that water pollution was far worse than first thought. About 70 percent of China's source water is unsafe. China tops the world in stomach and liver cancer deaths, mostly attributed to consuming polluted water. In addition, polluted water transmits the leading infectious diseases in China, such as diarrhea and hepatitis.

It's an awful situation, and the Chinese consumer, especially that growing middle class is increasingly aware of it. This is why water filtration products are selling so well in China. The market is huge.

A.O. Smith is one company in that market. It has a business in China that's been growing 25 percent a year for the past five years. It's been such a success that the company plans to duplicate the model in India, another place with mega water problems.

A.O. Smith has roots back to 1874, when it made steel baby carriages. It's always been involved in machinery and making stuff. In its 100-plus-year history, it has made everything from bicycle frames to brewery tanks.

It survives to this day in part because it was an American manufacturer that "got it" early on. Rather than become another dinosaur, it took its business overseas. Today, more than 90 percent of its manufacturing is done in either China or Mexico, with a new plant in Bangalore, India. Its low-cost operations are a big part of its success.

AOS makes water heaters and filtration products. AOS has a leading position in water heaters for residential and commercial use. The most exciting part of this business is the expansion in China.

It first opened a plant in Nanjing, China, in 1995. It's grown a lot since (see Figure 5.3). AOS bought a stake in Tianlong Holding Co. This is a highly

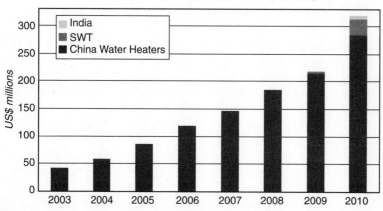

FIGURE 5.3 A.O. Smith in China—Nice Trend

Source: AO Smith.

profitable Chinese water filtration business in Shanghai, renamed Shanghai Water Treatment Co. (or SWT).

AOS makes its products in China for the Chinese market. Among its products are a tankless water heater and one that is wall mounted, both efficient in energy use and space. It released a balcony-mounted water heater that uses solar technology, which solves the problem of serving massive apartment complexes.

AOS sells through retailers, mainly Suning Appliance and GOME Electrical Appliances, both among the largest appliance retailers in China, as well as specialty shops. Market penetration is still low, only around 10 percent, and AOS has the dominant market share, at around 20 percent, so even if there is a bust in China, AOS has plenty of room to grow.

Yet there are other ways to play China's growing water needs. . . .

One Thing Plagues China's Growth More than Any Other

China has almost the same amount of water as Canada and a population 40 times as large. Furthermore, what water they have is in less populated areas. About 80 percent of China's total water supply lies south of the Yangtze River, but nearly half of China's population resides in the northeastern provinces, where only 14 percent of the water resources are located.

That's why it should come as no surprise that China is spending billions on water projects. The largest is a big dig to bring southern water north. Two large canals of the vast South-to-North project should bring water to a dozen cities, including thirsty Beijing, by 2014.

Scarcity, though, is only the beginning of China's water problem. Breakneck economic growth, ignoring environmental considerations, has converted China's water scarcity into a full-blown crisis. You can't fish or drink from most of the rivers in Chinese cities. The rivers come in a rainbow of colors,with some green, red, and even purple, depending on what chemicals are coming down from upriver. The vice minister of China's version of the EPA, Zhang Lijun, says: "Groundwater is now contaminated in about 90 percent of the nation's cities." I've seen reports saying 700 million citizens are without access to safe drinking water, 320 million of them in rural areas.

Only half of China's large cities even have municipal water treatment facilities. In nearly half of all China's 17,000 small towns, no wastewater treatment occurs. Sewage simply flows into the water supply. Dirty water causes 60,000 premature deaths every year in China and sickens about 190 million.

As previously mentioned, the main aquifer is being sucked dry. Beijing is sinking about eight inches per year. Meanwhile, Beijing's water demand outstrips supply by 340 trillion gallons a year. It's only going to get worse.

The price of water will go up. It has to. The South-to-North transfer project will triple what Beijing pays for water.

There aren't too many viable ways to create more fresh water. You find new supplies by drilling deeper, desalination of seawater, or by using existing supplies more efficiently, as with irrigation. All that takes time and money. One company based in Singapore has solutions for which China is willing to pay.

Meet the Water Queen

Hyflux (HYFXF:pink sheets) does gangbuster business with water filtration in China, the Middle East, and Northern Africa. This is another one of my favorite investment ideas for China and its water needs.

Hyflux has done well in all aspects of water, with its core strength in building desalination plants and using membrane technologies to purify water. Its Singapore desalination plant (completed three months ahead of schedule) provides 10 percent of Singapore's water needs. Hyflux built China's largest desalination plant in Tianjin. It makes 53 million gallons of water per year. Taken together, China and Singapore make up over half its revenues. Hyflux's water treatment facilities ensure that it gets a cut of revenues as China and other countries move toward global water rate averages.

Hyflux's CEO, Olivia Lum, knows exactly where this ship is going. They call her the "Water Queen." Since 2006, she has overseen an almost sixfold increase in net profits,from S\$15 million to S\$88.5 million. Lum grew up in Malaysia in a leaky shack without any running water. She got her start in business selling ice lollipops. Selling kaya toast funded her school tuition until she got to the National University of Singapore, where she graduated in applied chemistry. It was during her three-year stint at Glaxo that she saw the immense potential of the water treatment business.

Lum sold her condo and car to found Hyflux in 1989. She started selling her first water filters and chemicals off the back of her motorcycle. In five short years, she took Hyflux from a three-person company to its first million in sales.

Lum owns 30 percent of the stock, fully aligning her interest with shareholders, and her vision drives the company. Lum recently said her dream is to make desalinated water a cheap source of water, "as cheap as maybe ordinary river water treatment."

Hyflux will build the largest desalination plant in its home country of Singapore, which wants desal to supply 30 percent of its long-term water demand. Costs there, once the Hyflux plant is completed, should be at the bottom of the global range: 45 cents per cubic meter. That's cheaper than what it will cost per cubic meter for China's current South-to-North project.

Desalination's success in Singapore will train Chinese eyeballs on Lum's solutions.

Projects like these ensure Hyflux's order books stay plump. Most of its orders come from operations and maintenance on completed plants. Its biggest municipal water presence is China, where Hyflux has 11 plants. Hyflux covers a lot of ground there, with projects in 26 of the 31 provinces.

To start 2011, it gained two more lucrative contracts to build, own, and operate two wastewater treatment plants and a water treatment plant in Chongqing in addition to a wastewater plant in Guizhou. This steady growth in a water-poor country promises to provide great returns for Hyflux shareholders in the years ahead.

I've been writing about China's water crisis for years. It ties in, too, with related problems: desertification and declining amounts of arable land.

I noticed on the way to and from the airport that there was an abundance of young-looking trees lining the highway, often many trees deep. These trees serve a purpose beyond aesthetics. Beijing's trees help protect the city against the dust blowing in from the desert and help hold the soil in place.

Much of the land in north-central China lies on what is called loess. Basically, it's dry soil that has blown in from the Gobi Desert and other dry lands to the northwest. Over thousands of years, this soil can get deep, 600 feet or more in places. One commentator called it a "layered cake of dust." It's fertile, but fragile and dry. Even small streams of water can carve ravines hundreds of feet deep.

It used to be that China was covered in forests in the north, but the Chinese have stripped it bare over the years. In building the Great Wall, for example, experts estimate that each kiln-fired brick consumed 16.5 pounds of wood.

In any case, China has serious issues here with water and soil. It bodes well for the agricultural trends we talk about in other places in this book as other places of the world ramp up production to feed this growing giant.

Side Trip to Hong Kong . . . and a Cautionary Tale

In what other city can you legitimately use four different currencies to pay for things? On my last day in Hong Kong, I unloaded the last of my Yuan and HK dollars—and mixed in some American greenbacks for good measure to pay for my ride to the airport. The driver cheerfully accepted all of it and explained that Chinese Yuan, Hong Kong dollars, U.S. dollars, and euros are all good here.

Hong Kong boasts one of the freest economies in the world, as rated by The Heritage Foundation. The city has inherited a strong legal system and a rich pool of professional talent with expertise in matters of finance and international trade. No wonder it is an important hub of business activity in the region.

Taxes are low and simple. The corporate tax rate is under 20 percent; the top income tax rate is only 15 percent. One of the American expats living here told me it takes 15 minutes to fill out a personal tax return, which is only a couple of pages long. All capital gains are tax-free. Any personal dividends, bank interest, or foreign-sourced income is all tax-free.

As a result of its free market–friendly policies, the city has grown tremendously in economic importance. Hong Kong is the largest recipient of foreign investment in Asia, and it is the largest source of funds for the mainland. It's the fifth-largest stock market in the world and the third-largest in Asia (Shanghai and Tokyo beat it). To put that in perspective, just five years earlier, it was only the ninth-largest global market. It only had 915 companies listed. Today, it has 1,413 companies. So you can see as more economic activity and investment happen in the East, Hong Kong will be at the center of that mix.

Buying Hong Kong stocks these days is as easy as buying stocks that trade in London or Japan. And there are many to choose from. So far, though, I prefer to get my exposure to China from companies not actually headquartered in China (such A.O. Smith or Hyflux). As I write this, many China-based companies have issues with fraud or accounting misstatements. To be fair, the worst offenders are companies listed in the United States, but let me share a cautionary tale.

Investing always involves a leap of faith. Investors have to believe that the numbers they are looking at are real. They have to believe that the financial statements reasonably reflect reality. Without that trust, there is no point in going further. The investor is like a cook unsure of the safety of his ingredients.

This is why things like auditors, listing requirements, and boards of directors are so important. This is why due diligence is important: asking questions, talking to people on the ground. They give some assurance to investors that what they see is real, and not a fraud.

Sometimes the lines can be fuzzy. And sometimes the taint of fraud dogs a market, making all the stocks of that market cheap, whether they are fraudulent or not. Such a market is susceptible to rumor.

The market for the U.S.-listed China-based companies has that taint. That explains the cheap multiples that many such companies trade for. I'm talking about price-earnings ratios of three to five times for companies supposedly growing 20 to 30 percent a year.

There have been several cases of fudged numbers. Fuqi Intl. is a China-based jeweler whose stock traded on the NASDAQ. The stock dropped 37 percent one day in March 2010 after the company announced it would have to restate past results. The stock has continued to drop since. The stock had been $30 per share, but it trades for less than $3 today.

There have been other grim casualties. One veteran hedge fund manager, who would like to remain anonymous, told me how he was "very worried." There are too many scams, which is not good for the market. He said, "Another big development is these detailed negative research reports. There are three–four quality reports coming out each month from different outfits."

A company called China Marine Food faced challenges to its accounting. A website called chinesecompanyanalyst.com performs financial analysis of Chinese companies. In a highly detailed report, it contended that China Marine Food was a fraud. I can't do justice to the report here, but here is a damning snippet:

> I question how [the company] could generate $7.6 million of revenue, $1.7 million of net income and $1.2 million of operating cash flow in its first five months of operations with $44,000 of startup capital it received from its original founder [and] $414 of capex. . . .

China Marine Food dropped more than 20 percent on the day these allegations came to light. The stock has continued to fall.

Then there is Orient Paper. It seemed to have great fundamentals and traded cheaply. On June 28, 2010, a company called Muddy Waters released its "inaugural report" on Orient Paper contending that it was a fraud. The stock closed at $8.33 before the report. It dropped 13 percent that day, but the snowball was only just getting started. Two days later, the stock hit $4.11.

The Muddy Waters report was meticulous. The report authors talked to suppliers. Some of the suppliers offer a different view of Orient Paper's capacity than what Orient Paper claims. Muddy Waters tried to track down customers. Some of these they found did not exist or were small mom and pop shops. Yet Orient Paper reports millions of dollars in sales from such customers. Muddy Waters tried to match SEC filings with tax filings in China. They claimed to find major discrepancies. There are pictures of site visits showing old machines. There are other observations about the number of employees, trucks, and more.

It all adds up to a pretty damning dossier.

The point is to show you how tricky the market is for U.S.-listed China-based stocks. The people on the ground there can't even tell the frauds from the real companies. In my newsletter, I had positions in Harbin Electric, Zhongpin, China Boron, and others. We made money (and sometimes good money) on of all these positions save one, which made me quickly put up the white flag and sell all of our Chinese holdings.

The company was Duoyuan Printing. I sold it after the company announced it fired its auditor, Deloitte Touche Tohmatsu, CPA, and the stock fell 50 percent that day. I had checked it out as well as one can check these things out. I had my boots-on-the-ground Beijing contact, a veteran investor, Mandarin speaker, and specialist in the market of U.S.-listed China-based small caps, give it the all-clear sign after visiting with management and getting a tour. And DYP had a legitimate and internationally respected auditor, unlike many Chinese companies.

As my Beijing contact wrote to me the morning of DYP's announcement: "Nothing is safe. . . . " Not only did DYP announce it fired its auditor, but the CFO resigned, another bad sign. I knew DYP was speculative, but the numbers were compelling. However, that day I learned once again what the fish know, that the shiny flies often have lethal hooks.

After that episode, I've not invested in China-based stocks. Therefore, I'm going to recommend you follow my lead and not try it. Someday, things will be different, but we're not there yet.

A good year after I had made this discovery, John Paulson, the famed hedge fund manager, learned the same lesson in a public way. His disaster was Sino-Forest, which cost his fund over $700 million.

The Chinese Renminbi

Another question that comes up a lot for investors is whether China's currency is cheap or not. For U.S.-based investors, I think it may be one of the cheapest currencies you can own.

China fixes the value of the yuan against the dollar at the moment. This is a big bone of contention between American and Chinese officialdom. The charge is that China keeps holding the value of its currency down to make its exports cheaper.

Whatever the outcome of this spat, it seems as if some currency appreciation is inevitable over time. In the past, China has let its currency appreciate gradually. For example, the value of the yuan rose 21 percent from July 2005 to 2008 before China stopped it. What happened to commodities during this stretch is worth knowing. When China allowed its currency to appreciate, oil jumped 15 percent in the month after the news. Commodities across the board rose in dollar terms. The basic idea is that when the yuan is strong, imported raw materials in high demand in China, like oil, potash, soybeans, and iron ore, become cheaper, bringing more buyers.

So how cheap is China's currency? It is hard to say. Murray Stahl, the savvy investor who runs Horizon Asset Management, thinks it might be as much as 50 percent undervalued.

Purchasing power parity and currency valuation

Country	Dec. 2009 Value (USD)	July 2011 Value (USD)	Dec. 2009 Under/Over Value	July 2011 Under/Over Value
Hong Kong	1.72	1.94	−52%	−52%
China	1.83	2.27	−49%	−44%
Thailand	2.11	2.35	−47%	−42%
Russia	2.34	2.70	−43%	−34%
South Africa	2.46	2.87	−39%	−29%
Mexico	2.50	2.74	−33%	−33%
South Korea	2.98	3.50	−27%	−14%
Singapore	3.19	3.65	−19%	−10%
Argentina	3.02	4.84	−15%	9%
Canada	3.97	5.00	−6%	23%
Australia	3.98	4.94	−6%	22%
Japan	3.50	4.08	−3%	−3%
United States	3.58	4.07	0%	0%
Brazil	4.02	6.16	13%	52%
Euro Area	4.84	4.93	29%	21%
Sweden	4.93	7.64	38%	88%
Denmark	5.53	5.48	55%	35%
Switzerland	6.30	8.06	68%	98%
The New Arrivals				
India		1.89		−53%
Pakistan		2.38		−42%
Malaysia		2.42		−40%
Indonesia		2.64		−35%
Saudi Arabia		2.67		−34%

FIGURE 5.4 Big Mac Index: 2009 versus 2011

Source: Bloomberg, *The Economist.*

One way to look at this, though this hardly ends the debate,is through the famed Big Mac Index (Figure 5.4). It shows you how much it costs to get a Big Mac in different parts of the world. Based on this, one of the cheapest places to get a burger is China.

Put another way, China's renminbi is 49 percent undervalued versus the dollar. It's virtually unchanged from where it was in 2009. While that may not be the most accurate measure around, I do think it's meaningful. If it is that cheap, then U.S.-dollar-based investors stand to make a huge windfall.

Stahl estimated that if the renminbi truly floats, "one could expect returns of up to 100 percent from currency exposure alone." Regardless of what the exact percentage ends up being, playing for a rise in the yuan, as an American, seems the way to bet.

As a side note to this, Stahl points out how China remains underrepresented in the world's stock indexes. This is important because it helps give you a sense of where the big money, institutional money, will flow in the future.

Let's look at what you might call the "global S&P 500", the Morgan Stanley Capital International EAFE Index. (EAFE stands for Europe, Australasia, and the Far East.) This is the most widely used global benchmark for investment managers. That means the global index funds, ETFs, and other funds all look to ape this index or beat it.

Surprisingly, this index has zero allocation to China. China is the world's second-largest economy, and it has no weighting in this popular index. One would think this really doesn't achieve the goal of replicating world financial performance if China is not in the ranks.

Where you do find China, it is often a ridiculously small portion of the index. State Street Global Advisors has the MSCI All Country World Index. China is 2.39 percent (as of July 2011) of this index, the ninth-largest weighting. Japan, by contrast, has an 8.26 percent weighting. Investors thinking they are getting something representative of the world in the World Index are getting a skewed view of that world. If China got its proper weight, it would be 17 percent of the index.

The reason for the neglect is because there are not enough Chinese securities to fill out these indexes yet. The tradable volume of China's market is still small relative to the size of China's economy. As the market grows over time and as more securities come to the market, this issue will likely solve itself. As the investment dollars flow into China, it will create another source of demand for Chinese currency.

Why Coal Prices Will Soar

Beijing showed me firsthand the unfolding boom serving China's new and growing disposable incomes. Besides busy shops and restaurants, and 5 million cars on the road in Beijing alone, there is something more basic that underlines all of this. In fact, it is more fundamental to the entire story of Asia's new consumers and urban dwellers.

It is energy. Yes, all those factories require power, but so do iPods and air conditioners. So do cell phones and computers. The modern consumer economy is a plugged-in economy that eats electricity like locusts devour crop fields.

Richard Heinberg at the Post Carbon Institute estimates that "7–10 percent economic growth per year means doubling the size of your energy consumption every decade." That's huge. If China's 7–10 percent growth per year is real, then China's got to get more power and soon.

As a result, China has added power plants as fast as they can make them. China adds more every day, accounting for about 80 percent of worldwide construction. Where does the power come from? About 70–80 percent of it comes from coal. Awe-inspiring amounts of coal. Consider that in 2000, China used about as much coal as the United States. Here we are over a decade later and China consumes three times as much as coal as the United States.

There are a couple of problems with coal. One won't surprise you, but the other may. First, coal is a dirty fuel. Only a few days in Beijing or any of the big cities will show you what burning so much coal does to the sky. (Although I will say that Beijing circa 2010 is cleaner than I remembered it being in 2005.)

Such pollution creates many health problems in China, and the Chinese know this. Hence, there has been a lot of money flowing to alternative modes of power generation, like wind and nuclear.

The other problem with coal, which might surprise you, is that China may have a hard time making more of it. China burns over 3 billion tons of coal per year. In the last decade, it added 2 billion tons of production. That's quite a feat. But as Heinberg points out, it gets much more difficult from here.

"Imagine building mining and transport infrastructure three times the size of the entire U.S. coal and rail industries in just 10 years," Heinberg writes. "That's what it will take for China to maintain 7 percent growth rates."

Another limiting factor is water, of which the Chinese are relatively poor. Your average 500-megawatt coal-fired power plant uses about 2.2 billion gallons of water each year to create steam to turn its turbines. That's enough water to support a city of 250,000 people.

China will be pressed to produce the coal it needs domestically. In fact, after being self-sufficient in coal for years, China has begun to import coal.

In 2011, it will probably import over 100 million metric tons. It may seem a molehill compared with what it burns, but that molehill of 100 million tons is about 60 percent of Australia's coal exports, and Australia is the world's largest coal exporter, and growing.

In 2012, China will need around 145 million tons of coal to address its growing energy power gap. For the record, that's 20 million tons more than South Africa's national power company needs to power South Africa for an entire year.

This is fairly astounding math. And the first thing it makes me want to do is buy coal. It doesn't take a lot of brains to see that if this kind of demand scenario unfolds, it is going to drive up the price of coal everywhere. Beyond the obvious of investing in some way in coal, there are other opportunities that open up when you think about China's coal-based industry.

Let's look at three areas where China's coal-based industry may well lose its competitive position: urea, PVC, and methanol. Urea is an important source of nitrogen to make fertilizers. PVC, or polyvinyl chloride, is a plastic used widely in pipes, cables, inflatable products, and more. Methanol is a simple alcohol used in cooking and as an energy source. In China, methanol is like ethanol. It's used as an additive to gasoline.

China is a big supplier of these three things to the rest of the world. It has roughly 30 percent of the world's urea, PVC, and methanol capacity. With coal prices surging, these chemical producers will feel the pinch as their costs rise. Many will have to close up shop. China's coal-based chemical industry faces gradual extinction as rising coal prices squeeze it.

As always, though, crisis in one place creates opportunities in others.

The rest of the world no longer uses coal as a feedstock. It uses natural gas. It's cleaner, and in the case of PVC, the polymers made from natural gas are of a superior quality than those made from coal. Most importantly, using natural gas is a heck of a lot cheaper than using coal. In the United States, natural gas is cheap and abundant.

Now we have the pieces of an interesting investment proposition. We can answer the question of who stands to benefit from a rise in coal prices. Not the China-based, coal-using chemical industry. It will be the non-China-based, natural gas-using chemical firms.

These would include fertilizer stocks such as Agrium and CF Industries, which makes urea from natural gas. The main PVC players are Westlake Chemical and Georgia Gulf. The third choice is methanol. I've long recommended owning Methanex (MEOH: NASDAQ). Methanex uses natural gas to make methanol. It has a new plant in Egypt, and with rising coal prices putting upward pressure on methanol prices, it stands to make a lot of money.

The "Chinese Ethanol"

In the United States, corn ethanol may be king, but in China, where pure economics matter most, methanol is the dominant alternative fuel.

—John Lynn, president, Methanol Institute

The fact that China is going to have a lot of new cars on the road over the next decade probably does not surprise you. China has about 35 million cars on the road today. McKinsey Global Institute estimates that China will have 120 million cars by 2020.

What may surprise you is that China has adopted fuel-efficiency standards for vehicles that are even stricter than in the United States. What may surprise you even more is that methanol is the main alternative fuel. Think of it as the Chinese ethanol.

Methanol is a clear liquid alcohol made mostly from natural gas, though China makes methanol using coal. China produces and uses more methanol than anybody else. The main use is to blend methanol in gasoline. Taxi and bus fleets in China run on high-methanol blends. Retail pumps sell low-methanol blends, similar to the way U.S. gasoline stations have low-ethanol blends.

Even though China makes a lot of methanol and is adding more capacity, it still imports methanol. China's capacity is on the high-cost side of the spectrum, ensuring good profits for exporters to China. Prices for methanol in China are the highest in the world. Methanol is an old chemical with mature markets in many consumer goods, such as adhesives, paints, plastic bottles, pharmaceuticals, and many more. In fact, you'd be surprised how much methanol is in your home. But the exciting part of the story is methanol's newer and growing use as an alternative fuel.

Methanex controls 15 percent of the global market from its Vancouver, Canada, headquarters. It owns methanol facilities in Chile, Trinidad, New Zealand, and Egypt. We've owned it in my newsletter portfolio since April 2009, but the stock is a great play on rising methanol prices. It's well-run, pays a good dividend, and has high-quality, hard-to-replace assets.

China's Manufacturing Prowess: Geeks with Guts

I rested the butt of the AK-47 on my shoulder, aimed, and squeezed off a round. It was surprisingly loud, even with earmuffs. The gun didn't kick as much as I thought it would, and smoke smoldered from the barrel when I was done.

I completely missed the target, but it was fun anyway. It's something I'd never done and may never do again. We were firing machine guns at a weapons research center in Beijing, where they copy guns from all over the world.

You come here and walk into a room where all kinds of guns are hanging on the walls. You pick what you want to fire, an M-16, Uzi, M-1, whatever. Then attendants set it up for you at the firing range. We didn't even have to sign waivers or anything. It's all part of the freewheeling atmosphere we found in China.

In addition to the weapons, we stopped at a large market where you can buy knockoffs of just about anything you want: Rolex watches, Prada shoes, North Face jackets, even Apple iPods. We compared the faux iPod with the real deal. It was a darn good copy. In fact, everything was a darn good copy, at prices only a fraction of the real deal.

That's the prowess of Chinese manufacturing. I don't know that people appreciate just how large China's advantage is in this area. But when you look at where things come from, China is often the answer. Often, too, a single Chinese city dominates a certain item.

For instance, Yiwu makes one-quarter of the world's drinking straws. Datang produces one-third of the world's socks. Shenzhou makes 40 percent of the world's neckties. Wenzhou produces 70 percent of the world's cigarette lighters. Other cities specialize in all kinds of everyday items. Songxia turns out 350 million umbrellas a year. Fenshui makes pens. Shangguan makes table tennis paddles.

It's kind of odd how things have evolved, but China's advantage is more than just cost. It's speed and flexibility. You can often find a dozen manufacturers within a given area where you can drop off specs in the morning and have prototypes that afternoon.

China's prowess at making things extends into many areas. China has built the world's largest building (Beijing's airport terminal) and its longest transoceanic bridge. It has the world's fastest train and the biggest dam. As John Pomfret, former bureau chief for the *Washington Post* in Beijing, observes: "It is a nation of builders, of grand schemes, of gigantism." He calls China's engineers "some of the world's biggest risk-takers. Geeks with guts."

The Qinghai-Tibet railway was another engineering feat. Chinese engineers, considered the best railway builders in the world, built a railway on the complex and shifting permafrost linking Lhasa with Golmud, in China's western hinterlands. The railway stretches hundreds of miles across a treacherous plateau.

Author Abrahm Lustgarten in *China's Great Train* describes the area as one of "intermittently frozen marshes, lakes, and soggy permafrost that heave and shift more actively than almost any other geologic environment on Earth." In places, the quicksand is deep enough to swallow a tank. It is higher than any other railway on Earth, more than 16,600 feet above sea level at its peak. The cars of the train are pressurized as in an airplane, with oxygen pumped in.

With feats like these, China is pushing Germany for the chair of world's greatest engineers. In fact, in some instances, it has taken Germany's place.

China Takes the Ruhr

The Ruhr Valley was the heart of Germany's industrial might. For more than 200 years, the smokestacks in this northwest corner of Germany pounded out the steel and iron that would form the backbone of the nation's industry. And when the war drums rumbled, these factories supplied imperial Germany with its field guns, armored tanks, and shells.

Prosperous communities grew up around these old blast furnaces and mills. People took pride in the stuff they could make with their hands. Tens of thousands found work in the factories of the Ruhr. Generations passed with the knowledge that their sons and daughters could make a life here and carry on the legacy of such a place. For a long time, that was the way it went.

But the winds of change patiently grind away at even the most impressive advantages. In the early 1990s, the industrious workers of Asia powered the mortar and pestle that would crush the Ruhr's traditional way of life.

It was a slow process, but the endgame was not hard to see. While the South Koreans became the most-efficient producers of steel in the world, German workers were agitating for a 35-hour workweek. While the Chinese worked all day in their mills and new factories sprouted up like spring peepers all through China, Germany increased taxes and expanded its bloated government programs.

By the turn of the millennium, no one could ignore the stark reality any longer. The mills and factories of the Ruhr started to close forever. In his terrific book *China Shakes the World*, James Kynge tells the story of ThyssenKrupp's steel mill in Dortmund, one of the largest in Germany. The Germans called it the Phoenix, inspired by its rise from the ashes of bombing raids during World War II.

Within a month of ThyssenKrupp closing the mill, a Chinese company bought it with the idea of disassembling the entire mill and taking it to China, near the mouth of the Yangtze River. Soon after this Chinese company bought the mill, 1,000 Chinese workers arrived in Germany to begin the process of taking the plant apart and bringing it to China.

The Germans got an up-close lesson in why they could not compete against the Chinese who worked seven days a week for 12 hours a day. The Germans started to complain, so the Chinese, in deference to local law, took one day off.

In the end, the Chinese dismantled the mill in less than one year, a full two years ahead of the time ThyssenKrupp initially thought it would take.

When the Chinese departed, they left the makeshift dormitories and kitchens they occupied for a year neat and clean. There was, however, a single pair of black boots left in one of the dormitories. The boots carried the brand name Phoenix, which was the same name of the plant the Chinese just took apart. The boots carried the label "Made in China." Kynge writes, "Nobody could tell, however, whether the single pair of forgotten boots was an oversight or an intentional pun."

Over 5,000 miles away, the Chinese rebuilt the steel mill exactly as it was in Germany. "Altogether, 275,000 tons of equipment had been shipped," Kynge writes, "along with 44 tons of documents that explained the intricacies of the reassembly process." Doing all of this was still cheaper by about 60 percent than building a new mill. Plus, in China, the demand for steel was such that the mill could start producing steel immediately at full capacity.

As recently as 1975, China's entire output of steel could not match this one mill in Dortmund. Now the Dortmund plant itself stands in China. And in Germany, you have a dying industrial city, unemployed steelworkers, and the scarred earth where the mill once stood. Germany is thinking of turning the site into parkland and perhaps creating a lake and marina. But as one burly steelworker says in Kynge's book: "Do we look like yachtsmen to you?"

This remarkable vignette captures, on many levels, how the game has changed. Comfortable workers in the factories and mills of America and Western Europe have no idea what they are up against. Even so, the nature of global competition keeps shifting.

We tend to think of emerging markets, such as China, as occupying a place down on the food chain of the global economy. We tend to think of these places as sources for cheap labor and natural resources. But more and more, these emerging markets are home to world-class companies in all kinds of industries.

This is something Antoine van Agtmael, author of a book called *The Emerging Markets Century*, tries to drive home. Agtmael is the man who coined the phrase "emerging markets" to describe growing, but less-developed economies such as those of China, India, Brazil, Argentina, Mexico, Thailand, and other places. Before him, we called these markets "third-world," which brings to mind many negative associations. To sell the idea, Agtmael came up with "emerging markets."

I saw Agtmael give a presentation in Washington, D.C. Agtmael spent 30 years in these kinds of markets. "I have helped IranAir lease airplanes and hire crews in Ethiopia, was involved in financing Ghana's cocoa exports," he writes, "and grew wise to the ways, many of them laughably one-sided, that developed nations interacted with what were in many cases recent European colonies."

Agtmael selected 25 companies to profile in his book. All of them exemplify best practices and are widely recognized as leaders in their industries. All of them call an emerging market home.

Agtmael writes about spending time in High Tech Computer Corp.'s research lab in Taiwan in 2005 and how "Suddenly, my BlackBerry looked like a Model T." He writes about how the regional jets we fly are made in Brazil (by Embraer). How computers are not just made in China, but designed there. How Indian and Slovenian labs produce proprietary new drugs, and it goes on and on.

One more nugget from Agtmael: In 1988, when he started his fund, there were only 20 emerging market companies with sales of more than $1 billion. Most of these were banks or commodity companies. (Overwhelmingly, they were located in Taiwan.) Today, there are over 270 companies with over $1 billion in sales, and 38 with more than $10 billion.

Many of them are high-tech companies or provide consumer products and services. This bolsters Agtmael's point that many of today's emerging market stars do not rely on cheap labor, abundant natural resources, or protective government policies. Instead, they have developed competitive advantages in technology, design, logistics, and other areas.

Agtmael has tips for investing in emerging markets. The most important of these may be "Don't be afraid to invest in them."

What about the China Bubble?

It's a cliché, but it's true: It is hard to make generalizations about China. For example, there has been a lot of talk of a property bubble in China in the same way there was a property bubble in the United States. But whatever frothiness exists does not extend to all parts of China or to all sections of its big cities. I put the bubble question to nearly everyone I met: money managers, economists, entrepreneurs, and so on. It's the pressing question everyone wants to know.

"A bubble," the late Charles Kindleberger once wrote in his classic on the subject, "is an upward price movement that then implodes." Identifying a bubble after it bursts is easy. The NASDAQ in 2000 was a bubble. The recent U.S. mortgage bubble, since popped, was another.

Bubbles are a part of the weather patterns of markets. They appear every so often, like cloudy days. So what about China? In the big cities, apartment prices have doubled or tripled in the past three to five years. Over 50 million housing units have been added in the past 20 years. Bank lending is up fourfold from 2008, and the government stimulus package encouraged a lot of temporary activity in construction.

If we pull in for a closer look, we see that the urban population might increase by 13 million per year, but not all urban centers see the overwhelming growth that the government envisioned for them.

Daya Bay, former hide-out of pirates in the 1920s, was developed for 12 million people. Today, according to the government's own stats, 70 percent of the units remain empty. That story comes from a report by Adrian Brown interviewing various individuals from struggling couples to Hong Kong investment professionals. One such analyst, Tulloch Gillem, admits that such build-outs add to GDP, but "it's essentially the modern equivalent of building pyramids." Manzhouli, on the Russian border, was put together for 5 million people and even has its own airport and five-star hotel. How many residents currently live there? About 250,000. To get maximum capacity at the airport, everyone would have to travel at least every three weeks. Other overbuilt cities include Tianjin, coastal Dalian, and Wuhan.

However, the housing story is regional. Beijing, Shanghai, and Shenzhen have better supply/demand scenarios playing out. Some have gotten quite wealthy on it. China's Hurun Rich List, the Chinese luxury magazine version of the *Forbes* list, figures the housing sector spawned 7 out of the 10 top billionaires. A construction tycoon scored the top of the heap. Who knows just how much debt may lie beneath that pile of wealth, though. It could be quite a fragile pile.

The bottom line: There is surely a property bubble in China, but it is uneven. As one hedge fund manager put it to me, "China is many mini-economies." He is sure there is a bubble too, but I note he's still investing in basic areas like food and water, which are less connected to the property market.

Even if—and especially if—there is a property bust, one thing stands to do well: gold.

Visit to the Cai Bai Gold Market

China loves gold. Chinese are buying gold hand over fist. In 2010, they imported five times as much gold as they did the year before. In 2011, they will top those figures. In China, unlike the United States, the government actively encourages its people to own gold as part of their personal savings plans.

Well, I can tell you the Cai Bai gold market was bustling on the day I visited. A guard promptly stopped me when I pulled out my video camera, but believe me, there was a good crowd buying gold in all its forms, from jewelry to bars.

Back in central Beijing, we visited a Bank of China branch. There were 77 teller windows. In the central foyer was a display case with gold and silver coins for sale, as if they were pens or tote bags.

We talked to a customer service representative about opening an account. It's as easy for an American to open a bank account there as it is at Bank of America, maybe easier. But you can do things with this account that you can't do so easily in the United States. For instance, you can buy any currency you want. You can even buy and sell gold online. There are no fees. You pay only a spread of about 10 cents per trade, which is tiny.

The numbers coming out of China back my street-level view. My visit coincided with a peak gold-buying season in China, May, a popular time for weddings, taking gold sales up over 70 percent from a year earlier. The sale of gold bars has doubled from a year ago, according to CCTV, the large state Chinese television station.

CCTV reports a case that could become the norm across China. "Housing speculators from Wenzhou city in southeastern China are switching their money from property into gold following government restrictions on the real estate market." A high-end gold trading group reported that three groups of Wenzhou investors made gold purchases worth over 10 million yuan. Numbers aside, you can be sure a lot of buyers are coming to the market. It's a story we heard more than once on our trip.

While in China, I met with Patrick Chovanec, a professor at Tsinghua University in Beijing. We dined one night at a 500-year-old restaurant in town, amid a striking interior made up of thick wood beams and traditional Chinese woodwork. In addition to his professorial duties, Chovanec advises hedge funds and investors in China.

Chovanec is an expat and writes a blog called An American Perspective from China. Commenting on CCTV's gold story, he wrote:

"I find it very interesting given the analogy I've always drawn between the way Chinese invest in empty apartments as a 'store of value' and investment in nonproductive assets like gold. So it might very well make sense that, if they are no longer so certain stockpiled real estate will act as a reliable store of value, they would opt for gold as an attractive alternative."

We often heard that the Chinese buy empty apartments and just sit on them, treating the investment as a store of value. The other favorite place to park cash is gold. This is an interesting dynamic at work here. It gives us another big catalyst for a higher gold price, a buying surge from the Chinese, especially if some do get burned on real estate.

It's not just Chinese citizens who want gold. The government is looking to load up on gold. China has $3 trillion in foreign currency reserves, but a mere $48 billion of those reserves are in gold, a paltry 1.7 percent.

There are numerous guesses as to where that number might end up. But they are all several times higher than 1.7 percent. As Goldcorp founder Rob McEwen said, "China is out to have more gold than America, and Russia is aspiring to the same. China wants to show its currency has more backing than the United States."

For some perspective of just how big a buildup China and Russia need to pull that off, let's review a list of the top 10 countries ranked by their gold reserves (Fig. 5.5).

World's leading gold reserves

Rank	Country	Gold (in metric tons)	Gold's Share of Forex Reserves
1	United States	8,133.5	73.9%
2	Germany	3,401.8	70.3%
3	IMF	2,846.7	—
4	Italy	2,451.8	68.65%
5	France	2,435.4	67.2%
6	China	1,054.1	1.7%
7	Switzerland	1,040.1	16.4%
8	Russia	775.2	6.7%
9	Japan	765.2	3.0%
10	Netherlands	612.5	57.5%

FIGURE 5.5 If China (and Russia) Loaded Up . . .

Source: www.AgoraFinancial.com.

To top the United States, the Chinese would have to grow their gold reserves nearly eightfold; the Russians more than ten fold. Between the two of them, they'd have to add 14,438 metric tons to their stashes, equal to nearly six years of global mine production.

Gold miners, then, are another way to play China's lust for gold.

China Forecast: Cloudy with a Chance of Rain

Since my first visit to China, one of my favorite investment theses has been: "Buy what China needs to buy." I dipped the ladle into this idea bowl often. And the stocks of producers of potash, oil, iron ore, and other stuff from the earth did well. But the tides of fortune ebb and flow. Will these commodities be good investments in the future?

First, let me state again what every investor in commodities everywhere should know: China is your biggest buyer. Take another look at Figure 1.2 in Chapter 1, which shows you China's consumption of a given commodity as a percentage of world consumption. So to answer the question I posed above means you have to think about China's growth rate. China slows, bad for commodities. China grows, good for commodities. Makes sense, right?

If China slows down, then these things will get hit hard. In June 2011, China's manufacturing activity fell for the third straight month. The official purchasing managers' index stood at 50.9, down from 52 in May. Any number over 50 means expansion, and below that means contraction. Unofficially, things are probably worse, because officials have a way of dressing up doggy numbers.

What happened to commodity prices in those three months? Let's look at the Dow Jones-UBS Commodity Index (in Figure 5.6) which contains 19 commodities, everything from aluminum to zinc. Not surprisingly, it fell.

Keep in mind that China was still growing, just at a slower rate. Imagine what happens if China actually contracts?

It's one of those things that will seem extremely obvious in retrospect. But if you are worried about a slowdown in China, you should shy away from commodities near the top of its buy list. This is the exact opposite of what I've advised my readers to do over the past several years.

This means you should particularly avoid cement, iron ore, coal, pigs, and steel. You'll see that they were at the top of the list in my chart. You ought to feel better about food, wheat, and chickens, which are not as sensitive to China's buying. Oil, somewhat surprisingly, is far down the list, too, and is something of an exception. While the price of oil was down in the second quarter of 2011, China's imports were near record highs. This doesn't mean oil prices won't go down if China slows or contracts, but oil seems less susceptible than other commodities at this point.

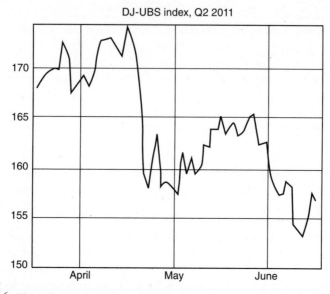

DJ-UBS index, Q2 2011

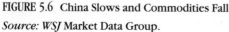

FIGURE 5.6 China Slows and Commodities Fall
Source: WSJ Market Data Group.

The other giant exception is precious metals. While China's imports of copper, coal, and iron ore are all down from a year ago, China still buys a lot of precious metals. We touched on gold above, but I think it's worth underscoring here. There are no official data, but estimates put Chinese imports of gold at 200 tonnes through June 2011. That compares with 250 tonnes for all of 2010, which was a fourfold increase from 2009. China has bought all of this gold despite being the world's largest gold producer.

This kind of analysis extends further. Certain countries, too, have been riding the coattails of China's buying binge. Brazil, for one, is a big supplier of China's raw material needs. No surprise, it was among the worst-performing markets in the second quarter of 2011, down more than 5 percent. So goes China, so goes Brazil. The same might be said of Canada (down 5 percent) and Australia. Russia, another big commodity market, was down 7 percent in the quarter.

This analysis is unsettling, I admit. But it is worth thinking about what happens if China slows further or even contracts. Every economy contracts at some point if only for a time. China's economy hasn't shrunk since 1976. That's 35 years, a long time between economic bowel movements.

On the other hand, people have been calling for China's demise for a long time. Most recently, Jim Chanos, the famous short seller forever known as "The Man Who Called Enron," has found many trouble spots in China's boom.

He points out that fixed asset investment in China is 50 percent percent of the economy. This easily exceeds figures from past bubbles in other markets. All that investment created "ghost cities with no people, high-speed rail lines to nowhere and empty apartments." He flags excessive debt engaged in real estate speculation. "The whole country of China has become a nation of real estate speculators on leverage," he says. Real estate as a percentage of the economy has reached levels associated with pre-bubble Ireland. Inflation is getting out of hand, hence the Chinese buying of precious metals to protect their wealth. Food and basics eat up 50 percent of the average Chinese budget.

All of this, too, is worrisome. What's more unsettling is that few people want to face the ugly possibility that perhaps it is time to lighten up on commodities. "We do not think this is the time to be lightening up on commodities," Barclays analysts declared emphatically as commodities fell, "quite the opposite."

That is the consensus opinion. It is the easy opinion, because so far it has been so right. According to Barry Bannister at Stifel Financial, "Commodity prices have reached the highest 10-year rolling return in 200 years." And in the past 10 years, the best-performing stocks have been those involved in commodity extraction. Figure 5.7 shows the Fact Set industry categories. It highlights the top and bottom five.

To date, "buy the dips" has been the right play in commodities. Perhaps the consensus will be right again. In fact, I hope it is. It is an easier world to

Total return indexes, March 2001–March 2011

	10-Year Annual Total Return
Non-Energy Materials	19.3%
Energy Materials	13.8%
Process Industries	12%
Consumer Non-Durables	10.8%
Health Services	10.7%
Consumer Services	8.9%
Distribution Services	8.4%
Transportation	8%
Industrial Services	7.9%
Retail Trade	6.5%
Technology Services	6.4%
Producer Manufacturing	6.1%
Utilities	5.4%
Consumer Durables	5.1%
Electronic Technology	3.7%
Communications	2.8%
Finance	2.8%
Health Technology	2.6%
Commercial Services	2%

FIGURE 5.7 How They Finished
Source: Fact Set.

invest in when you can count on China, the world's second-largest economy, bringing its best to the table.

But as I write, the skies on the financial horizon have darkened considerably for China. I think there will be some pain before the longer-term trend reasserts itself.

In some ways, China has often seemed on the edge of disaster. As Paul French writes in his new book, *Through the Looking Glass: China's Foreign Journalists from Opium Wars to Mao*: "From the 1820s, China's story was one of a country on the brink of collapse. . . . Of course, there is a story in China now—a massive and significant one. But in historical terms, it is tamer, far more stable. . . ."

I think China will both mint and destroy fortunes. There will be great opportunities and great dangers. In many ways, that's the way it has always been, and as French alludes to, whatever happens is not likely to be as wild and unstable as what China has endured to get to this point.

On this idea of making a fortune in China, I found inspiration in the life and work of one man who has been there and done that in China. His name is Carl Crow.

The Adventures of Carl Crow

No matter what you may be selling, your business in China should be enormous, if the Chinese who should buy your goods would only do so.

—Carl Crow, *400 Million Customers*

How many entrepreneurs have sat and thought, "If only the Chinese would buy my product. . . . Heck, if only one in 10 Chinese would buy my product, I'd be rich."

Finding a way to get rich by selling to the Chinese has got to be one of the great quests of moneymen everywhere, like trying to discover some magic key that unlocks the doors to untold treasures.

For the most the part, though, these dreams remain dreams. However, sometimes, someone, somewhere, figures it out. Carl Crow was someone who figured it out, and it made him a rich man.

Carl Crow led an adventurous life. Born in Highland, Mo., in 1884, Crow started out as a newspaperman. Eyeing his fortune, he started China Press in Shanghai in 1911, but Crow realized there was no money in newspapers.

In time, he turned his eyes to the great boom unfolding in China after the Great War, which in many ways reminds me of the China boom of recent years. There was a new and growing middle class, especially in the great city on the banks of the Huangpu River, Shanghai.

Crow followed the money. In 1918, he launched an advertising agency in Shanghai. As an adman, he basically tried to figure out how to help his clients sell their products to the Chinese.

His agency flourished, and it would make him rich. From his offices at 81 Jinkee Road, just off the city's landmark Bund, Crow worked out the great puzzle that is China. Crow's billboards peppered China, from Shanghai all through the Yangtze Valley and as far north as Hubei. Chances are if you flipped through a magazine in China between the wars, you saw Crow's work in advertisements for cars, matches, cameras, and many other goods.

He had a great run of 19 years. Then the war with Japan began in July 1937. Crow, who was outspoken in his criticism of the Japanese, fled the country. He could take none of his wealth with him. He lost everything: house, business, money. Back in the United States, Crow penned his classic book, which helped him start over again. It's still in print today.

The title of the book is *400 Million Customers*. If it sounds familiar, it's because James McGregor wrote a book in 2005 called *One Billion Customers*. You see, the dream only gets bigger over time. In Crow's book, he talks about his many adventures in the business world of China.

Along the way, you see how he learned many expensive lessons, which are funny to read about. For instance, Crow had a client who sold sewing needles. It sold a package with an assortment of sewing needles of different sizes. This product proved popular in other parts of the world and the needle maker wanted to get into China. However, no matter what, the Chinese didn't buy the needles.

After a while, Crow figured out why:

To offer a Chinese woman a packet of 12 assorted sizes [of needles] was like offering her a dozen pairs of shoes of assorted sizes. As only one pair would fit her, she wasn't interested in the other 11.

As you can imagine, Crow learns many things about the psychology of the Chinese consumer. Even in his business dealings, Crow quickly learns the ins and outs of negotiating. His observations are often humorous.

On using statistics and numbers to make an argument to Chinese businessmen, Crow writes: "Statistics bore them to the point of resentment. Figures will either confirm that they are right, which is unnecessary, or prove that they are wrong, which is unwelcome."

Then there are the little cultural nuances that make for entertaining reading. For instance, Crow was a large, fat man. Apparently, the Chinese liked to point that out to him. Crow discovered that being fat was indicative of being wealthy and eating well. Fatness denoted a sagacious calm. He writes: "When these [Chinese] go into ecstasies over my rotundness, they are really paying me very sincere flattery."

Many businesspeople still swear by Crow's book. As I say, the book is still in print. It's widely viewed as a classic and is surely one of the most-read books on China ever published. And from my own travels in China, I find myself agreeing with Crow's observations about the food, which is good.

Crow's book, though, shows how China was as much a money pit as a place where gold pieces grew in the bushes. It remains that way today, ever tricky and hard to figure out. For those who find a way, as Crow did, the rewards can be immense.

Let's face it: A market of more than 1 billion noses is one you shouldn't ignore. As for Carl Crow's excellent book, I recommend the Earnshaw Books edition, which includes the wonderful illustrations of Sapajou, a White Russian cartoonist Crow sometimes employed.

Five Key Takeaways

- China's pressing need for clean water is one of the most powerful investment trends in the country. Check out this pair of favorite stocks on the idea: A.O. Smith, which trades on the NYSE, and Hyflux, which trades in Singapore and on the Pink Sheets in the United States.
- Don't underestimate the power of China's gold purchases to push up the price of gold and gold stocks. Remember, the Chinese view gold as a store of wealth. And the Chinese government has lots of room to buy more gold.
- Keep an eye on China's coal needs. Coal miners are the straight-away play, but there is an interesting wrinkle in the challenges of China's coal-based industry. In particular, I like the methanol story, and Methanex is the stock to play that idea.
- Avoid the U.S. listings of China-based stocks. Even the experts have a hard time figuring out the frauds. In fact, tread carefully when investing directly in Chinese stocks of any kind.
- There have been many really good books on China in recent years. I mentioned several of them above. Here are two more to help you understand China's growing role in markets beyond China. To uncover China's economic ties to the Middle East, Ben Simpfendorfer's book *The New Silk Road: How a Rising Arab World Is Turning Away From the West and Rediscovering China* is the best I've come across. For what China is up to in Africa, read *China Safari: On the Trail of Beijing's Expansion in Africa* by a pair of Frenchmen, Michel Beuret and Serge Michel.

CHAPTER 6

India: Don't Drink the Tap Water?

"Don't drink the tap water or you'll be dead."
—Indian fund manager's advice to newly arrived foreigners

Since liberalization began in 1991, India began minting millionaires. The Sensex, an index of India stocks, is up nearly 500 percent in the last decade, a time when U.S. markets have barely budged.

Not bad for what Winston Churchill once called a "geographical expression." In his mind, it was "no more a united nation than the Equator." After independence in 1947, you would have been hard-pressed to find anybody taking even money bets that India would be around a decade later. That India would survive as a democracy for 60-plus years (and counting) seemed improbable to people at the time.

As the American writer Paul Bowles wrote in 1963:

Obviously, it is a gigantic task to make a nation out of a place like India, what with Hindus, Parsees, Jainists, Jews, Catholics, and Protestants [Bowles forgot Muslims], some of whom may speak the arbitrarily imposed idiom of Hindi, but most of whom are more likely to know Gujarati, Marathi, Bengali, Urdu, Telugu, Tamil, Malayalam, or some other tongue instead. One wonders whether any sort of unifying project can ever be undertaken, or, indeed, whether it is even desirable.

That it would be a place to get rich would have seemed even more improbable. Yet India embarks on the early stages of a massive secular boom. It is a fine place to see our thesis in play.

India has already created some massive fortunes. At one point, analysts at Agora Financial figured out that India minted 47 new millionaires every day. Moreover, there have been some high-profile billionaires, such as Lakshmi Mittal, founder of the world's largest steel company. Another is the head of Reliance Industries, Mukesh Ambani. He built a 570-foot tower in

Mumbai for use as a private home. It has 27 floors, a helipad, and 600 servants—as well as six floors of parking for 168 cars. The cost: a cool $1 billion.

Foreigners with patience can also make a fortune here.

The Japanese were the first major group to invest in India, according to Aaron Chaze in his book, *India: An Investor's Guide to the Next Economic Superpower.* There was a lot of failure in that early group, as you can imagine, but those that stuck it out have reaped great rewards.

Suzuki was one of the winners. Its joint venture, Maruti Suzuki India, produces about half the cars in India and about one-quarter of Suzuki's global profits. Honda Motors was another winner. Its joint venture, Hero Honda, helped make it the world's largest maker of motorcycles.

"Whatever the compulsions that drive future investment trends," writes Chaze, "the Japanese experience in India shows that the greatest reward to investors comes . . . to those who have decided to hang in there for the long haul."

It won't be easy as India goes through the sometimes painful birth shifting into a high-gear as an economic powerhouse.

For example, there is the notoriously rickety infrastructure. During my first visit in 2007, I got through customs and out of the airport with no problems. Getting to the hotel was another matter. The Taj Mahal Hotel is only about 12 miles from the airport, yet it took an hour and a half to get there because the traffic was so slow. Cars, motorcycles, and people crowded along Bombay's busy streets, giving me a firsthand taste of the poor infrastructure I had read so much about. The roads were hopelessly outmatched against the flow of traffic they carried. Seldom can you drive faster than 40 miles per hour, even on the highways. Ox carts and bicycles don't help matters. Then there are unpredictable lane changes and traffic laws no one enforces.

That is part of the opportunity. It's part of the catching-up process that is the theme of this book.

That is why India has many road projects in the making. More than one commentator has noted the parallels with America's efforts in the 1950s in building a national highway system. The so-called Golden Quadrilateral was a big step for India. It is a network of four- and six-lane highways, comprising more than 3,600 miles, which runs through 13 states and India's four largest cities: New Delhi, Kolkata (formerly Calcutta), Chennai (formerly Madras) and Mumbai (formerly Bombay). India has the second-largest network of roads in the world after the United States with much in the pipeline.

Roads such as these have a huge impact on development that often escapes the casual observer. India, for instance, actually wastes more fruit and vegetables than it consumes, according to *The Economic Times,* India's largest financial daily. India is the second-largest producer of fruits and vegetables in the world, but 30 to 40 percent never make it to their destination.

As the *Times* reports: "Gaps such as poor infrastructure, insufficient cold-storage capacity, unavailability of cold storage in close proximity to farms, and poor transportation infrastructure all are contributing factors." Routine brownouts and blackouts happen throughout India, often lasting for seven hours or more, which lead to food spoilage.

Somehow, so far, India has managed to overcome many of these obstacles. The economy has grown more than 6 percent annually for a long time. I saw more evidence of this, too when I spent some time going over a cross-section of midcap and small-cap Indian stocks with analysts in India. Many are growing 30–40 percent per year, and have done so for 15 or 20 years.

One of the people I met in India was Jayesh "Jimmy" Seth, who runs KC Securities, a large brokerage firm in Mumbai. I also met his son, Harsh, a then-22-year-old Northwestern graduate who returned home to make it in Mumbai.

Over lunch one day, Jimmy told me the advice he gave Harsh: "When you are in America, take note of all the daily conveniences you enjoy. Write them all down. Then, when you come back to Mumbai, check that list again. Whatever's missing, start a business around that."

It's a good piece of advice, as India has lots of gaps to fill, such as those basics of infrastructure. Some variation of Jimmy's advice applies to investors, too. Look for the gaps in these emerging markets. Find what they don't have but want or need. Invest in the companies that fill those gaps.

Still, It's Tough to Invest in India

My first swing through India in 2007 was the most ambitious. I started in the bustling port city of Mumbai, home to Asia's oldest stock exchange. Then I moved on to visit high-tech campuses in Bangalore and Hyderabad. The latter is only miles from the ancient city of Golconda, once renowned for its diamonds. From there, I was off to green Kochi (formerly Cochin) on the Malabar Coast, with its many coconut trees, rice paddies, and slow-moving rivers. I wound up the trip in the north, traveling to Jaipur, in hot and dry Rajasthan, then to Agra to see the Taj Mahal, and finally, to the dusty capital city of New Delhi.

In Delhi, I walked through the old market of Chandni Chowk, about which I had read so much. Camel trains came here from Kashgar. Traders carried jasper and sardonyx, cinnamon logs from Madagascar, and much more. Today, it's still a busy market, lined with shops where you can buy just about anything.

Unlike China and the Southeast Asian economies, India's economy does not hinge on exports. The explosive growth in India's economy is mainly a grass-roots-driven trend. About 200 million participating consumers are in India, with tens of millions added annually.

Unfortunately, it's just not an easy place to invest for the armchair investor. This was a common frustration as I traveled in India. The easy way to invest in India is to buy the polite merchandise. That is, the ready-made, off-the-shelf goods on the NYSE, listed Indian companies such as Tata Motors or Sterlite Industries, or even an Indian mutual fund.

Other ways take some digging. I'll give one such idea below. However, I think it is important to keep an eye on opportunities as they emerge. The world has never seen two economies the size of China and India industrialize so quickly.

You see the most immediate effects of this in the commodity pits. You see it in rising prices for all kinds of commodities. Rising prices for energy, food, and basic materials kicked off a major commodity boom in recent years. I think the second ripple effect is one we'll start to deal with soon: the health consequences of such rapid growth.

Indian Summer

The father superior stops. Finally, he reads: "Father Miguel . . . instructor of theology beginning Sept. 20, 1884, ordained in 1891, and . . ." The father lifts his face, and his serene eyes look straight at me.
"He died on Oct. 22, 1896." Silence. "No one lasts very long in this climate, dear sir."
　　　　　　—Guido Gozzano, *Journey Toward the Cradle of Mankind*

"Walking in this climate is such gentle agony," wrote Gozzano to open his book on India.

Gozzano (1883–1916), a distinguished Italian poet, visited India in 1912. He spent six weeks on the subcontinent and wrote letters about his travels. He made many observations about the heat. "Never have I been so glad not to be overweight in this climate," he wrote. "India is truly infernal for anyone with a few extra pounds."

Later, he went on to write about how the heat "creates mirages, dissolves in the air, makes it quiver and flutter on the horizon."

I wonder what Gozzano would make of India today. The first thing to hit me when I visited Mumbai was the pollution. Looking out at the Arabian Sea from my room in the Taj Mahal Hotel, I saw several boats bobbing along in coffee-and-cream-colored waters, but a fog obscured the horizon or, rather, a pollution-created haze.

I had a copy of Roderick Cameron's *Time of the Mango Flowers*, an account of his travels through India in the 1950s. It's an enjoyable companion to have while traveling India as Cameron has an eye for architectural details and tells interesting historical vignettes along the way. Cameron stayed at the Taj, but it was a different place then. He writes about how "rippling water reflections played over the bedroom ceiling." The water doesn't reflect much today because the sun doesn't seem to get through all that often.

I'd been warned I'd have a scratchy throat after three days, (I didn't), but this isn't some traveler's irritant. Pollution is a serious health issue for people who live there. According to Edward Luce's *In Spite of the Gods: The Strange Rise of Modern India*, air pollution causes about one-eighth of premature deaths in India. Hundreds of thousands of children die from exposure to contaminated water.

India is not alone in this. China, the other big rapidly industrializing nation on the stage, has big problems with pollution of all kinds, too. Air quality in China is awful, too, though improving in some areas. I remember the first time I visited China in 2005 and the stink when I opened my suitcase back home. It smelled like I had lived in a bar for three weeks.

Robyn Meredith, in her book on China and India, titled *The Elephant and the Dragon: The Rise of China and India and What It Means for All of Us*, comments on China's poor air quality. She writes one section from the city of Chongqing, an industrial city of 30 million people. (For perspective, that's about the number of people that live in the whole state of California.) "Sunlight barely reaches the ground, dimmed by thick, gray smog," she writes. "Skyscrapers just three blocks away are mere outlines because of the air pollution."

Meredith cites this alarming fact: "All but two of the world's 20 most polluted cities are in India or China." Writer James Kynge calls the environmental degradation a "concealed debt" that people will have to pay for eventually.

I think you get the idea. The rapid rise of China and India has come with a cost: serious environmental damage, on many levels. The governments know about the problem, and things are starting to change. Delhi was the worst-polluted city in the world in 2004, but the government has since taken steps to clean it up. Today, all buses run on natural gas for example.

Many other issues spin off from environmental degradation. The flip side is that all of this need creates great demand for the basics. Someone will work on the water systems. Someone will build new power plants. This is all unfolding, but it will take time.

India's Real Economy—Not What You Think

When thinking of India's economy, most investors probably associate it with its outsourcing companies, that is, India as the world's back office, with call centers and armies of computer programmers and engineers. But this part of the economy is still tiny, and much of India's strange economy is poor and backward.

The best book I found on India is *In Spite of the Gods*. The author was the South Asia bureau chief for the *Financial Times*, living in New Delhi from 2001 to 2006.

It seems Luce traveled everywhere in India, meeting with local officials, business people, journalists, and others. This is the kind of research I put a high value on. You learn things by being in a place that you simply can't from afar.

The portrait that emerges from Luce's work is one of incredible complexity, color, and contradiction. Here, he pokes holes in the image that India is all "outsourcing": "Fewer than 1 million, that is, less than a quarter of 1 percent of India's total labor pool, are employed in information technology, software, back-office processing, and call centers."

In fact, he goes on to share that most Indians work in an unorganized and primitive economy: working on farms, running small shops or street stalls, driving rickshaws, working as servants, serving as seasonal laborers, and other tasks.

There is a long way to go in India, which is, oddly enough, part of its great appeal to investors and businesses.

The Indian "middle class," depending on how it is measured, is between 50–300 million people. That class alone is larger than the populations of entire Western countries. Then there is brisk economic growth, so you can play around with numbers and get all kinds of wild results.

In 2003, for instance, Goldman Sachs made the following predictions about India:

- By 2020, its economy will be larger than Great Britain's.
- By 2040, it will be the world's third-largest economy.
- By 2050, its per capita income will have grown 35 times over.

It seems absurd, but four years after those predictions were issued, India's growth rate has been higher than the study assumed.

For these reasons, a long list of companies continue to try to crack the market. AIG, Citibank, Pepsi, and many others have become market leaders in their segments in India. Many more are trying to gain footholds.

"During my time in India," Luce reflects, "I have often been amused by the foreign executives I have met who spend years occupying the same hotel rooms while they await the green light for their company to invest in India, so they can set up a permanent office."

Since his book's publication, a couple of events stand out as interesting landfalls marking India's continued ascent.

India regained investment-grade status after a 15-year hiatus as the big ratings agencies removed the speculative tag from India's debt. This was important, as it lowered the cost of borrowing for many Indian companies.

Then, there was Tata Steel's big acquisition of Corus, its Anglo-Dutch peer, the first large acquisition by an Indian company. It has brought out a certain boldness in India's corporate culture. As one leading Indian commentator put it: "I look forward to the day when ICICI Bank takes over Citibank; when Infosys acquires IBM; when Reliance takes over Exxon; and Tata Motors takes over General Motors." Will the Tata Steel acquisition be something future historians muse over as a harbinger of a new trend, or will it be but a footnote?

In the short term, there are all kinds of obstacles to work through. Take the tangled and corrupt Indian bureaucracy. Its army of workers is immune to dismissal. Corruption is rampant and accepted in a way strange to Western eyes. This leads to some absurd circumstances. The highway department in India, for instance, employs 1.25 people per mile of road, the highest number in the world. The government pays them more than three times the market rate for such labor. "Many of these employees do not bother showing up for work," Luce writes "because they cannot be sacked."

The Indian bureaucracy is as expensive as it is useless. Much of the government's spending is tied up in paying itself. Salaries for its bloated payroll soak up money that could have gone to building better roads, power systems, and water and wastewater plants. All of these government employees have cushy pensions.

The legal system is a mess. Widespread corruption is one issue. It is so open that some judges have a menu of fixed prices. Luce writes: "You pay x thousand rupees to get bail if you are standing trial for a narcotics offense, y thousand for manslaughter . . . " Then there are lots of vacancies and the fact that judges don't work much, maybe from 10 a.m. to 3 p.m., with at least an hour for lunch. "Perhaps the biggest problem," Luce writes, "is the gigantic backlog of suits in India, which in 2006 amounted to 27 million cases. At the current rate at which India's courts wade through proceedings, it would take more than 300 years to clear the judicial backlog." By some estimates, 10 percent of the economy's capital is tied up in legal disputes.

Suffice it to say, this is a deep-rooted problem. I can only imagine the frustration of trying to do business there. This quote from the head of Procter & Gamble's India operations sums it up best: "In my 30 years in active business in India, I did not meet a single bureaucrat who really understood my business, yet he had the power to ruin it."

Plenty of head winds remain with or without government bureaucrats. According to the World Bank, the average Indian manufacturing firm loses

8 percent of sales per year due to power outages. India, like China, is a voracious consumer of energy and raw materials.

The daunting prospect of feeding India's economy bodes well for investors in energy and in all of the components of infrastructure. India currently imports 70 percent of its oil needs, for example, compared with only 30 percent a few years ago.

Rajasthan's Oil Prize and India's Energy Needs

Luckily for India, one of the world's newest and largest onshore oil discoveries is in the hot desert of Rajasthan. I've been to Rajasthan's largest city, Jaipur, sometimes called the Pink City. Rajasthan was once the seat of power for some of India's ancient kings. I visited the Amber Fort and rode an elephant from its base to the top of the hill. From the ramparts, you get an impressive view of the city and the dry, windswept lands around it.

Little did I realize back in 2009 that oil might lie beneath that breathtaking scenery. Later, a story emerged that there was a big oil project out in the desert of Rajasthan.

A company called Cairn India discovered oil in the Thar Desert, near the Pakistan border. Cairn then built an oil processing facility there, the Mangala terminal. It is the size of 200 football fields and processes the oil from Cairn's Rajasthan fields. Cairn estimates production will peak at 175,000 barrels per day.

Here is an example of the kind of backdoor plays you can sometimes find and for which I am always on the lookout. Cairn India lists in Bombay, but Cairn Energy owns 65 percent of it. Cairn Energy trades in London with the ticker CNE. So for a while, you had a neat opportunity to snatch up great assets at a hefty discount.

First, a look at Cairn Energy in Figure 6.1.

The market said Cairn Energy was worth $4.18 billion. Look at its 65 percent-owned interest in Cairn India in Figure 6.2

Cairn Energy's investment stake in Cairn India was worth $4.98 billion on the Bombay exchange, which is $802 million more than the price for which Cairn Energy itself was trading.

Cairn Energy Plc Share Price in pence	2,170 pence
Cairn Energy Plc Share Price in dollars	$31.90
Shares outstanding (in millions)	131
Market Cap of Cairn Energy (in millions)	$4,178

FIGURE 6.1 Market Says Cairn Energy Worth $4.18 Billion

Source: Bloomberg.

Cairn India Share Price in rupees	202.95 rupees
Cairn India Share Price in dollars	$4.05
Shares held by Cairn Energy (in millions)	$1,227
Value of Cairn Energy's stake (in millions)	$4,980

FIGURE 6.2 Get Everything Else Cairn Owns For Free

Source: Bloomberg.

So, you could've bought Cairn Energy in London and gotten Cairn India for 20 percent off what it would have cost you to buy it in Bombay. Plus, you get everything else Cairn Energy owns for free.

What else did Cairn Energy own? It owned an exploration company called Capricorn. Capricorn had exploration efforts in Greenland, Tunisia, Bangladesh, and Nepal, among other places. I don't know what any of that was worth. But if it was worth more than zero; it just added to the value proposition here.

I first wrote about this idea in April 2009, and if you had bought Cairn Energy (the London shares) then, you would have enjoyed a 50 percent gain in about a year's time. Plus, the Rajasthan project is exciting. It more than doubled Cairn Energy's production. And there was something like 1.5 billion barrels of oil spread over 20 discoveries in the process of evaluation.

A *Financial Times* article was the bird dog that got me looking at the idea. ("Cairn Lifts India's Energy Profile" by Joe Leahy.) In that piece, Leahy makes the point that the Indian government is supportive of the project since it will cut India's oil import bill. A big gas project was off the east coast of India. Reliance Industries was about to start production there. These two projects together had a total production of about 30 percent of the Gulf of Mexico.

As Leahy writes: "The Cairn and Reliance projects are the poster children for government efforts to increase domestic oil and gas production in India."

India has potential as an energy producer, which makes it worth keeping an eye on as an investor in energy projects. For instance, India has vast coal reserves, and India is tapping coal bed methane trapped in those coal reserves.

Meeting the energy demands of its growing economy will be a big challenge. To that end, India is set to become one of the big players in alternative energy. Renewable energy sources represent 11 percent of power capacity, and much more is on the way.

One interesting tidbit on this front: India is the world's fifth-largest producer and consumer of electricity, but if you look at consumption per person, it is still only 30 percent of the global average. This shows you just how much more India's power consumption could grow over time.

Coal currently powers more than half of India's energy needs. Coal India is the state-run near-monopoly in coal. It had an IPO in November of 2010, and within six months, it was up more than 60 percent.

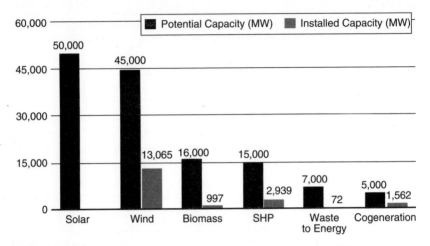

FIGURE 6.3 Potential and Installed Renewable Energy Capacity in MW

Source: Financial Times.

Coal India has the largest coal reserves in the world, at 10.6 billion tons, just edging out Peabody Energy, at 9.3 billion tons. As of May 2011, you could get those tons for about $2 each, compared to a global average of $7.40. It had net cash that was one-sixth of its market cap. Another example of the interesting opportunities such markets can offer.

Still, India will continue to be a net importer of energy, so it is has an ambitious plan for renewable energy. Over the next 10 years, just based on planned investments, this sector will grow 17 percent per year, an astounding rate, and three times faster than China's. See Figure 6.3.

The alternative energy source of choice is wind. India is third in the world by installed wind capacity, and wind is 70 percent of the total renewable energy capacity in India. Anybody who is anybody in wind is there: Vestas Wind Systems, Gamesa, Siemens, and others.

Wind used to matter a lot in the old days. In fact, you could say wind powered Marco Polo's famed explorations to the region in the first place.

The Malabar Coast

When the traveler leaves Ceylon and sails westward for about 60 miles, he arrives in the great province of Malabar. It is indeed the best part of India.

—Marco Polo

The Malabar Coast is on the west coast of India, facing the Arabian Sea. It has been a center of trade for centuries. I spent some time in Kochi, an important port city in the province of Kerala. Marco Polo, too, made his way up the Malabar Coast in the thirteenth century. It's amusing to read his comments today.

"The climate is amazingly hot," he writes. Polo deduced this was why the people "go naked." "If it were not for the rain," Polo adds, "the heat would be so oppressive that no one could stand it."

The account we have of Marco Polo's journeys comes from Rustichello da Pisa, who wrote down Marco's stories. They were prisoners of war together during the fighting between Genoa and Venice. As you may have guessed, the authenticity of these stories is questionable. Nonetheless, I found it entertaining reading.

Polo comments on the spice trade: "In this kingdom, there is great abundance of pepper and of ginger, besides cinnamon in plenty and other spices and coconuts." Today, the region is still an important source of spices. Over the years, Chinese, Portuguese, English, and other traders coveted this area for its spices.

Kochi has a worldly feel because of the influence of these other groups. They left their indelible mark. The Chinese, for example, were here in the thirteenth century. You can see their influence in the distinctive architecture of Kerala. I visited a fishing area where the fishermen still use nets created from the original Chinese design.

There are plenty of markers left by other groups as well. I visited various buildings built by the Portuguese centuries ago. You can see tall rain trees, the Brazilian trees they brought with them.

All of this cultural history is fascinating to me. I couldn't help but wonder what it must have been like for, say, a Portuguese trader to gaze out on the lush green landscape of the Malabar Coast. It must've seemed a paradise on earth. Coconut trees are everywhere (Kerala means "land of coconuts") and so are the distinctive banana trees.

This is the prettiest part of India I've seen yet. I can see why *National Geographic Traveler* named it one of the "50 Places of a Lifetime." I took a ride down a canal from Alleppey to Kumarakom on a neat houseboat constructed from coconut wood and teak. On the boat, I had a delicious meal of grilled fish, rice, cabbage cooked in coconut milk, curried chicken, cucumbers, sweet pineapple, and fried bananas. This is a typical meal for this part of the country, or so my guide told me.

In my hotel room in Kumarakom at night, I could hear a hard rain outside and see lightning flash through the window, punctuated by rolling thunder. In Kerala, the monsoon season was still on. Kerala gets plenty of rain.

At this point in my travels, the power had gone off in every hotel I'd stayed in, if only for a moment. It happened briefly in Kumarakom, and my room was dark, save for the light from my battery-powered laptop screen.

When in Kochi, I met with a government official about investment opportunities in the province. It was not helpful, but the meeting had some comical aspects. My favorite answer was to the question "What about corruption?" The official answered: "We are the least-corrupt state in India." Still corrupt, mind you, just "the least corrupt."

But he did confirm something else I heard on my trip. When asked what the province's most-pressing need was, in terms of investment dollars, he said, "Hotels. We need rooms."

It seemed odd he would say that, but when I dug into it more, I could see why. India attracts many visitors, both tourists and business people, every year, more than ever. The better hotels sell out quickly.

Before landing in Kochi, I spent some time in Hyderabad and Bangalore. Both cities are home to significant technology companies. I visited the campuses of Satyam in Hyderabad and Infosys in Bangalore. Satyam and Infosys both maintain their own housing quarters onsite for visiting employees because they cannot rely on the city's existing hotels.

I met with a pair of private equity managers about real estate development opportunities in India. Hotels were at the top of their list, too. They presented a surprising slide (Figure 6.4) that showed how all of India has fewer hotel rooms than the city of Orlando.

I thought that was an interesting observation, something you wouldn't think of if you were drawing up a list of investment opportunities in India. I know it would've taken me a long time to get to hotels.

I stayed at wonderful hotels during my trip, such as the Rambagh Palace in Jaipur, the Oberoi Amarvilas in Agra, and the Taj Mahal Hotel, which I'd recommend anytime you come to Mumbai. (After spending a day in the chaos and noise of the city, its poolside Ionic pillars and palms make for a

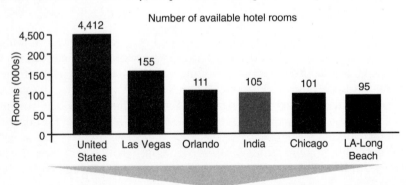

Significant under-penetration in the Indian hospitality sector creates a large demand/supply imbalance.

FIGURE 6.4 Get a Room! (Hard to Do in India)

Source: Equitymaster.

welcome retreat.) Still, the room rates were so out of whack with everything else. The supply-demand balance was so tight that the average room rates in some cities reached the $400 level. Overall, room rates in India were higher than the current average room rates for New York, London, and Singapore. That $400 can go far in India, which is not true of the dollar in too many places of the world these days.

The hotel situation is one that's not going to get a lot better anytime soon. The number of tourists visiting India will likely increase at a 15 percent or better clip for years, according to the World Travel & Tourism Council. That would make India one of the fastest-growing tourist destinations in the world, to say nothing about the business travelers. Some companies have gone ahead and put up their own hotels on land they own. They run these hotels for employees and business visitors. They can't afford to sit around and wait for government approvals to build new hotels.

Thus investment opportunity number one would be to develop and run hotels in India. Unfortunately, there is no way for you as an investor in publicly traded stocks to do that. I heard a couple of developers talk about hotel and resort projects they have on tap. These were attractive, I thought, promising 30 to 40 percent annual rates of return on modest assumptions for hotel occupancy and room rates.

Mega Money Enters India's Housing Market

One Mumbai morning, after an Indian breakfast of mutter masala and a cup of chai, I set off for a day of meetings at the Cricket Club. The club is a short ride from the Taj Hotel. Lined with large banyan trees, the white-walled Cricket Club proved a nice location for meetings. I had a good day talking with some Indian money managers about the market there.

The real estate market is hot in India all around, and it's attracting some mega money flows. Goldman Sachs calls India "the most exciting real estate market in Asia." All told, the market could grow from $15 billion to $90 billion by 2015. Kind of mind-boggling, isn't it?

So it's no surprise to me that the money managers saw opportunities in real estate.

One was an Indian mortgage company, HDFC. The Indian market remains far behind the United States in this regard. Mortgages generally run for only 11 years. Borrowers typically put down 35 percent. This makes borrowers naturally debt averse. There remains virtually no secondary market for mortgages. Banks make their loans, and they are stuck with them. This makes them naturally debt averse, too.

DLF, a big property company, had a record IPO in India around 2007 when I was there the first time. There were many more property companies in the pipeline looking to raise billions in the public market. Overseas investors have an especially big appetite for real estate.

As with any market, there are pockets of opportunity as well as danger zones. As far as danger zones go, the Indian property market looked frothy then. In fact, one money manager told me that some public companies changed their names to include the word "property," even if that had little to do with their actual business. This was eerily reminiscent of the United States tech bubble in the late 1990s, when companies wanted "dot-com" as part of their name. Just that moniker alone sent a stock soaring.

However, one can't argue that demand is being outstripped by supply. There are shortages in play in India, especially clustered around major new employment centers in the big cities.

Bad government policies get in the way here, as they can anywhere else. For example, Mumbai has some great old buildings with wonderful architecture. The shame of it is that many of the buildings appear worn down. I learned later that much of the city is under strict rent control, and the rates tenants pay are well below market value. The rent in some of these buildings is only $100 per month for a 3,000-square-foot apartment in prime real estate.

Therefore, there was no incentive for the owner to pay a lot of money to keep the building in good shape. It's painfully obvious which buildings have rent control and which don't. You'll see a nice building, painted and scrubbed, right next to something that looks as if it's going to fall down any minute.

Apartments in southern Mumbai, the kind without rent control, go for $1,000 per square foot, sometimes $2,000. That means you'd pay $3 million for a 3,000-square-foot apartment, at a minimum. And I hear the quality is not all that great. Nonetheless, real estate is in high demand and short supply in this part of Mumbai.

Our next stop, Hyderabad, is actually the second-fastest growing center for commercial real estate.

The View from Hyderabad

Hyderabad is a 400-year-old city of over 6 million people. It's famous for being the home of the wealthy Nizam of Hyderabad, who once ruled this part of India. Today, it's mostly a dirty, bustling, and noisy city.

Hyderabad is home to a number of technology companies. I'm more interested in some of the other stories developing in India—such as the water and infrastructure issues. However, the technology companies are an important part of the growth story. You can learn a lot about doing business in India by listening to them.

For example, as I mentioned before, many of these technology companies have their campuses with schools, hotels, and even their own sources of power. They can't wait for the city of Hyderabad to allow for the construction of another hotel, for instance, so they build their own on land they own. They secure their own sources of water and power.

The strengthening Indian rupee was big news while I was there the first time in 2007. The rupee put in a fresh $9\frac{1}{2}$-year high against the dollar. It has affected the earnings of Indian technology companies as their dollar profits convert to smaller amounts of rupee profits on the voyage home.

So, there is often some commentary in the papers on the dollar and a move to possible alternatives. I read articles about how resource-rich economies will move away from the dollar to protect their earnings as the dollar's slide accelerates. As an example, one writer cited the fact that Iran sells 85 percent of its oil exports in non-U.S. dollar currencies. The same writer speculated that the Russians may soon try pricing commodities in some other currency, possibly rubles.

Whether any of this happens or not is beside the point. More important is how the Indians talk about using currencies other than the dollar, something that you would not have heard 20 years ago. Spreading doubt and worry over the long-term value of the dollar is becoming more and more of an issue.

This brings us, once again, to gold.

Buying Gold in Mumbai

On one of my trips to India, I spent some time just working there, mostly out of my publisher's joint venture office in a part of Mumbai known as Churchgate. I got a different perspective simply living there on a day-to-day basis in October 2009. I got a sense for more-mundane things, like the harrowing daily commute. I got a better feel for how the city works. Mumbai looks and feels chaotic and messy, but for millions, it gets the job done.

Some parts of Mumbai are tough to stomach, such as the widespread and seemingly hopeless poverty. While at a stoplight, little kids came up to my car window begging. One was carrying a little baby, barely clothed and dirty.

Great poverty in this city walks beside great wealth. For instance, we visited the oldest gold market in the city. It was part of a larger market that housed a temple to the goddess Mumbadevi, from whom some think the city got its name. This market was packed with people. Cars, including mine, rolled slowly down the narrow streets, honking their horns at indifferent pedestrians.

Old, dilapidated buildings lined the streets with shops selling everything from linens to pineapples. In the gold market, I saw several blocks of merchants selling gold in all its forms. I stopped to visit the largest market maker for gold in the city, with slums towering around it.

I entered a decrepit building and got in a creaky elevator little bigger than a phone booth. An attendant opened and shut the door. The elevator looked about a hundred years old. I got to the right floor and went down a filthy hallway so narrow that you had to turn your shoulders to get by other people in the hall. Finally, I arrived at this gold merchant's office.

When I got inside, we entered a modern-looking office that had clean, wooden floors, air-conditioning, and a wall-mounted TV playing the Indian version of CNBC. You'd never know the squalor and chaos that exists just outside the door.

I was led to a small conference room where I waited. After a short time, the gold broker walked in. He was a big bear of man with gold hanging on his neck, his wrists, and even his eyeglasses were rimmed with gold. He represented the prosperous side of Mumbai.

This man has a great business. He is, as I said, the largest market maker for gold in India. He brings buyers and sellers of gold together. He runs an online trading system. I happened to be here during Diwali, the festival of lights. People buy gold during Diwali, which is considered good luck. The gold markets were busier than normal.

I got his take on the gold market. He's bullish, which you may discount, but remember he's a broker. He makes money on transactions, not on the gold price. He sees India's strong and growing demand for gold. India has long been a net importer of gold, since it makes little gold itself. Yet, it makes up nearly a third of total demand for gold. "People here buy gold routinely, as a store of wealth," he said. "People from the villages even buy gold and bury it in their backyards."

As I'm compiling this book, I see that India's gold imports have more than tripled since the prior year. Why? Rajesh Shukla of the Center of Macro Consumer Research puts it simply: "People in India have accepted high inflation as a reality of life."

It's something I've found often on my trips. People are increasingly buying gold, whether in Dubai or Mumbai. For these cultures, unlike for most Americans, buying gold is a social norm, a rather mainstream place to park your wealth. India, as it continues to grow in wealth, should be a steady buyer of gold for years to come.

Crop Prices Matter Here

Speaking of inflation, I said earlier that commodity prices tell you a lot about the growing Asian economies. The basic things, like crop prices, matter more in emerging economies than they do in the West. I suppose this is no secret, but living in the West, you might start to think that an economy is all about bank loans and retail sales. That seems to be what the mainstream media cover and what our politicians seem to think signifies wealth.

It's different in the emerging markets.

After working in Mumbai, I got a better sense of how basic these kinds of economies still are. This is why, though, the most commodity-intensive phase of their growth is still ahead of them. We have mainly reliable electricity, safe tap water, and (mostly) functioning highways. They don't, not yet.

Every morning, I'd grabbed the *Economic Times*, India's largest financial newspaper, along with the *Times of India*. I'd be fascinated by the topics of daily concern that made the business headlines . . . the price of palm oil or the state of the garlic crop . . . the dip in cashew exports or the drop in yellow pea imports from Canada.

Agriculture is a still a sizable part of the economy here, so the monsoon rains make a big difference. About 80 percent of India's precipitation falls between June and September. Much of India still lives off rain-fed farmland. If the monsoon season is light, then Indian farmers get hurt.

Certain popular policies will exacerbate the problems in agriculture. I find it incredible that India would aggressively pursue a biofuels program, given the lack of clean water. But it is. To meet its requirements, India will have to boost its production of sugar cane significantly. The International Water Management Institute released a study in which it warned that India's (and China's) plans to produce more biofuels could cause water shortages.

"Crop production for biofuels in China and India would likely jeopardize sustainable water use," said the study's lead author, "and thus affect irrigated production of food crops." These places have growing populations and booming economies, each of which soaks up a lot of water. The last thing you'd want to do is overlay that with biofuel production, which is water intensive.

Plus, large parts of India's population are incredibly poor. Any rise in water or food prices could cause hunger and massive political instability. India has a possible solution in a hardy bush called jatropha, which uses little water and requires no fertilizer.

But a poor monsoon season isn't a bad thing for everybody, and the entire economy isn't all focused around commodities. More days of cloudless skies, for instance, mean that construction projects can continue. Cement companies in India enjoy strong demand, reflecting the construction site nature of many of India's largest cities.

As I met with other analysts, money managers, and business people, a picture of busyness emerged. Construction projects are all over the country, building roads, power plants, power lines, and pipelines for water and wastewater.

In different sessions with analysts of our joint venture partners, I got a look at a mixed grill of companies building and making all kinds of things and growing 30 to 40 percent per year. Some did much better. Srei Infrastructure has enjoyed a sizzling compound annual growth rate of 88 percent for the last three years.

Anybody involved in building out India's demand for food, water, power, and infrastructure is doing well. The opportunities are mind-boggling. As one analyst wrote in his report, "Over 1.6 billion people in the world lack access to electricity, and 25 percent of them live in India."

That's not only a roadblock to economic growth. It has an effect on the basic "safety of people who are forced to light their homes with kerosene lamps, dung cakes, firewood, and crop residue after sunset."

Yet India has managed to grow at a high rate for years. While I was in India in late 2009, the most industrial output numbers came in at 10.4 percent for the month of August, this while most of the rest of the world was stuck in a bog of recession. More recently, industrial output numbers hover around 5–6 percent, sluggishness particularly hitting car and textile manufacturing.

India, as you may have guessed, is the second-largest market for cell phones in the world, behind only China. Cell phone rates average about 7/10ths of a U.S. penny per minute. The industry has, like an ice cream truck circling a playground, attracted millions of customers and billions of dollars in investment.

But just to show that macro trends can be tricky, the average revenue per user per month has fallen, and telecom carriers have cut back on investing in India by about 42 percent. Take a look at Figure 6.5, which dates from March 2011.

The trend may have changed by the time you read this, but it doesn't matter. It stands as a case study of how local policies and super-competitive markets can make for a poor investment, even if the big-picture story is compelling.

The next big thing might be the Internet. Though India has more than 500 million cell phone users, it has only 40–50 million Internet users. The existing telecom network can't handle the data-intensive nature of the web.

That's changing, too. You may have heard of Ajit Balakrishnan, the founder of Rediff.com, an Indian social media site. Well, more than a third of India's Internet users visit Rediff every day, mostly for email. "The sheer size of the market is mind-boggling once it gets going," Balakrishnan said in a *Financial Times* piece ("How I made it: Ajit Balakrishnan" by Stephen Wilmot).

Or take Zee Network, a media company. My Mumbai sources emphasized that India is the largest "manufacturer" of films in the world, cranking

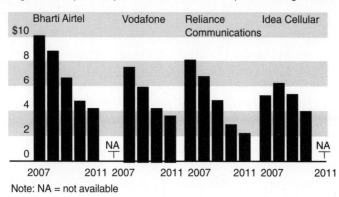

Average revenue per user per month in India for the quarter ending March 31

Note: NA = not available

FIGURE 6.5 Losing Ground

Source: Bharti Airtel, Vodafone, Reliance Communications, and Idea Cellular.

out some 1,000 films per year. Only 53 percent of Indians have a television, so the room for growth here is ample.

In some ways, I think of India as the United States rolled back about 100 years. For instance, most of the wealthy are industrialists. Names such as Tata, Agarwal, and Mittal own large interests in manufacturing, metal, and steel companies. It's not unlike early twentieth-century America, when names such as Carnegie, Rockefeller, and Morgan dominated American business. India has the added twist of having a bevy of technology and service companies that boost its growth profile.

As in early twentieth-century America, the stock market is still finding its sea legs. I asked a local analyst who the Warren Buffetts and Peter Lynches of India are. He said there really aren't any. The leading stock market speculators are men of ill repute. They have shady reputations for manipulating markets, just as early U.S. speculators did.

And numerous speculators exist. In this, it's the same as the early U.S. "bucket shops" famously written about by Edwin Lefèvre and others, where the working Joe would gamble on stocks, hoping to get rich.

Few companies pay any significant dividend in the Indian stock market. A 4 percent yield is a lot. It makes sense, though, given that India is a rapidly growing market. Reinvesting the money is often a better choice than paying a dividend.

India is a giant country, and I can't hope to do more than just paint a small corner of an enormous canvas. Every country has its own complexities, its own ever-changing story. I have just snapped a few pictures to give you an idea of how the world is changing and what part India will play in it.

Five Key Takeaways

- Though a number of Indian mutual funds exist, I like the Quantum Mutual Fund family. I know the chairman, Ajit Dayal, and trust him and his process. His team has delivered good results over the years and will get you exposure to India you will find hard to get otherwise. (Note: There are restrictions to the Quantum Funds. Check to see if you qualify.) More on Quantum here: www. quantumamc.com/.
- Check out Equitymaster, one of the few sources for independent research on Indian companies. Again, I know this team as well, including Rahul Goel, who heads up the group. There is a wealth of resources here: www.equitymaster.com/.
- There are several Indian companies that trade on U.S. exchanges: Tata, Sterlite, ICICI Bank, and Infosys, for example. I'm not as fond of this investment option as I am the two above, but you could probably create a decent homegrown mini-portfolio around owning these India names.
- Lazier options include the Wisdom Tree India Earnings Fund (EPI), which invests in Indian funds that have at least $5 million in earnings and meet certain liquidity requirements. The PowerShares India Portfolio (PIN) is another relatively easy way to gain exposure to Indian equities.
- I'd recommend Edward Luce's readable *In Spite of the Gods*. An older travelogue worth hunting down if you are going to India is Roderick Cameron's *Time of the Mango Flowers*.

CHAPTER 7

The Emirates: Penthouse Gypsies

A s the sun sets over this desert country, the still cranes perched on unfinished buildings look like ruins bathed in golden light.

But when the sun disappears, and inky darkness fills the sky, Dubai's cityscape lights up and takes on a magical quality. "I love Dubai at night," my host and friend, let us call him Andy, said as we sat out drinking and chatting on the balcony of his flat. "It's like something out of *Arabian Nights*."

Andy is an example of what I have come to call a "penthouse gypsy." They go where they are treated best, wherever in the world that may be. They have money, own businesses, and invest in real estate. They are smart, independent, and value their privacy. And they aren't living in the United States, the United Kingdom, or Europe.

Andy's apartment sits on a man-made island in the middle of a man-made lake. It's called The Old Town Island even though it's brand-new because it looks like a part of old Arabia, or at least the old Arabia of Hollywood and Westerners' dreams.

The Old Town Island stands in sharp contrast with the ultra modernity of Dubai's signature buildings, with their curves and sail shapes washed in multicolored illuminations. These structures give Dubai the air of an eccentric tycoon's playground, with its seeming indifference to how much things cost. Only the rich could build such things in deserts.

For example, The Old Town Island sits next to the Burj Khalifa, which is the world's tallest structure, at 2,717 feet. That's over twice as tall as the Empire State Building. The Middle East, by the way, held the record for tallest building for 3,900 years, thanks to the Great Pyramid of Giza, even before the West took the crown.

The Burj Khalifa is a symbol of Dubai, its ambition and can-do spirit, its boldness, and its wealth. Everywhere in the world, there is a tug of war between usefulness and a desire to build pretty things. In Dubai, though, usefulness seems to lose often. Instead, the goal is to build the largest, the longest, the tallest, or anything else they can append an "-est" to.

At the world's first Armani hotel, nestled in Burj's first eight floors, the smallest suite is 7,200 square feet. The electricity needs of this building in the desert are enough to power a small city. Think of just the power needed to pump water to its upper floors, so you can flush a toilet. No wonder Dubai, and the UAE as a whole, is starved for power.

No wonder, too, that the UAE has one of the top three carbon footprints per capita of any place on Earth. People here use more water, 145 gallons per day, than any people anywhere. Yet there is no river and hardly any water resources. The water resources Dubai enjoys come from turning seawater to fresh water.

One question I kept asking myself when I was in Dubai during its latest boom was how sustainable all this is or could be. That leads to some interesting and surprising answers about why Dubai exists at all.

It's a mistake to assume that Dubai is another Las Vegas, an Arabesque Disneyland in the middle of a desert. There was a reason why people settled there long ago, and why people continue to live there today.

The old Dubai actually had the best creek of the southern Gulf. I visited the twisted old creek while in Dubai. The dhows still make their way across the Gulf to Iran, India, and East Africa and back again, as they have for centuries. There isn't a container in sight in this old port.

For a long time, there was not much here. Alan Villiers writes about sailing the rim of the Indian Ocean in the 1950s in his book *Monsoon Seas: The Story of the Indian Ocean*. He mentions, in passing, "the roadstead of Dibai," which is still an inconsequential port, especially compared to larger regional ports such as the one in Muscat, Oman.

Jebel Ali in Dubai is the main port, not only for Dubai, but for the entire region. It is the world's largest man-made port. But in this old port, goods are offloaded by hand, largely on the backs of Pakistani and Indian workers. The goods are stacked right offshore, sacks of pistachios, crates of cigarettes, boxes of toothpaste, and other goods.

Dubai was, and remains, a port city. Its main business is trade. The ruling sheiks opened up Dubai as a free port to the world, no taxes, no hassles. "Free trade was mother's milk for Dubai," writes Jim Krane, author of the excellent *City of Gold: Dubai and the Dream of Capitalism*.

Trade is what made Dubai wealthy. Dubai has more in common with Venice of the twelfth century than with Singapore or Hong Kong today. As with all free ports, it has had a history of being a haven for smugglers. Early on, traders would smuggle gold through here on the way to India. Gold, guns, slaves, diamonds, and drugs all ran through Dubai, and still do today, according to Krane. (Robin Moore, author of *The French Connection*, wrote an awful thriller around it called *Dubai*, with bad sex scenes and wooden dialogue. The book is banned in the city.)

The real boom in Dubai, though, kicked off only recently. There is a picture that you'll run into more than once if you start reading about Dubai. It's a snapshot of the main thoroughfare through Dubai in 1990. There were just a handful of buildings along an otherwise empty desert highway. The transformation since then has been breathtaking.

My friend Peter Cooper has seen the whole rise and fall. I was fortunate to meet Peter, a British expat and journalist who has been in Dubai for fifteen years and knows the city in and out. Peter is from Salisbury in England. "My old city of Salisbury has hardly changed since I was a boy," he told me. "That is quite endearing, but it does mean people live in the same rather small houses, use the same roads, and even the same school buildings, hotels, and pubs. Not much progress, really. Dubai was a fleapit when I was a boy, and look at it, with the world's tallest building and all those hotels. I have an agent showing me a few penthouses on the Palm soon, even the land was not there 10 years ago!"

Peter Cooper is a self-made millionaire and author of the book, *Opportunity Dubai: Making a Fortune in the Middle East,* in which he tells his tale. Today, Peter writes ArabianMoney.net, a useful site for keeping track of things in that part of the world. He edits a newsletter focusing on investment opportunities in the region. Peter was my main guide in Dubai, and you couldn't ask for anybody better. We'll hear more from Peter as we go.

Anyway, after spending some time here, chatting with Penthouse gypsies like Andy and Peter, I would boil down the more important ingredients of Dubai to these:

- **Low regulations, low tax.** This has probably been a Dubai advantage for a hundred years, but people here told me repeatedly how easy it is to set up shop in Dubai, and how your privacy is protected. There are no income, property, or corporate taxes. Zero. Imagine no IRS, no annual tax reports.

  The city funds itself with taxes on hotel occupancy, liquor sales, and restaurant meals, as well as permits for roads and such. Part of the budget comes from the emirates' business interests, such as Emirates Airlines, which handles more international traffic than any airline in the world, and aluminum smelters.
- **In 2002, Dubai allowed foreigners to own property in so-called freeholds.** That was a big milestone that kicked off a wave of immigration. So, there are these freeholds where the Penthouse gypsies live in high style in nice communities. This was impossible before 2002.
- **The backlash of September 11.** Before September 11, Middle Eastern oil-exporting countries reinvested $25 billion a year in the United States. After September 11, that slowed to about $1.2 billion a year. Arabs no

longer felt welcome in the United States and feared what might happen to their wealth,so guess where the money went?

Arab wealth started flowing back to its home countries. The economies of the eight states of the Gulf Coast grew 60 percent from 2001 to 2008. "Cash poured into Dubai," Krane writes, and Dubai's growth rate topped China's, averaging 13 percent per year.

Essentially, the repatriation of Arab wealth from the United States was a big driver and still continues to be today. As the Middle East region gets wealthier, a good chunk of that wealth will flow through Dubai.

■ **The UAE fixes the value of its currency to the dollar, at least for now.** For a time, this convertibility helped the UAE. But it means that as the United States prints dollars, the inflationary effects will be felt in Dubai. This is where Dubai got into trouble. Lots of speculative capital flowed into building islands in the shape of date palms or creating residential and shopping communities with a robotic dinosaur park from Japan. Dubai is suffering through a massive real estate bust as a result.

Still, Dubai's important position in world trade is many layered, like a wedding cake. As Krane writes: "Dubai today is the Middle East's capital of commerce, one of its biggest recipients of foreign direct investment, its top financial center, biggest port, and airport, and home of the largest number of foreign businesses."

Quite a list, considering air conditioning arrived in 1967. Today, Dubai is a key crossroads. It fills a gap between New York/London and Singapore/Hong Kong. As long as Dubai is kind to money, the Penthouse gypsies will come.

Dubai Circa 2007: Boomtown, Arabia

I had been to Dubai before the bust, back in 2007. It was an impressive scene, a glittering boomtown. I remember standing out in front of my hotel with Joel Bowman, who co-edits the *Daily Reckoning* and lived in Dubai at the time. We were waiting for a taxi.

"I think this might be one," I say.

"Nah," he says. "It's not a Lexus. Look for a Lexus."

What is a luxury car in America was but a common taxi in Dubai. That's some small measure of the wealth of this place, at least on the surface. (The plights of immigrant workers tell another story entirely.) But it hardly tells the whole story.

It is hard to believe how rapidly this part of the world has changed. On a desert safari, I got to enjoy a little of the land outside the city. After slipping and sliding over dunes in a Jeep and going camel riding, we finally settled at a camp, smoked shisha, and watched the sunset and the moonrise over the desert. It wasn't so long ago that nomads wandered this arid region, the Bedouin fished and dove for pearls in the Gulf, and Persian traders built little courtyard houses of coral and gypsum. Even 10 years ago, Dubai was nothing more than a port town with a single business thoroughfare.

Today, the desert remains, but the nomads have settled down, and the sleepy trading post is a memory. A vibrant, modern, and rich city stands on what was once only a sea of sand, punctuated by an occasional oasis. Skyscrapers and dealmakers, not camels and nomads, dominate contemporary Dubai.

As we whipped along new highways through the city, we saw construction cranes all over the place. In one little area, I counted over 25. Dubai is only 1,500 square miles. It's tiny. Yet there were over 5,000 construction sites.

Then there are the buildings themselves. I mentioned the Burj Khalifa tower, but there are many other signature buildings. There is the Burj Al Arab, the self-proclaimed seven-star hotel with its distinctive sail shape. There are the famous palm-shaped man-made islands. The abandoned Dubai Waterfront was to be a crescent-shaped man-made island twice the size of Manhattan. Dubai is just one architectural marvel after another. One writer described Dubai as "a goulash of Las Vegas, Zurich, Disney World, Rodeo Drive, and Miami Beach."

At the height of the boom in 2007, the Emirate had gone on a buying spree. Dubai, for example, paid $825 million for U.S. department store, Barneys. It bought a 19 percent stake in the NASDAQ. Dubai International Capital (its main shareholder is Dubai's ruling family) bought a $1.25 billion stake in American hedge fund Och-Ziff Capital Management. This followed a $1.5 billion purchase of Madame Tussaud's wax museum, a $1.2 billion purchase of United Kingdom engineering firm Doncasters, amid numerous other purchases.

Saudi Arabia, Qatar, and Kuwait jumped in, too. They bought up banks, stock exchanges, energy companies, ports, airports, and other infrastructure. They tend to like real estate, having picked up prime Manhattan properties and beachfront property in South Africa. This is reminiscent of the 1980s when Japanese investors snapped up trophy properties in America. Middle Eastern money seems to follow that path globally, with hotel deals in Shanghai, Beijing, Jakarta, and Singapore, as well as properties in Los Angeles, San Francisco, Miami, and Chicago, and resorts in the Caribbean.

They like the emerging markets. A Kuwaiti fund manager said: "Why invest in 2 percent-growth economies when you can invest in 8 percent growth economies?" He shifted more money to India, China, and Southeast Asia. As for currencies, he preferred the South Korean won, Malaysian ringgit, and Indian rupee over the dollar, euro, or pound sterling.

A good part of the buying comes from the so-called sovereign wealth funds. They are major players in international finance. These great pools of money are something relatively new under the financial sun, in that we have never seen them attain such a massive scale before.

Four of the eight largest funds are from the Gulf, with the Abu Dhabi Investment Authority at the top of the charts, weighing in at nearly $1 trillion at its peak. That was three times the size of the big California pension fund CalPERS.

Dubai 2009: The Bust

To me, it was a quite alien attitude, this casual confidence in the notion that things can be made to happen according to plan. In the Gulf, it was an instinctive habit of mind.
    —Jonathan Raban, *Arabia: A Journey Through the Labyrinth*

One of the greatest real estate bubbles of all time hatched and died on the hot sands of Dubai. The story of Dubai is something of a cautionary tale, and its bubble is worth reflecting on a bit because it was so stunning, both in the inflating and the popping.

In 2009, when I landed in Dubai, it was a different story from the boom in 2007. From my hotel window, I could see the sun peeking over the horizon illuminating two buildings with cranes over them and in the distance another building in scaffolding. But it was not the same as the frenzy of only a couple of years before.

As late as September 2008, realtors could claim that no one had lost money in the Dubai property market. That's no longer true. By 2009, the market had too much of just about every property type. One headline story noted how 32,000 homes were about to come on the market next year, which is a big number to choke down in any city. Dubai had a huge property boom and must suffer the flip side.

I was in Dubai during the Cityscape exhibition in 2009. If you didn't have any background on this event and just walked in, you'd think this was a healthy and bustling real estate market. There seemed to be a good crowd. The exhibition spread out over several large halls, and there were models of ambitious real estate projects every 10 feet.

Some of these projects were outlandish and others just ridiculous, so much so that it will be a long time before I forget them. Take the Falcon City of Wonders, for instance, a residential development with its own smaller versions of the Eight Wonders of the World . . . the pyramids here, the Leaning Tower of Pisa over there, the Taj Mahal. . . .

Or the City of Arabia project, which is another residential property, with a Jurassic Park–like vision, replete with imported robotic dinosaurs from Japan, some of which, apparently, wander around. . . .

Or the man-made islands in the shape of the world, called, appropriately enough, "The World." Or "The Universe," with man-made islands in the shape of the sun and the planets. . . .

But the facts betray the surface appearances. Commercial real estate prices dropped by 50 percent in some cases after the bubble collapsed. (After Singapore's great real estate boom in late 1980s, for instance, prices fell by 80 percent in 18 months.) There were too many malls, too many empty buildings, too much of everything. All of it was overbuilt on a flood of cheap credit. Then there was a sea of unfinished projects, on hold or abandoned entirely, as the money ran out.

Peter Cooper showed me around Dubai and helped give me the broad perspective. He told me that the exhibition was about half the size it was the year before. The old zing of boomtown Dubai had been replaced with a more subdued atmosphere. No A-list movie stars. No Donald Trump athough Donald Trump Jr. was there along with his sister.

This is what happens after a real estate boom, and this was one of the greatest booms in history. By 2008, Dubai had as much property under development as Shanghai, even though the latter has a population six times as large. And as Krane points out in his book *City of Gold: Dubai and the Dream of Capitalism*, demand was so intense at the height of the boom that developers were raising their prices by the hour. In six years, the city quadrupled in size and doubled its population.

By 2009, things had stopped dead in most parts of the city.

The hotels, too, were mostly empty. I stayed at what was the new Address Hotel downtown, an impressive place. It had been open for only 25 days. I was the first person to stay in my room, which had that new carpet smell.

I wandered down for breakfast and was alone in a cavernous dining room. The hotel was brand-spanking-new, and everything looked wonderful, but was mostly empty. There were more hotel workers there than guests.

In Dubai in 2009, revenue per room was down 35 percent from the year before. Yet there was still an expansion going on. In 2010, estimates called for a 15 percent increase in the number of rooms. This would mean a 40 percent increase in two years.

Thus a bust is a somewhat relative thing. For example, there I was having coffee and eating cookies and chocolates in comfy chairs on the second floor of a large sales booth, a sort of villa almost, set up for the City of Arabia project. I mean, we're talking about a crisis and how bad things were, but everyone seemed comfortable to me.

Abu Dhabi—One of the Richest Places on Earth

Another surprise at Cityscape was the commanding presence of Abu Dhabi, the capital of the UAE. Plus, thanks to its ownership of 96 percent of the UAE's oil, it's the richest emirate. Ironically, water, not oil, made Abu Dhabi. The story goes that in 1761 a Bedouin hunting party was following a trail of desert gazelles, or dhabis. They set up camp and discovered fresh water nearby. As that was a valuable thing in Arabia, a settlement grew up around it over the years. The island became known as the father, or "abu," of the dhabi.

Today, the UAE supplies about 10 percent of the world's oil. In fact, this is one of the richest places on Earth. Abu Dhabi is only about an hour and a half drive from Dubai via Sheikh Zayed Road. However, that road didn't link the two cities until the mid-1990s. And it goes to show that while Abu Dhabi and Dubai are part of one country, it's a loose federation. The two are not as integrated as you'd imagine, even today.

I visited Abu Dhabi and lunched at the Emirates Palace. It's a self-proclaimed seven-star hotel. The phrase that came to mind was "numbing opulence." Marble was all over the place. "Acres of marble," as Peter put it. Even the public bathroom was stunning. I had to take a picture of it.

Abu Dhabi was then behind Dubai in building a new city. Much of Abu Dhabi seemed thrown up in the 1960s and 1970s, with rather tame concrete high rises of no particular distinction. But there were newer buildings as wild as anything in Dubai, such as Ferrari World. The main structure looks like something from *War of the Worlds*, a giant sprawling red creature of a building, with tentacles of halls leading out to the sands.

Abu Dhabi seemed to have its own little building boom in progress. Just driving on the roads, I couldn't help but notice all the cement trucks. We hadn't seen any in Dubai.

Real estate isn't everything. Back in Dubai, we stopped off at the Mall of the Emirates for lunch. Mall traffic seemed busy enough. This is where the indoor ski slope is. For research purposes, we had to give it a look. We ate at a little Lebanese restaurant overlooking the slope.

Again, this was quite an experience. You completely forgot you were in the middle of a desert. It was strange to walk in from 90-degree weather outside and then see people bundled up in ski jackets inside. "People say management is the art of the possible," says an Emirati in Jim Krane's book on Dubai, *City of Gold*. "Not in Dubai. In Dubai, management is the art of the impossible."

It's a fascinating place to me, and in some ways, Dubai confirms a few Westerners' stereotypes of Arab countries. You get thrown in jail for bouncing a check or skipping out on a debt. If you are caught drinking and driving, you used to get 30 days in jail, no questions asked, but the jail is so full of bad debtors, there is a fine. Camels are protected: You get fined if you should kill or maim a camel, say, with your car on the highway. And on my laptop screen, I met Salim, a cartoonish Arab figure, "Your Cyber Security Adviser," which cheerfully pops up and blocks you from accessing certain websites in the UAE.

I found some of the cultural wrinkles amusing. There is the use of the word "inshallah," for example. As one of our Dubai friends explained to me, it means something like "God willing." "When my gardener says, 'I'll trim the tree, inshallah,' I know he won't do a darn thing," my friend told me. "People here use it in the sense of 'it will happen when it happens . . .' like never."

Having said all that, Dubai is a real mixing bowl of people and culture. Seth Stevenson, writing for *Slate* some years ago, seemed to get at the nub of Dubai's attraction: "To me, here's what's promising about the cultural dynamic in Dubai: It throws different people together within a peaceful and prosperous setting."

Krane uses the analogy of tenth-century Cordoba for what Dubai aims to achieve. Spain's Cordoba was one of Europe's largest and most enlightened cities. It had libraries of books and research universities that were the envy of the world. It was an architectural marvel. It was a mercantile hub, where traders swapped goods from as far away as China. "Cordoba remains the pinnacle of Arab achievement," Krane writes. "When it fell apart in 1031, the Arab world sank into a long and debilitating decline. It has never regained its greatness."

Dubai had its brush with oblivion, too, beyond just a property bust . . . albeit rumors of extinction were wildly exaggerated. Everybody loves to kick a success story when it goes wrong.

Dubai's Debt Crisis

Dubai, as in America and everywhere else, took on lots of debt to build real estate projects it didn't need and that the market couldn't support, like giant palm-shaped islands in the Gulf. You can do that for only so long before the game is up.

As a side note, though, it's worth pointing out that the first palm-shaped island was a great success. It cost $275 million just to dredge it. But the asset itself is worth $25 billion and is a neighborhood all its own with thousands of residents. The problem was, as often happens, a good idea turns into a bad idea when overdone. Dubai quickly built a second palm-shaped island, and before the second one was done, it started on a massive third one. These were complete busts.

In late 2009, Dubai admitted that the debt it inhaled finally licked Dubai's ability to pay it. Specifically, Dubai World, owned by the emirate of Dubai, suspended its dividend payment and asked its creditors to "stand still" for six months. As a former banker, "stand still" sends chills down my spine. It means you're probably not going to get paid.

The Dubai debt crisis set off a mild panic. Remember, this was not long after a slew of American financial institutions failed or had trouble. If Dubai doesn't pay, who is left holding the bag? Perhaps some bank failure would follow as it disclosed how much Dubai paper it owned. Making the whole thing worse was a series of bad news in the same week Dubai made its announcement. Problems in Greece boiled over, and Vietnam devalued its currency. People started to think again about the whole fragility of the Rube Goldberg contraption that is the world's financial system.

It was true that Dubai had a lot of debt, about $80 billion. But perspective helps. When Lehman Bros. failed, it had $613 billion in bank debt. When the United States propped up AIG, it spent $180 billion. I'm not minimizing $80 billion, which is a lot of money for Dubai. I'm just giving you some perspective.

This debt, too, was no secret. When I was in Dubai in 2009, I remember sitting at a restaurant one evening on the Old Island. Around the table were a variety of Dubai entrepreneurs and businesspeople. We discussed the fate of Dubai's debt and what might happen to it all. It was a hot topic of conversation then. But I think the consensus was that some combination of a bailout from Abu Dhabi and asset sales (perhaps of Dubai's prized Emirates Airline?) would get things back to some kind of balance. An outright default would've surprised that crew.

Abu Dhabi is the home of the central bank. The analogy we kept hearing was that Abu Dhabi and Dubai were brothers. And just as you'd like to help your brother when he gets in trouble, you don't mind seeing him suffer a bit first to make sure he's learned his lesson. In fact, the Maktoums, who have ruled Dubai since 1833, came from Abu Dhabi originally.

But as I said above, while Abu Dhabi and Dubai are part of one country, the United Arab Emirates, the two operate largely independently. So, although it was not automatic that Abu Dhabi would bail out Dubai, I thought it likely. Abu Dhabi needs Dubai and vice versa. Abu Dhabi had the means to do it. And in the end, Abu Dhabi did extend Dubai that lifeline.

The Future of Dubai

There is no doubt that the real estate bubble in Dubai was one of the most extraordinary bubbles in history. There is also no doubt that Dubai still has a lot of debt to work through. Still, I think it would be a mistake to dismiss the place. Singapore recovered from its real estate bust and remains a key city in global trade. Dubai has a similar role to play in the global economy, a role that is likely to grow in importance over time.

As Jim Krane writes, summing up the thing nicely:

Observers should be careful not to dismiss Dubai as an Arab Monaco or Las Vegas that has fizzled out. It's more than a playground. It's the most stable and comfortable city in a fast-growing and volatile region of 1.5 billion people. It's the natural place for the region's wealthy to invest, take their companies public, set up distribution centers, and buy second homes. As the wealth of the Middle East and South Asia increases, it will percolate into Dubai.

I would agree, and that's why I came to Dubai in the first place. I think this whole region, with its young and growing populations and more open markets, will create some noise on the global stage, particularly in its demand for commodities such as water, energy, and food.

What the Emirates Need

We did try to smoke out where the opportunities might be, but what we found tended to confirm what we knew. First, this is a great place for infrastructure companies. The UAE, along with the other Gulf states of Bahrain, Qatar, Oman, Kuwait, and Saudi Arabia, collectively, the GCC, are spending gobs of money on things like airports, ports, pipelines, refineries, power stations, desalination plants, and the like.

Strains are showing. Developers have been known to delay projects because of lagging connections to power and water supplies.

According to the Dubai Electricity and Water Authority (DEWA), the increase in demand for power and water rises by an average of 20 percent and 15 percent, respectively, each year. There's a clear need for infrastructure investment, which is coming one way or another.

People are enterprising. They will not wait for the government. While I was in Dubai in 2007, a front-page story reported that the private sector was set to overtake the government as the main supplier of new water and electricity supplies in the Gulf. A business intelligence group, MEED, called the private sector a "cost-effective way to get new infrastructure built." By 2011, Dubai changed the laws to end the Dubai Electricity and Water Authority's monopoly on water and power supply. Private sector companies have come through the door. More will follow. Shades of what I have heard in India, where large tech companies like Infosys and Satyam maintain sprawling IT campuses with their own water and power supplies, and many other places. Shades of what we see in America, where cities auction off highways and water utilities. It's a trend we'll see more of around the world.

Over breakfast at the Address Hotel, I perused my complimentary copy of the *National*. One of the things I like to do in a foreign city is to read the local newspapers. (I'm kind of a newspaper junkie anyway—I get three dailies delivered to my doorstep at home.)

An array of stories caught my eye, all about power and infrastructure. There was the arrival in Doha of a new LNG tanker, fresh from Seoul's shipbuilding docks. (Liquefied natural gas, or LNG, is a big investment theme, which we'll tackle more later in the book.)

Abu Dhabi was looking to raise $100 billion for infrastructure projects. From the *National*: "The emirate needs to fund new transport, electricity, and telecommunications schemes."

Dubai's own ambitious infrastructure plans aren't just about water and power. Around the city, you could see the new Dubai Metro stops along the way, which, lit up as they were in soft blue and white twinkling lights, looked like something out of the future.

Peter and I rode on Dubai's new metro rail. It is driverless, smooth, and gives you a great look at the city. It cost over $7 billion to build and was the first urban railway among the Arab Gulf states. Here we made our first cultural faux pas. In a rush to grab a train, we stepped in the "Women and Children Only" car. An attendant politely told us to get out. (Women and children can go in any car they want, but the men can't go on these special cars.) We sheepishly hustled off.

Incredibly, the Dubai government spent about 45 percent of its budget on infrastructure projects, mostly on the roads and ports. There is a lot more on tap, as the *National* reports:

> *Dubai could invest as much as $20 billion in desalination projects in the next decade alone as it increases its water output by 2.72 billion liters a day. . . . [There are also] plans to add 14,405 megawatts by 2017. . . . Construction costs for those new plants amount to $11.6 billion, while infrastructure costs, including substations and transmission lines, will be about $11.6 billion.*

This massive build-out is not unique to Dubai or even the UAE.

Another similarly fascinating story has developed in Qatar. I was there in 2009, and it was a red-hot economy. In 2008, it grew 18 percent, and in 2009, expectations were for another 16 percent. I saw the headlines in the *Gulf Times*, which proudly told the tale.

Qatar's greatest asset is its natural gas reserves. In fact, the largest gas field in the world is there. Its discoverers were disappointed when they found it in 1971. They were looking for oil.

The boom Qatar enjoys is the result of some daring investments in liquefied natural gas (LNG) back when people thought doing such a thing was a little batty. Faisal Al Suwaidi, the head of Qatargas, deserves the props for his wager, which have paid off handsomely. Today, Qatar produces about one-quarter of the world's natural gas.

Qatar supplies such far away customers as Japan, India, and China. Qatargas operates the largest LNG terminal in Europe, at South Hook on the Welsh coast. This facility provides Britain with a fifth of its gas needs.

Qatar's dominant position has filled its coffers and changed the country forever. On a per capita basis, it is one of the wealthiest countries in the world. Even the world's growing energy demands and the appeal of clean-burning (and cheaper) natural gas when compared with oil, Qatar seems in a good position. It's copying Dubai with massive expansion of its airline and airport and has secured the World Cup for soccer in 2020, which will require $60 billion or more for air-conditioned stadiums.

Big infrastructure projects of all kinds are under way everywhere in India, China, and other emerging markets. This infrastructure build-out theme drives several investment ideas that we'll tackle in this book.

But there's one last idea for us to explore. You might say it's the most basic thing that makes the Gulf tick in global markets.

The global economy is like a vast spider web, and little vibrations in one corner of it can travel the length and breadth of the web.

As Peter Cooper wrote on his blog, ArabianMoney.net:

> *As a regional hub for trade, multinational headquarters, finance, tourism, and aviation, Dubai still makes excellent business sense. It has been the great business economics of these operations that has made the city rich and will do so again even if the recession proves to be a double dipper, and there is more pain yet to come.*

Why Dubai Still Matters

"Just about everything that comes into the Gulf from the Indian Ocean gets to Dubai," writes Jonathan Raban in his classic 1979 account of his travels through Arabia. Today, Dubai is still much the trade hub Raban portrayed. Raban, an Englishman, upon arriving in Dubai, noted:

> *I fell into step. Anywhere else in the Gulf, I would have been marked an outsider; but Dubai was different. The crowd absorbed strangers easily: Indians, Iranians, Pakistanis, Arabs congealed into the careless cosmopolitanism of an old port which has always been used to beaching the tide wrack of the Gulf and the India Ocean.*

My used copy of Raban's classic made for a good companion because much of what Raban saw playing out is still happening today. Dubai is still a port city, still a trade hub, and still absorbs strangers easily. It is more cosmo-politan than ever. Some 95 percent of Dubaians are foreigners.

In May 2011, the Economic Intelligence Unit of *The Economist* put out a report titled *GCC Trade and Investment Flows: The Emerging-Market Surge*. The GCC stands for Gulf Cooperation Council and is a political union that includes the United Arab Emirates, Bahrain, Saudi Arabia, Oman, Qatar, and Kuwait. Dubai is part of the UAE and thus part of the GCC.

The report backed up much of what we've gone over here. It frames how the region sits on some of the world's largest reserves of oil and gas, and how the massive influx of cash that goes with selling them has been plowed into infrastructure projects and investments abroad.

Importantly, the report emphasizes the GCC's vital role in trade:

New markets are being sought around the world for a growing range of nonoil goods and services while, on the investment side, both the well-capitalized sovereign wealth funds and an increasing range of private investors have built up wide-ranging investment portfolios. Emerging markets, especially in Asia, are becoming increasingly impor-tant economic partners for the GCC.

In another turn of our world right side up thesis, we see markets beyond Western Europe and North America playing a bigger role. The latter made up 85 percent of all GCC trade only 30 years ago. However, today, nearly half of the GCC's trade comes from markets other than these. Trade with the rest of the world is growing twice as fast as trade with Western Europe and North America.

The GCC's physical location is a blessing. It finds itself in the middle of the spiderweb of trade, the focal point of movement across this web. John Grant, senior vice-president of a U.S.-based route-development company, Airport Strategy and Marketing, says in the report that "the Middle East is almost an acronym for the middle of the world."

Many multinational companies base their operations in the region here. It's not only a crossroads for trade with Asia, but a great staging area for Africa.

"In the coming years," the report goes on, "more will use the area as a base for their growing activities in Africa and South Asia, especially when doing business in countries with weaker infrastructure and higher political risk. For instance, a spokesman for Unilever, a consumer goods multi-national, notes that, for his firm, 'The GCC is an attractive market in its own right on account of a young, growing, and increasingly affluent population, but it also provides a base for operations into Africa.'

Africa will play a particularly important role for the GCC as these countr-ies import about 80 percent of their food needs. The vast open areas of

Africa have great appeal, and great potential, for agricultural investment. (We'll take a look at Africa in the next chapter.)

The GCC's investments will likely stay in "tried and tested areas of competitive strength," which the report lists as "chiefly energy and services industries and sectors, such as port operations, tourism, retail, financial services (especially Sharia-compliant finance), and telecoms. Financial investments will go into agriculture, minerals, and real estate in a broad range of emerging markets."

Trade with Latin America is rising, though from a small base. Most of it relates to Brazil, again for food-related imports. Peter, our man in Dubai, notes there is a massive expansion of air routes to South America, with Dubai's Emirates Airline adding Buenos Aires and Rio as well as increasing the number of flights to existing Eastern destinations.

Currently, the Arab world is roiled by waves of popular unrest. In contrast, Dubai is trying to get on with business as usual. Oddly, the crises in the Middle East may help Dubai.

In early 2011, the Dubai market rebounded 22 percent and is near where it was before the unrest broke in Egypt. A harbinger of things to come? I think so.

My friend Peter summed up what he saw from his perch in the City of Gold:

> *The Dubai economy is definitely picking up traction, and cash is flowing in from oil revenues, from Arabs shifting their wealth to a safe haven, from regional refugees (families and businesses), and from money spent by governments such as Saudi Arabia. This is a bit different from the TV image of Arab unrest, Dubai just gets on with making money.*
>
> *After all, this region has traditionally played an important role in world trade and finance. Countless European adventurers and traders risked their lives to reach the great cities of Alexandria, Cairo, Baghdad, and Aleppo, among others. The tradable goods of East and West passed through many hands in the region on their way to markets far from home.*

The Story of Ibn Battuta

High tide for a cosmopolitan and open Islamic world was probably the thirteenth and fourteenth centuries. In this case, the story of Ibn Battuta is one that informs. He led a truly amazing life. His tale is retold in Ross Dunn's book *The Adventures of Ibn Battuta: A Muslim Traveler of the 14th Century*.

Ibn Battuta's story began in 1325, when at the age of 21, he left his home in Tangier, Morocco. Tangier was a port, a link in a chain of trade that stretched from the North Atlantic and the Mediterranean to Arabia and African ports beyond. It was a maritime town and reflected the international character of its itinerant population. Some of this wanderlust from this frontier town must have rubbed off on Battuta. In any event, this was the beginning of Battuta's journey, a journey that would prove unlike any other.

Ibn Battuta did not see Tangier again until he was 45 years old. In those intervening years, he wandered the globe. Battuta crossed over 40 modern countries and covered over 70,000 miles, around three times the distance Marco Polo claimed to have covered. Battuta is the greatest traveler the world has ever seen.

(His adventures are admirably retold by Tim Mackintosh-Smith in a trio of books in which the travel writer attempts to follow in Battuta's footsteps. Start with *Travels with a Tangerine* and enjoy. Mackintosh-Smith's fascinating documentary about his journeys, called *The Man Who Walked Across the World*, is worth seeking out.)

Battuta left behind a travelogue of his life's journeys filled with details on the places, people, and politics of medieval Eurasia and North Africa. This period was the peak of the trading prowess and economic might of the Arabic world. Cairo, for instance, was a teeming market with a population likely 15 times that of London at the same time. An Italian traveler noted that the city had a population greater than all of Tuscany and that "there is a street which has by itself more people than all of Florence."

There were thousands of shops and seas of vendors. There were warehouses full of pepper, cloves, ivory, and pearls, Chinese porcelain and fruits from Africa, silk, sugar, and precious metals. You could find whatever the world at that time had to offer. The affluence of this part of the world astonished visiting Europeans. This was a view that would prevail for centuries.

Battuta's experiences reveal, as Dunn writes, "the formation of dense networks of communication and exchange." These networks "linked in one way or another nearly everyone in the hemisphere with nearly everyone else."

"From Ibn Battuta," Dunn continues, "we discover webs of interconnection that stretched from Spain to China, and from Kazakhstan to Tanzania." Even in the fourteenth century, an event in one part of Eurasia or Africa might affect places thousands of miles away.

In reading the book, this multinational aspect of Ibn Battuta's world really fascinated me. The Mongol states allowed merchants to travel freely in their realms, regardless of religion or origin. This led to the creation of a worldly, prosperous, and traveling elite, transmitting ideas as well as goods across countries. For these traders, the focal point was not countries, but cities. They were, in Dunn's words, "free from the grosser varieties of parochial bigotry." It is one reason why some historians say that during the medieval period, the Islamic cultures came closer than anyone else in creating a common social order.

Needless to say, it was a time of great growth and trade. Households enjoyed porcelain from China, pottery from south Arabia, gold and ivory from Africa, animal skins from India, rice from the Ganges Delta, and more.

Ships sailed the Volga, filled with grain from the steppes, timber from the mountains of Crimea, and furs from Russia and Siberia, along with salt, wax, and honey—all carried by a hodgepodge of peoples: Egyptian traders, Turkish nomads, Greeks, Circassians, Alans, Florentines, and Venetians.

China, too, played an important role. The huge Chinese junks, the ocean liners of the day, expanded trade across the Chinese seas to the Bay of Bengal. Populations soared, and cities multiplied along with a vast network of canals and roads. Ross contends that the people of the Mediterranean rim, the Middle East, Greater India, and China formed a "single field of historical interaction and change."

The Middle East may never attain the heights it did during the thirteenth and fourteenth centuries. But what we are seeing, particularly with the explosion of trade in the GCC, is closer to the kind of world that existed during Battuta's time than the violence-wracked backwater most North Americans think of when they think of the Middle East.

Five Key Takeaways

- Check out ArabianMoney.net, which is Peter Cooper's blog from Arabia. There is a wealth of material there, all for free. For those who crave more, Peter pens a good newsletter, too. He's written a book on his adventures in Dubai, titled *Opportunity Dubai.*
- The National Bank of Abu Dhabi's NBAD OneShare Dow Jones UAE 25 ETF is the Gulf region's first exchange-traded fund. It gives you exposure in 25 blue chips from across the UAE. The downside: it isn't available to U.S. investors. Try an Emirates NBD mutual fund instead.
- If you had to buy only one share, Emaar Properties is the largest real estate company in the region and one of the largest in the world. It owns many premium assets and will come back someday. The stock has completely washed out in the wake of Dubai's debt crisis and trades for a small fraction of its high. While it may never scale those heights again, it ought to deliver a good return from there.
- Peter offers up other ideas for long-term investors: Union Properties (a Dubai landlord whose debts will slowly turn to gold); Shuaa Capital (Dubai's top investment bank whose profits would surge in a stock market boom); First Gulf Bank and the Abu Dhabi Commercial Bank. "The strategy is simple," he says, "You buy these stocks and sit on them until the market turns around." They are not easy to buy, so you'll have to work with your broker.
- Jim Krane's *City of Gold* is the best book on Dubai.

CHAPTER 8

South Africa: Rainbow Capitalism

There is an old joke about South Africa: When God created it, He told St. Peter it would be His greatest masterpiece.

"Mountains that pierce the sky, great forests that shelter all manner of wonderful creatures, endless plains, and deserts and grasslands to far horizons. All these things this land will have," God said.

Peter was impressed, but God went further, saying, "Beaches as fine as powdered gold, washed by clean water and caressed by tropical zephyrs. And beneath the mountains and rivers, a treasure-trove of gold and diamonds, platinum, and uranium, rich beyond dreams."

"This is wonderful," Peter said. "But won't the other nations of the world be full of envy?"

"No, they won't."

"Why not?" asked St. Peter.

"Wait till you see the government I am going to give them."

The above is an edited version of the joke as told in Gavin Bell's book on South Africa, *Somewhere Over the Rainbow: Travels in South Africa,* which I tucked in my bag for my May 2011 trek there. People from other richly endowed but politically challenged countries tell variations of this joke. Russians over vodka in smoky bars, Argentines over slabs of grilled meats, and many others besides, all spinning their own variants to laugh and maybe to erase a little of the pain that comes with knowing what might have been.

I heard many jokes about security in South Africa, where crime is a serious problem. One old joke goes that when pilots land there, they tell their passengers, "The safest part of your journey is now over."

A lot has changed over the past 10 years in South Africa, but a lot has stayed the same. I'll sidestep the politics, but the gold and uranium are still there as are the diamonds, the coal, and the mineral wealth. South Africa has a few other cards to play.

The BRICs, Brazil, Russia, India, and China, dominate the emerging markets discussion, and like a quartet of bright suns, they seem to blot out the smaller stars. But in April 2011, on the island of Hainan in China, the BRIC countries held their third summit, and South Africa was invited to attend for the first time.

South Africa may seem small with an economy about 1/16th that of China's and slower growing than the BRICs, estimated at around 3.5 percent in 2011, but it has other ways in which it is far ahead of them.

For instance, in the Transparency International's annual corruption index, South Africa ranked 54 out of 178 countries. This was well ahead of Brazil (69), China (78), India (87), and Russia (154). This doesn't mean you can't have your pants jerked down investing in South Africa, but it seems less likely than in these other countries. In terms of financial systems, South Africa scores well. The Global Competitiveness rankings put out by the World Economic Forum have South Africa at sixth in the world for bank soundness and first in the world in securities regulation.

These rankings are interesting, but nonetheless abstract. I have a natural tendency to distrust them somewhat, especially when it comes to investing, which is why I go get some boots-on-the-ground perspective.

South Africa has been a winner as the global appetite for commodities soared in recent years. It reported a trade surplus in 2010, its first since 2003, its chief exports being gold, precious stones, metals, and minerals. South Africa is a good base for companies investing more broadly in southern Africa and the rest of the continent. Africa is rich in natural resources, and there are mining projects all over.

Beyond the resource story, there is a growing consumer base in Africa. More people use cell phones and banking products, eat a richer diet, and buy cars. This huge area of opportunity seems to get overlooked in the hunt for natural resources, but that, I think, may be the better story.

The investment equation is simple. There is a massive latent demand for consumer goods, the things we enjoy every day, but that are in short supply in Africa. Therefore, African companies can earn high returns on capital supplying these things because Africa is capital starved. Put another way, there isn't much competition. That is how Africa can claim to have had the world's best returns on capital over the past 10 years, according to the International Finance Corp.

To see how this can work, look at cell phones. Mo Ibrahim was the founder of one of the early African mobile networks, Celtel, in 1998. There were hardly any cell phone users, but great latent demand for them. By 2000, there were 9.8 million mobile phone users in Africa. By 2010, there were 547 million users.

Wouldn't you like to catch a wave like that? In a way, I was on a big game safari in South Africa, except I was looking for something that might turn into an elephant one day, Ike Ibrahim's Celtel. (Ibrahim, by the way, sold Celtel for $3.4 billion in 2005. He is chairman of an investment firm, Satya Capital.)

Let's have a look.

Johannesburg: The City Built on Gold

I landed here for the same reason that has driven many people here since 1866, to find ways to make money. In Johannesburg, that traditionally meant gold mining. Downtown Johannesburg has no white Dutch gables or mountain backdrops, as in Cape Town, but I took some pleasure in thinking I was in the stomping grounds of the old Rand Lords. In truth, Johannesburg was not what I expected, which was a city more decidedly "third-world," to use the non-P.C. term. Today, Johannesburg is the financial center of sub-Saharan Africa. It is to southern Africa what Dubai is to the Middle East, what Singapore is to Southeast Asia, what New York is to North America, and what São Paulo is to South America.

It has an airport you could drop in any city in the world, and it would be a top-notch airport. Jo'burg's network of smooth-running highways connect plenty of areas that would not be out of place in the better parts of any American city. Still, it's something to arrive in Johannesburg and see all the houses with eight-foot walls and two feet of electric wire across the top. I saw lots of security system signs and warnings about "armed response." My room even had a "panic button."

I suppose you get used to these things if you live here. Gavin Bell made it sound like an urban hell of crime in his book: "No dinner party is complete," he writes, "without anecdotes about people being shot/robbed/raped/blown to bits." He was right.

One night, I had dinner with a reader of my newsletter, Jacobus, and his family, who graciously hosted me with a home-cooked meal. Jacobus fired up a braai (a traditional South African barbeque) with all sorts of goodies and a feast of side dishes. Jacobus's father brought a couple of bottles of excellent South African wine, too. We had a fascinating discussion about all things South African. Jacobus had an impressive setup of security cameras, and he told me about the neighborhood watch system, in which the neighbors all look out for each other. They have hand-held CBs and check in with each other nightly. The idea is if something happens, you put out a call on the CB, and your neighbors drop everything to go help, which is faster than waiting for security to arrive. Jacobus has a handful of dogs to help in the effort.

Jacobus told me stories of the neighborhood watch nabbing burglars and making a bunch of arrests. But things have slowed down. Jacobus seemed to miss the excitement of it all. "Not much happens these days," Jacobus told me, half-joking. "It's getting rather dull."

That may be how he feels, but the real dull days were pre-1886. There was nothing here and no reason for anything to be here. In fact, Johannesburg is the largest city in the world not located by a river, lake, or coastline. It sits on a featureless plateau, about 5,000 feet above sea level.

A discovery of farmer George Harrison changed everything. He stumbled on some shiny stuff he correctly identified as gold. But he must not have been an entrepreneurial sort, for he quickly sold his claim for 10 pounds, and so gave up the richest gold field on the planet. Not long after rich mining men paid out tens of thousands of pounds and more to farmers. There is a story of the great mining magnate Cecil Rhodes counting out 20,000 sovereigns on the kitchen table of a farmhouse.

Wagons full of prospectors poured in. The tents went up, and in a few years, a city grew around this, the biggest in southern Africa. It was a rough frontier town, a boomtown. By 1900, it had 97 brothels and over 1,000 prostitutes, one for every 50 white inhabitants.

The City of Gold was built around a gold-bearing reef that extends for more than 100 miles. The Witwatersrand, or "ridge of white waters," is the source for about 40 percent of all the gold ever mined.

It was a kind of freak of nature. In an ancient age, a great river ran through Africa and flowed into a lake that is the Rand. Gold particles settled on the bottom of the lake and eventually were covered with mud and sand. In time, these turned to shale and quartzite. The sea dried up, and the bed bent and warped as geological shifts did their thing over millions of years. Finally, a piece of the rim of the seabed broke through the surface, tipping off a great gold sandwich that extended deep beneath the Transvaal.

Author, diplomat, and traveler Alexander Powell was Johnny-on-the-spot in 1910 to record his impressions during part of the mining boom. He called the city a place where:

> *European civilization met and mingled with the last frontier. Standing beneath the porte-cochère of the palatial Carlton Hotel, one could hear the click of roulette balls, the raucous scrape of fiddles, and the shouts of drunken miners issuing from a row of gambling halls, dance halls, and gin palaces still housed in one-story buildings of corrugated iron.*

He writes of boozy prospectors saddling up to the bar and rubbing shoulders with groomed financiers. It was a freewheeling boomtown. Powell continues, "The mine workers were paid big wages, the miner managers received big salaries, the mine owners made big profits, and they all spent their money as readily as they made it."

You can still see the effects of that history today, especially in the mine dumps, these tall mounds of earth from all the digging over the century. Author Martin Flavin called them "ocher-colored hills growing into modest

mountains . . . the monuments of Jo'burg, night soil of successful enterprise, excrement expelled in 60 years of eager, unremitting gluttony."

Other travelers looked at them more charitably. Henry Morton, in over-
the-top prose, wrote they are "what St. Paul's is to London, what Table
Mountain is to Cape Town, what the Acropolis is to Athens: the landmark
that all eyes see and know to be a symbol of the city, its true coat of arms."

Men and machines have eaten away at that great sandwich of gold for
more than a century and a half. In Johannesburg, you can see the effects of
all the digging that ensued since Harrison's accidental find. If you think
about it, you have to put the dirt you dig up somewhere. From a distance,
you think the mine dumps are small hills. You find them all over. In fact,
some enterprising miners are going back to process this ore, as it still holds
some gold. Even after all that, new gold mining continues there. Gold companies are developing smaller deposits around the reef today at much shal-
lower, and thus more accessible, depths.

The Chinese Beat Me to It

While in Johannesburg, I met with Gold One, one of these enterprising
shallow miners. I had a meeting scheduled with Gold One set for Tuesday,
May 17. This was one of my favorite companies in South Africa, and I was
looking forward to meeting them.

On Monday, May 16, one day before my meeting, a Chinese consortium
bought a 60 percent stake in the company, and the stock jumped nearly
20 percent, to 51 cents per share, on the Australian exchange, where the
price has stayed since. I was a bit bummed out by the timing. I would've
liked to have recommended the stock to readers of my newsletter first, but
the Chinese beat me to it.

The Chinese are all over Africa. China-based companies (often state-
owned) have been buying natural resources in Africa, everything from coking coal to agricultural goods, such as coffee from Uganda and sesame from
Ethiopia. China's trade with Africa has gone from only $10 billion in 2000 to
$129 billion last year, surpassing the United States as Africa's largest trading
partner. Importantly, Africa supplies China with one-third of its oil.

There are plenty of connections specifically with South Africa, which
is home to the largest Chinese population in Africa, more than 250,000
people. About a quarter of all Chinese direct investment in Africa winds
up in South Africa. The China Construction Bank and the China Eximbank
set up headquarters in Johannesburg in 2009. Then China's largest
bank took a 20 percent stake in South Africa's largest bank, Standard
Bank, for $5.5 billion. At the time, that was the largest purchase of a
foreign asset by a Chinese bank.

I find China's investment activities on the continent fascinating, both as a curious cultural drama and as a development story. If you want a good read on the subject, I recommend *China Safari: On the Trail of Beijing's Expansion in Africa,* by a pair of French journalists. It's a complex topic and one that will probably stay with us for a while as foreign investors jockey for African assets.

So given all this, I'm not surprised about the Gold One transaction. Plus, the Chinese love gold. According to Reuters, "China produced 340 tonnes of gold in 2010, and investors locally bought 571.5 tonnes, according to official data, for a gap of 231.5 tonnes." To make up that gap, China goes abroad. India is still the largest buyer of gold, but China passed it as the largest market for gold bars and coins.

What the Chinese got in Gold One was a shallow gold mine in Johannesburg with mines that have relatively low technical risk and produce gold at high profit margins. Gold One is the lowest-cost producer of gold among South African gold miners. (Hence, the reason it attracted my attention.)

What is fascinating about Gold One is its place in the development of Johannesburg's gold mining industry. You would think that after more than a century of mining the great reef in Johannesburg, most of the gold would be gone. Well, the giant deposits are mostly drilled out. Most South African miners go deep, miles underground, to get at the remaining gold.

However, many smaller deposits were left untouched. The history of Johannesburg is a history of big mining companies and big mines. This was never a culture of junior miners as in Canada. Only now are the smaller players exploring and putting together interesting assets, the crumbs, you might say, left over from the days of the great Rand Lords.

These assets are big enough to build a $600 million company, which is the valuation the Chinese transaction puts on Gold One. And Gold One still has room to grow. It recently acquired Rand Uranium, a company with significant gold and uranium in the West Rand, about 11 miles from Jo'burg.

Entrepreneurial Gold One shows you what can still be done in South Africa. More broadly, it highlights the attraction of greater Africa. On this point, the *Financial Times* profiled Algy Cluff, the 71-year-old chairman of Cluff Gold and a longtime mining man in Africa ("Air of Derring-do as Africa Pioneer Eyes New Ground" by Christopher Thompson).

The interview took place at Cluff's St. James office in London, which resembles "an explorer's den," filled with exotic objects. Cluff had just returned from "shooting guinea fowl in the Kalahari Desert." Sounds like somebody out of a H. Rider Haggard novel.

Cluff Gold is Algy Cluff's fourth company and the third focused on Africa. Cluff Gold produces about 94,000 ounces of gold in Burkina Faso and the Ivory Coast. But what I found most surprising was Cluff's comment that Africa is becoming less of a frontier market. "By and large, countries are approachable," he says, "and you're operating under English or French law, so you know where you stand."

If you have qualms about investing in Africa, perhaps that comment will put you at ease. Certainly, the Chinese seem comfortable investing in Africa. I think it will be hard to ignore the opportunities on the continent in the years ahead.

In Search of African Rainbows

One of the more compelling themes I heard about in South Africa was investing in the mining of platinum group metals, or PGMs. These include platinum, palladium and rhodium. The bird dog that first put me on this trail was African Rainbow Metals (ARM), a company I visited in Johannesburg.

I wanted to meet with them for a few reasons. First, as the name implies, the company produces a rainbow of stuff—gold, copper, iron ore, coal, nickel, manganese, chrome, and PGMs. With such a range of views into so many different markets, I figured ARM might have some good intelligence on the relative merits of investing in each.

Second, the company has an interesting history. It was South Africa's first black-owned mining company. The founder, Patrice Motsepe, is one of the richest men in Africa and has made the Forbes 500 list. South Africa, post-apartheid, has encouraged black ownership of business through black empowerment laws and such. Another contact described the policies as "like your affirmative action in the States . . . except on steroids." As a result, ARM surely enjoys favored son status in South Africa, something that is significant in mining, which is often as political as it is economic.

Lastly, I was attracted to ARM because of its low costs. (You may detect a theme. Yes, I prefer investing in low-cost producers of commodities. It is really the only sustainable competitive advantage you can have in mining.) ARM has a stated goal of being in the bottom 50 percent of the cost curve, and they have succeeded. All of ARM's operations produce at costs better than at least 50 percent of the population of producers.

So, I made my way over to Sandton, which is a wealthy area of Johannesburg and home to many businesses. When crime got out of hand in downtown Johannesburg in the 1990s, this is where many businesses moved. It's the premier business district in the city. Two of the four largest banks in South Africa maintain headquarters there. The Johannesburg Stock Exchange is there, too.

I met with one of African Rainbow Metals' executive directors, with the great name of Stompie Shiels. Stompie is a 50-something-year-old who has seen the passage of many mining cycles under African suns, and I enjoyed hearing him talk about doing business in Africa. He is no pie-eyed optimist, either, as he spent quite a bit of time talking about the challenges of mining in Africa.

ARM itself is an interesting investment idea to kick around. Not only does it have low costs and a diversified portfolio of commodities, it has long-lived assets, a good balance sheet, and is still growing at a good clip. Stompie told me ARM could double production in five or six years.

As we went through the different markets, the one that stood out as the cheapest was the PGMs. Stompie said so emphatically, and this proved a good tip that was repeated later in a meeting I had with Dr. Prieur du Plessis, a money manager in Cape Town. That's one of the benefits of doing trips like this. When people begin to repeat ideas, themes emerge.

The essence of the story is one that will get any commodity investor salivating. Mine output is dropping, and it's hard to make more; it is hard to find good deposits, and demand looks to soar.

PGMs are scarce metals, and there are not many economically viable ore bodies. The main sources are concentrated in Russia and South Africa, which produce 80–90 percent of the metals. The market is tiny. Total production is only about 15 percent of gold's and 3 percent of silver's. That production is struggling, too. Since 2006, palladium mine supply has fallen 15 percent, and platinum has fallen 12 percent.

South African miners face rising costs as they mine deeper. In addition, there are power and water limitations, shortages of skilled labor, and a rising rand, which makes South African production more expensive.

Yet demand for platinum and palladium is strong. The main demand driver is car production, as these metals are used in catalytic converters. And as emissions standards go up, so does the amount of PGMs used in a car.

Stillwater, a large PGM miner, says that the market will be in deficit by about 3.6 million ounces by 2018. This market currently produces about 12 million ounces, and about 2 million ounces come from recycling. So, that 3.6 million ounces is a wide gap to make up.

The metal prices have room to run because for most applications, it's still a small piece of the total. For example, total PGM costs for a car run about $300, a small fraction of the typical purchase price of a car, which is often a hundred times higher. It's a good thing, too because the price is going to have to go up a lot, even to just keep production where it is.

Beyond this, there is investment demand for PGMs. People hold them as they would gold or silver, as a store of wealth. This demand has been met through the proliferation of exchange-traded funds that allow investors to easily buy the metal. Figure 8.1 shows you that such ETFs hold 2.5 million ounces.

The impact of the buying (and selling) in ETFs can have a big impact on prices. In the last week of May 2011, Deutsche Bank launched an ETF for the

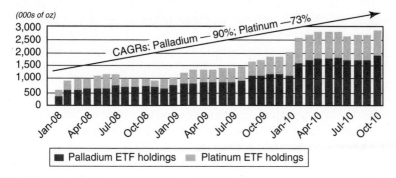

FIGURE 8.1 More Investors Hold Palladium and Platinum

Source: ETF Securities, publicly available information.

third member of the PGM trio, rhodium. The price of rhodium rose 20 percent that week.

I don't think this demand is temporary. The demand to hold these metals has always been there, but it's only recently, through ETFs, that it has become so easy to do so. As with gold and silver, the PGM ETFs will likely be much larger in a few years.

In any event, PGMs as a long-term investment theme was compelling to me. Because of all the problems in South Africa, the best bets would seem to be outside South Africa, such as Stillwater and North American Palladium.

Postcard from Cape Town

It is remarkable to be told, when you are on top of Table Mountain, that you are 2,300 feet lower than Johannesburg. It is, I think, one of the many surprising things about South Africa that nearly half of the country is higher than Table Mountain. The great mountain ranges of the Cape, which look so high from sea level, are, so to speak, a rampart on top of which lie the Free State and Transvaal.
—Henry Morton, *In Search of South Africa*

While in Cape Town, I met with Dr. Prieur du Plessis, president of Plexus Asset Management. Du Plessis added to my case for investing in platinum. Du Plessis was a perfect gentleman in all respects, and I enjoyed my meeting with him, in which we discussed many topics.

Du Plessis, you may have guessed, is a French name. French Huguenots faced persecution in the seventeenth century, and some of them wound up here in South Africa. Of these Huguenots, author H. V. Morton notes in his book *In Search of South Africa* (1948), "their true memorial is . . . the great wine industry of the Cape. With the Huguenots came men who knew all the secrets of the French vineyards."

Therefore, it was appropriate that we met du Plessis at one of these celebrated vineyards in the Durbanville Wine Valley's Cassia Restaurant. It's only about 20 minutes from Cape Town, and I highly recommend it should you ever get to this part of the world. Over fresh line fish and excellent wines, Du Plessis gave me some interesting insights on platinum. This commodity sold off heavily after the Tohoku earthquake that struck Japan in March of 2011 and wrought so much destruction there.

Platinum's biggest use is in automobiles. Post-quake, the Japanese auto industry produced about 535,000 fewer cars in the month of March compared to the year before, a drop of 57 percent. This trend continued into April of that year. Du Plessis estimates that from March to May, the total loss in vehicle production will be about a million vehicles.

Doing the math, Du Plessis figured the total lost demand for platinum could exceed 100,000 ounces. "While it seems small," du Plessis continued, "the 100,000 ounces should be compared to the average investment demand of approximately 55,000 ounces (2008–2010). That is huge!"

Platinum, like gold and silver, enjoys a certain demand solely as a means of storing wealth, as we've discussed. It is one of the precious metals. To see platinum's price weakness most clearly since the Tohoku quake, du Plessis plotted it against the price of gold. As you see in Figure 8.2, by this measure, platinum is quite cheap relative to gold.

"I think it is only a question of time before platinum's premium to gold will be restored," du Plessis offered. I know it may be all different by the time you read this, but I found it a useful lens to view platinum, and you can easily update the ratio at your leisure. The historical patterns tend to repeat.

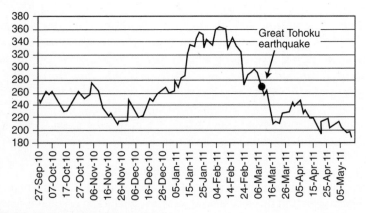

FIGURE 8.2 Platinum Premium to Gold

Source: Plexus Asset Management.

After the meeting, as I headed back to Cape Town, head swimming in good wine and bright sunshine, I had a lot to think about. I left with a good opinion of Dr. du Plessis, as gracious a host as one could hope for and a sharp-eyed observer of financial markets.

Cape Town's Biggest Industrial Site

In Cape Town, I visited the biggest industrial site in Western Cape Province: Chevron's refinery. By global standards, it is small, turning out about 100,000 barrels per day. However, this particular refinery has long been seen as a strategic asset, a key refueling point for navies sailing around the southern tip of Africa.

Built in the 1960s, a lot has been added and replaced since. Because of this, birthdays for refineries can be deceptive. The refinery is a jumble of pipes, towers, and machinery. It is here where the magic of converting crude oil into useful products such as gasoline, diesel, and jet fuel takes place. This extremely complex process can be dangerous. Refineries have a tendency to blow up every now and then.

So there is no fooling around at these things, and Chevron's focus on safety was readily apparent. Even as a visitor, I had to pass a Breathalyzer test upon entering the facility and watch a short safety video. There is beefy security, including a triple-layered fence system laced with generous amounts of razor wire. There are bunkers in the refinery built to withstand explosions. As the general manager at the refinery told me, "This is among the safest places you can be."

Refining is a tough business, and not only because of the complex chemistry involved, for which everything must be just so, but because of the economics. The price of the chief input (crude oil) does not move in lock step with the price of the outputs (such as gasoline and diesel). Plus, there is a time lag. For example, the refinery must buy crude oil three months in advance, so if you are not careful, you can find yourself in trouble quickly, and many refineries have struggled in recent times.

Much of the crude comes from the Middle East, which is 17 days away, and from West Africa, which is only four days away. However, where the refinery buys the crude is itself a math problem with several moving parts. It's not just about distance, but about yield (i.e., how much they can get out of the oil) and price. Surprisingly, little of the crude oil is actually Chevron oil.

The refinery does not speculate on the price of oil and tries to manage these risks to produce a 15 percent return on capital. As I say, it is a tough task.

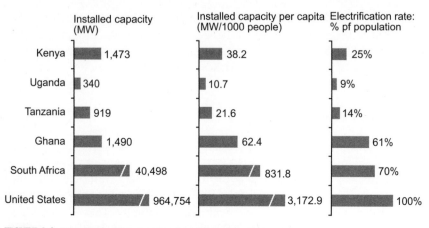

FIGURE 8.3 The Under-Penetration in African Power

Source: KPLC Rights Presentation, November 2010, U.S. Energy Information
Administration, 2009 (EIA).

The toughness is made tougher operating in an emerging market such
as South Africa. One of Africa's biggest chronic problems is unreliable electricity. You may hear about rolling blackouts in Nigeria. Or Zambian farmers
losing electricity two times or more per week, using charcoal to keep chicks
warm after hatching. Well, even a biggie like Chevron has to deal with
power outages here in South Africa. What's the holdup? Rising generation
capacity can't get ahead of demand, not by a long shot. And South Africa is
the most developed country of the bunch (Figure 8.3).

The World Bank's recent report *Africa's Power Infrastructure* puts it in
stark terms: The entire generation capacity for the entire sub-Saharan Africa
(SSA) region is equal to that of Spain. That's 47 countries working, refining,
living, and mining on just 68 gigawatts of power.

But it gets trickier. Take South Africa's 40-gigawatt contribution out
of the picture, and you're looking at a capacity the size of Argentina's to
power the rest of SSA. During normal times, South Africa has been the one
to fill in the gaps, but no longer. A 2007 *New York Times* article predicted
seven years of electricity shortages. Here we are five years later, and the
problem isn't fixed.

In a six-month span, for instance, Chevron's plant has had something
like five shutdowns because of power outages. For a refinery, it is not a
simple matter of flicking a switch and turning it on again. It takes weeks to
restart the refinery, which means millions in lost sales.

Then there are other issues South African businesses like Chevron face,
such as dealing with the nearby poor community. In an emerging market,
social investing activities are not simply philanthropic. They are necessary in

keeping things working smoothly. You may recall Serafino Iacono's comments about dealing with the locals in the Colombia chapter. Building the mine was easy, but dealing with the locals was more important. Because if you don't bring them into the process and win them over, you can lose the project.

In South Africa, the same can happen. The gap between rich and poor is especially wide here. The Chevron folks told us a story about an R$70 million project that was stopped because of community protests against it. So reaching out to the large poor community is a critical part of keeping the refinery operating without interruption. Chevron has done so in an impressive way.

Haymish Paulse is the manager of public affairs here, and he gave an overview of how Chevron works with the community. They have monthly meetings with community leaders. They explain everything that's going on, so there are no surprises. I am not doing justice to the effort here, but suffice it to say it was thorough, involved, and well thought out.

The name of the poor community is Dunoon. About 100,000 people here live in shacks in a surprisingly small area. About 50 percent of the population suffers from HIV/AIDS. There is approximately one toilet for every 400 people. It isa violent place. There were 17 murders committed here in one month. In short, it is the kind of poverty you often find traveling through emerging markets. This is not the worst place I've seen—Indian slums still take the prize—but it is a difficult place all the same.

We embarked in a van marked with the Chevron logo, which I felt was like an immunity shield of some kind, guaranteeing our safe passage. Chevron has done much for the community here, and the people seem grateful.

I saw tangible results of it by visiting a school for which Chevron rebuilt the library and stocked it with relevant books, computers, and a full-time librarian. They could be kids anywhere in the world. As neat and trim as they looked, it was hard to believe the squalor they go home to every day.

I noticed a few of the posters on the wall of the library. One read, "The Young Entrepreneur" and included "Eight Steps to Start Your Own Business." Another read, "The Business" and showed how businesses work: inputs, outputs, marketing, profits—it was all there. I thought to myself, many American schools could benefit from such an emphasis.

It was good to see it all. Visiting the refinery made me appreciate everything a bit more, my own comfortable circumstances, yes, but that humble product called gasoline. A lot goes into creating needed energy products that many people take for granted.

Oil companies are easy whipping boys, but I think if more people had the opportunity to spend the day with Chevron, as I did, they might see things differently.

My Favorite Way to Play Africa

South Africa is a great staging area to get access to the broader sub-Saharan African market. There are multiple opportunities of different shades in, for instance, Namibia and Angola (offshore oil and gas), Zambia (copper), Mozambique (agriculture), and even Zimbabwe.

It surprised me to hear a team of investment managers and directors talk so enthusiastically about Zimbabwe, or Zim, as they called it.

This team is Imara, an investment bank and asset manager with an expertise in sub-Saharan Africa. We met at Nelson Mandela Square in Johannesburg over lunch at the renowned Butcher Shop & Grille. Not a cloud was in the sky, and we ate out in a covered veranda next to the square.

Imara is a Swahili word meaning "strong," and Imara's emblem is an African scarab, a sort of beetle capable of carrying 800 times its body weight. The Imara story is rooted in Africa, going back to 1938.

As for Zim, it may seem crazy to invest in a country run by Robert Mugabe, an aging Marxist thug whose policies have brought the country to ruin. But the market is extremely cheap. The theory goes that the worst has passed and owning a basket of Zim stocks is a ticket to future wealth many times what you put in today.

Zim's stock market is not among the biggest in Africa, but it has a depth and breadth of securities. Its first stock market opened in 1896 in Bulawayo to raise money for gold miners. But today the market has 81 securities in companies that do everything from manufacturing to pharma.

Most stocks reported earnings growth of 40 percent last year. Imara forecasts 20 percent growth this year. And yet many stocks trade for low-multiples of earnings, some as little as two or three times.

Zim, for all its problems, has a generous reserve of natural resources. In particular, it produces chrome, coal, diamonds, gold, and platinum. It enjoys a high degree of literacy among its people and a dynamic private sector. (Imara's website has a lot of information on Africa and ways to invest through Imara-managed funds. Worth checking out.)

As I traveled in South Africa, though, a broader theme emerged. It is the most compelling big picture theme on the continent. Perhaps it is best to illustrate with an anecdote.

A billionaire investor named Anand Burman controls a company called Dabur. This company makes consumer goods such as packaged honey and hair oil, as well as medicines. It began in India but is expanding in Africa.

This is significant because India is a huge market opportunity itself. Why go to Africa? As CEO Sunil Duggal put it: "The African market is the epicenter of our growth prospects for the future. The upsides in some of these markets are as much, if not bigger than India."

It's a telling comment. At least the minds behind Dabur have concluded they can sell a lot of honey and hair oil to African consumers. As to just how many consumers, there are many fancy guesses with numbers and assumptions that hide their unreliability. But the best way to see the African consumer in action is to look at the little stories. For example, one that sticks out in my mind is from Vijay Mahajan's recent book, *Africa Rising*.

He writes about a man and his family living in Nairobi on $400 a month. The family hardly sounds like much of a consumer group to get all worked up about, yet they buy food at a local supermarket, have a television set and a radio, and several cell phones. The family manages to pay for private education for its three daughters. They took out a small loan to pay for solar panels that provide electricity to their three-bedroom home, which they own.

So, you see, in Africa, your perspective needs serious recalibrating. It is easy to write off the continent as a basket case, but I think that would be a mistake. Many of the trends happening in other emerging markets are happening in Africa. More people moving to cities. More people joining the ranks of global consumers.

I saw this with my own eyes in South Africa. I visited a Fresh Stop convenience store at a Caltex gas station. The Fresh Stop was like a mini-grocery story offering fresh fruits and vegetables. It was clean and well attended. It was busy. There are many more examples.

Anecdotal evidence paints a picture that bloodless statistics fail to capture. If you need further proof, dwell on the African operations of major companies. You will find them growing and profitable. SABMiller, the giant brewer, for instance, recently reported brisk sales of beer in Africa, 20 percent–plus growth in some markets. And consumption is here near saturation levels.

Turning again to Imara, a report recently called sub-Saharan Africa "the last cement frontier." It is a market where prices are 200 percent above those in other emerging markets. Demand is huge and yet "Africa's cement companies are cheap," Imara opines.

No surprise that China is all over Africa. It's set aside billions for investment in farming and infrastructure. Trade with Africa was only $10 billion in 2000. Last year, it topped $129 billion. Africa supplies the Chinese with much-needed raw materials, including oil. All that money sloshing around means more Africans using banks, grocery stores, cell phones, and the like.

How to play such a cornucopia of opportunities? As you might expect, I have a favorite.

Bet on the Inevitable

On my first full day in Johannesburg, I made my way over to Melrose Arch. This is a relatively new area of wide streets and sidewalks. There are cafes, restaurants, and stores. I was early for my meeting, so I stopped in on one of the wine shops and bought a bottle of wine. The experience was like one that you would experience in any better wine store in the world, except that I got a good South African cabernet for about $10.

Then I headed over to meet with Francis Daniels, who manages the African Opportunity Fund. We had a good chat about investing in South Africa and greater sub-Saharan Africa. His fund is my favorite way to play Africa.

"I look for trends that I know are going to happen," Francis told me, "unless there is a nuclear explosion or something. Things are that inevitable. So . . . I like consumer finance. I like retail. I can say with confidence that, eventually, blacks will have the same access to consumer products as anyone else. That's a trend that's unfolding now."

The best way to see that is to look at specific companies. We looked over some of his largest holdings at the time, which are useful to recap if only to see what kinds of opportunities exist as investors.

He owned African Bank, for example, which had "wonderful financial ratios," Francis related. A capital base stocked with 20 percent equity (most U.S. banks never top 10 percent and, hence, often get in trouble). It was profitable. "Blacks are underserved," Francis goes on, "and you can command above-market rates."

Even here, though, you can see how things have changed. Francis Daniels had owned African Bank for 10 years. In 2001, it was charging 80 percent interest rates. The argument then was that blacks had no credit history. They've collected the data and competition has done its part. Francis showed me an ad in which they charge 11 percent to finance furniture purchases. It may seem high, but remember where they started from.

"Blacks have had very little access to credit," Francis says. "They still have little credit. But they have been at it for only 20 years or so. Over time, it will normalize. That's what we're betting."

The fund's second-largest position was Shoprite, the largest South African food retailer, with over 1,100 stores in 16 countries in Africa. It serves over 14 million shoppers annually. While I was on my trip, I heard this name come up at least three different times as an investment idea. The one catch is that it is not easy to buy Johannesburg-listed stocks. (There is a Pink Sheets version, but it trades infrequently.)

Francis owned Shoprite's shares in Zambia, which trades at half the price there, even though it is the same security. This then, is another reason to buy the fund. Francis will ferret out deals you could not find on your own.

He owned Sonatel, his largest position. Cell phones are big in Africa. Ten years ago there were maybe 10 million users. Today, there are 540 million cell phone users. Sonatel is a fast-growing mobile phone provider in Senegal and neighboring countries. It used to be a state-owned company.

"They had a monopoly," Francis says, "and managed to lose money." But today, Sonatel serves as a case study for what you can buy in Africa.

Sonatel is the second-most-profitable telecom in Africa, with net profit margins of 31 percent. At the time, it had a sizable market cap of $3.7 billion and a price-to-earnings ratio of only 10 and paid a 6.7 percent dividend yield. Sonatel had little debt and over 10 million subscribers. It is an example of what the Africa Opportunity Fund seeks out, a company with high returns on assets at a cheap price.

He owned bonds in Old Mutual, Africa's largest life insurance company. The bonds pay 16–20 percent and enjoy a thick cushion of protection. This position was nearly 13 percent of the fund.

In fact, the fund focuses on its best ideas: Sonatel, Shoprite, African Bank, and Old Mutual represented about half of the portfolio.

The rest of the portfolio is a smorgasbord of opportunities: a rubber plantation, a leading media company, and a stake in AICO. The latter is the controlling shareholder of Seedco, which makes seeds crucial to improving African agriculture.

In Africa, it pays to be a stock picker, because fortunes of companies and economies can diverge widely. Francis tells the story of buying Nigerian debt and making 35 percent during a time in which the Nigerian market fell 48 percent. There is opportunity for arbitrage, or buying the same thing in a cheaper market (as Francis had done with Shoprite in Zambia).

However, there are social and political risks that go with investing in Africa, Francis warns. Income inequalities are highly visible and extreme, often fall along racial lines, and stem from a legacy of oppression. This makes for fertile ground in which to whip up nationalization or asset seizure sentiments. In fact, as I write this, there is a discussion about the state seizing certain mining assets in South Africa.

It is too early to tell how this will go, but it highlights a risk an investor in these parts must think about. Mining and oil are industries where these sentiments flare up more often, probably because it is easier to seize such assets than it is to seize those of an IT company, where most of the value is in the heads of people or in software. Nonetheless, such businesses can still be hit with higher taxes and costly regulations.

It is, as Francis put it, "a non-trivial risk." Francis often has to handicap such risks by thinking about who has the incentive to be reasonable. One interesting example is Zimplats, a Zimbabwean platinum miner. It produces a raw material, called matte, that needs refining. The refineries are in South Africa. Moreover, the refiner owns a majority stake in Zimplats. So, there is little incentive for Zimbabwe to nationalize Zimplats because Zimplats' product has no value without the refiners, which it can't touch. (This thesis is being tested as I write, though it's worked out well for years as Zimplats expanded even as Zimbabwe's economy crumbled.)

These incentives shift and change over time, depending on circumstances. Zambia, for instance, nationalized its copper mines in the 1960s, and it was a great failure. After reversing that policy, today Zambia is the top copper producing nation in Africa. By 2013, it will be a top-five global producer of copper. Its economy is growing at 6 percent–plus clip per year and is generally seen as having a positive investment climate. Nothing is forever, Daniels points out, but at least in Zambia, the risk of nationalization is not something to worry about in the present.

In short, the social and political risks are complex in Africa. They are beyond the scope of this book. But you should be aware of them.

Francis Daniels had 16 years of experience investing in Africa. He is steeped in the picky value investing tenets set out by the great Benjamin Graham in the 1930s. His partner, Robert Knapp is an experienced and successful investor with a large stake in the fund. They've worked together for a decade. The Africa Opportunity Fund, as a team, had a great track record. If you had put $1,000 with them beginning in 2003, you would have had nearly $6,000 by the end of 2010. That includes a difficult period for most investors.

The Africa Opportunity Fund is a great way to play South Africa (which is about a third of the fund) and broader Africa. And best of all, the fund's insiders eat their own cooking. About 25 percent of the fund's capital was their money.

Five Key Takeaways

- Buy the Africa Opportunity Fund to invest in the long-term growth of Africa under the steady hand of a proven (and relatively unknown) value investor. The fund trades in London under the ticker AOF. Check out the website, where you can read past shareholder letters. Francis Daniels, the fund manager, gives an excellent review in his annual report, and it contains valuable investment wisdom. Make it a part of your regular investing diet: www. africaopportunityfund.com/index.php?menu=2.
- Check out Imara and its funds. The company's annual report includes fascinating information on investing in Africa. The website gives you access to its Monthly Communiqué and Investment Notes. (Click on "Asset Management" and then "Publications.")
- The PGM group metals have serious supply and demand issues at least through 2018, which make PGM mining stocks attractive. However, because of the chronic power issues and other challenges in South Africa, the best opportunities may be outside the

country. See North American miners such as Stillwater and North American Palladium.

- Look at the shallow gold miners in South Africa. They have a lot of running room in and around Johannesburg. They have lower costs and simpler operations than the deep miners. Gold One, which I talk about in this chapter, is a good example. Great Basin Gold is another.
- Read *China Safari* for an in-depth look at China's activities on the continent and *Africa Rising* for a more business case study of what's happening. If you like travelogues, Gavin Bell's *Somewhere Over the Rainbow* is excellent. The historically minded may want to hunt down Henry Morton's *In Search of South Africa*, which made for good reading while I was traveling there.

CHAPTER 9

Down Under and Beyond: Australia and New Zealand

When the great explorer James Cook bumped into Australia in 1770, he sailed right by Sydney Harbor. Botany Bay, some miles south, impressed him more. Sydney Harbor has a narrow entrance, only three miles across. Unless you sail past its great rocky headlands, it won't strike you as a great harbor.

So, in 1788, when the British Empire charged Capt. Phillip with the task of setting up a penal colony in Australia, he sailed for Botany Bay. Phillip, though, soon did sail past those headlands and established what is today Sydney.

Another irony about Sydney, and Australia generally, is that many of the people sent here initially were petty criminals. Australia was a penal colony, a place to dump convicts. By 1840, when penal transportation ceased, there were 87,000 convicts in the province of New South Wales, where Sydney is, and 70,000 free Britons. Yet from this cauldron of outcasts and societal riff-raff came some great entrepreneurs. There would be no Australia without the efforts of these remarkable people.

You see the legacy of these entrepreneurs in Sydney today. I saw Juniper Hall, built by a former convict who made his fortune in gin. Another convict turned millionaire dubbed his own hall Frying Pan Hall, because he made his fortune selling iron cookery. Australia's history has many such manacles-to-millionaire stories.

One of my favorites is the tale of Mary Reibey (pronounced Ree-bee), whose face graces the Aussie $20 note. She got seven years when he she was only 14 years old for stealing a horse. She claimed she was only borrowing it—a timeless excuse. But Reibey must've been a force of nature. It was hard enough for a convict, but a female convict especially. Yet by 17, she ran her own general store. By 35, she was well-off. And by the age of 50, she owned two ships and eight farms and was quite rich.

Australia's third great irony is that the world's naval powers largely overlooked it. On the far side of the world, Sydney, one of its great cities, was not a link in any great trade route. It was no crossroads of any sort.

Jan Morris wrote in her history of the city, *Sydney:* "Born a concentration camp thousands of miles from the next town, maturing so improbably on the underside of the world, more than most cities it seems artificial of purpose. It really need not exist at all."

But today all that's changed.

What began as a penal colony, an afterthought of the great British Empire, has since exceeded the riches of Great Britain. Australia is, depending on how you measure it, the fourteenth or sixteenth largest economy in the world. On a per capita basis, Australia is richer than the United Kingdom, France, or Germany. It ranks sixth in quality of life, according *The Economist's* much-followed index.

Today, Australia has a great seat overlooking the unfolding Asian boom. Australia holds many of the resources so needed by Asia's growth economies: Iron ore. Coal. Wheat. There is gold there. And uranium, nickel, and lots more. Massive natural gas deposits lie offshore. Its close proximity to these resource-hungry Asian markets is its biggest advantage.

All in all, Australia is in a good position, and plenty of opportunity exists.

The Middle East of Gas

In Sydney one sunny morning, a group of readers and I met with Kris Sayce, editor of the *Australian Small-Cap Investigator*. Sayce talked about what could become Australia's biggest resource boom yet. Australia is on its way to becoming to natural gas what the Middle East is to oil.

In my own research before the trip, I wrote to my readers about the liquefied natural gas (LNG) boom, and we picked up a great way to play the growth in LNG spending over the next several years. (More on that in a bit.)

The LNG boom is really an Asia story, and that makes it an Australian story, too, as we'll see. As Sayce pointed out, Asia is the fastest-growing market for LNG. Sayce presented Figure 9.1, which shows the dramatic increase. ("Non-OECD Asia" excludes Japan and South Korea.)

Currently, Japan is the largest buyer of LNG. Japan and South Korea together make up 53 percent of current global re-gasification capacity, which is the ability to import LNG and turn it back into a gas for consumer and industrial use. Pressed against this new demand is an aging supply base in

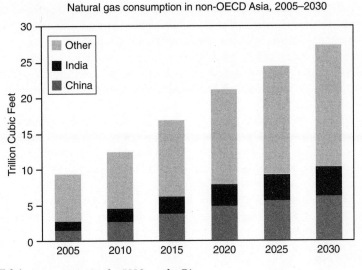

FIGURE 9.1 Asia's Appetite for LNG on the Rise

Source: **Port Phillips Publishing.**

places. For instance, there are old LNG fields in Malaysia and Indonesia that are coming to the end of their useful lives.

So how will the market meet this surge in Asian demand? That's where LNG from nearby Australia comes in. It's hard to miss this story when you take a look at the Australian resource markets. It's in the papers nearly every day, and the amount of money going here is just staggering.

The Gorgon project alone, a joint venture between Exxon Mobil, Chevron, and Shell in Australia, will cost some $50 billion. It has supply contracts from India and China worth $60 billion and will surely get more before it opens in 2014. There are other firms pushing ahead with aggressive LNG ambitions. Woodside Petroleum, an Aussie oil and gas company, wants to be the leader in LNG by 2020.

As a result of all this activity, Australia will challenge Qatar as the world's largest LNG exporter. One analyst quoted here said: "The numbers are phenomenal. When you look at them, it's mind-boggling. It's going to be LNG boom times."

Asian buyers love Australia because it's closer. Even better, the gas doesn't have to pass through the war zones of the Middle East or the pirate-infested waters off Somalia. For most buyers, Australian gas doesn't even have to pass through the congested Straits of Malacca, either.

Australia has loads of offshore natural gas. Explorers continue to find sizable new discoveries, which means new projects may yet come on board. Most of these are in Western Australia's waters. But Sayce shared with us the new discoveries made in Queensland, off the east coast. Queensland has big reserves of coal seam gas. This is naturally occurring methane trapped by water deep underground. You can convert coal seam gas to LNG.

The big energy companies are moving in. Shell, BG Group, Conoco-Phillips, and Malaysia's Petronas are among those developing projects in Queensland. The growth in LNG production from Queensland alone has tripled in recent years.

With all these projects, it's quite possible that in the next decade, LNG will pass coal as Australia's most valuable export. The government is certainly supporting LNG projects, for they will add a gush of tax revenues to its coffers. Look at what oil did for the Middle East; the same kind of thing could well happen to Australia.

I often hear the objection that LNG won't ever catch on in the United States, at least not in a big way and not anytime soon. I don't disagree, but we have to think beyond just the United States.

It may help here to take a short digression. . . .

The Case for LNG

I present you two numbers. The first is the price of natural gas in the United States, which is less than $4 per million British thermal units (mBtu) as I write. The second is the price of natural gas in Asia, where people will pay $10 per mBtu for natural gas that they import from overseas.

This disparity will allow someone to make a lot of money. The only reason it exists at all is because the natural gas market is still mainly a local market. It is not as easy to ship natural gas into a country as it is to ship oil. You have to super cool it, so it liquefies. Then you can put it on a tanker and ship it to a terminal where your buyer can re-gasify it. This is the LNG trade.

There are other problems. U.S. energy companies, before the shale gas boom changed everything, thought the United States would need to import natural gas, so the United States had about 10 LNG import terminals and two more in the works. With a natural gas glut in the United States, these terminals are pretty much useless.

Owners of these terminals want to turn them into export terminals, where the gas is liquefied and shipped out. As the *Financial Times* reported, "The United States could soon be competing with Russia and the Middle East to supply the world with natural gas, a shift that would reshape energy markets over the next decade." Even if the United States exported just 10 percent of its natural gas, it would become the largest exporter of LNG in the world. Few countries can match the United States in natural gas resources or in its low costs.

So where will the natural gas go? This is an interesting question because it yields some surprising answers.

I attended one of the ASPO conferences in Washington, D.C. (ASPO stands for the Association for the Study of Peak Oil & Gas). Jonathan Callahan, founder of Mazama Science, gave a fascinating presentation around one key development.

He looked at natural gas through the lens of the import/export markets. This is a good thing to do for any commodity because it can tip you off to what's happening in that market. When China went from one of the biggest exporters (sellers) of soybeans to the biggest importer (buyer), the effect on agricultural markets was huge.

Anytime a big exporter becomes a big importer, you can bet that spells opportunity for that commodity. China, for instance, remains a big importer of oil and iron ore, which has been good for investors in those commodities. China will soon become a big importer of coking coal, used to make steel. So will India and Brazil. This is good to know if you are an investor, as it will drive demand for coking coal.

Callahan creates nifty charts to capture these import/export trends. For example, take a look at the United Kingdom in Figure 9.2.

You can see that the United Kingdom was an importer through the 1980s and 1990s. Then there was the North Sea boost, matched by a step-up in consumption. Finally, as the North Sea supplies dwindle, the United Kingdom has gone deep in the red as an importer. This chart exhibits a pattern we see time and time again. Consumption is sticky and stubborn. It doesn't go down much.

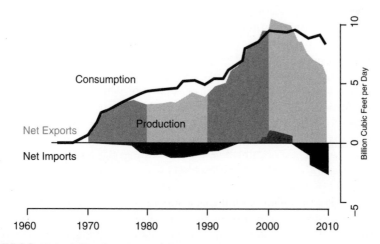

FIGURE 9.2 United Kingdom: Natural Gas

Source: mazamascience.com.

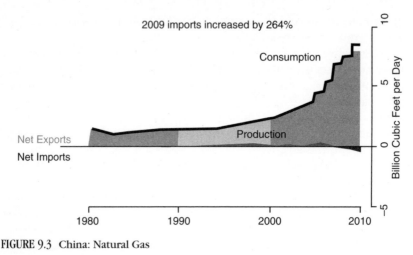

FIGURE 9.3 China: Natural Gas
Source: mazamascience.com.

Callahan charts all the big producers and consumers of natural gas. We know the big buyers: Japan, South Korea, and Taiwan. All of the gas they import comes from LNG tankers.

But what about, say, China? Here is another one of Callahan's charts (Figure 9.3). Note it is just starting to turn negative, which means China is becoming a net buyer of natural gas. Per capita consumption, Callahan points out, is only a fraction of its neighbors. He predicts, and I agree, that China will soon be a huge importer of natural gas.

Combine China with Japan, Taiwan, and South Korea, and Callahan concludes: "Clearly, East Asian demand for LNG will not be letting up anytime soon."

What about the Middle East? Callahan's data suggest that the Gulf region is consuming ever more gas and that its exports may peak soon. The data do not lie. The Arabian Peninsula is alive with new petrochemical plants and desalination plants and growing consumer power demands. "We should not be surprised to find that these nations consume an ever increasing amount of their indigenous oil and natural gas supplies," Callahan says. Despite expectations that Qatar will boost LNG exports in the next five years, "the region as a whole may see declining LNG exports by the end of the decade."

The UAE is typical. The UAE became a new importer of gas in 2008. What about South America? A turning point lies ahead there, too. To date, SA has been largely self-sufficient in gas. However, it's becoming a source of LNG import demand. Argentina has peaked, causing shortages in the Southern Cone. Bolivia and Venezuela are rich in gas but are sealed off from markets because of political issues.

And if you look at the construction of LNG import terminals in Argentina, Brazil, and Chile, you will see a market that will soon import a lot of gas. "The region is on track to become a significant importer of natural gas over the next decade," Callahan concludes.

The same style of analysis applies to Europe, where Callahan predicts Norway is peaking, and many European countries will only import more gas.

The impact on the global market seems clear. "If shale gas doesn't turn out to be as prolific as hoped," Callahan wraps up, "we can expect to see increasingly expensive natural gas in the next decade. Forewarned is forearmed."

So put together Callahan's data on exports and imports with the glut in the United States and the lack of export terminals. I think it's pretty clear we'll see more export terminals in the United States. It's too big of an opportunity to ignore. The United States could well become the leading exporter of natural gas in the next decade.

Worldwide, we'll see the LNG trade grow significantly to make up the shortfalls that are emerging in South America, Asia, Europe, and the Middle East.

How to play this trend?

You want to own the companies that put together the Erector Set that LNG needs to operate. There are cold boxes that turn the gas into liquid. There is special insulated pipe. There are storage systems. There is a whole complex of materials that has to be put together.

By owning one of the companies that make all of that stuff, you don't take on the enormous risk that goes along with these huge capital projects. Fifty billion dollars, the latest estimate, for Gorgon is a gargantuan bet, too big for any single oil company to go it alone, hence the joint venture. Then there is price risk. No one can say what the LNG will sell for or what kind of returns it might generate.

It's simpler to own the companies that put it all together. They will enjoy fat cash flows and swollen order books for years to come. Lately, the financial crisis has put some projects on hold, but that's what gives you the opportunity today. Longer term, the case looks solid to me.

My favorite here is an American company called Chart Industries. Chart makes the mission-critical LNG equipment that all these projects need. The company is number one or number two in all of its markets, important in a business in which failure of equipment is not an option. Chart is still a small company in a fragmented market.

Management highlights two key pieces of the big picture in their presentations. The first is that global gas demand is likely to rise by 25 percent by 2020, while the use of LNG is set to surge by 40 percent. The second is that we need $220 billion in annual investment in the entire gas-supply infrastructure through 2030. Chart stands to profit from these trends.

Chart has three business segments.

Energy & Chemicals, or E&C, which makes up about 40–45 percent of sales. This segment is the one that deals with liquefied natural gas. (Remember, liquefying natural gas makes it easier to ship and store.) Chart makes cold boxes and heat exchangers that cool liquids and turn them into gases. Chart makes the insulated piping for LNG terminals. This is where the headline-grabbing LNG awards would go.

In China, Chart has opportunities. The Chinese have made a commitment to develop as much of their own natural gas resources as possible as well as use their LNG import terminal facilities. Noteworthy activity is in the Middle East, Kazakhstan, and Russia.

Then there is the **Distribution and Storage** segment, or D&S, which pitches in about 40 percent of sales. This segment sells tanks to store gases and has a wide range of applications: chemical companies, restaurants, food processors, oil and gas producers, and more. About 43 percent of sales go to energy companies. D&S sells all over the world, too.

It's a business that has enjoyed record orders from China. According to CEO Sam Thomas, "The activity in China . . . is continuing to increase across all of our products, with a particular bright spot being LNG-related vehicle fueling."

The wider adoption of natural gas as a fuel for fleets (like city buses) is an opportunity few analysts on Chart talk about. At a recent conference, Chart management estimated that there could be up to 10,000 fueling stations built worldwide at a cost of $1–8 million per location, a potential $10–80 billion market. About a quarter of those costs would come from hardware that Chart supplies. That could be a huge revenue generator for Chart for many years. (Chart did less than a billion dollars in sales in 2011.)

Finally, there is the **Biomedical** segment. This segment mostly sells cold storage systems to animal breeders and biotech researchers. It sells things like oxygenators to nursing homes and hospitals. Thomas said, "Particular bright spots come from cord blood banking and large cell bank opportunities globally that are driving demand for the large freezers."

Those are the three main legs of the stool that is Chart. There is a fourth leg if you consider its steady acquisition business. Chart has been a good acquirer, a rare quality. It looks for engineering firms that are number one (or have the potential to be number one) in their niche. Management has said that it won't invest unless it can see at least a 35 percent annual return on its investment.

Sometimes it does much better than that. One cherry pick was its purchase of Covidien's oxygen therapy business. It bought a business generating $60 million in sales for $11 million. Covidien neglected it, and Chart thinks it can get this business to generate 20 percent profit margins.

If so, then, essentially, Chart paid less than one times profits—a steal! This means that if you value the business at just 10 times profits, Chart bought a $120 million business for $11 million. Not only that, but Chart picked up a business that gave it an 80 percent market share in the portable liquid oxygen market with little competition and big barriers to entry (like regulatory hurdles).

But back to Australia, where there is more to see. . . .

As I usually do, I read some of the older books and travelogues on Australia, just to get a sense of the history and how it all fits in. There are a couple of things all travelers in Australia seem to comment on.

First, there is the Aussie accent, supposedly derived from eighteenth-century cockney thieves' slang. Mark Twain wrote about hearing "tyble" for "table" and "piper" for "paper" in his book *Following the Equator*. "In the hotel in Sydney," Twain reports, "the chambermaid said, one morning—' The tyble is set, and here is the piper; and if the lydy is ready I'll tell the wyter to bring up the breakfast.'"

The other thing travelers often commented on was how cheap it was to travel in Australia. In 1913, American writer E.W. Howe wrote about how he paid $2.62 per day to stay in a good hotel. That price included three regular meals, early morning tea, and supper at 10 p.m. "The meals and rooms at the Hotel Royal are so good," Howe wrote, "that we are almost ashamed to accept them at $2.62 per day each."

Well, the accent remains, but the low prices do not, at least for those of us carrying U.S. dollars. Everything is quite expensive. Currencies go in cycles, but the current cycle certainly has favored the Aussie over the U.S dollar.

The United States wallows in heaping piles of debt against a relatively weak asset base, blowing money on insolvent financial institutions and propping up an overbuilt housing market.

By contrast, the Australian dollar is strong and the Australian economy rich in natural resources. Although there were rumblings of potential trouble while I was there in 2010. Personal debt levels were on the rise, and Australia's housing market in the big cities was starting to get a bubbly feel to it.

Later, it did begin to unravel. By mid-2011, prices were beginning to fall in the major cities. Delinquency rates on mortgages hit all-time highs. We've seen this movie before, and it doesn't end well.

Australia's ties to Asia are both a boon and a curse in some ways. Australia may be on the far side of the world as viewed from Europe or the United States, but it is on the doorstep of growing Asian markets hungry for the natural resources Australia has in such abundance. Lines of ships as far as the eye can see ferry coal to China, and the iron ore mines run around the clock. But it means that as China goes, so goes Australia. As we saw in our look at China, its boom faces serious short-term obstacles. In any case, the boom and bust action could be severe in Australia. Investors be warned.

Front Line on Ag Investing: Melbourne

Driving around the countryside of Melbourne, I saw pieces of the agriculture economy at work. Australia is an important agricultural player. It is, for instance, a large exporter of wheat. Take a look at Figure 9.4, which shows you how all the major wheat exporters face declines in wheat exports save three—Canada, barely, Australia, and Kazakhstan.

Australia will be an agricultural hot spot as the world's growing population presses against a dwindling supply of arable land and low inventories of grains. We'll need to produce more food. We can do it; but it's going to absorb more resources and eat up more inputs, like fertilizer.

One of the farms I saw outside Melbourne is bigger than Denmark. I saw dairy operations that typically range from 700–1,400 cows in this part of the world. Their rotary machines milk 50 cows at a time. My guide was a former dairy farmer named Bruce. He told me more than you would ever want to know about dairy ops.

Bruce delighted in telling stories of people meeting bad ends in Australia: bushfires and people burning in cars and homes, unable to escape, suicides on bridges that he drove us over, and a kangaroo horror story in which the marsupial kicked the stuffing out of a man and landed him in the

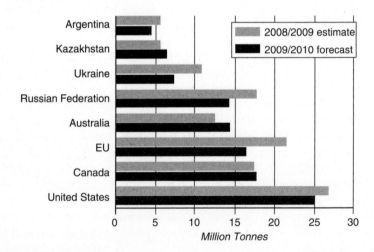

FIGURE 9.4 Wheat Exporters

Source: Financial Times.

hospital. His relish in recounting such tales had me calling him "Bruce the Morbid Tour Guide."

Beyond the investment scouting, I enjoyed the sights and sounds of Australia, great restaurants, a colorful history, and some amazing natural wonders. In Melbourne, I took a drive down the Great Ocean Road, which hugs a spectacular coastline.

And the Australians seem to love Americans. One day, I met with a 75-year-old guide who told us the story of how the Americans came to Australia's aid in World War II and the great Battle of the Coral Sea. "People my age will never forget that," he said. "That makes us mates, and that's the way it is."

On to New Zealand

While on this end of the Earth, I ventured to New Zealand. In Queenstown, my hotel overlooked the dark blue waters of Lake Wakatipu. Jagged green mountains, called the Remarkables, surround the lake.

Just driving around, you get a sense this is an agrarian economy, which in this day and age is a good thing. Sheep dot the foothills, grazing in wide-open pastures. In fact, there are more sheep than people. New Zealand is a country of only 4 million people but some 45 million sheep.

The Kiwis' most valuable exports are dairy products and meat. The third-largest export is oil, surprisingly. New Zealand's oil industry produced 21 million barrels of oil last year. Not enough to topple Saudi Arabia or make a dent in global oil supplies but enough to bring home $2.8 billion.

Oil from the offshore Tui field in Taranaki makes up 64 percent of total oil exports. But the country has a strong resource sector. Gold and silver production hit a record high last year. Moreover there is an estimated $140 billion of mineral wealth still in the ground, plus another $100 billion of lignite, which is a kind of low-grade coal.

Another way to look at the prosperity of the resource sector is to look at how much it's paid in taxes, up 470 percent from the year before, or about $519 million.

All is not rosy, however. I've been reading in the papers about how some New Zealand farmers took on too much debt in the last dairy boom. The farmers wanted to increase the size of their farms or buy additional farms. They have to look elsewhere for fresh capital to help clean up balance sheets and reduce debt.

It's a story told a thousand times in a thousand places, isn't it? Something in the human heart makes us overdo it, like a kid who can't say no to another scoop of ice cream and gets sick as a result.

Now many farms trade for prices a third of what they sold for at the height of the boom only two years ago. Cash yields for dairy farms are in the

6–7 percent range, which are not all that exciting, but a lot better than what you can get at a bank. And the risk is lower than the stock market.

The reorganization of the farming sector in New Zealand is creating some opportunities for investors because the main source for new capital comes from non-farming investors. As the *Star-Times* notes:

> *Suits are replacing gumboots on many dairy farms as non-farming investors take an increasing stake in this country's dairy industry. . . . One of the most popular ways for farmers to access capital from non-farming investors is through the use of equity partnerships . . . where a farm is sold to a group of private investors who employ a manager to run it.*

New Zealand has seen booms and busts in dairy farming before. The celebrated Victorian traveler George Augustus Sala visited New Zealand in 1885. He commented then on the "fearful depression" brought on by too much debt and low prices for mutton and wool:

> *Every child that comes into the world in this beautiful land is handicapped from his first entrance into life with indebtedness to the extent of 55 pounds sterling. Imagine such a load of pecuniary embarrassment on a baby's head before even the sutures in its tender young cranium are knit together.*

Imagine what Sala would think about the last U.S. housing bubble. He wouldn't believe a people could go so overboard.

Investing Advice under a Pohutukawa Tree

My merry band of readers and I gathered around on a white sand beach under the shade of a giant pohutukawa tree, sometimes called the New Zealand Christmas tree for its brilliant red blossoms. We looked out to the cool blue waters of the Firth of Thames. It was a sunny, cloudless afternoon. There, Rick Rule, resource investor extraordinaire and founder of Global Resource Investments (now part of Sprott Inc.), held court.

We had just ridden about an hour north of Auckland to see Rick Rule at his farm. The roads there wind around in a pattern akin to that left by a bug dipped in an inkwell and allowed to run wild. When we arrived, he and his wife served us a wonderful lunch. We ate sweet plums and apricots, picked that morning from local trees. After pleasantries, some walking along the beach, and more than a few glasses of wine, we started to talk about markets.

He began with cautionary warnings, like a lighthouse marking dangerous shoals and treacherous reefs. "All the causes of the 2008 crash are still with us," he pointed out. It's a function of a society living beyond its means. There is too much debt and leverage in the system. Balance sheets were and remain strained. A balance sheet recession, Rick continued, can't be cured without fixing those balance sheets.

The government's response of dousing markets with lots of liquidity and bailout money is not helping. "It's like we had a tequila hangover, and we decided to substitute rum," he said.

With those warnings out of the way, Rule warmed up to the opportunities in today's market. He expects markets will be extremely volatile, which he considers a gift. It's what allows you to pick up assets on the cheap.

"When a stock falls by half," Rule advises, "you have to be able to have the courage to buy more and not let the market sway you." You have to be careful, but many of the great investors I've met and studied over the years have made their best scores in ideas in which they bought a lot of it over time and often in the face of declining prices.

Rule's favorite stocks occupy the natural resource sector. His simple reason is that for a long time there was little investment in the sector, and we will catch up. From 1982 to 2000, there was no net investment in the resource sector, Rule maintains. This is a sector that is slowly self-liquidating. If you run a mine, for example, every day you run it, it gets smaller.

At the same time, we had a massive global boom in demand. Here Rule essentially laid out ideas similar to those we've talked about it in past chapters. In a nutshell, the emerging markets are large and growing and closing the gap with the West.

This is particularly bullish for commodities. Rule said: "When Indonesians make a little extra money, they buy stuff. They upgrade from bicycles to cars. They buy air conditioners for the first time. They buy refrigerators." All of these things use basic materials—steel, aluminum, and other metals. They use energy.

Rick sums it up this way: "When we spend money, we buy services. When poor people spend money, they buy stuff." He points out that China's use of oil is 3 percent of the United States' on a per capita basis. If China were to get to the demand of South Korea on a per capita basis, which is 16 percent of the United States', then China's incremental oil demand would account for all of current world production.

Not surprisingly, Rule's favorite resource is energy. "Energy is cheap, and it's not going to stay cheap. Gas is the same price as it was in 1980 on inflation-adjusted terms."

Demand is going up, and supply is problematic. Rick points out that most of the oil in the world is produced not by the Exxon Mobils and Chevrons of the world, but by national oil companies, like those of the Venezuela, Peru, Iran, Mexico, Indonesia, and others. The NOCs are starving their companies of much-needed reinvestment, so they can spend the proceeds on social programs and for political ends. Many of these countries are in immediate danger of no longer exporting oil.

Another factor is "carbon hysteria." Skirting the issue of whether global warming is real or not, there are consequences to the current drive to reduce carbon emissions. For instance, "coal is bad" from a government point of view. If you found a bunch of coal in Australia or New Zealand, Rule says, and wanted to develop it, you probably couldn't. Governments hate coal, despite the fact that most of the world still relies on it.

There is something that does meet government approval, and that's what Rule calls a "lonely trade." He likes lonely trades best.

"I really like geothermal," he says. U.S. political consensus says geothermal is good. Power companies want it and are willing to pay up for it. They pay for it because it's green.

Political subsidies make the economics of geothermal really compelling. Rule maintains you can earn a 22 percent internal rate of return with a cost of capital less than 5 percent. One of the companies we met while in Australia was a geothermal company called Hot Rocks. It showed us how geothermal stacks up to alternative energy and renewable sources in terms of cost (Figure 9.5).

This chart equalizes all sources of power to 23.6 MWh generated over a 30-year period. So it's a full-cycle cost analysis. Geothermal wins this comparison handily. (Capacity factor is how much actual power is produced as percentage of capacity; O&M is basically operating costs).

"I can't say when geothermal will take off," Rule said. "But the businesses work stupidly well. They really work. It almost doesn't matter what stock you buy, just own the sector." A few names to investigate here are: Ram Power, Nevada Geothermal, and U.S Geothermal.

They are speculative little ventures, but owning a basket is probably a good move. As for the speculative nature of the stocks, Rule said the best stock he ever owned was an Australian penny stock. "I bought it for 1.5 cents per share and sold it for $10 per share," he said. "It was the best stock of my life."

He likes uranium, the feedstock for nuclear reactors. Uranium had a mania, then the price collapsed and the stocks with it, but the businesses

	Geothermal	Wind	Solar
Plant Size (MW)	100	300	360
Construction Cost ($M)	$400	$600	$2,800
Capacity Factor	90%	30%	25%
MWh generated — 30 years	23,652,000	23,652,000	23,652,000
O&M Costs: 30 years ($M)	$108	$135	$371
All-in-costs: 30 year plant life	$508	$735	$3,251

FIGURE 9.5 Geothermal is the Best of the Alternative Energy Lot
Source: Hot Rock Limited.

kept getting better and better. "The uranium story that fed the mania is still in place."

Rule said we consume more uranium than we produce. "The uranium price has to go up. More importantly, it can go up." In other words, the price of uranium is small. It could double and still not have any meaningful impact on the economics of a nuclear plant. "People don't care much about uranium today, but in three years, they are going to care a lot."

I was on board with uranium idea for a time. Then we had the quake and tsunami in Japan in March 2011 that led to the near meltdown of nuclear reactors in Fukushima. I got out of the sector right then. By late 2011, it looked like I did the right thing.

However, the long-term story of uranium is still interesting and compelling in a contrarian sort of way. As usual with commodities, I think it comes down to two basic reasons, supply and demand.

In looking at supply and demand, it seems clear that we'll need more uranium than we mine. At least if we expect to run all the power plants that are on the board. The World Nuclear Association (WNA) reports there are 50 nuclear reactors under construction around the world that'll need some 23 million pounds of U308. (U308 is the oxide you get when you mine uranium ore.) There are 432 more on the planning board. Based on these projects, the world's nuclear power production will more than triple from 2008 to 2030. The incident in Japan will slow the growth of reactors. How much is hard to say.

Not surprisingly, China has a big role to play here. Its power needs are growing dramatically. Some think that the boom in Chinese nuclear power is a lot like what happened in the U.S. nuclear boom between 1970 and 1980. America's reliance on nuclear power doubled as a percentage of total power generation in the 1970s and then doubled again. From 1972 to 1990, total reactors in operation in the United States went from 40 to 110.

Something like that may happen in China. Today, China has only about a dozen reactors, which supply about 3 percent of its power needs. But the growth curve is steep. The WNA say there are 15 more under construction, which will more than double China's nuclear capacity. It has another 114 either planned or proposed. If everything gets built, that will be nearly a fourfold increase.

So where is the uranium that will power all those plants going to come from? Not China. In fact, China represents only about 1.7 percent of the world's uranium production. Take a look at Figure 9.6, which shows you the top five producers, which make up nearly 80 percent of the world's production:

Note that Australia clocks in at number three, right behind Kazakhstan. While it may surprise you, Kazakhstan is home to one-sixth of the world's

Country	2008 Production (in tonnes)	Share (%)
Canada	9,000	20.3
Kazakhstan	8,521	19.2
Australia	8,430	19.1
Namibia	4,366	11.1
Russia	3,521	8.6

FIGURE 9.6 The World's Biggest Uranium Producers

Source: World Nuclear Association

uranium reserves. It's one of the fastest-growing producers. By 2012, Kazakhstan may well double its production of uranium. But most of the new uranium mines are in Africa.

Namibia, the former German colony, gained independence from South Africa in 1990. It's mostly a coastal desert of 2.1 million people. It's politically stable and has good infrastructure with a long history of mining. Namibia is generally thought to be a less risky place to do business than China, Russia, or Kazakhstan.

Another point: All the best mines are in production. The new mines are all of lower grades and will be higher-cost sources of uranium: 14 of the 20 largest deposits in the world are in production. New mines will be smaller, raising production costs. All of this bodes well for higher uranium prices in the future. The higher price is the lure that will bring the fish.

So on the supply side, the market should tighten. It's living off stockpiles that are dwindling, and, as is the case in much of the resource world, the low-hanging fruit is gone.

I want to say a few words about the uranium mania of 2007, which cracked in 2008, along with most things. In 2007, there was certainly a uranium rush. Besides the small circle of established players that were actually producing uranium, there were over 750 exploration companies created to look for more. Almost all of these flamed out in 2008 as the uranium price sank and the credit crisis finished off the wounded.

Thinking in contrary fashion, it looks to me that uranium is due for an upturn. Investing well often requires you to buy what is out of fashion or what has done poorly. Uranium is a good candidate.

The four big uranium producers worth thinking about are Cameco, Uranium One, Paladin, and Denison Mines. These are the ones I watch. If the uranium story plays out over the next decade as we speculate it might, then these stocks ought to deliver market-beating returns.

New Zealand's Economic Place in the World

New Zealand today is a highly productive agricultural economy, an exporter of dairy, meat, and other agricultural products, as well as wool from its ample stock of sheep, which dot the countryside.

New Zealand's biggest customer is Australia. So you should expect its economy to somewhat mirror its bigger neighbor. Although it too has housing bubble troubles and debt worries, it is has its natural resources that it's tapping to good effect. In 2011, it recorded its biggest trade surplus ever.

What it sells, chiefly, is dairy products such as milk, butter, and cheese, which make up a quarter of its exports. One-third of world dairy exports come from New Zealand. It's like the Saudi Arabia of dairy. It was not always so. New Zealand's bounty is a product of fertilizer and the application of modern farming techniques.

I have an old book on New Zealand by W. Pember Reeves. It's a 1927 edition, well-worn by the passage of years and illustrated with beautiful watercolors. Reeves, who visited New Zealand on two extended trips about 25 years apart, was in a good position to note the changes. He writes about the productive growth of New Zealand agriculture from 1900 to 1925:

Millions of acres had been converted from fern, scrub, or forest into fine pasture: Hundreds of thousands of acres of heavy swamp had been drained and turned into dairy farms. The use of fertilizers had made large areas, once hardly profitable, very productive. The application of electric power to dairy farming, factory work, and domestic purposes, had transformed industry and life both in town and country.

The importance of fertilizer is something we touch in other chapters. I think this sector will continue to offer up worthwhile opportunities in the next decade as we figure out ways to feed a growing planet eating richer, more complex diets.

To wrap up New Zealand, our crew spent an afternoon in Arrowtown, tucked away in the mountains on the banks of the Arrow River. This was a gold rush town back in 1862, when prospectors found gold flakes shimmering in the river. You can still see some of the buildings from the Chinese mining settlement there. And you can still pan for gold as a tourist.

Back in Queenstown, another New Zealand city with a history of gold mining, I picked up a book on the New Zealand gold rushes. The book, *Diggers, Hatters & Whores* by Stevan Eldred-Grigg, maintains that "the gold rushes were the single biggest event in the history of colonial New Zealand."

It's easy to see why. In 1863, the population of Otago, a southern region on the South Island where Arrowtown is, jumped 28 percent. That same year, the region produced 40,000 pounds of gold, more than the contemporary gold rush in California.

Gold rushes boomed all over New Zealand, from Auckland to Dunedin. By 1880, though, the great gold rushes of New Zealand were all over.

Gold rushes come and go. Historically speaking, the idea of gold rushes is relatively recent. There were no gold rushes in ancient India or China, as far as we know, or in Africa or the Middle East. The first great gold rush, according to Eldred-Grigg, was in Brazil at the end of the seventeenth century.

Brazil was a colony of Portugal, and the Portuguese traders mostly hugged the coasts, growing sugar. But some of them began to work their way inland through the wooded hinterlands, where they found gold. The gold fields became known as Minas Gerais, or General Mines, a name that still sticks. Minas Gerais still produces gold today. Within a few years, Eldred-Grigg tells us, Minas Gerais produced "more gold than had been dug anywhere in the world for whole centuries, with output peaking at 31,000 pounds annually."

The second gold rush was in the great forests of the taiga, in Siberia. In the 1830s, folks found gold in the shingle riverbeds of the Yenisei. A rush set in, and gold peaked at about 47,000 pounds annually.

But the big gold rushes didn't happen until a bit later, powered by the Industrial Revolution. As Eldred-Grigg writes: "Worldwide gold fever was unthinkable before the middle of the nineteenth century. The thrilling scramble for nuggets or flakes or even dust was powered almost wholly by the Industrial Revolution and its steam technology."

Today, the dynamics are all different. Today, what drives the gold markets is not the desire to get rich, but the wish to avoid the poorhouse. It is fear, not greed that makes the yellow metal dance. When people worry about the creditworthiness of paper currencies and fret over the worth of the paper in their pocket, they turn to gold. It's been that way for a long time.

All the forces that drove gold to record heights are still hanging around. The U.S. government has a monstrous budget and enormous obligations, which it cannot meet without printing a lot of money. All of that means the dollar is a doomed currency. Gold, on the other hand, has been a store of wealth for centuries—millennia even.

Gold is an idea that touches on many markets, so let's end our glimpse at these two in the far corner of the world. I am wary of investing directly in these countries, given their long booms and trouble spots in housing.

Wait for those storms to blow over first and for asset prices to come down. Follow the interesting trends and ideas, though. Long term, both countries should benefit from their proximity to hungry Asian markets and a world turning right side up.

Five Key Takeaways

- I encourage you to check out Jonathan Callahan's website: http://mazamascience.com/. You can see his presentations and read his useful blog. You can play around with the tools on the site to make your own import/export charts on energy use.
- Stock to watch: Chart Industries. Explore its website: www.chartindustries.com/.
- Rick Rule's website is www.gril.net/. The site is updated regularly with useful articles on all manner of investing topics. Rule is an extraordinary investor, and you should investigate using his services.
- Keep an eye on the geothermal basket: Ram Power, Nevada Geothermal, and U.S. Geothermal.
- Consider these uranium producers worth following: Cameco, Paladin Energy, and Denison Mines.

CHAPTER 10

Southeast Asia: Travels Through Thailand, Cambodia, and Vietnam

I received an email late one night from my contact in Bangkok. "I would strongly recommend you delay or cancel your trip to Bangkok," she began, "as the flood situation is getting from bad to worse."

Stability and calm seem rare cards in the greasy deck of human outcomes. Instead, we reel from one crisis to another. Some are small. Some are large. But the transitions are rarely smooth. Big, influential events dominate the history of markets and men.

"Big gains and losses concentrate into small packages of time," wrote Benoît Mandelbrot, the late great iconoclast of finance. He points to how the dollar lost value against the yen from 1986 to 2003. Half of the losses happened in only 10 trading days out of 4,695 such days. In the 1980s, nearly half of the gains from the S&P 500 occurred on one-half of 1 percent of the trading days. These are just a pair from a fat file full of such examples of big gains and losses in small packages of time.

The rising floodwaters surrounding Bangkok gave us another example. The floods had a serious economic impact.

"More than 2 million people in 23 provinces have been suffering from floods for months," our correspondent continues, tapping out her worried lines, staccato style, in the wee morning hours from Bangkok:

More than 350 people have perished. Rice fields in nearly all industrial estates in the Central Plain have been inundated. Floodwaters have entered parts of the city. The government has no serious measures of how to deal with billions of cubic meters of water entering from the north. Bangkok is currently able to pump 300 million cubic meters a day. Meaning it will take at least 40 to 60 days before we see dry land again. This is worse than the tsunami. Waters just keep coming for weeks toward the city. We can't even get drinking water and basic food from supermarkets for days due to logistical difficulties. This is serious.

More than 200 major highways were impassable. Factories closed. People put up barricades of sand and tarps. Bottled water supplies were running low. Estimated losses totaled $6 billion and rising, enough to shave off two points from economic growth in 2011. Some towns north of the city were under six feet of water.

Rains had been harder than normal. For months, rains pounded northern Thailand. In March, rains were 334 percent above normal. In April, they were 76 percent above normal. The months rolled by, and totals stayed high: 41 percent-plus in May, 43 percent-plus in June, 43 percent-plus in July, 22 percent-plus in August, and 46 percent-plus in September.

However, there was more to the story. Seasonal floods are common in Southeast Asia. Monsoons are an essential part of the hydraulics of these economies. A healthy monsoon season means well-watered crops and plump rice fields. This disaster, though, stemmed from more than just abnormal rains.

Not that long ago, thick forests and dense wetlands used to soak up floods. But in recent decades, industrial parks, highways, and housing projects grew to surround the city of Bangkok. As recently as the middle of the last century, Bangkok had only 1 million residents. Today, there are 12 million people living in and around Bangkok. It alone is nearly 40 percent of Thailand's economic output.

This growth is part of a pattern of Asian cities. In 1950, 237 million people lived in Asian cities. Today, there are over 1.8 billion. Bangkok is the heart of one of the fastest-growing economies in Asia.

The growth of these cities has not been entirely well thought out. Bangkok is not much above sea level. That fact did not stop people from building homes, hospitals, schools, and more on flood plains. Worse, the population put tremendous pressures on the groundwater beneath Bangkok. As the city pumped out the water, it actually compacted the earth beneath, sinking the city even closer to sea level.

Incidentally, Bangkok gets its name from the marrying of the Thai word for village (bang) and for a species of wild plum that grew along its riverbanks (kok). Translated, Bangkok is the village of wild plums (its official name has 167 letters, making it the longest city name in the world).

It's a poetic name for a city that used to be a kind of Asian Venice, with its famous canals (called klongs). As with most Asian cities, it has undergone radical change in the past 50 years. I flipped through some old black and whites of the city. The tall buildings of today are relatively new. As late as the 1950s, when the Oriental Hotel installed an elevator, it was a novelty to have a building of any height.

That's because the soil in Thailand is soft, and parts of the city actually lie below sea level. You couldn't put tall buildings here if you wanted to. But as so often happens, technology got better. Once people figured it out, a building boom commenced in the 1970s. It accelerated as the years progressed. In 1982, there were 48 condo projects in the whole country. By 1992, there were 220 in just Bangkok, and many were over 30 stories high.

High-rises sprang up all over. The Thais filled in many of the canals. (This reminds me of something the old long-serving foreign correspondent Keyes Beech once wrote of Bangkok. "If somebody should ask you what happened to Bangkok, you can tell them, 'They paved it.'")

Venice is probably a good analogy for Bangkok, even without the canals. As that city slowly sinks in the mud, so too, does Bangkok, at a rate of about two centimeters per year.

American cities are not so well thought out, either. Witness the destruction of New Orleans. We've built large cities in some areas where if you had to do it over again, you wouldn't. Or at least you'd have done it differently.

Bangkok: From Behind the Floodwaters

Despite the warnings, I went anyway.

I arrived at the airport, which was mostly empty. There was hardly any traffic on the streets. When I got to the hotel, it was a little eerie seeing the sandbag defenses up around the building. In fact, most buildings had sandbags around them in case the floodwaters broke through. And when I walked in the hotel lobby, I was greeted by name. "Welcome, you must be Mr. Mayer."

I must have been the only nut checking in that night.

Tens of thousands have already fled Bangkok. The floods, too, have certainly affected the flow of travelers here. Some foreign governments have advised their citizens not to go to Bangkok. Tourism numbers were down. Business meetings have been cancelled.

As a result, hotel vacancies were up. The *Wall Street Journal* reported that the Shangri-La Hotel had an occupancy rate of only 30 percent, compared with the 70 to 90 percent rate the hotel usually enjoys this time of year. I'm sure that's typical.

As Bangkok is about 40 percent of Thailand's economy, what happens in Bangkok is important to Thailand. The floods were the big topic of conversation everywhere I went. Bangkok has been hit with a number of business-stopping events in recent years. There was a military coup in 2005, protests that closed the airport in 2008, and more protests in 2010 that left 90 dead. (Some of this unrest is, likely, economic, whatever the political motives offered. The average manufacturing wage in Thailand is about $250 a month, compared with $400 in China. Ten years ago, the countries' relative positions were the other way around.) The floods add to the list.

You might be surprised at the global impact of these floods. Thailand is the world's second-largest producer of disk drives, for instance, at about 40 percent of global supply. Western Digital was particularly hard hit, with 60 percent of its production in Thailand. Key suppliers to the industry were submerged in water. Nidec, for instance, has a 75 percent share of the motor market for disk drives. Its Thai plants were at one-third of production. As a result, components were scarce, and the prices of disk drives shot up about 20 percent after the floods began.

Japanese companies, in particular, rely on Thailand as an offshore production base. Toyota and Honda have plants in Thailand (and so does Ford). Both had to scale back their global production of vehicles because of shortages of Thai-made parts. These facilities were literally underwater.

My first meeting in Bangkok was at the Spice Market at the Four Seasons. It was empty during what normally would be a busy lunch hour. I met with Lan, a Cambodian-born Thai of Chinese descent who has worked in the brokerage business for more than 20 years. (Lan is on "permanent sabbatical," she tells me.)

She gave me a good overview of the scene here, besides giving me a crash course in Thai cuisine. Lan brought up the historical curiosity of Thai independence. By dint of diplomatic skill and luck, Thailand has never been occupied. Unlike other nations of Southeast Asia, the colonial powers never ruled it.

I'm not sure what this means in practical terms. Lan thought it important enough to mention and said it may account for the relative enduring openness of the Thai economy to foreigners. Thais don't have the baggage associated with the legacy of colonialism.

Buying Thai stocks is easy, for instance, and the Thai stock market is interesting on several levels. In that respect, my timing was good. Later in the afternoon, I got a bird's-eye view from Andrew Stotz, a strategist at Kim Eng Securities. He had a neat way of presenting his ideas on the Thai market and its stocks in a flipbook publication that he puts out monthly, called *Stotz Stocks*.

The gist of his latest view was that Thai stocks were attractive at about 11 times earnings with low debt, hefty dividends (a near 4 percent yield), and healthy returns on equity (around 20 percent). Those are the averages. A little stock picking can you get you even more enticing goods. Plus, foreign ownership of Thai stocks was down to where it was in 2009, at around 35 percent. This may be a contrarian indicator, as foreign investors owned 41 percent of the market before the crash in 2008. And contrary to the Western world, Thailand has low debt levels. No sovereign debt crisis there!

According to Stotz, historically, Thai stocks do well from this 9–12 price-earnings ratio range, with an 18 percent return in the year following and an 11 percent annual return over five years. A blunt instrument to play Thai stocks is the MSCI Thailand Index Fund (THD). Thailand has been through worse crises before and has always rebounded.

So as bad as the flood appears, I am inclined to think this, too, will pass. It seems a temporary setback for Thailand's markets, which, like bamboo, bend but do not break from the stresses put on them.

Needless to say, the Bangkok I saw on my visit was not typical, but I am glad I lingered there. It was supposed to be just a stopover on my way to Cambodia and Vietnam. But thanks to Lan, my contact and new friend, I had a productive time there that included one fantastic meeting that turned up what may well be the best idea of the trip.

This idea has a 20-year track record of wealth creation that is almost too good to be true. Based in Bangkok, it boggles the mind that the man behind it is not more famous.

The Warren Buffett of Thailand

No road is ever straight in Bangkok.
                    —Carol Hollinger, *Mai Pen Rai Means Never Mind*

The best meeting I had in Bangkok was with a special investor who, I am told, meets with few people. I think the floods worked in my favor here. He probably thought, if this poor guy was willing to brave the floods, I guess I'll meet with him.

His name is Doug Barnett. We met at the Sukhothai Hotel in Bangkok. Barnett must be the best investor in Thailand and one of the best ever. He's not well known, probably because his specialty is in a small corner of the financial world: Thai stocks.

He had an unlikely start to his career. Doug was an engineer, designing oil refineries for Chevron. Later, he decided to go to business school, and then worked for Morgan Stanley as a security salesman. He was a lousy security salesman, by his own account. But his best customer was a friend of a rich family with a bunch of money in the Thai market. Asked to manage it, Doug said yes, and when the family moved their investments to Russia, Doug decided he'd rather stay in Bangkok and continue to invest in Thai stocks. He needed investors.

The first guy he turned to was Julian Robertson, the famed hedge fund manager. Doug had gotten to know him as Julian occasionally passed through Bangkok. Doug had offered some trading ideas that worked out well. Robertson approved and became Doug's first major investor. His second was George Soros. Not bad company to start out with.

Since 1990, Doug has produced an annual return of about 18 percent for investors in his Thai Focused Equity Fund. That's incredible, and if he were in the United States, he would be feted as one of the best investors around. Heck, he's outgained Buffett by a healthy three percentage points over that time. Do the math, and it means you wind up with about twice as much if you had put your money with Doug instead of Warren Buffett.

That performance is even better than it looks because of the market Doug is in. While he was banging out an 18 percent annual return, the Thai market gave investors a zero return. In fact, it was down 1 percent over the same time frame. Only 29 Thai stocks even had positive results. The best Thai stock over that period—Banpu—was up only 1,090 percent. Doug's fund was up 3,111 percent.

So how does he do it? Doug, the man behind the Thai Focused Equity Fund, answers for himself below.

The first thing to know is that Thai stocks are volatile. Their volatility is like the NASDAQ. The Dow Jones industrial average has had 33 moves of 20 percent or more in 80 years. Thailand's market has had 38 such moves in just the past 20 years. "Is that how you got your gray hair?" I joked. "I've always had gray hair," Doug answered.

So investing there is not for the kind of investor who worries when he is down 25 percent. In fact, when we spoke, Doug's fund was down 25 percent for the year. (The SET Index of Thai stocks was down 7 percent; it was the worst-performing market in Asia in September.) Last year, the fund was the best-performing fund in Asia, returning 96 percent.

In his September 2011 letter to investors, Doug wrote about the attraction of Thai stocks. This might be best summed up in Figure 10.1.

"In addition," Doug wrote, "listed companies that pay normal taxes at 30 percent of pretax net profits will get an additional 10 percent after tax net income boost due to the new government's corporate tax reduction from 30 percent to 23 percent next year. Meanwhile, Thailand has a strong balance sheet with surpluses in both the trade and current accounts.

	P/E on 2012 Estimates	Earnings Per Share Growth Rate	Dividend Yield
U.S. stocks	10.2	11.7%	2.3%
Asian benchmark	10.7	14.6%	3.0%
SET Index (Thailand)	9.0	14.1%	4.6%

FIGURE 10.1 Why Thai Stocks Look Good Right Now

Source: Quest Management, Inc.

Furthermore, Thai commercial banks have strong financial status with nonperforming loans of 2–3 percent on average and no investment in any overseas debt. As a result, we believe that the SET Index will outperform based on strong fundamentals, higher earnings growth, and a discount in P/E valuation."

But back to our conversation and that volatility . . .

"You get compensated for having a more volatile path to achieve your goal," Doug told me. "Of course, at times like these, your resolve is tested. We're down this year because one of our biggest positions is doing everything right fundamentally, but the stock is down from $61 to $23."

"Ah, a common lament for a long-term, fundamentalist investor," I said.

"Yes. . . . We've underperformed a lot worse than this in the past. You just have to believe that in the end, you'll win." Skittish investors who buy and sell on rumor and gossip dominate in the short term. Yet over the longer term, the market sorts things out rationally. Doug has run tests that show a strong correlation between earnings per share growth and total return. One such test looked at dates from 2006 through the first quarter of 2011. He took all the Thai stocks Bloomberg has data on. Then, he took the 20 percent that grew their earnings the most and compared them against the bottom 20 percent.

The top 20 percent growers returned 239 percent, the bottom only 33 percent. "This is during a period when we had coups, exchange controls, tsunamis, bird flu, red shirts . . . every conceivable exogenous variable that could've affected the market negatively," Doug said, "but the market discriminated and rewarded good companies. This is why I say that politics doesn't matter, and any drops on political fears are great buying opportunities."

He talked about a company called Indorama Ventures (IVL), which accounts for about half of the fund's 2011 unrealized losses to date. IVL is one of the world's largest makers of PET (polyethylene terephthalate, used to make plastic bottles and containers). It has facilities all over the world. It's a good example to look at because it shows you what kind of stocks Doug likes.

So far, earnings this year are 60–70 percent higher than a year ago. For the first quarter, earnings jumped 662 percent compared with a year ago. Mostly, this was due to one-time factors, and perversely, the market sold off the stock. IVL has a price-earnings ratio of eight or nine times and should grow earnings at least 38 percent over the next 12 months.

"The math is inevitable on something like that," I said.

"That's what I think," Doug said. "I have tens of millions of dollars in this company. Five years from now, this company will be 5 or 10 times bigger than it is right now in terms of earnings . . . and my 20 million will be 100 million or 200 million."

Let's look at one more holding, Banpu Coal.

Banpu recently acquired Centennial Coal of Australia for $2 billion. It gets 14.5 million tons per year in capacity with 9.6 million locked up in long-term contracts at $45 per ton. The spot price for the same coal is $98 per ton. But the key to this acquisition is that Banpu gets the ability to add another four million tons of capacity for only $380 million.

"We think," Doug wrote, "the Centennial Coal investment will show good results over the next couple years, as legacy contracts with Australian power companies at $45 per ton are renewed at current spot prices near $100 per ton, and their mine capacity has increased from 15 mm tons/year to 20 mm tons/year, all of which can be sold at spot prices." Banpu trades at just 9.9 times 2012 earnings, and Doug believes it can grow earnings per share at 15 percent per year over the next two years.

So that gives you a look at the kind of things that make up the fund's holdings. Overall, the fund's companies ought to enjoy 25 percent earnings growth in 2012. Yet the portfolio trades for about eight times earnings. There is a lot of implied upside in numbers like that.

Doug runs a concentrated fund, which contributes to that volatility, and performance. He often holds only 8 to 14 stocks. The top four or five positions might be 50 to 70 percent of the portfolio. Last year, he had 45 percent of the fund in one stock, because that stock kept going up. He does hedge positions at times to lock in gains. And he is not afraid to hold cash when good ideas are scarce. At times, the fund has had 50 percent of its assets in cash.

Doug does deep bottoms-up fundamental analysis and meets with management. He might meet with 100 to 200 companies a year. The Thai universe is a relatively small one, and he knows it well. There are about 450 listed companies. Of these, there are maybe 210 that meet his liquidity standards. And of those, there are about 80 that Doug would think about owning at some point in the cycle. The secret, then, is to drill down to select companies and get as close to them as possible.

I asked him what the management teams were like here. Were they easy to talk to and transparent? Doug made it sound as if it weren't much different from any other market.

There are, as in all markets, some control groups who "screw investors on a regular basis," he said. Doug told me about a company that has private companies around the public one, and how it sells assets back and forth to transfer wealth out of the public company and into the private company. An investor who had put money in its subsidiary that had the country franchise for 7-Eleven, when it had only four stores at its founding in 1993, would not have made a cent until 2009, even though the company has 6,000 stores.

"Wow, from four to 6,000, and nobody made any money," I said.

"Nobody except the management," Doug added.

Conversely, are there managers and entrepreneurs you'd follow anywhere? "There are lots. It's more of the rule than the exception," Doug said.

One fascinating thing about Doug's fund is that 60 percent of the assets are from other hedge fund managers. "They know what we're doing, and they never call," Doug says. "They just add more."

Doug and his associates make up 27 percent of the fund's assets. So you have vested insiders here who eat their own cooking. A value-based fund of funds and two high net worth individuals own another 24 percent, and the rest is spread out among 80 or so smaller investors. Total assets under management come to about $160 million, and Doug said he would not market the fund above $250 million.

The big drawback here is that the minimum to invest in Doug's fund is $100,000. That will price a lot of folks out, I know. But if you can do it and stomach the inevitable volatility, the fund is worth a commitment. You've got a 20-year track record behind it, and Doug is, by all accounts, a stand-up guy.

Cambodia: Kingdom of Wonder

Your eyes believe what they see. Your ears believe others.
—A saying found in a fortune cookie, as related in
The Entrepreneurial Investor

I received an unusual email one day while planning my trip, which put me on the trail of one of the best investment stories in Southeast Asia.

I was excited to see its high-growth economies, such as Vietnam and Thailand, for myself. I had planned to start in Singapore, the financial hub of Southeast Asia and then on to see the bustle of Ho Chi Minh City, Hanoi, and Bangkok. I added Cambodia because I wanted to see Angkor Wat and the ruins of the Khmer Empire. It seemed a shame to go all that way and not visit one of the world's great historic sites.

Thankfully, a reader alerted me to my oversight by email:

"Your Southeast Asia trip omits the best investment story of all, Cambodia. You should go beyond the conventional wisdom that Cambodia is merely Angkor Wat, and instead, focus on the fact that it is one of Asia's least-regulated, lowest-taxed, most-open, and most-politically stable economies. Its youthful population makes even Vietnam's population look old. The country offers large-scale agricultural and mining potential and, possibly, some oil as well."

It was a wake-up call. I never seriously considered Cambodia, but the more I started to look into the opportunity, the more I liked the idea.

First, I should introduce this reader. His name is Douglas Clayton, and he is the founder and CEO of Leopard Capital. "We manage the first invest-ment fund in Cambodia," Doug told me. "We have invested in the country's largest bank, largest cell phone operator, only seafood processing plant, best brewery, a power grid, a rice farm, and a housing project, with more to come."

I like to explore the fringes of the investment universe. I've invested all over the world in all kinds of businesses, and I've traveled all over the globe, but Cambodia? I mean, isn't Cambodia that awful place where the killing fields are? And Pol Pot? And all that?

It was.

"A popular view on Cambodia," Clayton tells me, "is that it remains forever rooted in the Pol Pot period that ended 33 years ago, as if Germany's or Japan's future economic prospects in 1978 could be eval-uated only by delving deeply into the Hitler and Hirohito periods, or America's future can best be understood by analyzing the Gerald Ford period. One must remember that around two-thirds of Cambodians to-day were not even alive during that period and are mainly interested in getting a job, cell phone, motorbike, and Internet connection. This is what investors should be looking at."

On the youthfulness of Cambodians, there is no doubt. More than 60 percent are under the age of 25, and the median age is only 21. Not only are they youthful, they are mostly literate. The literacy rate in Cambodia is about 75 percent, and the workers here are the cheapest in Asia.

No wonder the investment dollars are flowing. Mostly, it's the Chinese, Vietnamese, and Korean money moving in. As Clayton pointed out, "It's un-related to the West."

Vietnam's investments are worth around $2 billion. These include in-vestments in oil, rubber, mining, and power. Viettel, a Vietnamese telecom operator, has more than 40 percent of Cambodia's mobile phone market. Trade between the countries is worth over $1 billion annually.

South Korea is Cambodia's third-largest investor, mostly in construction and banking. (When I finally got to Cambodia, which I'll relate more in a bit, I saw a POSCO sign on a work site across from my hotel in Phnom Penh. POSCO is the large South Korean steelmaker.)

China, though, is Cambodia's biggest investor, making up nearly half of total investment all by itself. Much of this has gone toward building infra-structure. China, for example, is building and financing the construction of Phnom Penh's second river port, which will triple capacity. China is financ-ing a $400 million hydropower project that will double Cambodia's current generation capacity. It will supply half of Cambodia's power needs. China built the Prek Tamak Bridge, which crosses the Mekong north of Phnom Penh.

The economy is growing rapidly. In fact, Cambodia has done better than many of its much-more-celebrated peers. As Clayton points out:

Cambodia somehow outgrew India, Vietnam, Thailand, Indonesia, the Philippines, Malaysia, Singapore, Japan, Korea, Taiwan, and every other economy one can name in Asia (except China) from 2003– 2008—right up until the United States collapsed in 2008.

Furthermore, virtually all Cambodia's social indicators achieved significant improvement—this wasn't the case of an economy being boosted by the opening of a giant copper mine or oil field or hydro dam.

Lastly, I would invite skeptics to name any other post-conflict nation that has bounced back so vigorously while being criticized by so many.

There is political stability. The prime minister has held power since 1985. The ruling party won a decisive election in 2008, and most of the key ministers are long-serving members with experience. Moreover, the government is open to new investment. Foreigners can own 100 percent of businesses, unlike the restrictions in other Asian countries. Repatriating profits is easy. There is even a stock market, which opened in 2011. (As I write, it has no listed securities. It seems more a response to received ideas about what a modern market economy ought to have than a functional exchange created out of need.)

Cambodia has a lot going for it. It has some of the most fertile land in Southeast Asia. Millions of hectares of land remain uncultivated because of lack of capital. There are oil and gas resources here that could be worth 10 to 20 times Cambodia's current economy. There are untapped deposits of nickel, lead, zinc, bauxite, and iron ore. There is a growing tourism industry and a need for new hotels. There are 274 miles of unspoiled white sand beaches open for development and 61 islands. There are more opportunities in banking and telecom among others.

Clayton saw how bad things were in Cambodia. "Having seen Cambodia in a more-disheveled state in 1991," he told me, "I have admiration for its unexpected achievements and undiminished optimism about its potential. Cambodia's glass is 'half full' to me."

Clayton is a hands-on frontier investor. He eloquently describes his own métier. "Find me in a forgotten frontier, investing in and building up simple businesses facing minimal competition, like creating a national beer brand or hooking up rural homes to a power plant or lending farmers money at 2 to 3 percent a month, instead of the 4 to 5 percent monthly loan shark rate, or seeing if we can boost rice yields by using tractors, instead of cattle, or teaching fishermen's wives to process and export the shrimp their husbands catch, and so on"

So, I had to get to Cambodia to see it myself.

Phnom Penh: The Pearl of Asia

Phnom Penh is a thriving city of 2 million people at the confluence of the Tonlé Sap, Bassac, and Mekong Rivers in Cambodia. Historically, travelers often describe Phnom Penh as a pretty French colonial town. It was once known as the "Pearl of Asia." Keyes Beech's description in a 1971 book is typical: "Phnom Penh is a lovely city of stately homes, broad, tree-lined avenues, and golden upswept-roofed pagodas. . . . It is a leisurely city with not too many cars."

These descriptions do not ring true today, as there are swarms of cars, tuk-tuks, and motorcycles that manage to navigate crowded intersections, often without the benefit of traffic lights. The golden upswept-roofed pagodas are still there, architectural marvels of their own, as is the royal palace.

Even so, some of the bones of the French colonial era remain. I stayed, for example, at the Raffles Hotel Le Royal (for a mere $120 per night). It dates from 1929 and oozes old-world charm. The hotel is a majestic presence, with its French vanilla-colored exterior and immaculate grounds shaded by palm, bamboo, and rain trees.

You may be thinking, "But what about the Khmer Rouge?" There are no visible stains of that dark period, which closed 33 years ago. I did visit the famous Tuol Sleng museum. Pol Pot and his minions converted the former secondary school into a prison, known as S-21. It was the largest in Cambodia. Some 14,000 people were held there (and some estimates put the number as high as 20,000), but only seven people survived. Yes, seven.

One of the survivors was there the day I visited. He was a little old man, seated behind a desk under an awning, sipping at a fruit drink through a straw and taking pictures with tourists. I wondered what the man must've felt sitting in a place that was such a hell 30-odd years ago.

Hell is what it must've been. Vietnamese soldiers found it in 1978, when Vietnam invaded Cambodia and toppled Pol Pot's regime. They took pictures of what they found. And those pictures hang on stark walls in the prison. Dead and mangled bodies on steel bed frames, blood-splattered floors and implements of torture scattered about and hung on walls. My stomach turned, standing there in the same rooms in which such awful deeds took place.

There are hundreds of pictures of the victims, with sad, worried eyes staring back at the camera, as the Khmer Rouge documented what they did here. You can peruse the tiny cells and see the pile of clothes from the victims, asked to strip before interrogations. S-21 is an overpowering portrait of evil. It's a terrible, somber place.

On the other hand, I thought about how resilient people are. The ability and determination to rebuild always astonishes. You would never know any of these awful things happened tooling around Phnom Penh today. The people I met in restaurants and shops were warm and friendly, and young. They are not interested in Pol Pot any more than American youths today are interested in the Vietnam War. They want good jobs and the goodies we take for granted. They want a better life.

This is contrary to what many mainstream journalists want you to believe. I read Joel Brinkley's new book, for instance, *Cambodia's Curse: The Modern History of a Troubled Land*. He writes, "Cambodians by and large are a dour people. . . . In fact, it was quite rare to see Cambodians laugh at all. Given their desperate situation, they seldom even smiled." Well, I don't know what Cambodia Brinkley visited, but it's not the same one I was in. There is certainly suffering and poverty in Cambodia, as Brinkley details. Another story of Cambodia is seldom told. That's the one I focused on.

A definite energy here, a good vibe, is here. The restaurants and bars are hopping at night. There are a number of scaffolds on buildings being renovated or cranes atop new ones. There are old French colonial buildings being restored as hotels, restaurants, apartments, and more.

Foreigners do all these renovations, so I'm told. Perhaps because restoring old buildings is something done by rich cultures after certain other needs are met. The prices of real estate are high, and the renovations are not particularly rewarding financially. In Cambodia, there are lots of other needs and better uses of capital. Let me highlight one that deals with a favorite theme: farmland.

I met with the chief investment officer of Leopard Capital, Scott Lewis, in a little Mediterranean bistro called Ocean Restaurant tucked down a quiet side street in Boeung Keng Kang.

Scott ran through the appeal of the idea. The big picture, if you've been reading to this point, you well know. We're going to need to produce more food to feed a growing and increasingly affluent global population that's eating more complex diets. The land to do that has to come from somewhere. Cambodia is one of those land banks.

Land is cheap, available, and of pretty good quality. You can get a 20-year concession for only $400 a hectare. Rubber prices are favorable, so the business is attractive. So much so that it's attracting Malaysians and Indonesians, who produce a lot of rubber but are running out of space in their homelands.

There is plenty of room to modernize agriculture here—to use better seeds, irrigation, and fertilizers to boost yields. An acute need exists for better storage and drying facilities, milling, and processing plants. These would allow Cambodians to capture more of the value of their crops, instead of shipping them elsewhere for processing.

Scott laid out the basic economics of acquiring farmland. You buy the hectares for $400 a pop. You have to invest about $3,500 per hectare to get it to production. So, let's say you're all in for $4,000 per hectare. Meanwhile, producing rubber plantations go for $15,000–20,000 in Cambodia and pay a 9 to 10 percent yield. So, that's a four-bagger, with yield, too. Sounds like a winner, right?

Ah, but there is a catch. Land is sensitive everywhere. I have been at this long enough to know. It's true in Saskatchewan, and it's true in Brazil. I have firsthand experience with both. Nowhere is it easy for foreigners to start gobbling up farmland.

So, the catch is that it can take a long time to get approvals. Leopard's been working on it for over a year and is close. Plus, when you start to factor in the time value of money and other expenses incurred along the way, the deal does not look quite as sweet.

But at some point, the land will get to production because the economic incentives are so great. It's just a matter of time. Still, it illustrates, in a tangible way, that what sounds great from a macro-perspective can be tough to implement in a micro way.

Leopard Capital: Visionary Investors of Frontier Markets

I met Doug Clayton at Leopard Capital's headquarters in Phnom Penh, where the company operates out of a refurbished colonial home. (This was actually the fourth time we'd met. We managed to hook up in Medellín and Bogotá, as well as Vancouver, of all places. But I'd never before made it to his neck of the woods.) Inside hang maps, classic 1930s-era travel posters, and various examples of Khmer art.

In a kind of war room, fitted out with a white board (streaked with lines and arrows left over from some brainstorming session) and a big map of Cambodia, Doug laid out some of the big-picture trends in more detail.

Two big themes are keys to unlocking rapid growth in Cambodia: better transportation networks (mainly roads) and improved power.

As to the former, 10 to 15 years ago, no paved roads existed. Today, two-lane highways connect the country at various points. A variety of countries including China, Korea, and Japan funded these efforts. "This is a big deal," Doug said, equating the creation of a road network in Cambodia with the creation of the U.S. highway system in the 1950s.

The roads allow trade to open up across the country, and even remote areas can become economic centers. Transportation costs drop, which unlocks tremendous economic potential as transportation costs in Cambodia are high compared with neighboring countries. To get a container from one point to another may cost three times as much as in Thailand over the same distance.

Cambodia was behind even its poor neighbors, as far as roads go. Even Laos has Route Nationale 13, which connects Luang Prabang with Vientiane.

(Laos has a stock exchange, which opened six months before Cambodia's, with two stocks trading on it.) Laos' road is not a great road, but it is a paved road. RN 13—the number 13 is considered lucky in Laos—ran right to the Cambodian border. There, according to author John Keay in *Mad About the Mekong*, "The pristine tarmac slithers into a tangled wall of undergrowth and expires at the base of a stately dipterocarpus. Until Cambodia recognizes road building as relevant to national reconstruction, there is no reciprocal highway to which RN 13 can connect."

That was in 2005. Cambodia gets it now.

Then there are railways. China is building one, a $250 million project that will link Phnom Penh with the port city Kompong Som. Some sections are already open. "China looks at the map of Asia and thinks in terms of decades," Doug said. They want the agricultural goods from Cambodia, and providing better links to get the goods from here to China serves their long-term interests.

"Relations with the Vietnamese are warm at the government level," Doug said, "and they've reopened the borders." This leads to more regional integration, which is how a poor country catches up with its neighbors. As investors begin to arbitrage away the opportunities, the gaps narrow.

In addition to transportation, the other big deal Doug pointed to was power. There is no electrical grid, but rather, 24 isolated power systems, much of it high-priced, unreliable, and oil-powered. However, the country is moving toward hydropower, and by the end of 2015 will be self-sufficient in energy. If Cambodia can do that, its power costs will plunge, and as with its roads, it will unleash more economic potential.

So, two shackles to high growth, high transport costs and high power costs, ought to melt away. This is a story no one is telling about Cambodia. "What it took a hundred years to do in the United States, from the Oregon Trail to the Eisenhower-era highway system, will happen in 20 years in Cambodia," Doug says.

The country's labor pool is a plus, all those young people, willing to work and no wage pressures at the unskilled level. Cambodia will enjoy a demographic dividend for the next 20 years. From the expanding population of workers alone, the economy ought to grow 3 percent per year, even if it does nothing else. Add in the roads, power, and investment dollars flowing in to the country, and this should be a high-growth economy for years.

As far as industry goes, there have been a number of successes already. The garment industry in Cambodia has over 300 factories that employ over 300,000 people. It ships goods mainly to U.S. customers. It is all International Labor Organization inspected and compliant with fair-trade rules. There are no sweatshops or child labor issues, which is an advantage for Cambodia over certain other countries in the region.

The garment industry is useful as a source of talent. It's where people learn to work in a factory and all that is involved with that, as opposed to living as a farmer (which 60 percent of Cambodians do).

Tourism on a relative basis is more important here than in many countries, at maybe 15 percent of the economy. Mostly, tourists are visiting the ruins of Angkor. There were 2.5 million visitors to Cambodia in 2010, and 2.8 million as the 2011 totals come in. They drive a lot of business in a country of only 14 million. The ministry of tourism expects 7 million international visitors by 2020. That demand will drive the creation of more than 1,000 restaurants (the country has about 900) and create 40,000 jobs.

Then there is agriculture, in which the beginnings of agro-industry are taking hold. Currently, Cambodian agriculture is about rice and rubber, and, to a lesser extent, corn, cassava, and forestry.

Doug sees the potential to create branded Cambodian products. If you go to a grocery store, you see mostly Thai and Vietnamese products, and not much in the way of Cambodian brands.

Kingdom Breweries, which Leopard started, is the first national brand. Though not made from Cambodian ingredients (save for the water), it is made in Cambodia, and it's a premium brand. Its Pilsner won a gold medal in Belgium in its first year. Kingdom is an example of what can be done. I visited the plant, atop which sits a comfortable rooftop bar. I sampled the latest brew, a dark lager. It's dark as a Guinness and tastes more like a lager.

Next, Leopard would like to try to create a mineral water brand. There is no local competitor. The bottled water here is from French companies. So Leopard went looking for a good source of mineral water and found a spring in Koulen, which has special historical importance and meaning to Cambodians. "It is kind of a holy mountain," Doug explained, "and in the foothills, there is good mineral water."

Leopard has invested in a shrimp-processing plant, the only one in the country, in the south off the Gulf of Thailand. Food processing is another attractive area, turning local raw materials into an exportable product to capture more value, rather than export everything for processing and packaging. The seafood-processing plant is the only one in the country. (Leopard, if you haven't deduced as much, likes to do things others aren't doing.)

On paper, it looked like a surefire winner, but there have been a number of challenges at the micro level, and the plant is not yet profitable. Leopard has brought in a new manager, a financial play doctor, so to speak, to see if he can get it going.

His name is Leonard Minster, and he is an American that has been running shrimp-processing plants in Thailand for the past 18 years. The Thais have mastered the shrimp game, and he'll take what he's learned there and apply it to Leopard's plant. I met with Leonard at his office. He said there wasn't much of an aquaculture industry in Cambodia, and it was harder to get reliable, quality product. He pointed to the lack of certain hardware, like cold storage. On the other hand, he was optimistic about the people and the potential of the seafood resource itself. Finding buyers is not a problem because the Japanese will buy everything Leopard's plant will produce. The challenges are operational.

So, this is frontier-market investing at its best. Internal capital markets don't exist. The country has a stock exchange but no listed companies. The one major listed Cambodian company is Naga, listed in Hong Kong, which is the Phnom Penh gambling monopoly.

I asked Doug about the business class in Cambodia, is there a thriving entrepreneurial community, I wondered? Doug said that the genocide wiped out much of it. What's left are the kids who are growing up to assume those roles. So the human resources of Cambodia are coming back after being depleted. The gap between Cambodia and the rest of Southeast Asia will narrow over time. "It may not ever get to where Singapore is," Doug adds, "but it can get where Thailand was 10 years ago." That would be a big improvement.

The richer Cambodians tend to be traders, people who have taken advantage of the system in some way and have recycled their wealth into land development and real estate. This is how fortunes get made in the early stages. Politically connected groups grab hold of tracts of land ahead of development, as happened in Thailand.

At this stage, most Cambodians don't have electricity in their homes. They don't have toilets or cell phones. There isn't much spending power. The elite are a small group of 2 to 3 million that do have cell phones, cars, and bank accounts and whose kids go to school. There are nine cell phone companies and 30 banks in Cambodia, all competing for this slice of affluent Cambodians.

Doug cites the main risk for Cambodia as political in nature: What if something happens to the old man (Hun Sen) before the son, a popular, Western-educated, progressive-minded fellow currently being groomed as his successor, is ready to assume his father's role? Sen is 60 years old, so there is some succession risk if that happens too soon.

"But the government has never deviated from the open economy model," Doug said. "We don't consider the government a problem from an investment point of view. Social issues are another matter. But political reform happens when a middle class emerges. What you won't find here is Putin-style episodes of foreigners getting robbed. . . . It's a good track record, for the most part."

Leopard Capital's Cambodia fund had $34 million under management. The goal is 20 percent per year. Leopard had made 10 investments and sold two that exceeded this hurdle. It has invested $26 million and had $4–5 million to go.

But Leopard is a visionary investment group. Everyone I met, I liked immediately. They were smart, global in their outlooks, and adventurous. When I visited, they were exploring funds for Haiti, Bhutan, and Burma. It's a group to keep an eye on, follow, and invest if you can. Leopard will undoubtedly find niches in the investment world long before the mainstream catches on. And when the rest of world catches on, Leopard and its investors should make a lot of money.

The Ruins of Angkor, Tonle Sap, and the Mekong

I did get to see those ruins.

To do that, you first go to Siem Reap, where the ruins are a short drive from the center of town. A few things surprised me immediately about Siem Reap. The airport was nice, even beautiful, with a pond and plenty of greenery around it. (It might've made Douglas Adams eat his words. He wrote, "It is no coincidence that in no known language does the phrase 'As pretty as an Airport' appear"). I grabbed a cab and, on the ride from the airport, was struck by all the big new hotels along the road. I stayed at the Hotel de la Paix, in the heart of town, within walking distance of the Old Quarter, a lively maze of streets full of cafes, restaurants, and vendors.

The next morning, I visited Angkor, which I heartily recommend to anyone coming through this part of the world. Built by the Khmer empire between the ninth and fifteenth centuries, the whole complex encompasses over 80 square miles. It is a sprawling network of tombs and temples, moats and causeways, a maze of sandstone and laterite, where the trees and vegetation intertwine with the stone to create an otherworldly setting. Henri Mouhout visited in 1860 and brought it to the world's attention. He found it, as Phil Karber wrote, an "almost deserted and neglected tangle of jungle profusion like a botanical Pompeii." The center piece is Angkor Wat, still a functioning temple.

The great ruins have been described better than I can ever hope to describe them, so I won't dwell on them. The investment conclusions are thin anyway, but it does make you appreciate how important water was to the Khmer civilization and to present-day Cambodia as well. Plentiful food from its well-watered floodplains made the great Angkor possible. Even today, Cambodia's economy is a hydraulic economy which is heavily dependent on the Tonle Sap Lake and Tonle Sap River.

The two have a unique relationship. Let's start with the lake, which is filled with fish and provides Cambodians with 75 percent of their fish and more than half of their protein intake. Tonle Sap Lake is the largest freshwater lake in Asia and the fourth-largest captive fishery in the world. The lake irrigates nearby rice paddies.

Then there is the river, which changes its flow depending on the season. During the rainy season in June, water floods the Mekong pushing water up into the lake. It reverses course again in November, as the waters recede. This is the time of a big festival in Cambodia called Bom Om Tuk, or Festival of Reversing Water.

Rivers are almost always important to the development of human societies. In Southeast Asia, the great river is the Mekong. It's vitally important to the region and remarkably different from other rivers. John Keay's *Mad About the Mekong* is a pleasure to read if you want to learn more about the river. Keay follows the Mekong Expiration Commission's historic journey up river in the nineteenth century, interspersing it with modern-day observations.

As Keay points out, the river crosses through six countries, unlike most major rivers, such as the Mississippi, Yangtze, or Nile, that flow through one or two countries. Along about a third of its length, it serves as an international border. Unlike other rivers, it did not unite those living along it, nor did it historically bear much traffic. The Mekong is extremely difficult to navigate. Until recently, no bridge ever spanned it. We didn't even know its exact source until 1994, when a French adventurer found a bubbling spring more than 16,000 feet above sea level in a pass in eastern Tibet.

The rich sediment of the Mekong, though, feeds a great many people. As Key writes, "A cup of Turkish coffee, heavily sugared, has less sediment per cubic centimeter. In its suspended grit, modern propeller screws get so quickly blunted that riverside repair shops offer a regrinding and replacement service. To offload this sediment, a sludge of mica and minerals from Tibet, Yunnanese phosphates, nitrogenous Burmese clays, and leafy loams from Laos . . . it deposits its burden in a silk-glistening tilth of prime growing potential."

The delta has belonged to Cambodia for centuries but now belongs to the Vietnamese. That's our last stop on our Southeast Asian tour.

Vietnam: A Country, Not a War

In recent years, there has been a great deal of interest in Vietnam from investors. Why? Well, Vietnam has a large, young population—86 million people (the thirteenth-largest in the world), with about half under 25 years old. The country is slipping out of its communist shell, a process that began with doi moi (the renovation) in 1986, a tilt toward more open markets that saw the light of day when Le Quean, the head of the communist party, died.

There is a perception, rightly or wrongly, that Vietnam is the next China, a booming market soaking up resources and consumer goods, buying banking services and cell phones with gusto. Investors love a good story. In 2006, the Vietnamese market went up 145 percent and 50 percent the next year. The problem is that investing there has never been easy (it fell 70 percent in 2008) and still isn't. Karber writes about the billions slated for Vietnam but how only a fraction makes it through the bureaucracy. "In the manner of a simple guest house in Saigon," Karber tell us, "the investor was required to have almost 100 permits."

Finally, perhaps the interest has something to do with the unique historical relationship with the United States that goes back to the Vietnam War (or American War, as it is called here).

Already, Vietnam has made a number of remarkable transformations, which are hard to ignore. One of the books I read ahead of my trip is *Vietnam: Rising Dragon* by BBC correspondent Bill Hayton. Again, you see the same patterns repeat. "Vietnam is in the middle of a revolution," Hayton writes, "capitalism is flooding into a nominally communist society, fields are disappearing under new industrial parks, villagers are flocking to booming cities. . . . It's one of the most breathtaking periods of social change anywhere, ever."

The nudge toward markets opened up huge untapped potential within the country. For instance, Vietnam was an importer of rice in the 1970s and 1980s. But following the privatization of land and markets, farmers looked to improve their yields since they could keep more of the profits. Better seeds and irrigation led to huge gains in crop yields. Vietnam enjoys food security and is the second-largest exporter of rice after Thailand. (The story of the demise of the collectives is told well by Hayton.) The rich Delta yields two to three crops per year.

I started in Saigon, a hot, polluted, chaotic, emerging market city if there ever was one. Evidence of petty capitalism is everywhere. On seemingly every corner stood someone selling street food. A charcoal grill spread with pork and chicken, a bahn mi stand, a pho stall, it seems you can't walk a block without running into one. Then there are the fruit and vegetable carts loaded with the abundance of the delta. You never go hungry in Saigon.

You quickly learn, though, that this is still a country dominated by the government. The largest companies are state-owned enterprises (SOEs). Despite selling off SOEs in recent years, there are still large plums in the state's embrace. Moreover, the government has a hand in nearly everything.

I met with Marc Djandji at the Coffee Bean & Tea Leaf on the corner of Thai Van Lung and Le Thanh Ton. Marc is the Canadian-born head of research at Viet Capital Securities, which has won a shelf of awards for its equity coverage of Vietnamese stocks.

Marc has been in country since 2003. The stock market of Vietnam was only set up in 2000, with only 14 listed companies at the time. There are almost 700, though there are a lot of small companies with $500K or $1 million market caps that wind up being orphans. The practical universe is about 35 to 40 companies. They get all the attention.

"The valuations are getting more and more attractive," Marc told me. "But I talk to a lot of foreign investors, and nobody is pulling the trigger." Vietnam has issues, such as rampant inflation of about 20 percent while I was there. Then there are worries about the banking system and what losses it may be hiding.

The big opportunity in Vietnam is the potential sale of plum government businesses to private investors (so-called equitizations or what we'd call privatizations). This has been put on the back burner since 2008, but there is talk of getting it back on track because the government needs the money. "It's always been about getting Vietnam Airlines and Mobilphone, the crown jewels," Marc told me. "Maybe 2012 for the airlines and telecom. . . . "

This is what foreign investors are looking for. "The government has to sell out these crown jewels," Marc says, "and they need to sell out a good chunk of it so that government does not have a controlling interest. The government has to let go. That's a hard thing for a country that believes it can control everything."

There are other opportunities in Vietnam's supply chain. "Investing anywhere across the supply chain to facilitate the moving of goods and agriculture is a good opportunity right now," Marc said. "Let's just take a look at the agriculture sector. The storage facilities in the country are in such a state that 10 to 20 percent of goods are lost to spoilage, which is a huge economic loss. So, we are seeing some companies putting in better storage facilities, rice silos, cold storage, and things like this."

The big rice exporting companies are just aggregators, collecting the rice from small farmers. But they are all paying spot because they don't have rice silos. (Spot prices are what the market will pay for immediate delivery. Futures prices are what the market will pay for rice out a number of months. Usually a market has both prices, and buyers and sellers transact along the curve. This doesn't seem the case in Vietnam, at least not on the scale it should for a market this size.) If they did, they could sit on the rice for up to a year, and it would make for a better market. Farmers could have greater control over when they sell and at what prices.

The other catalyst here is the 20 percent inflation rate. "If it comes down, then you could get a nice lift for valuations," Marc said. He is long-term bullish on Vietnam but worried about the near term. "I need to see more from the government that it will tackle the inflation problem. And the question is how much it comes down, 10 percent, 15 percent. . . . It matters."

We talked about how the Vietnamese are buying gold and paying premiums of 9 to 11 percent over the world price because of import restrictions. With inflation so high, one place to protect your wealth is gold. Vietnam is one of the highest per capita consumers of gold in the world.

I headed north to stop in Hanoi and visit contacts there. For the most part, I got the same kind of story.

Hanoi: City of Lakes

Hanoi is one of the fastest-growing cities in the world. Situated on the bank of the Red River and dabbed with 17 lakes, Hanoi seems to have more open space and greenery, which lend it a certain enchantment. The traffic is horrendous, though, with seas of motorcycles and many cars honking and weaving their way impossibly through thickets of other cars and motorcycles. There are about 6.5 million people here, and there is a motorcycle for every two of them. The roads can't handle it.

It's hard to imagine that when the French left in 1954, the smoldering city had one quarter of its housing stock impaired and only 300,000 residents. Even then, it was overcrowded for the infrastructure in place. By the 1960s, American bombers badly damaged Hanoi. Yet somehow there are many French colonial buildings still standing.

The pollution was among the worst I've experienced in Southeast Asia. I didn't need to see any statistics. I could smell it. You could see people wearing masks on their motorcycles, a probably futile attempt to inhale less exhaust fumes. The skies over Hanoi are often smoky, like some brooding capital in Northern Europe.

Beyond air pollution, the city suffers from poor wastewater management. Those lakes may look pretty from afar. But get a closer look and you'll see piles of floating garbage and patches of dead fish. Officials are beginning to crack down on pollution, but it's going to take some time. These are problems all rapidly growing and industrializing emerging market cities face. Cleaning it all up will be an opportunity for investors over the years in companies engaged not only in clean energy, but that tackle the issue of clean water.

Whatever happens, Hanoi will endure. It is a testament to Vietnamese sovereignty and has been the capital for over a thousand years.

Vietnam is one of the countries that history tells us one should not invade. This goes beyond the American experience. The Chinese have tried many times before. "For over 2,000 years," Phil Karber wrote, "China has tested the sovereignty of Vietnam. Time and again, they have been repulsed. The Mongol armies of Kublai Khan, arguably the most powerful empire in history, went home empty-handed from Vietnam."

Wars were the farthest thing from my mind, though, as I slipped into the comforts of the Sofitel Metropole, one of the world's great hotels, which first opened its doors in 1901. Somerset Maugham stayed here in 1923 to finish his book *The Gentleman in the Parlour*, an account of his travels in Southeast Asia. (There is a suite named after him at the hotel.) Maugham rendered a tough judgment on Hanoi:

"Here I had the intention of finishing this book for at Hanoi I found nothing much to interest me. It is the capital of Tonkin, and the French tell you it is the most attractive town in the East, but when you ask them why, they answer that it is exactly like a town, Montpelier or Grenoble, in France."

I came here, too, to finish this book. It is a wondrous thing to be cocooned in this hotel, an oasis from the noise, crowds, and pollution just outside its doors. I didn't want to leave. This is a place of great history. Noel Coward, Graham Greene, and Charlie Chaplin are among the prominent guests and residents at the hotel. Among all the teak wood and ceiling fans and posh service (the hotel employees charmingly address you in French, "Bonjour, monsieur!"), you can drift back to the golden age of travel. There is even a pair of classic 1956 Citroens out front if you are feeling nostalgic for a lost age (and want to spend some money).

By the poolside bar, I met with a contact of my contacts in Hanoi.

"Welcome to Vietnam," he said. "Your timing is no good."

I am withholding his name at his request. He is close to the prime minister and others of political power in Vietnam, and I wanted him to be able to talk freely. As it happened, I don't think he said anything controversial. "Vietnam is in a very dangerous situation where you have huge budget deficits and high inflation," he said, reiterating what it seemed everyone knew. "And I am not sure that the prime minister has the willingness to fight inflation. Vietnam will probably suffer a lot."

The SOEs soaked up a lot of capital, spent freely, often in unrelated lines of business, and took on tons of debt. People are wondering how and if they can pay it all back. It's a wait-and-see market.

"This is a good time for patient long-term investors, with 5- to 10-year time horizons to start thinking about what they want to buy. In 2007, prices were too high, and we didn't buy anything," he said, speaking of his group's investment activities, which buys whole companies. "Now, you can buy the same assets for a fifth of what it would cost you in 2007, if you have the political capital to make the deal. You need government support. You can't buy anything without government support."

He said, echoing what I heard elsewhere, that something bad is going to happen, but timing is uncertain, as it often is. Vietnam had a great run, but there is some trouble to work through. My swing through Vietnam didn't uncover an investment thesis that I wanted to act on anytime soon, so I'm not going to spend as much time on Vietnam as I might. But I still wanted to include it in this book, because I think Vietnam, over the longer term, will be an important market, and I think it illustrates more of the trends we've been talking about in this book to this point.

After all, this was a country in tatters in the 1970s. Today, it is a bustling emerging market. You can travel around safely, eat well, and stay in nice places, all relatively cheaply. There is much to see and do. The country has changed a lot in a relatively brief span of time, and such change is at the heart of what this book is about, something we've seen recur in history.

The Adventures of Mr. Shaplen

In the 1950s, Japan was the hot story. In the postwar era, Japan's economy began to industrialize in a big way. Investments poured in from all over the world. Steel mills, power plants, and factories sprouted up like bean plants. Japan soon became a big producer of ships, electronics, petrochemicals, photographic equipment, synthetic fibers, and automobiles.

The Japanese people moved from rural areas to the cities in large numbers. The population of Tokyo, for example, more than doubled in less than 10 years. With that came a hunger for new consumer goods. People ate better, which is always the first thing to change. But these new consumers coveted the goods that make life easier, such as washing machines, refrigerators, and television sets.

In fact, demand was so high for these three goods that people called them the "three electric treasures." Sales of washing machines quadrupled in the years 1953–1955. Then sales doubled again in 1956. The number of TVs went up nearly fivefold in the 1957, and the number doubled again in 1958.

Yet while this was going on, there were still a lot of growing pains. There was still widespread poverty. Masses of people huddled in tiny apartments. Sewage facilities were inadequate. Water was often unsafe to drink. Traffic was terrible since road building couldn't keep up with the ballooning number of cars on the road. Pollution was a big problem.

Does this sound familiar? It could easily be China or any number of emerging markets today.

I owe these observations on Japan to the late Robert Shaplen, a longtime Asia correspondent. Shaplen first arrived in Asia in 1944, near Leyte, in the Philippines. He was a war correspondent with the 1st Cavalry Division, and he landed on a beach softened up by U.S. Navy artillery. Walking through the surf, Shaplen recalls the acrid smoke and shattered coconut trees. What a way to begin a long tour in Asia. But his departure was even more dramatic. In 1975, he would leave from Saigon aboard a Sea Stallion helicopter flown by U.S. Marines taking communist rocket and small-arms fire near the American defense compound at Tan Son Nhut Air Base.

In between these poles, Shaplen managed 30 years of distinguished reporting on the Far East as a *New Yorker* correspondent. I've read pieces of his *A Turning Wheel* (the 1979 edition). It's a summary of his 30-year tour of duty in the Far East, based on thousands of interviews and his own research and observations traipsing throughout Asia over that time.

In his book, Shaplen has striking observations about that other superstar of the period: South Korea. "Seoul became Asia's biggest boomtown," Shaplen writes, "a throbbing metropolis of 7.5 million (one-fifth of the South's population) and the hub of what was probably the fastest-developing nation in the world except for the petroleum powers."

The pattern of development was the same. A man living in Seoul then saw the factories sprout out of nowhere. In came the steel mills, cement plants, and shipyards. He saw apartments and high-rise office buildings and industrial centers fill the city blocks. He watched the massive migration of people from the farms and villages to the cities. New subways and hotels opened. It became hard to find an empty taxi, and good restaurants stayed crowded until 10 at night. People got richer. Per capita income in 1977 was four times what it had been 10 years before.

As for this sudden and surprising nature of change, let me end this section with a note on Singapore, which is the regional financial center for Southeast Asia. It is, as some say, the Asian Switzerland with its low taxes and status as a haven for the wealthy. There are other similarities as well: low crime, rule of law, and good infrastructure to name a few. Both places have few natural resources and no military influence.

As Lars Tvede wrote, Singapore is far richer. "Today the country has not only caught up with Switzerland in most senses, it is now actually pulling quickly ahead." Singapore's wealth per capita is higher. "It was therefore no coincidence that it was Singapore that during the recent crisis came to the rescue of the Swiss giant bank UBS, which Singaporeans now sometimes as a friendly joke refer to as "Union Bank of Singapore" How things change!"

The next big story in Southeast Asia will probably be Myanmar, formerly Burma. At a restaurant on the riverfront in Phnom Penh, I met with two French brothers who are active in buying real estate in Yangon (the old Rangoon). They were excited about the place and found much to like—but that is a story (and a trip) for another day.

I think Southeast Asia will be on more investors' radar screens in the years ahead.

Five Key Takeaways

- Doug Barnett's Thai Focused Equity Fund is a great way to invest in Thailand with a proven investor who eats his own cooking. Visit his website at www.questthai.com/, where you will find shareholder letters and useful information on the Thai market.
- Check out Leopard Capital at www.leopardasia.com/. You can read past newsletters for free, and they make for fascinating reading You'll get a window into a world of opportunities you didn't know existed.
- For Vietnam (and Marc Djandji's latest commentary) check out Viet Capital Securities website where all their research is currently free www.vcsc.com.vn/default.aspx.
- There are a few good books I recommend on the region. *The Indochina Chronicles: Travels in Laos, Cambodia and Vietnam* by Phil Karber is one of my favorites. It's filled with history, cultural insights, colorful characters, and touching vignettes stemming from the war years. For Bangkok, William Warren's *Bangkok* is a compact, readable narrative tracing the outlines of the city's development written by a long-time expat who's lived there for 50 years.
- To explore Vietnam further, read *Vietnam: Rising Dragon* by BBC correspondent, Bill Hayton. *Mad About the Mekong* by John Keay is a good history focused on the exploration of the Mekong River.

CHAPTER 11

Other Places, Other Opportunities: Mongolia, Argentina, Russia, Turkey, and Central Asia

We're coming close to the end of our globe-trotting investment field trip. There are many more markets and many more opportunities we won't be able to visit this time around. They will have to wait. Nevertheless, there are a few more markets that I want to tell you about before we make our way back home.

Let's start in the "Land of the Blue Sky."

The story of Mongolia's resurgence is mouthwatering for investors for one reason. Mongolia is rich in natural resources, and it sits next to the world's most voracious consumer of those resources, China.

Beneath Mongolia's rugged mountains and slumbering sands lie huge untapped resources of copper, coal, gold, uranium, iron ore, oil, and more, only recently discovered. In 2010, this country exported about $2 billion worth of minerals. But based on mining project startups, exports ought to grow to $20–80 billion per year. That's a 10- to 40-fold increase in just a couple of years. Some $30–50 billion in new investments are set to flow to this economy in the next few years.

But there is a long way to go. Production of coal, iron ore, and crude oil should rise ten fold over the next 10 years. The 10 largest deposits are worth over $1.3 trillion. For perspective, Mongolia has a $4.5 billion economy. (Yes, billion.)

Oyu Tolgoi is one of those big deposits. It is the world's largest new copper and gold mine, with some 80 billion pounds of copper and 46 million ounces of gold. It is a joint venture between Ivanhoe Mines and Rio Tinto. Here is the mind-boggling part: This one mine will represent about 30 percent of Mongolia's economy when it starts producing. Just one mine.

Another big one is Tavan Tolgoi, which is in what may be the largest undeveloped coking coal district in the world, with more than 6 billion tonnes of coal. These are staggering piles of wealth for a nation of only 3 million people. Some believe these resources could turn Mongolia into another Qatar or Norway.

Qatar is an example of a country that got rich after exploiting a massive natural resource. In Qatar, it was natural gas. The Qatari stock market went from $4 billion in 1998 to $104 billion by 2010—a 27-fold increase.

Another example is Kazakhstan, as Brad Farquhar, my friend from Saskatchewan, points out. We will hear more from Brad in the next chapter on Canada, in which we'll look at his canola fund and Saskatchwan farmland. In addition, Farquhar has an interest in Mongolia and has been making regular investing field trips there, enthralled by the opportunity he sees there.

"The Kazakhstan stock market went from something like a billion-dollar market cap to $100 billion in eight years," he writes:

Mongolia, I think, is on a faster growth track with a more diverse resource base. It has better logistics to access markets in China, Eastern Russia, Japan, and Korea than Kazakhstan. Plus, Mongolia is a free and open democracy. For what it's worth, Mongolia's president has photos of Ronald Reagan and Margaret Thatcher on his office wall. In addition, the Mongolian stock market surpassed the $1 billion market cap mark in 2011.

That stock market was the best performing in the world in 2010, up 125 percent. My guess is that it is only the beginning of a long bull market. Eurasia Capital estimates that Mongolia will be the fastest-growing economy in the world over the next decade.

The Mongolian currency, the tugrik, has been among the world's best-performing currencies against the dollar. Farquhar sent me a neat little stack of fresh Mongolian tugriks. It's colorful money. The blue-green five spot features Sükhbaatar, an important figure from Mongolian's struggle for independence in 1921. On the reverse side is a pastoral scene of horses eating grass with mountains in the background.

"I went to Mongolia last summer," our correspondent continues:

I came home convinced that the country will do incredibly well over the next decade. In order to try it out myself, I opened an account on the Mongolian Stock Exchange in early November, and I have been searching out companies on other global exchanges that have significant Mongolian exposure. In the first four months, my own Mongolia-specific portfolio is up 84 percent, and I have some friends and colleagues clamoring to get in.

So, Farquhar decided to open up his own "super-exclusive Mongolia-focused micro-hedge fund."

Other opportunities should occur, too, outside of mining. Mongolia will need to double its power output in the next five years at a cost of at least $2 billion. It needs highways and railroads. All that mining will require water. Mongolia has water in deep aquifers beneath its deserts, and there are northern rivers it could divert, but all this, too, costs money. Somebody has put all that together.

In fact, one group is focusing on everything but mining. Mongolia Growth Group is a recently formed company trading on the Pink Sheets. It intends to invest in real estate, industrial, and service companies in Mongolia.

The company had an interesting beginning. It started with Harris Kupperman, who was running a hedge fund. He took a trip to Mongolia in the summer of 2010, poking around for investment ideas. Bowled over by what he found, Kupperman started Mongolia Growth Group and moved to Ulan Bator. "The Mongolian economy is far more robust than I had ever imagined," he writes. "Unable to find an ideal way to invest in Mongolia, I have instead set out to build my own diversified entity." He eats his own cooking, too, as Kupperman and his management team own 58 percent of the company.

I caught up with Kupperman by phone. He was in Ulan Bator. I was in Maryland. It was 1 a.m. for him. "Welcome to finance in Mongolia," Harris told me, a veteran of many wee-hour conversations.

Kupperman reiterates that Mongolia is a place of rich mineral wealth. "Every time someone puts a shovel in the ground, they seem to find something valuable," Harris said. But Harris isn't playing the commodity boom. The mining companies tend to be fairly valued and well covered. Instead, Harris looks to play trends in real estate and finance, places that ought to prosper as people have more money. This seems a good idea.

In fact, the reason for my call to Harris was a piece in *The Wall Street Journal* noting how luxury brands such as Louis Vuitton, Burberry, Zegna, Emporio, Armani, and Hugo Boss all have stores in Ulan Bator. Burberry plans a second store in the Shangri-La Hotel, currently under construction. Ferragamo and Dunhill are looking to open stores. This in a place that doesn't even have street names and only recently introduced ZIP codes.

Something big is going on. Harris looked at buying existing Mongolian companies but has since given up. They are impossible to figure out.

He tells some funny anecdotes about meeting with Mongolian companies. One CEO was so happy to see him, he posed for pictures. He had never had investors visit before. Then there was the time he was thrown out of somebody's office for asking for a copy of the financials. Or the time when they gave him their latest figures from 2007. Or the time when the company couldn't even tell him how many shares were outstanding. Or the CEO he met who was most proud of the production awards the plant won in the 1960s under Soviet rule. Or the time he asked a company why he hadn't received the stated dividend. They told him to drive 500 miles to the mine and pick up the check himself.

Nonetheless, Harris bought a basket on the theory that if Mongolia did well, it'd do well. Still, Harris wanted to put more money to work, so he started his own company.

"We're buying about $1 million of property a week," Harris told me at the time. They are cherry-picking the best assets. On the residential property, you can get double-digit yields, but if you spend a little money to make it look nice, you can get 20 percent yields. And prices are increasing 2 to 3 percent per month. Rental rates have doubled in two years.

Harris told me the story of a $400,000 property sale settled in cash. The seller was a little old lady, about 4'2" and weighing 95 pounds. Harris arrived with a large brick of money. When the closing was all done, she put the money in a bag and walked out. "I offered to drive her home," he said, "but she thought that was crazy. It's really very safe here." I can only imagine that woman tottering out in the street with $400,000 in a shopping bag.

Real estate is probably the most exciting thing MGG is doing. "When another fund comes along to replicate what we're doing, these assets won't be there," he said. Harris pointed out how small an area downtown was. Harris knows of funds being raised in the hundreds of millions to buy real estate there, and as the money came in, prices had to rise. "The only way for yields to get to 5 percent here, as in the rest of the world, is for prices to triple."

MGG got its insurance license for its wholly owned insurer, Mandal General Insurance. The first policy underwritten will be Harris' SUV. There is tremendous demand for insurance. MGG was getting calls before they even had their license. Today, Mandal General is a 17-employee operation with $5 million in capital.

The beauty of insurance, as Warren Buffett famously profited from, is its ability to generate "float," or the upfront cash from the premiums collected. Until claims are paid, this float is MGG's to invest. Harris is a proven investor. His hedge fund is up over twenty fold since its inception in 2003, and I suspect his ability to invest this float is a big cherry atop the MGG financial sundae. "In a market in which structured debt products routinely yield better than 20 percent and where rental properties earn double-digit yields," Harris writes in his latest shareholder letter, "I am hopeful that we can produce very attractive returns on this float."

MGG is super shareholder friendly. Harris takes no salary and no stock options. He makes money only if the stock goes up. He put $3.5 million of his own money in MGG and owns 17 percent of the company. His board includes noteworthy investors, such as Bill Fleckenstein (who owns nearly 9 percent of the company).

Next up for MGG? Harris says the company is near profitability. He wants to start paying a regular dividend to show investors what they are doing is real. He aims to list on the Toronto Stock Exchange. "There is a huge secular tail wind under way," Harris sums up. "This tail wind will go on for decades, and the assets are simply not priced for the upside that we see."

To sum up: Mongolia has waited a long time for another turn at bat in a big game. In the thirteenth century, Mongolia was the seat of the largest territorial empire the world had ever known. The hordes erupted out of Central Asia, conquered Russia, China, and most of the Middle East. (Only the powerful armies of the Mamluks of Egypt checked the hordes' advance at the Battle of Ain Jalut.) Pax Mongolica reigned until the arrival of the Black Death. As far as the rest of history goes, Mongolia hasn't registered much since.

Thanks to its mineral wealth, it looks like Mongolia will enjoy another turn on the big stage with the eyes of the world watching, and some getting rich, besides.

Argentina: Ruining a Good Thing

"There's an old expression in my family, in every Argentine family," my guide Maria told us as we zipped down a new freeway heading out of Buenos Aires to a town called Tortugas. "Buy the bricks . . . always buy the bricks."

In that little nugget lies the key to successful investing in Argentina, or anywhere, for that matter, where holding cash for any significant length of time is problematic.

The Argentines have learned the hard way. In 2002, the peso was on par with the dollar, one for one. Today, that exchange rate is closer to four pesos for $1. Put another way, the peso has lost about 75 percent of its value against the dollar in 10 years.

If you had money in the bank denominated in Argentine pesos, such as a certificate of deposit, a bank account or other paper assets, you lost big.

To preserve wealth in that environment, where the currency is flaming out like a lit match, you needed to own tangible things. "Buy the bricks" refers to buying houses and buildings. When Maria's family got some extra money, they'd put it into a house.

More broadly, though, we can think about it in terms of buying tangible assets: land, precious metals, vineyards, timberlands, oil in the ground, or what have you.

In Tortugas, I met a businessman and investor who had interests in real estate properties and retail operations. He was a partner in a private investment firm. Federico took us to his house, one of the original group built in this development 60 years ago. We had drinks while sitting on his back porch, which looked out on a beautiful garden and pool. Federico was frank in his assessment of Argentina.

"Argentina, the piece of land itself, is a paradise on Earth," he told me. It is rich in natural resources, plentiful green land, lots of trees and water, a long growing season, and no hurricanes or snowstorms. It seems to have everything. The problem has been the government. Federico said doing business in Argentina is "like spending all day with God, only to have dinner with the devil."

Argentina was once among the richest countries in the world, and Buenos Aires among its most sophisticated and cosmopolitan cities. As late as the 1920s, its only rival in the Western Hemisphere was New York. There was a large, educated middle class in Buenos Aires. There was the grandeur of its Beaux-Arts architecture. It had the largest opera house and the finest newspapers and universities in Latin America. It has fallen a long way since.

Walking around the city, one can easily imagine how great and wealthy this city once was. There are reminders everywhere: beautiful European-style buildings, broad avenues and plazas, and narrow, cobbled side streets lined with cafes and small shops. It is sad to think of the opportunity wasted. This place should truly be among the richest cities on Earth.

Federico, though, had not yet given up hope. "Argentina is a country of the future," he said. "There is plenty of opportunity here."

Later, Federico took us on a helicopter ride over Tortugas, which is only about 20 minutes from Buenos Aires. There is a freeway that connects Buenos Aires with suburban towns like Tortugas. Federico pointed out the large swaths of land and trees in the area. "Imagine what it could be," he said. He told us of projects in the works or in the planning stages: houses, shopping centers, golf courses, and more.

There is tremendous potential here. It's a developer's dream, with lots of land, water, mature trees, relatively flat country. It is a palette of possibility.

Real estate is cheap. With what it costs to rent an apartment in London, you could buy 10 in Buenos Aires. That's why Americans and Europeans have been among the most active buyers of property in Argentina. They are real estate bubble refugees, you might say. They cashed out of their expensive and inflated properties in the United States and Europe, and then they came down here and lived like kings. The inflated prices deflated, and these people look particularly smart.

The effects are tangible on the streets on Buenos Aires: busy restaurants, packed seaside resorts, and all the usual trappings of prosperity.

When in Argentina, I traveled around rural areas in Salta. I spent some time at a ranch and viewed properties owned by American and European investors seeking to develop them into residential communities, golf courses, vineyards, and more.

There are some 60,000 acres here at this ranch. It has livestock and grows alfalfa, tobacco, and corn. This place was owned by a group of overseas investors who had plans to carve off lots and develop the property while maintaining it as a working ranch.

Besides the potential for development, the agricultural lands out here should grow increasingly valuable. As I've written elsewhere, several factors are fueling a boom in the agricultural markets. Argentina and South America should prosper from these trends. Argentina is one of the great food-producing countries in the world, with cereal, sugar, fruit, wine, tea, and cotton among the crops grown there. Finally, Argentina is a big producer of beef.

This creates opportunities through the back door, like in fertilizers and farm equipment. I couldn't help but notice the ranch's small fleet of John Deere tractors. Basic infrastructure is vital. Water resources are critical for any kind of agricultural concern. Cafayate has plenty of water. The owner of the property proudly told me several times about the abundance of water on the property and his ownership of the rights.

In other places, clean water is a concern. In San Rafael; for example, a region that produces 70 percent of Argentina's wines, as well as olives and other fruit, there was concern over pollution affecting the water and soil.

Politicians can get in the way of the best ideas with wars, stupid policies, taxes, and excessive regulation. And talking to people there, there is a wary sense about how the government will screw it up again. The basic problem with government there, and nearly everywhere, is that there is too much of it.

In Cafayate, which sits in a valley surrounded by rugged, red-speckled mountains, I walked a property owned by investors who have a compelling vision for what could be. It doesn't take a lot of imagination to see how property here would be an attractive place for expats to buy a second home, a place to escape the cold winter months, or just as a place to come recharge your batteries and get away from it all.

Cafayate is wine country. The weather is pleasant with 320 days of sunshine a year. There is plenty of water. We visited a vineyard and plucked juicy, flavorful grapes right off the vine. I'd never tasted grapes with so much flavor.

Development is still in the early stages. Ultimately, Cafayate will have a golf course, hotels, and more to cater to a growing stream of tourists and snowbirds. They will live well for little money. One night, we had a dinner party of eight. We drank wine and ate appetizers and steak. The bill was almost laughably low, about $70. Later, we had six beers and coffee for a total of $7.

The next day, we met with some gauchos and rode horses through the lush ranch in Salta.

The gauchos are some tough hombres and good with horses, as you might expect. We were riding through a lush ranch in Salta, Argentina. The gauchos wore what looked like slippers, not at all like the long leather boots American cowboys wear. They were small men compared with the average American, but tough as leather. Their clothing had seen many hard days under the sun, and they wore long knives behind their backs tucked under their belts.

This American investor was able to buy the land at good prices because the Argentines had been through such a nasty crisis that they couldn't wait to unload it. It's as if they'd been wandering in an economic wasteland so awful that when an American came waving some cash under their noses, they could scarcely believe it. Their first instinct was to take the money and run.

Every place has its special genius, its unique gift. In the Pampas, the wide fertile plains of South America, that gift is climate. The growing season is long. It's a great place to grow things. Corn. Tobacco. Alfalfa. Soybeans. This particular ranch had it all, as well as heads of cattle and pigs. In fact, we sampled the latter. Later that evening, we enjoyed a traditional asado, which consists of a variety of grilled meats cooked over an open wood fire. The pig we ate was killed the day before. It was a terrific meal.

You could scarcely imagine a place with more natural advantages. Will Argentina make it back to the big time? I have my doubts, but the potential is there.

Mother Russia: Full of Surprises

Investing in Russia [is] like entering a rich gold field studded with land mines: laced with veins of rich treasure and riddled with pockets of pure poison.

—Mark Mobius, *Passport to Profits*

In Russia, he who draws the longest bow makes the rules. The powerful and the powerless square off every day—even in the trivial matter of simply getting from one town to the next.

In his fascinating book, *Murderers in Mausoleums*, Jeffrey Tayler travels the back roads from Moscow to Beijing. (The murderers in mausoleums are Lenin in Red Square and Mao in Tiananmen Square.) As Tayler makes his way across Russia, he notes, at one point, that of the four hours he's been on the road, he's spent at least an hour and a half at six or seven checkpoints along the way. Russian law requires everyone in Russia to carry ID papers in public. Tayler seems to be constantly dealing with officials checking his papers, stamping them, and soaking him for bribes.

Riding shotgun with Tayler, you pick up a lot of anecdotes and snap-shots of life in Russia. You appreciate what a seething boil of ethnic tensions exists in parts of Russia. Some of these small republics within the Russian Federation are home to dozens of ethnic groups and languages. They are marked by age-old blood feuds and outbreaks of violence and crime. You come to appreciate how bleak life in Russia is for a lot of people.

Russia has more incidences of tuberculosis and HIV than anywhere else in Europe. Drugs and drinking are serious health problems. Regular terrorist attacks and disasters seem to be happening, killing hundreds at a time: the Kursk submarine disaster (118 dead), the incident at the Dubrovka Theater in Moscow (at least 129 hostages dead), and the hostage situation at a school in Beslan (at least 385 dead). Perhaps it is not surprising that the life expect-ancy of a Russian male is only 58 years, the lowest in the developed world.

Russia's population falls by about 700,000 people every year. Demogra-phers predict that Russia could slip to only 100 million people, from 143 mil-lion currently, by 2050. By objective measures such as health statistics and life expectancy, life in Russia is miserable and hard for most.

Yet Russia holds undeniable investment appeal, despite the perils. As the old Russian proverb says, "It's not the horse that draws the cart, but the oats."

It was only 2004 when investors lost their shirts in Yukos, the biggest oil company in Russia. The Russian government seized Yukos for back taxes totaling more than $30 billion. The move was widely regarded as a political act, checking the ambitions of its billionaire CEO. Investors howled, but at the end of the day, foreign investors lost over $6 billion.

You would think after that experience, any mention of Russia would be like (as P.G. Wodehouse once wrote) trying to cheer up Napoleon by talk-ing about winter sports in Moscow. You would think Russia's mere name would hurl investors into alternating fits of rage and despair. Not so. Inves-tors are forgiving, or forgetful, or both.

State-owned oil giant OAO Rosneft went public in 2006. What makes this all the worse is that this, in part, is the old Yukos. Rosneft is the company the government folded Yukos into. In other words, it stole this asset from investors and then turned around and sold it back in an initial public offering.

Why the enduring attraction to Russia? Russia's magnetism can be summed up in two words: "cheap assets."

Russia is still the largest country in the world, in terms of land area. The expanse covers 11 time zones and nearly every conceivable type of land-scape, from frozen tundra to hot deserts, from lush, wet lowlands to high, dry mountains, from dense forests to open plains.

And buried amid all that are rich veins of natural resources, Russia is a veritable storehouse of Mother Nature's useful goodies. Russia is the largest, or among the largest, producer of palladium, platinum, diamonds, nickel, and gold. Russia is rich in oil and gas. Rosneft, for example, has more proven oil reserves than Exxon Mobil. It's bigger than any oil company in the world on this basis, save for its sister company Lukoil. It is the world's biggest producer of natural gas.

Eric Kraus is our man in Moscow, where he is a money manager. We'd only swapped emails before, so I was glad to finally meet him in person at the Agora Financial Investment Symposium in Vancouver. I liked his presentation, which included some surprising ideas on Russia.

For instance, of all the ballyhooed BRIC countries, Brazil, Russia, India, and China, do you know which market has done the best over the last decade? Russia. See Figure 11.1.

Now, many people, including me, had worries about investing in Russian companies. As I mentioned above, we all remember what happened to Yukos.

Our Western sensibilities, though, cloud our vision on Russia, said Kraus. A big part of his message in Vancouver was to say that the Western orthodoxy of free markets, democracy, and transparency has little to do with picking winners in the market. The chart above makes that clear. As Kraus put it, "Ideologically driven disinformation can cost you a fortune."

Still, Kraus used a lot of words you don't normally associate with Russia. Kraus described Russia as "very low risk" with "stable macroeconomics and

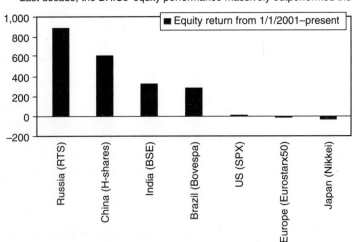

FIGURE 11.1 Russia: Best BRIC of the Past Decade
Source: GS Global ECS Research.

politics . . . where reform is going on far faster than Europe, but slower than Asia." Russia is "by far, the wealthiest of the BRIC countries," Kraus said.

He called it "a middle-income, moderately high-growth (5 percent) middle European country with the world's largest resource base." It has abundant oil and gas but lots of farmland and fresh water and hydropower. Once one of the world's largest grain importers, it is a top exporter.

Russia has plenty of cash, the world's third-largest foreign currency reserves. Poverty has been cut way down. So things actually look pretty good for Russia. "Of course, the Western press hates it!" Kraus said. "If you have a long-term time horizon, Russia is a no-brainer." The easiest way to buy Russia is to buy the Market Vectors Russia ETF, which trades under the ticker RSX on the NYSE.

Kraus is particularly bullish on Russia, not only because he thinks the shares are cheap, but because he believes the price of many commodities will rise. "Peak Oil is a mathematical certainty," he said. Not in the sense that we are going to run out of oil, but that prices will rise as we reach for more expensive sources of oil.

"And it's not just oil," he continued. "Grades of copper, nickel, and bauxite ores are now being mined, which no one would have bothered digging up a couple of decades ago . . . peak water! A lot of places are running dry, and this will have scary effects upon agricultural prices.

"The predominance of the West is an anomaly in history," Kraus went on, echoing the thesis of this book. "It ended with the turn of the millennium." It is a "multipolar world" in ideas and commodities. Instead of the traditional New York–London axis, the economic world will spin on different poles from Beijing to São Paulo.

Central Asia: History's Geographical Pivot

Ukraine and Russia had a nasty spat in 2009, as Russia cut off natural gas supplies to a host of European countries. Tired of relying on Russia, the European Union looked for alternatives. Its eyes wandered to Turkmenistan.

In October 2008, while the world was busy putting out the fires of a financial crisis that still burns, little-thought-of Turkmenistan made a bombshell of an announcement. It seemed to gather little notice at the time. But Gaffney, Cline & Associates, a British consulting firm, completed an audit of Turkmenistan's Yoloten-Osman natural gas deposits. Based on GCA's first results, the fields have a minimum of 4 trillion cubic meters of gas and as much as 14 trillion cubic meters of gas, a truly staggering sum. The announcement put Yoloten-Osman among the four or five largest natural gas fields in the world.

The country's biggest field was Daulatabad, a rich and extraordinary field in its own right. Yoloten-Osman is at least five times as large. Turkmenistan has many gas fields not yet explored.

"Without doubt," the *Asia Times* weighed in, "Turkmenistan is closing its gap with Russia and Iran, hitherto listed as having the world's largest and second-largest gas reserves. . . . If the GCA results are confirmed, Turkmenistan will have reserves just 20 percent lower than that of Russia and outstrip Iran by far."

Turkmenistan has the potential to rival Russia's clout in natural gas and provide an alternative for Europe. By creating a pipeline from Turkmenistan, through Azerbaijan, Georgia, and onto Turkey, the European Union could bypass Russia entirely.

You can be sure the Russians won't like that. Again, from the *Asia Times*: "[Russia] is no longer the superpower in the world of natural gas, as was widely regarded. . . . Turkmenistan is, unquestionably, a gas superpower of comparable muscle power to Russia."

The effort to bypass Russia via a southern route is an old game. Tamerlane, the fourteenth-century conqueror of Central Asia, wanted to do the same thing when he sought to divert trade from the northern Silk Road, controlled by the Golden Horde, to a more southerly course through Bukhara and Samarkand (in present-day Uzbekistan).

Today, the five Islamic republics that were once part of the Soviet Union are back on the center stage of geopolitics. Kazakhstan, Kyrgyzstan, Tajikistan, Turkmenistan, and Uzbekistan all have huge oil and gas reserves. The names sound odd today, perhaps. But someday, Americans will get to know their names as well as they know those of Iran, Iraq, and Afghanistan.

The race is on to court these countries of the steppe, taiga, and desert. In this, China may have a lead, as it often seems to when it comes to securing energy supplies. Beijing offered to finance a pipeline through which natural gas would flow from Central Asia to China. It's doing its best to cozy up to the fab five.

Russia, too, is close to them. Russia relies on Turkmen gas to meet its obligations to Europe, for instance. But the powers that be in old Ashgabat have been sticking it to Russia. They're making Russia pay up for its gas supplies. In 2007, Ashgabat raised the price to $100, from $65, per 1,000 cubic meters. Then in 2008, the price went to $130 and to $150 by June. Today, Russia is paying about $250.

As the *Asia Times* remarked, "Russia will have to rework its bonding with its Central Asian partners." It's as if Turkmenistan drew an ace face up, and Moscow is sweating a bit. Turkmenistan has more clout to peddle with eager Americans, Europeans, and the Chinese, who all want Turkmen gas and the opportunity to build out the infrastructure. Russia will have to play the game like everyone else. Turkmenistan is in the driver's seat.

This story goes beyond just Turkmenistan, which is why I relate it to you. It looks like Central Asia will become a grand chessboard of sorts. Some have long seen the region as a key to world commerce and global influence. The first was a British geographer named Halford John Mackinder, widely regarded as one of the founding fathers of geopolitics.

In 1904, Mackinder submitted a paper to the Royal Geographical Society titled "The Geographical Pivot of History." In it, he developed his "Heartland Theory," in which he defended the idea that Central Asia would be the seat of global power. Mackinder thought that the Eurasian heartland would come to dominate the fringes, or coastal regions, of the world with the invention of the transcontinental railroad. He thought the Eurasian heartland would be the "geographical pivot of history."

It didn't turn out quite that way. Today, sea and air power dominate. Most of the world's manufacturing and wealth continues to be found on the oceanic fringes. In fact, over half of the world's population lives within 60 miles of a coastline.

Still, was Mackinder wrong? Authors Ronald Findlay and Kevin H. O'Rourke offer their perspective in their book *Power and Plenty.* "The railroad has not overtaken the steamship as he imagined it would," they write of Mackinder, "but the oil and natural gas pipelines of the world, so necessary to sustain all that coastal manufacturing, are increasingly running overland across Central Asia."

Central Asia, or the Heartland, as Mackinder called it, once again finds that the lifeblood of the West's mighty industry flows over its steppes. "In turn," Findlay and O'Rourke finish up, "this vital overland trade is raising familiar problems of control over bottlenecks and monopoly power."

Maybe Mackinder was right after all, in a sense. He was just about 100 years too early.

Turkish Delights

In northern Iraq, there is the Zagros oil belt, which holds the super-giant Kirkuk field. All around this area in northern Iraq, Iran, Syria, and southeastern Turkey lie rich, prospective, and productive oil fields.

The Selmo oil field, for example, has produced 85 million barrels of oil in its life, the second most in Turkey. Discovered by Mobil in 1964, there are an estimated 600 million barrels of oil in place. Then there are many other prospects and leads in this mostly unexplored country.

The Selmo oil field is 100 percent owned by Trans-Atlantic Petroleum (TAT:amex). It owns other prospective acreage all around southeastern Turkey. I'm not saying that the Turkish acreage is of the same size or as oil rich, as that in Iraq. But Turkey is largely unexplored and offers a big upside and is much safer.

Turkey has abundant natural gas embedded in shale, as in the United States, but the hydraulic fracturing technology is new in Turkey. Trans-Atlantic was the first company to frack a well there. So the idea is that Trans-Atlantic can create the same kind of boom enjoyed by the U.S. shale producers.

Trans-Atlantic, though, enjoys some major benefits over its U.S. brethren, beyond the fact that it has little competition and operates in virginal territory. (Trans-Atlantic's CEO and largest shareholder, Malone Mitchell, said that the level of development in Turkey is like that of the Permian Basin in Texas in 1938. Read: Lots of upside.) Natural gas in Turkey fetches prices more than double those of the United States since Turkey must import to feed most of its growing energy needs. There is no glut in Turkey; the market is tight.

It may be helpful here to say a few words about Turkey, which is fascinating in its own right.

First, let me say that the Turkey of today has about as much in common with the Turkey of 10 years ago as rigatoni con la pajata has with moo goo gai pan. Ten years ago, Turkey was a basket case, waist-high in debt with spiraling inflation, busted banks, and unstable politics.

Today, it is an economically resilient place. It suffered in the 2009 recession, but it bounced back and grew faster than any EU country. From 2002 to 2008, its economy grew by about 6 percent per year.

Young people are economic catalysts, and Turkey is a young country of 72 million people. The average age is only 29 years, compared with 40 for the European Union. About 60 percent of the population is under the age of 35. Demographers predict it will have over 100 million people by 2050, making it the most populous country in Europe.

Foreign investment is flowing in. In the bad old days, investments used to get about $1 billion a year. Today, it's closer to $20 billion a year. Turkish companies make all kinds of things: cars, furniture, shoes, televisions, and cement (of which it is the world's largest exporter). Some call it the "China of Europe" because of its many busy workshops. It is the world's sixteenth-largest economy.

As you might imagine, Turkey's appetite for energy, in particular for natural gas has risen. You can see in Figure 11.2, courtesy of Mazama Science.

You can see the consumption bar stepping up over time. There is no discernible production line because Turkey produces so little, hence the big, yawning net imports. Natural gas is Turkey's fastest-growing energy source.

Overall, the rise in energy consumption reflects the pattern of industrialization we've seen time and time again in China, Brazil, India, and many other places. This big deficit makes energy investing in Turkey attractive

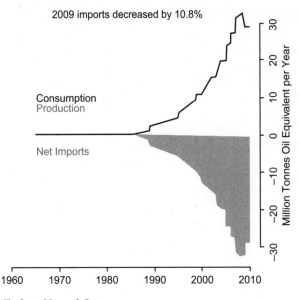

FIGURE 11.2 Turkey: Natural Gas

Source: BP Statistical Review 2010.

because it will welcome you with open arms. Taxes and royalties in Turkey are low because it would like to encourage investment.

Jonathan Callahan at Mazama Science points to Turkey's geographical importance as a transit country. "Turkey has long occupied an exceedingly important geographic location: the bridge between East and West," he writes. "The Anatolian peninsula is centrally located between Asia, Africa, and Europe."

That too has helped fuel investment. As way stations along the new Silk Road, once-drowsy towns are springing to life. Read this passage from an *Economist* correspondent on the city of Gaziantep, the sixth-largest in Turkey, with a population of 1.3 million people:

> *Until recently, Gaziantep (Antep, for short) was a sleepy, poor, provincial town. A smattering of tourists were drawn by its fortress, its ancient history, the Roman mosaics of Zeugma, the Euphrates River, a few old Armenian churches and houses, and its traditional produce of pistachios, hazelnuts, and what it claims to be the world's best baklava (a sticky pastry).*

Antep suffered the same ailments as much of "old Turkey." The roads were poor. The city was up to its eyeballs in debt. Unemployment was high. Its best days seemed well behind it. (The city is known for its valiant stand against French forces in 1921. Even though the city fell, its heroics earned it the honorific "Gazi," or "warrior.")

Today, Antep is booming. Its factories churn out carpets, shoes, packaging, and many other goods. The city ships out more than $4 billion worth of exports per year. The airport is busy. The roads are better. The government offers liberal tax cuts and incentives.

All of this forms the backdrop for Trans-Atlantic Petroleum, whose prize assets are in its huge acreage in largely untapped Turkey.

The other key part of the Trans-Atlantic story is the aforementioned Malone Mitchell, who studied agriculture at Oklahoma State University. It was fellow alum T. Boone Pickens who got him interested in oil and gas. Today, both are rich men with fortunes built on getting oil and gas out of the Earth.

Mitchell made his bundle by building up a company called Riata Energy. He started with a $500 loan in 1984. It became one of the nation's largest privately owned drillers. In 2006, he sold a 46 percent stake to Tom Ward for $500 million. You might know of this company as Sand Ridge Energy. Then Mitchell sold the rest of what he owned in Sand Ridge in 2008 for another $500 million.

Mitchell has seen it all in the oil and gas business, seven busts and six booms over nearly three decades. He's proven adept at navigating the ups and downs of the business. He had the foresight to sell his holdings in 2006 and 2008 while the going was good. What he did with that money was prescient. Trans-Atlantic has been public since 2007. It is Mitchell's latest investment vehicle in the oil and gas business. And he has an idea of how to get rich all over again.

This Oklahoma oilman, who cut his teeth in the oil and gas fields in Colorado and West Texas, decided to go abroad. In an interview with *The Energy Report* in March 2009, Mitchell explained his thinking:

> *We started looking about a year and a half to two years ago more seriously at the international market. For the last 20 years, we've seen prospects come to us that, typically, had a number of things in common. There had been a few wells drilled by a large oil company 20 years ago that had what would be considered by U.S. standards very good oil and gas shows, but that had not led to full-scale development by the large company.*

Mitchell was intrigued. He studied a number of foreign countries and prospects. He started to form some ideas on what he wanted. He wanted to be in a country that was a big importer of oil and natural gas, so the local powers would look favorably on new domestic supplies, and so he would have an eager and nearby market for his product.

Mitchell focused on areas that allow licensing, rather than production-sharing agreements." This means you can own your reserves," he says. He looked for stable governments and low taxes and royalties. Mitchell sought out large acreage positions where he could make big finds. "I like finding oil and gas," he says. And that's a good thing for investors, because that's where the big money comes from, finding new fields. Mitchell is looking to hit home runs, not singles and doubles.

Mitchell loves Turkey. It is virgin territory. "Drilling onshore in Turkey is like going back in time 50 years," he says. "During the last upswing in Texas, there were over 800 drilling rigs running. In either Turkey or Romania, you may have no more than 10 rigs capable of drilling at any one time. The level of development here is comparable to the Permian Basin in Texas in 1938."

He's bringing modern techniques to these new markets, including "fracking" that process of injecting water and sand down a well to break up rock and release gas. That has become something of a lightning rod in the United States, where people worry about the groundwater. Not so in Turkey.

Most of the big players aren't looking at big finds onshore. They are busy looking to grab a piece of Turkey's share of the Black Sea. They think the onshore stuff isn't big enough.

Mitchell thinks otherwise. As he says, Trans-Atlantic owns the second-largest oil field in Turkey. "It's been developed on a density basis of about 5 percent of what any comparable field and reservoir would be in the U.S., so we'll have the opportunity to see if our deeds can match our words."

Given Mitchell's track record, I wouldn't doubt it.

Economic Impressionism in the Dark Corners

Robert Smith has spent more than 30 years traveling to some of the most troubled economies in the world. Smith and his firm, Turan Corp., trade debt in battered economies. In his book *Riches Among the Ruins: Adventures in the Dark Corners of the Global Economy*, Smith recounts his experiences in the nascent debt markets of El Salvador, Vietnam, Nigeria, and other tricky places.

For example, Smith was working in Saigon during the Vietnam War. "On nights when the occasional VC rocket would land near my apartment," he writes, "I'd climb under my bed, where I kept an M-1 rifle I never fired, and wait for things to quiet down."

Smith's adventures make for entertaining reading, but you get a sense for how the world's markets have changed. Vietnam is a vibrant, emerging market, which we saw in an earlier chapter. And when Smith started in the 1980s, the global debt trade for emerging markets was less than $300 million a year. Today, it's nearly $2 trillion a year. Today's markets are sophisticated, electronic, and global.

Smith's methods are worth keeping in mind. He relied on what he calls "economic impressionism." It's a fancy word for old-fashioned detective work. It's how he learns about a country, by talking to bankers, business-men, diplomats, and money-changers. "My education about a country . . . began at the airport," he writes, "and continued in the cab as I picked the brains of the driver."

It's not scientific, but his ground-floor view made him lots of money over the years. In my own investing, I've always put a premium on such on-the-ground views and primary sources. (Economists and market strategists babbling away about charts and what they found while grazing on the Inter-net hold no interest for me.) Smith's success is something to remember as you weigh the research and information you read in making your invest-ment decisions.

Smith's inspirational perspective shows how staying ahead of changes in markets at the fringe and not getting stuck in outdated views can help seed a fortune.

Five Key Takeaways

- Mongolia is an exciting market in the early phases of a long, steep growth curve. Check out Mongolia Growth Group at www .mongoliagrowthgroup.com.
- Argentina is a wonderful place to visit. Buenos Aires is a great city, and if you want to explore a little further afield, I recommend La Estancia de Cafayate. Find out more here: www.laestanciadecafayate .com/.
- Russia is another fascinating market to follow. Keep an eye on the RTS as a proxy for that market. Eric Kraus is my favorite commenta-tor on Russia. You'll find his work here: www.truthandbeauty.ru/.
- Turkey has many opportunities in oil and gas. Trans-Atlantic Petro-leum (TAT:amex) is a great play on that idea.
- Mackinder's lecture is worth reading for the historically minded. Tayler's *Murderers in Mausoleums* and Smith's *Riches Among the Ruins* are fun and informative reads.

CHAPTER 12

Canada: A Breadbasket's Great Comeback

O nce flyover country, Saskatchewan is a focal point in Canada's growing economy. So I couldn't resist dropping in on this resource-rich province. It has become an agricultural power.

Many things come from this one province of Canada that many Americans would have a hard time finding on a map. (Brad Farquhar, who we will hear from shortly, relates the following story: "Once on a flight from Memphis to New Orleans, I sat next to southern woman who asked me where I was from. I told her Saskatchewan. When I told her it was north of Montana and North Dakota, she said to me, [with southern drawl] "Son, there ain't nothin" north of North Dakota!") Yet, Saskatchewan makes up a large percentage of the world's exports in a number of goods:

- 67 percent of the world's lentils
- 56 percent of the world's peas
- 25 percent of the world's mustard
- 40 percent of the world's flaxseed
- 18 percent of the world's canola
- 33 percent of the world's durum

As far as natural resources go, fortune has smiled broadly on this land between the forty-ninth and sixtieth parallels. It is the world's largest producer of uranium and potash. The former is a critical component in the "nuclear renaissance." The latter is a key fertilizer. It is rich in oil and gas.

These resources have produced abundant cash flows, which you can see in the tax records. At a time when governments everywhere faced gaping budget shortfalls, Saskatchewan has been awash in cash. In 2008, when the financial crisis hit, the province reported a $3.1 billion surplus on a budget of $9.4 billion. Not needing so much money, the government announced the largest cut in personal income taxes in its history. It paid off 40 percent of its provincial debt. Prudently, the government decided to sit on a $2 billion cash cushion, just in case. Today, the government still maintains a surplus, although not nearly as large as in 2008.

Now, once-sleepy Regina is coming into its own as the commercial hub of Canada's hottest economy. Regina reminded me of Omaha, another city in a prairie-ocean. The downtown is small, and the city looks and feels mostly new.

I stayed at the elegant Hotel Saskatchewan. Its Manitoba Tyndall stone façade and richly appointed interior are a piece of history, built by the Canadian Pacific Railroad in 1927. Down the street, I saw the headquarters of Viterra, a leading grain handler and processor. Around the corner, a new 20-story office tower was in the works as new headquarters for the fertilizer giant Mosaic.

Brad Farquhar, vice president and partner of Assiniboia Capital, showed me around. (You may remember him from our brief visit with Mongolia). I also met with Doug Emsley, co-founder and president of Assiniboia. I first started writing about Saskatchewan's farmland in 2008. After my first story, Brad wrote to me. That was in November 2008, and we've been correspondents ever since. I'll have more on Assiniboia in this chapter, but first, let's investigate how far Saskatchewan has come.

From the beginning, people had large ambitions for the province. They thought the population would grow by millions of people and that Saskatchewan would be a great breadbasket, a thriving new land. It didn't work out that way. Today, the population of the province is only about 1 million people.

The legislative building in Regina reflects what people thought that it would be. It is a massive building, completed in 1912. It's a big building for the province, even today. In fact, it is the largest capital building in Canada. But events, man-made and natural, would thwart those early ambitions.

The Great Depression hit Saskatchewan with particular force, as it did the American prairie states. Beginning in 1929, Saskatchewan suffered through nine consecutive years of drought and crop failure. The province suffered what must be one of the biggest declines in income suffered by any people anywhere during peacetime. "Incredibly," writer Edward McCourt tells us in his book *Saskatchewan*, "the net agricultural income for 1931 and 1932 were reported in minus figures."

I have a minor hobby interest in the implosion of the 1930s, so I had to explore this a bit further. A reporter in 1934 described the landscape in southern Saskatchewan as "lifeless as ashes . . . for miles, there was scarcely a thing growing to be seen." He went on:

> *Gaunt cattle and horses with little save their skins to cover their bones stalked about the denuded acres, weakly seeking to crop the malign French*

weed which seemed to be maintain some sickly growth. . . . The few people in evidence in the little towns appeared haggard and hopeless.

I can only imagine how difficult it must have been to carve out a living in this unyielding landscape. It reminds us that no matter how good things look, any agricultural enterprise is at the mercy of the weather.

The Great Depression would have a long-lasting effect. It helped push Saskatchewan politics decisively collectivist. The government would clamp down on enterprise for decades afterward, including a decision in 1975 to nationalize the potash industry. It only recently started to go the other way and loosen up.

Our conversation on these matters led Brad to muse: "In some ways, this place is only now starting to get out from under the effects of the Great Depression."

Today, the trend is more toward opening up for business. The province, as I pointed out earlier, runs a surplus, virtually unheard-of in governments today, and maintains a AAA rating. Moreover, because of that long, moribund period from the Great Depression until just recently, large chunks of Saskatchewan's resource-rich land remain untapped.

And that helps explain Assiniboia Capital's success here, too. Brad and Emsley had a good idea and fortunate timing. They saw an opportunity opening up in Saskatchewan farmland, thanks to the relaxing of restrictive rules on farm ownership. (For a time, non-Saskatchewan Canadians couldn't own Saskatchewan farmland.) From 1974 to 2003, you had to be a resident to own farmland.

"During this period, Saskatchewan was a net exporter of people," Farquhar's prospectus points out. "It was a province whose population was in decline." Doing away with these restrictive ownership requirements in 2003 has unlocked some of the value. Annual declines in farmland values immediately began to reverse.

Double Your Money on Cropland

Brad and Doug saw 55 million acres of opportunity in Saskatchewan. Almost half of all the farmland in Canada is found in its golden prairies. Wheat, canola, and barley represent three-quarters of the crop acres in the province. So they started Assiniboia with the idea of investing in farmland. Today, the company is the largest farmland fund in Canada, with over 110,000 acres managed and owned.

Saskatchewan farmland has a lot of ground to make up, though. Only 22 years ago, farmland here was more valuable than in neighboring Manitoba. But today, Manitoba's farmland is more than 50 percent higher than

Saskatchewan's. The Saskatchewan discount is attracting ranchers and grain farmers from neighboring Alberta, as well as immigrants from abroad. The government of Saskatchewan actually has a fast-track program in place to assist immigrants looking to farm in the province.

Statistics compiled by the Canadian government show that the average farmer in Saskatchewan is 52 years old. That leads Assiniboia's team to conclude in its prospectus: "The aging farming population in Saskatchewan has created a buying opportunity that [we] believe may not return for another generation." Brad adds that the average age of Saskatchewan farmers (53) is not out of line with the rest of Canada, and is in fact less than in the USA (55.3 years). "The challenge is the drop in the number of younger farmers as a percentage of the whole." This next generation is less interested in farming. The older generation will, in many cases, have to sell to folks beyond kith and kin. Folks like investors in Assiniboia.

Assiniboia's farmland LP has delivered superb returns so far. At inception in December of 2007, the NAV of the fund was $25 per unit. By October 31, 2011, the NAV was $41.48 per unit.

That doesn't include $2.37 in distributions made along the way through December. Brad likes to call farmland "gold with yield," because farmland prices tend to correlate with gold, but it pays its investors income. All told, that's a 75 percent return since late 2007, during a time when the U.S. stock market has been firmly in the red.

Even now, Saskatchewan farmland is still a bargain, trading at a significant discount to its neighbors on a per acre basis (Figure 12.1).

Crop prices still promise a good return for farmers, but financing is harder to acquire. Farming is a capital-intensive business. You need to spend a lot of money before you see a dime. So farmers often put off expansion simply because money is tight.

Say you were a farmer in Saskatchewan, and you wanted to add acres to your farm to take advantage of market prices. You'd have to purchase or rent more land. You'd probably need new tractors and combines to handle the extra workload. You'd need more on-farm storage. You'd need fertilizer, seed, and chemicals.

How much would all that cost? Brad Farquhar said it is normal for farming expansion to cost $150–$300 per acre. That means a 2,000-acre expansion needs an investment of $300,000–$600,000. (Those costs do not include land costs. Buying the land would add another $400 to $1,500 per acre in cost.)

Some farmers have the financial capacity to do that on their own, but most typically turn to a local bank or credit union. In the credit crisis meltdown days, it was tough for anybody to get a loan. Credit is not as easy as it was in the balmy days of no-doc loans and no money down.

So while a farmer could make an extra $100 an acre in revenues for every $30–50 an acre spent in fertilizer, he doesn't necessarily do it. In fact,

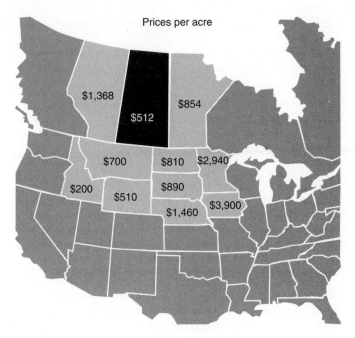

FIGURE 12.1 Saskatchewan Farmland Is Still a Bargain!

Source: Assiniboia Capital.

farmers cut back on fertilizer in the meltdown days, from which we are rebounding. Then, too, there are timing issues. Nitrogen fertilizer is often cheapest in July, right when farmers have maxed out on their borrowing capacity. That means that they can't take advantage of the lower prices.

These funding gaps are where Brad's Assiniboia steps in to fill the void. They provide the funding as an investor, with the profits shared between the farmer and Assiniboia. The firm has a simple truism as its mantra: "The returns are highest where capital is scarce." Saskatchewan farming (and agriculture generally, at least at the farm level) is one such place.

You'd think something like this would have evolved sooner. But it was a new concept when the firm began approaching farmers in 2009. As Brad describes it, after a lot of time at farmers' kitchen tables and hundreds of cups of coffee later, farmers began to sign up for Assiniboia's program.

Canola: Canada's Most Valuable Cash Crop

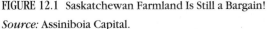

His firm is high on canola. Why canola? The heart of canola country is right in Assiniboia's backyard, in Saskatchewan. It's like the Silicon Valley of canola. Brad points out that "recent genetic developments are pushing yields to whole new levels." These breakthroughs are happening in Saskatchewan and lead to better economics.

Peter Phillips of the University of Saskatchewan calls canola "one of our visible and uniquely Canadian success stories." About 20 percent of the world's production comes from Canada, which is eager to ship to drought-parched China. Last year's exports there topped $1.8 billion. It's currently a $15.4 billion industry, surpassing wheat. And Brad's investors have a direct play.

Brad's firm ran a pilot program in 2009 on about 25,000 acres. Even though it suffered through an incredibly wet summer in 2010, the partnership broke even, proving the durability of the model. It remains an attractive and more aggressive way to investing in farming.

"Average crops should provide good returns, but any above-average production or commodity price makes the return numbers take off," Brad says. "And the majority of the downside is covered by crop insurance. So it's like having a perpetual call option on canola."

Brad prepared the next chart, which shows a few scenarios of how a share in his limited partnership (LP) might fare depending on crop yield and price. You can see that a low yield and a low price make for a poor result. But the range of outcomes skews to the upside. A bumper crop and a strong price could hand you a 101 percent gain. (Note: In Figure 12.2, "bu" stands for bushel.)

One other thing I like about this model is that farmers have skin in the game. About half or more of the profits will go to them, so they have every incentive to make it work.

Brad drove me over to a canola farm. It's beautiful, flat country. We walked around to check out the canola crop. Along the way, we stopped to scope out the red lentil crop coming in.

Just to see it all, touch it, and walk on it, the experience makes everything more real. It's no longer just numbers I imagine when I think about Saskatchewan farmland. I'll think about how this summer's yellow blooms

Crop	Farmer Average Yield per Acre	Actual Yield per Acre	Price	Net Value of LP Share per Acre	Pre-Tax Rate of Return*
Canola	31 bu	35 bu (Good Yield)	$9.00/bu Average Price	$112.59	+12.59%
Canola	31 bu	24 bu Low Yield	$8.00/bu Low Price	$ 86.40	(13.60%)
Canola	31 bu	45bu Bumper Crop	$15.00 Very Strong Price	$ 201.15	101.15%

*Returns presented here are net of management fees.

FIGURE 12.2 How Canola Can Boost Your Portfolio

Source: Assiniboia Capital.

will turn into green pods, with their small, narrow seeds. How the seed will go off to the local crusher. I'll remember these plains. This farm. (Investors have a tendency to get lost in abstractions. Stocks become only ticker symbols, and they don't think about what they own, what those shares represent. I've always tried to resist that kind of abstracting.)

Having seen it for myself, I think the boom in Saskatchewan farmland still has lots of legs.

The Topsoil Crisis

Taking the long view, we are running out of dirt.
—David R. Montgomery, geologist

The world needs to boost its production of food. The United Nations estimates that the world will need to boost investment in agriculture by $83 billion a year, that's a 50 percent annual increase—to feed a growing population. Its estimate may prove an errant shot from an uncertain bow into an unpredictable future. But it doesn't matter. Investing is more like horseshoes and hand grenades, as the old saying goes; close counts.

If the United Nations is half-right—others have done similar work with similar conclusions—then we're talking about a healthy bull market in all things green. The question is where does the boost in production largely come from? One answer is Brazil, as we discussed in another chapter of this book. However, Saskatchewan is part of that food equation, too.

Quality soil is the thing in demand. The world continues to deplete its base of arable land. Until the final decades of the twentieth century, the amount of new farm acreage added to the mix by clearing land offset the losses on a global basis. In the 1980s, the amount of land under cultivation began to fall for the first time since humble early humanity began to farm the rich land around the Tigris and Euphrates. It continues to fall today.

Though it's been going on for some time, the dramatic blows are showing their effect. In East and North Africa, in the plains of India all the way to Turkey, the story is the same. Some of it is just human carelessness about the land. Some of it is climate-driven: the declining snow melts of the Himalayas and more-frequent crop-killing heat waves in places such as India.

Climate change has been going on for a long time, too. As Peter Matthiessen points out in *The Snow Leopard*, the Gobi Desert was once fertile. In Central Asia, he writes, "broad lakes vanished in dry pans, and grasslands turned into shifting sands." Many of these changes happened in only a few hundred years. "The death of a civilization can come quickly; the change in climate that dried up rivers and destroyed the savannas of the central Sahara scattered the great pastoral civilizations of [Africa] in just a few centuries after 2500 B.C."

Such changes impact economics as well. We are close to passing some giant milestones. China is the largest net importer of soybeans in the world. A mere 15 years ago, it made more than it needed and exported soybeans. Some think that India could import as much as 2 million metric tons, the most in the world. Traditionally, India has been the world's third-largest exporter.

During the summer 2008 grain crunch, Iran bought a large amount— more than 1 million tons—of wheat from the United States. That's something we'd not seen in 27 summers. In Iran's case, a tough drought cut the wheat harvest by a third, forcing the country to look abroad. Nevertheless, the fact that Iran had to come to the United States is telling. It's like Lee asking Grant for rations in the summer of 1863. As one analyst put it: "Do you think Iran would come to the United States if they had any place else they could buy it. . . . They're searching the world for wheat. They're buying from the United States because it's the only thing they can buy."

Markets, like great, unscripted dramas, develop their own plotlines as time rolls on. The new drama surrounds the fewer options for importers looking for large quantities of high-quality grains. But it points to a deeper issue: the emerging shortage in fertile soil. Yes, we're running out of good dirt.

In fact, fertile soil, good dirt, may become more important to land values than oil or minerals in the ground. Some say it is a strategic asset on par with oil. As Lennart Båge, former president of a U.N. fund for agricultural development, says, "Now fertile land with access to water has become a strategic asset."

Doubtful? Consider rising export restrictions around the globe, which act as a sort of fence keeping the goods within borders. India curbed exports on rice. The Ukraine halted wheat shipments altogether. The number of grain-exporting regions has dwindled, like the vanishing buffalo herds. Before World War II, only Europe imported grain. South America, as recently as the 1930s, produced twice as much grain as North America. The old Soviet Union, for all its faults, exported grain. Africa was self-sufficient. Today, only three major grain exporters remain: North America, Australia, and New Zealand.

It is no surprise, then, to find faith in the global food supply at generational lows. So begins the scramble to secure farmland. Saudi Arabia, for example, is particularly at the mercy of the winds of global agriculture. It has little ability to produce its own food. "The kingdom," reports the *Financial Times*, "is scouring the globe for fertile lands in a search that has taken Saudi officials to Sudan, Ukraine, Pakistan, and Thailand." Saudi Arabia's quest is not one it pursues alone. There are many hunters.

The UAE has been looking to lock down acreage in Sudan and Kazakh-stan. Libya wants to lease Ukrainian farms. South Korea pokes around in Mongolia. Even China is exploring farmland investments in Southeast Asia. You'll recall that China does have plenty of cultivable land, just not plenty of water.

"This is a new trend within the global food crisis," says Joachim von Braun, the director of the International Food Policy Research Institute. "The dominant force today is security of food supplies." Food prices reflect this crimp in supply.

The mainstream press focuses on issues such as population, dietary shifts, and the impact of biofuels. One thing that doesn't get talked about much may be the most important thing of all: a growing shortage of quality topsoil. Call it the topsoil crisis.

Quality soil is loose, clumpy, filled with air pockets, and teeming with life. It's a complex micro-ecosystem all its own. On average, the planet has little more than three feet of topsoil spread over its surface. The *Seattle Post-Intelligencer* calls it "the shallow skin of nutrient-rich matter that sustains most of our food."

The problem is that we're losing it faster than we can replace it. And replacing it isn't easy. It grows back an inch or two over hundreds of years.

This is not lost on certain far-seeing investors. Jeremy Grantham, the curmudgeonly head of the money manager GMO, wrote about soil deple-tion in a recent quarterly letter. "Our farmers are in the mining business! Yes, the soil is incredibly deep, but it is still finite." For every bushel of wheat produced, we lose two bushels of topsoil.

Erosion, development, and desertification eat away our topsoil. "Globally, it's clear we are eroding soils at a rate much faster than they can form," notes John Reganold, a soils scientist at Washington State University. Estimates vary. In the United States, the National Academy of Sciences says we're losing it 10 times faster than it's being replaced. The United Nations says that on a global basis, the rate of loss is 10 to 100 times faster than that of replacement.

In any case, it seems safe to say that good dirt is in short supply. The obvious investment conclusion: Buy farmland.

A firm called Agcapita prepared this little graphic (Figure 12.3) that sum-marizes where we are in terms of arable land per person. For the first time, we're in danger of slipping below one acre per person.

We don't need 2.8 acres per person anymore because of advancements in agriculture over time. Over the past 40 years, we've increased the yield per acre by 2.1 percent percent per year. But the pace of those gains is slow-ing. Since 2000, the increase in yields per acre has averaged less than 1 per-cent per year.

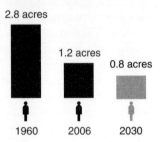

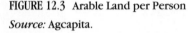

FIGURE 12.3 Arable Land per Person
Source: Agcapita.

We may see new innovations in seeds or other technology that we can scarcely imagine. But it seems that any solution would take some time and money to implement. Meanwhile, the world's agriculture markets get tighter and tighter.

In 1974, the cereal crop consumption was about 1,500 bushels per second. Today, it's 2,600 bushels per second. So, we have a double effect here. We have increasing population with an increasing amount of consumption per person. Agcapita estimates that cereal crop consumption will double again over the next 20 years. The pressure on the global food supply network is enormous. This again is a reflection of people eating better and eating more meat, which requires exponentially more grains to produce.

There is another wrinkle to the story. And that is that most every oil-consuming country has put in place biofuel targets. These nations include the United States, the European Union, Canada, Japan, Brazil, India, and China. To meet their targets, according to work by Agcapita, we'll have to commit some 240 million acres to biofuel production. That represents about 50 percent of the arable land in North America. Or you can look at it as 6 percent of all arable land in the world. The biofuel craze puts further pressures on farmland demand.

Outpace Inflation with Farmland Investing

The other appealing aspect of farmland is how well it did in the inflationary environment of the 1970s (see Figure 12.4). If you believe that we will continue to feel the bane of inflation, as I do, then farmland's performance in the 1970s will give you some comfort.

So you see that while you lost half of your money in the S&P 500, your farmland kept its value nicely. Again, I think that's rooted in the fact that farmland is intrinsically useful.

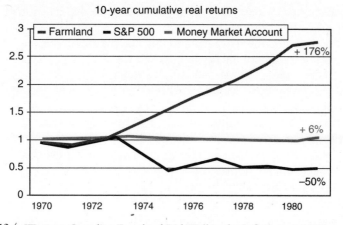

FIGURE 12.4 Western Canadian Farmland Did Well in the Inflationary 1970s

Source: Agcapita.

Now imagine what farmland might do in today's climate. We have not only the likely prospect of inflation, but a tightening supply of farmland and rising demand for its crops. I imagine you'll do quite a bit better than the 1970s vintage.

There's another way to reap the value of good soil: Own farming assets in grain-exporting countries. We'll explore a couple of ideas in a bit, but first, let's tackle another big challenge in expanding crop production.

The Case for Pulses

Yet another obstacle to increased food production has to do with water restraints. Some of the largest cities and population centers happen to be in areas with little water, like China's urban north.

This creates water-based food bubbles. A water-based food bubble forms when farmers tap into more and aquifers and food production rises. But the rate of water extraction exceeds the aquifers' ability to recharge. So you have a water-based food bubble, meaning production is unsustainable and will collapse at some point as water supplies run out.

The best example of this dynamic is Saudi Arabia. For years, pumping water from aquifers allowed Saudi Arabia to be self-sufficient in food. But wheat production is collapsing as the aquifers run dry. The Saudis will soon import all of their grain needs.

According to Lester Brown at the Earth Policy Institute, Saudi Arabia is one of 18 countries with water-based food bubbles:

Altogether, more than half the world's people live in countries where water tables are falling. The politically troubled Arab Middle East is the first geographic region where grain production has peaked and begun to decline because of water shortages, even as populations continue to grow. Grain production is going down in Syria and Iraq and may soon decline in Yemen. But the largest food bubbles are in India and China.

The World Bank estimates some 175 million Indians and 130 million Chinese are fed by water-based food bubbles. That's a lot of mouths, nearly equal to the population of the United States. What happens when the aquifers run dry in China and India as they did in Saudi Arabia? I am sure you can guess the answer.

The simple fact is that we have to change some things about how we produce food, where we produce it, and the mix of what we produce. One particular crop in great shape to benefit is a group called pulses.

Pulses are crops harvested for the dry seed. They include lentils, chickpeas, peas, and a variety of beans. They are an efficient source of protein by weight, giving you almost as much protein as chicken and more than beef (Figure 12.5).

Most importantly, pulses require far less water. It takes only about 40 gallons of water to produce one pound of pulses. Compare that to the nearly 2,000 gallons of water to produce one pound of beef. Agriculture is the

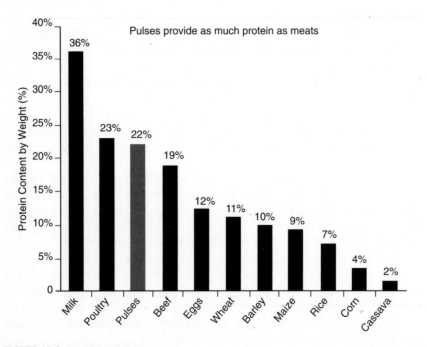

FIGURE 12.5 Eat More Pulses
Source: Alliance Grain Traders.

single-biggest user of water on the planet, accounting for about three-quarters of all water drawn from rivers, lakes, and aquifers. And across large swathes of the Earth, like China, South Asia, the Middle East and North Africa, current water extraction rates are unsustainable, as I noted above.

So this is a big deal and a giant plumed feather in pulses' humble cap.

Pulses are much cheaper than meat. It's no surprise that pulse crops are becoming a growing source of protein in emerging markets, especially those in dry regions or in places where water is problematic, such as the Middle East, India, and China.

The World Bank projects demand from emerging markets will grow to 45 million tons by 2030. Major importers such as India, Turkey, and Egypt will only import more. And China, which has been an exporter, will soon flip to a net importer of pulses. We know what happens when China becomes a net importer of something. It really juices the market. We're only in the beginning of that wave for pulses.

There is another great benefit to pulses' key to the investment thesis. Pulses have nitrogen-fixing properties. They fit well as part of a crop rotation system. By alternating pulses with wheat and canola, farmers don't have to leave the land fallow in the summer. Pulses naturally replenish nitrogen in the soil, and they thrive in the dry prairies of Saskatchewan. This reduces your need for nitrogen fertilizers. Since nitrogen fertilizers make up half the energy costs of most North American farms, planting pulses makes good sense. I would not be surprised to see the practice spread in developing countries.

So I like the long-term story on pulses. And I've found a keeper, a great way to play the pulses.

Bringing Crops from the Producer to the World

I sat down in a quiet Italian restaurant (owned by Persians) in Regina, Saskatchewan. At the table were Murad Al-Katib, the president and CEO of Alliance Grain Traders, and his older brother Omer, head of investor relations. Both were born and raised in a little town in Saskatchewan, from a family of Turkish descent. What I learned made me respect Alliance Grain Traders all the more.

The Al-Katibs are passionate about their business. I felt we could talk all day about the world of lentils, peas, chickpeas, and beans. They love this stuff, which is a good sign. They are owners. Insiders and employees own about 35 percent of the company, which I love to see as an investor. In fact, Murad started it all 10 years ago with a simple idea.

He saw that Saskatchewan farmers harvested their lentils and shipped them out raw and unprocessed, bugs, dirt, everything. Somewhere else the crop was processed, cleaned, peeled, split, polished, sorted, and so on. These activities add value.

So, Murad thought, why not process the crops here, close to the source, sell the byproduct to the feed markets, and maximize the value of the product? He wanted to capture more of that value, control the logistics, and manage those relationships with farmers and buyers.

AGT grew out of that kernel of an idea. Today, AGT is one of the largest lentil- and pea-splitting companies in the world. Its 26 facilities occupy the best pulse-growing regions in the world, primarily Canada and Turkey, but also the United States, China, and Australia. It ships pulses to 85 countries. The company's slogan captures it all: "From producer to the world."

AGT continues to grow, both organically and by making neat-fitting acquisitions. "It's like I see what the completed puzzle looks like," Murad said. "And now I just have to fit in the pieces." While I was there, AGT announced picking up another pulse processer in Australia.

I have a greater appreciation for how AGT's business works and fits together as a result of the tours and time spent with the Al-Katibs. Let me try to explain it simply.

You can imagine a raw crop that comes right off the farm. It's a long way from landing on your table. So let's look at how AGT gets more value from lentils.

AGT cleans them, peels them, and sorts them. It can sort them by size, for instance. Different-sized lentils command different prices. If you just bag them all without sorting them, you lose some value there. AGT can sort them by color and reject bad lentils. I saw this process firsthand, and I can tell you it is amazing. Imagine a machine with a carpet of lentils flying down a screen in a blur. Yet there is this optical computer sorting them, rejecting individual lentils, looking for sizes, colors, faster than you can see. In this way, AGT can "grade" its lentils, selling premium lentils in one bag and a lower grade in another, and make more money than if it just sold the bag unsorted.

AGT can split the lentils. Split lentils are easier to cook, and they command a higher price. AGT can polish them to varying degrees, which adds more value, so they can charge more. AGT even bags them. There are different kinds of bags. If you want a certain premium bag, AGT charges more. This is something the Al-Katibs hammered home: AGT performs lots of services, and for each, it charges something. This is what they mean by "value added." The term gets thrown around a lot, I know. It's kind of lost its meaning, but here you can see what it means. The things AGT does are not easy to imitate, and, clearly, alter the product.

First, you just can't buy these machines off the rack. AGT's lentil-splitting operation is proprietary. While I was there, they wouldn't let me take pictures of certain aspects of the production. Even if you could replicate the machinery, you'd need people, and this business is as much art as science. There is a need for skilled labor, of which there is something of a shortage in the province. AGT hand-picked some dozen Turkish technicians and brought them to Saskatchewan.

This is because AGT merged some time ago with Arbel (a Turkish pulse processor) and has a strong connection to that country. (The family that owned Arbel remains big investors in AGT.) The Arbel Group, operating within the AGT fold, produces pulses as well as rice, semolina, bulgur, wheat, and wheat flour. Through Arbel, AGT picked up Arbella Pasta, the third-largest-selling brand of pasta in Turkey, which is sold in 50 countries worldwide (though not in the United States). This is a natural extension of processing and milling and fits well with what AGT does. The Al-Katibs gave me some samples of the pasta, which my wife and I prepared when I got home. It was good pasta, and the kids loved it.

In short, once product leaves AGT's plant, it's ready to be used as food. This is why Murad told me AGT was "more a food story than a commodity story." And when I asked him what he thought the biggest opportunity ahead was, he didn't hesitate. It was transitioning more and more to a food ingredients company.

Remember, this is a key part of the attraction of pulses. They are low in fat, high in protein, and provide a low glycemic index; they are a good source of fiber, complex carbohydrates, vitamins, and minerals (especially potassium, phosphorous, calcium, magnesium, copper, iron, and zinc). They are relatively inexpensive and use less water to grow.

These attributes encourage food companies to add lentil flour to cereals, breads, cakes, and baby foods to bolster the nutritional value of their products. They do this to satisfy increasingly health-conscious consumers and to get a leg up on competitors. This is a trend that is only starting, and it's a huge opportunity for AGT!

These food companies are not just going to buy from anybody. You don't mess around with food ingredients. AGT provides that confidence with its top-of-the-line facilities and track record. I saw machines that would pick out pieces of metal smaller than the tip of a pencil. I watched AGT's inspectors work. They track everything, and they know the chemical composition of everything that leaves their plants down to every shipment. It's an impressive operation.

Beyond this, I want to say a few more words about AGT's informational advantage. The market for pulses is global, and accurate pricing information is a competitive asset. It's not as if there is a liquid exchange with price quotes for split lentils of a certain grade. AGT has a network that extends the world over. It uses this information to its advantage.

I asked Murad how the company makes decisions about which lentils to sell or split, for instance. The company has a lot of trading decisions it could make. It can move around in this value chain of pulses to maximize returns.

Murad told me all the decisions are made centrally. So, all the information captured every day by its processors around the world feeds back up to Regina. There, with this worldly window, AGT can decide how to buy and how to sell.

Importantly, AGT is not speculating on pulse prices. It's always covered, and it holds minimal inventory. It's more a business about capturing a spread between a raw product and a finished good.

This is not a quarterly earnings story; this is about long-term wealth creation. Murad is not going to manage this business to produce a quarterly earnings number. In fact, Murad doesn't even provide quarterly earnings guidance or any guidance at all. He doesn't play Wall Street's dumb game. And thank goodness for that. He'll manage the business as an owner because he is an owner himself. I can't stress the importance of this kind of orientation enough.

Recently, two family-owned processors of pulses and other crops merged. They merged with the idea that they would go public and use the proceeds to build a new canola-crushing plant in the United States.

According to AgCanada.com:

> *On Monday, Roy Legumex of St. Jean Baptiste, Manitoba, and Walker Seeds of Tisdale, Saskatchewan, announced their merger under the name Legumex Walker Inc. (LWI) and their filing of a preliminary prospectus for an initial public offering (IPO).*

The combined LWI becomes what's billed as "one of the largest processors of pulses and other special crops in Canada," combining Roy Legumex's plants at St. Jean, Morden and Plum Coulee, Manitoba, and Regina with Walker's processing and packaging facilities at Regina, Saskatoon, Brooksby, and Runciman, Saskatchewan, plus, a stake in a plant at Avonlea, Saskatchewan.

Brad sent me the following note on the Legumex Walker IPO:

> *I see this merger-IPO as being driven by the success of Alliance Grain Traders. AGT has been able to gobble up plants all over the world and become a dominant player because it had access to capital from the public markets. We're going to see a lot more of this as many agricultural enterprises scale beyond the ability of their founders to bootstrap them, coupled with the need of the founders to find liquidity for family and estate-planning purposes.*

I agree. And Alliance Grain Traders has a big leg up on the competition. (Legumex-Walker went public in the summer of 2011 and now trades on the Toronto Stock Exchange.)

The Toll Road for Grains

Another long-term grain play I like is Viterra. The name is new, perhaps some amalgamation of "vital" and "terra," but that is only a guess. The old name, Saskatchewan Wheat Pool, reflected its old-world trade.

Viterra is in the grain moving, storing, processing, and cleaning business. But, Viterra is not a straight-up commodity play in the sense of selling grains. You would do better to imagine a toll road. Volume is the name of the game. Volume and efficiency, not grain prices, dictate the profit profile here.

Its largest business is grain handling, chipping in 65 percent of sales. Viterra has lots of those tall grain elevators you may have seen in grain country. About two-thirds of Viterra's grains eventually head west by rail and ultimately wind up in the Asia Pacific region. So it's a fine back-door play on the booming demand in Asia and its people's rapidly evolving diets. A falling Baltic Dry Index, which measures shipping costs, bodes well for Viterra. Cheaper shipping costs make Western Canadian grain cheaper for Asian buyers.

Viterra's second-largest business is selling agricultural products, such as fertilizer, seeds, and crop protection products, as a retailer and distributor. The company has 276 retail locations across the Canadian prairies. Like any other retail business, the drivers here are volume and margin. In these two lines, Viterra is the biggest dog on the block, with 45 percent market share in Western Canada.

In the big-picture sense, Viterra's profits tie more closely with seeded acreage and the mix of crops so planted. These tend to be stable variables over time.

And just to juice up the mix a bit, Viterra has a 34 percent interest in Canadian Fertilizers Ltd. (CFL), a nitrogen fertilizer plant in Medicine Hat, Alberta. Here CFL earns a spread on the difference between fertilizer prices and natural gas. This business is not particularly significant at the moment, but it is an interesting asset, nonetheless.

Viterra has numerous options in how it uses its cash and balance sheet. These could include acquisitions, which, in a market where cash and credit are hard to come by, and may lead to some bargains among smaller, less-financed operations.

Though it has little bearing on the share price, Viterra may be the only publicly traded enterprise run by a former NFL wide receiver. Mayo Schmidt, CEO of Viterra, played wide out for the Miami Dolphins in a brief stint. More importantly, though, Schmidt deserves credit for making many great moves, such as the acquisition of Agricore in 2007. He's proving a savvy chieftain.

There are more moving parts here, but I'll simplify for the sake of brevity. The bigger picture is what I want you to focus on. In Viterra, we have a well-financed and well-managed company. It's expanded globally with a large presence in Australia and a growing presence in New Zealand and the United States. The company has big winds in its sails. The best way to think about Viterra is, again, to think of it as owning the global toll road for grains. I don't see any decline in the traffic on that toll road over the next several years.

Of Course, There's More to Canada than Saskatchewan

There is more to Canada than Saskatchewan. But as this book draws from my own personal travels and interests, Saskatchewan is where I've focused this chapter, since I think it's a story you don't hear much about.

More broadly, I think Canada will be fine in a world turned right side up. Saskatchewan is emblematic of why. It has loads of coveted natural resources, and the trend is toward unlocking that wealth. Canada has become a leading producer of a long list of commodities. (See Figure 12.6.) For investors, there are many opportunities.

Canadian companies make up an increasingly large portion of my portfolios, as Canadian markets have seeded a number of companies in oil, gas, and mining that offer compelling rewards for shareholders. What's more, Canada has produced a stable of large, globally significant players: Cameco in uranium, PotashCorp in potash, and several others.

I'd like to end the chapter with two favorites of mine, Canadian Natural Resources and Brookfield Asset Management.

Canadian Natural Resources (CNQ:nyse) is one to keep. As I write, it is a $40 billion enterprise, a behemoth in oil and gas. It is one of the largest

Canada is a leading producer of natural resources

Canada's Global Rank	
Category	Rank
Oil production	6
Natural gas	3
Electricity exports	2
Diamonds	3
Nickel	2
Uranium	1
Wheat exports	2
Water	3

FIGURE 12.6 Canada's Natural Resource Wealth

Source: EIA, Global Insight, U.S. Geological Survey, EU Energy, USDA.

producers of heavy oil in Western Canada and the second-largest producer of natural gas. It has a long history of boosting production and reserves. It has an enormous asset base to continue on such a path for many years to come. Canadian Natural's operations are low-cost and long-lived. Every quarter, the team gives a detailed view of the business that should satisfy the great stickler for disclosure.

However, there is something else special here. Its management team owns a good stake in the business. That's important. They act like owners because they are owners. Figure 12.7 makes the point.

All things being equal, you should always prefer to invest with owners, rather than management teams that own token amounts of the companies they manage. The decisions owners make are better over time.

In a similar vein, I like Brookfield Asset Management for the long-term investment. It is quite a different company. It is focused on real estate, hydropower assets, and infrastructure. Brookfield manages over $150 billion in assets for clients. Its real estate is only high-quality property in big cities like New York and Toronto. Its hydropower portfolio is one of the largest in the world, high-quality, long-lived assets that produce free cash flow and are hard to replicate. Its infrastructure assets are the key components of trade: ports, rail, pipelines, and transmission lines.

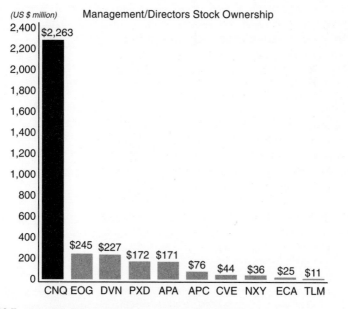

FIGURE 12.7 Canadian Natural Resources—Run by Owners

Source: SEDI and Thomas Financial.

Management has a 19 percent stake in the business. Led by CEO Bruce Flatt, it is a talented group with an exceptionally good track record, reflected in Brookfield's market-beating share price. The company is conservative, carrying lots of cash to buy when things get ugly. It's frequently made its best purchases by picking over the carcasses of busted competitors. *Canadian Business* once featured Brookfield in a memorable profile titled "A Perfect Predator." It is.

I view these two as core positions, and this chapter rich in those sorts of ideas. One could do well over the next decade by building core positions in my favorites: Alliance Grain Traders, Viterra, Canadian Natural Resources, and Brookfield, to say nothing of a position in Saskatchewan farmland.

The countries poised to grow and prosper in the next decades need all the things Canada has and does well. Canada and Saskatchewan will have great market share from MENA, China, and beyond.

Five Key Takeaways

- For more on farmland investing in Saskatchewan and lots of other good related information, visit Assiniboia's website: www.farmlandinvestor.ca/.
- Agcapita is another firm offering a wealth of information on farmland in Saskatchewan. Visit the website at www.farmland investmentpartnership.com/.
- Alliance Grain Traders is a great way to play the world's need for more food as it is the leading processor of pulses: lentils, chickpeas, peas, beans, and more.
- Viterra is another leading grain processor of commodities such as wheat and has a worldwide reach.
- Two long-term core Canadian holdings to check out: Canadian Natural Resources and Brookfield Asset Management.

CHAPTER 13

The United States of America: Home Again

Boredom lies only with the traveler's limited perception and his failure to explore deeply enough.
—William Least Heat-Moon, *Blue Highways*

Blue Highways, by William Least Heat-Moon, spent 34 weeks on the best-seller list from 1982 to 1983. He recounts a three-month road trip exploring small-town America.

When the kids were out of school for spring break, my wife and I took the family for our own mini–*Blue Highways* tour, poking around the Maryland portions of the Delmarva Peninsula. (I had my copy of *Blue Highways* tucked in my bag and I reread pieces of it along the way.) The peninsula gets its name from the three states that occupy it, Delaware, Maryland, and Virginia. We visited little towns including Berlin, Snow Hill, and Pocomoke City.

Each has deep roots in Maryland history and its own reasons for being. Berlin got its start in the 1790s. It gets its name from an old tavern called the Burleigh Inn. If you say it five times fast, you can see how over many generations "Burleigh Inn" became "Berlin." Snow Hill is even older, having been settled in the 1680s by Londoners. They named it after a favorite neighborhood back home, which explains why there is no hill anywhere (nor is there ever much snow).

We stopped off at a museum in Pocomoke City, on the banks of the Pocomoke River. Local tradition has it that the river got its name from an Algonquin word for "dark water." (I share with Heat-Moon an interest in knowing why a place came to be and why it has the name it has.) The river water is naturally tea-colored, stained by the tannic acids from the roots of the many cypress trees that grow all along its banks. It is thought to be one of the deepest rivers in the world for its width. Though dark, Pocomoke's waters are home to catfish, rockfish, bass, perch, among other things, including a long monster called a gar.

The plentiful supply of local cypress and pine formed the basis of a shipbuilding industry that boomed along the river in the late 1800s. The cypress was a prized wood as it was resistant to rot and decay. Skipjacks, schooners, bugeyes, and steamships were put together there.

That's just a snippet of the rich history along this river. The museum put me in a philosophical mood. I gazed into those black-and-white pictures, into the eyes of traders, sailors, and farmers long since dead. I wondered about what they were thinking then. All the little daily concerns that make up a life surely seem absurd with the passage of time. How might they have done things differently, I wondered, if they got to do it all over again? (I shared these thoughts with my wife. "A little deep for vacation," she said.)

All these sleepy little towns have only a few thousand people or so. Each has its own main street, peppered with antique shops, cafes, churches, and a curious mixture of Victorian-style homes and 1950s-style bungalows.

Outside the towns, we drove around mostly flat lands and farms. This area of Maryland is known for its poultry farms. You can see the long warehouse-like structures filled with birds. Perdue is the big producer out here, although I noted a small sign near a driveway that read, "Tyson."

You could smell them well before you could see them. After my commenting on the stench, my wife said, "Nothing irritates rural people more than city people coming around talking about how it smells." Maybe so. I guess you get used to it if you live out there.

These places did not seem economically prosperous on the surface. We saw a lot of homes for sale. We saw more than a few boarded-up shops. Later, I looked up some stats and found that about 15 percent of the population in these towns is below the poverty line. The median income is only $28,000–32,000, depending on the town, well below the national median of $44,000.

I reflected on this land of antique shops, B&Bs, and churches. I often get the sense, when I visit these kinds of towns, that they were once thriving and busy places, and that today, you see only fragments of what was. The B&B was once the home of a well-to-do merchant. The museum was once a trading goods store. And so on.

But this may be something of an illusion. The history of these places is a history of boom and bust. They boomed with tobacco and then busted. (There once were warehouses along the river where you could store tobacco and write drafts against them to pay for things. Tobacco was as good as money. The warehouses are no more.) They boomed with shipbuilding and then busted again. The familiar arcs repeat themselves.

Maybe they will boom again. Perhaps this region's ability to grow enormous amounts of food will fuel a new boom. It seems doubtful, but you never know.

This is one of the fascinating things about markets, the tidal ebb and flow of fortunes, the uneven march of "progress," and the uncertainty of it all. Maybe Heat-Moon is right. "Instead of insight," he wrote, "maybe all a man gets is strength to wander for a while. Maybe the only gift is a chance to inquire, to know nothing for certain."

America holds an uncertain position in the world right side up. It has been on top for a long time. Surely, in the United States, there is a lot to worry about, without even considering what's happening abroad. Still, the historically anomalous gap between the Western world and everybody else will continue to narrow. This means Americans, accustomed to dining at the best table alone, will have to share their table with others.

For some, this will be a hard adjustment. But it need not mean that America's quality of life will decline in absolute terms. There are still many areas where America is rich and competitive. It may sound simple, but we have to do more of what we do well and less of what we do poorly. There is still a rich set of opportunities in the United States as this section will highlight. As has been the case throughout the book, this is my own idiosyncratic and eclectic collection of ideas from own travels and rooting around. It's not meant to be a comprehensive look at investing in the United States.

Let's begin on the natural resource side of things.

The Greatest Resource Shortage You've Never Heard of

The Argana Café, off Jemaa el Fnaa Square, was a popular spot in the city of Marrakesh, at the foothills of the snow-capped Atlas Mountains in Morocco. The square is the heart of the city, alive with food stalls and crowded with people. It is a great place to watch the sunset over Jemaa, enjoying tea and snacks.

In 2011, a terrorist attack upset that enchanting scene. A bomb detonated in the café, killing 15 people and injuring at least 20 more. A few days later, thousands marched in Moroccan cities, demanding a faster transition toward democracy and denouncing terrorism.

You know what's happened in Libya, Tunisia, and Egypt. The Middle East and North Africa were in political turmoil in 2011. The politics of it all are beyond my beat. But there is a reason these countries are important to us. Investors will want to focus on a particular critical commodity that has a hand in 40 percent of the world's food supply.

I'm talking about phosphate. And these four countries in North Africa account for 80 percent of the world's supply (Figure 13.1).

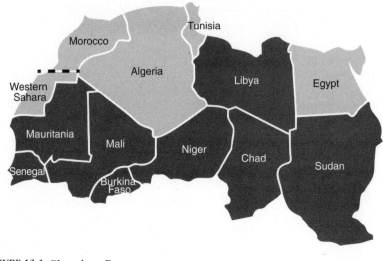

FIGURE 13.1 Phosphate Powers

Source: Stonegate Agricom.

You'll note the dotted line between Morocco and Western Sahara. This is disputed territory. The Moroccans claim it, but so do the native Sahrawi. When Spain left Morocco in 1975, the Moroccans and Sahrawis fought for it over 16 years until they agreed to a cease-fire in 1991. Since then, the fate of Western Sahara has been in limbo.

I won't get into all the particulars of this dispute, except to point out that some of Morocco's richest phosphate beds lie in this disputed territory. They contribute 11 percent of the country's phosphate production.

Thus, a good chunk of the world's phosphate resources lies in questionable political circumstances. Should any disruptions occur, it could lead to spikes in the price of phosphate.

Such spikes have happened before.

In the 2008 food crisis, phosphate prices peaked at $500 per tonne. You can see how phosphate prices broadly tracked the FAO's Food Price Index in the following chart. (Note Figure 13.2 shows average annual prices for phosphate.)

As food prices continue to climb, the price of phosphate rock ought to follow. That's because it is crucial to the world's food supply, for which it serves as a fertilizer, and there is no replacement. Most of the world's mines are in decline. *Foreign Policy* magazine called it "the gravest resource shortage you've never heard of." Phosphate helps plants develop stronger roots and use water more efficiently. It improves yields and gets plants to mature faster. To get it, you have to mine it. And there are only so many large-scale deposits around. This brings us to our opportunity.

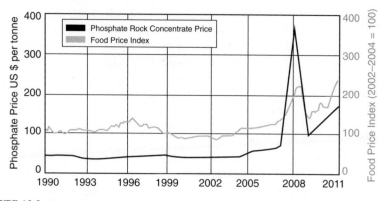

FIGURE 13.2 Phosphate and Food Prices Go Together

Source: Stonegate Agricom.

I believe investing in food production is a good place to be in general, for some simple reasons, many of which we've discussed in this book. One of my favorites is to look at how diets have shifted over time. China, India, and the rest of the emerging markets have gotten a lot bigger in the last decade. They've gotten richer. As part of that, they are eating a more calorie-rich diet. This is exactly what we would expect as there is a reliable relationship between income and calories consumed. Take a look at Figure 13.3.

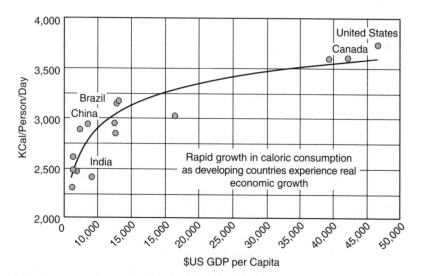

FIGURE 13.3 Income Levels Impact Food Consumption

Source: Stonegate Agricom.

So, as these countries move along this curve, they will propel investment in agriculture and food production.

The source of arable land available per person has shrunk over the years as well. Cities traditionally grew near farms, and as cities have expanded, they have consumed the surrounding farmland. (This is true where I live. What was once all farmland is a suburb of Washington, D.C.) In any event, it means we have to be more efficient with existing resources. Fertilizers mean higher yields, more crops per acre, and hence their critical role today.

You may not be surprised to learn that four countries consume about 60 percent of the world's fertilizers: China (30 percent), India (13 percent), the United States (12.7 percent), and Brazil (5 percent). India's yields are half that of China's, and India has no phosphates. Chinese are well-endowed with phosphates, but they use much of what they produce. China maintains stiff tariffs on phosphate in order to protect its supply.

As is usually the case in mining, grades have declined over time. In other words, we have to mine more rock to get the same amount of phosphate. The big mines are old and harder to replace. Phosphate deposits may well become a strategic asset in the future, indeed, the Chinese seem to treat it as such with their high export tariffs.

I visited one of the most promising new phosphate deposits in the United States, not far from Bear Lake, Idaho.

Reporting from Bear Lake

> . . . the sudden changes and chances of Fortune, who delights in making the miner or the lumberman a quadruplicate millionaire, and in "busting" the railroad king.
>   —Rudyard Kipling, From Sea to Sea

The waters of Bear Lake are turquoise blue, thanks to limestone deposits suspended in the water. It is beautiful country, once the stomping grounds of Shoshone tribes. A smooth-riding Pilatus PC-12 from Salt Lake City took me there.

I was in Idaho to have a look at Stonegate Agricom's Paris Hills property. Paris Hills is one of two phosphate deposits Stonegate is working on. The other is the Mantaro deposit in Peru.

The Paris Hills property is in an area where there has long been mining. Exploration in these parts began in the 1900s. In fact, there are three old shafts on the property from mines operated intermittently until the 1940s.

Within 50 miles of Paris Hills, there are three active phosphate mines owned by Monsanto, Agrium, and Simplot. (The latter is one of the largest privately held companies in the world.) This is important because it means there is infrastructure all around (roads, rail, and power). There is plenty of water. Everything that you need to build a successful mine.

Stonegate bought the property in 2009 from a distressed seller, a firm called RMP Resources, which bought the property to explore for vanadium. RMP bought it from Earth Sciences, which did extensive evaluations of the property in the 1970s, drilling 46 holes. Stonegate paid only $4 million for the property and began drilling in September 2010. Stonegate's emphasis, from the start, was to develop a phosphate resource.

Looking at the maps of Paris Hills made me think about the importance of the railroads in making or breaking towns in American history. Montpelier, northeast of Paris Hills, is the largest town in Bear Lake County, with nearly 3,000 people. Pioneers settled it in 1863, arriving by way of the Oregon Trail. Stonegate could truck the phosphate up to Montpelier, and then it would likely go to Florida (to the big fertilizer company, Mosaic) or perhaps to a seaport on the West Coast, from where it could go anywhere. There used to be a railroad from Montpelier to Paris, but the rails were pulled for scrap. The bed is still there though.

When the West was still a blank canvas, towns sprouted up, sometimes for no reason other than there was a railroad junction or terminal there. Railroad magnates had considerable influence over the towns that dotted the prairies and plains. James J. Hill, the magnate behind the Great Northern, once got the town of Spokane to knuckle under to his demands. Back in 1892, he threatened to have his railroad go around the town, a practical death sentence. Spokane caved.

My own hometown of Gaithersburg, Maryland, began in 1765 as Log Town. There was not much here but farms and orchards until William Gaither convinced the B&O to build its line through the town in 1873. It was such a big deal the people named the town after him.

On the map, I found the airport where I arrived. From there, I then rode through the small town of Paris, population 576. It has an impressive sandstone tabernacle, completed in 1889, with a capacity nearly four times the town's population. We then drove down through Bloomington, a town half the size of Paris, and then over to the property. These towns are mostly economically depressed, and Stonegate has found a welcome reception (particularly from the local restaurants).

The Paris Hills property is set back in the hills, in rolling ranch land covered with sagebrush and wildflowers. Stonegate was still drilling on the site while I was there. Save for the two rigs, the property looks much like it did to the pioneers who came here in their covered wagons. If anything, the land looks more inviting than it was. Winters could be harsh. As I gazed out over the pretty view, I thought how hard it must've been to carve out a living here initially. It's not like there was a

Home Depot and Safeway nearby. It made me think that America is still a big place in its vast and relatively empty middle. As Stonegate is proving, there is still much wealth in the land.

Stonegate's rigs have been turning up some good-looking phosphate drill core samples. The Paris Hills deposit itself sits in a formation that occurs mostly in southeast Idaho and has an estimated 146 billion tonnes of phosphorous. The geology of Idaho is interesting, as it was once the western shoreline of Pangaea, the supercontinent that existed 250 million years ago. As the Earth's crusts shifted and pushed west, the collisions created the Rocky Mountains, as if you pushed one rug into another. This explains the marine phosphorite rock found in this corner of Idaho, along with dark shale and black carbonite.

The deposit itself has extremely high grades. They are high enough, in fact, that Stonegate ought to be able to ship concentrate directly with little or no processing, which means lower costs. The deposit is uniform and predictable, another attractive feature.

I stopped in to visit Stonegate's office in Paris Hills, which sits next to an antique store selling all kinds of cool things, including World War II flight jackets, steel helmets, and even a stuffed mountain lion. Over lunch, we talked about what the mine might look like. Paris Hills could produce one million tonnes per year for 15 years just from the lower zone. The upper zone could add another 15 years at least.

I pay a lot of attention to who is in the stock, and who is running the show. There are proven insiders here. Ian McDonald and Kerry Knoll (co-chairmen and significant stockholders) are proven company builders. They have created and sold companies and made a lot of money for their investors. They have done it not once, not twice, but three times. Eric Sprott owns a third of the company. Sprott is one of the smartest small-cap resource investors around. Put them together, and show me where to sign.

The CEO, Mark Ashcroft, is a big fellow, raised in the cold country of Northern Ontario in a mining family. I enjoyed listening to him talk about the market for phosphate and Stonegate's projects. He is one plugged-in guy. After I said goodbye, he was off to meet with Simplot. He seems to know everybody in the industry and has an encyclopedic knowledge of phosphate projects and mines. He was handpicked to lead the company by McDonald and Knoll, and he enjoys the full support of Sprott and the board.

Stonegate Agricom is an example of the natural wealth still here in America if only we tap it. (The irony is not lost on me that the company's management team and primary backers are Canadians.)

You can find a lot of little companies doing interesting things with old U.S. assets. Consider this next one in Colorado.

Rocky Mountain Coal Meets Steel Demand

Metallurgical coal (called met coal or coking coal) is a high-grade coal used in making steel. Met coal prices go for two or three times the price of coal used to generate electricity. It is a prized strategic asset for steelmakers, for which they are willing to pay a lot of money to secure.

The industry knows that we'll need significant expansion in new mines to meet demand for met coal. Rio Tinto's own estimates call for an annual growth rate of nearly 6 percent through 2020. That translates into 88 million metric tons of new production needed to meet demand.

In essence, Chinese, Indian, and Brazilian steelmakers have expanded capacity and built many new mills along their coastlines, ready to import met coal. China doesn't have enough and has been a net importer since 2009. India suffers from chronic shortages of met coal, and Brazil will have to import a lot of coking coal.

The big producer is Australia. The second-largest exporter is the United States, which sits on some of the best coking coal deposits in the world. Opening a new mine in the United States is not easy, but one company has succeeded. It built its mine on the skeleton of an older mine complex.

About 25 miles west of Trinidad, Colorado, there is a long valley with a coal-producing history that stretches back into the nineteenth century. The storied Colorado Fuel and Iron Co. built met coal mines here. CF&I used to be a giant steel company in the United States, a Rockefeller-controlled company that traded on the NYSE and was part of the Dow Jones industrial average.

CF&I had a big steel mill in Pueblo, and the coking coal for that operation came from what is today the New Elk Mine, until 1989. CF&I had its troubles and went through several bankruptcies. It no longer exists, though the met coal in the old mine still does. The New Elk Mine had been mostly idle since 1996, until a new company bought it in the summer of 2008 and began the process of bringing it back.

That company is Cline Mining. In the July 2011 issue of *Coal & Energy Price Report*, an industry publication on pricing trends and gossip, Cline got a mention, as a potential takeout target, according to "one sharp Wall Street source." The ramp-up to 3 million tons, annually, of high-volume B-grade coal is a big deal. And the grade might prove even better than B. Try B+.

The source points out that two rail options allow the New Elk Mine to ship out coal, either domestically or internationally, through Corpus Christi, Texas, which Cline has locked down. The source flatly stated Cline "should be bought" by Arch, Cloud Peak, Alpha, Peabody, Cliff, or "anyone with the financial wherewithal to do it." Cline is a juicy target because it is cashed up after an equity raise. It has $80 million of noncore assets to sell. Meanwhile,

Cline's enterprise value is only $400 million. Based on discounted cash flow, the source argued that those 3 million tons of high-volume "B" are likely worth two times what the market values Cline at today.

No doubt, Cline will be on somebody's shopping list before too long and may not exist by the time you read this. Nonetheless, it serves as an example of a much-prized resource that the United States has in relative abundance and that makes for good opportunities for investors.

There are other such opportunities in oil, too. For that, we'll head to Cook Inlet and the Bakken.

Journey to Cook Inlet

Captain James Cook (1728–1779) is my favorite explorer. When I was in Melbourne, Australia, I made sure to see Cook's Cottage in Fitzroy Gardens, which commemorates the great explorer's "discovery" of the southern continent.

On my office wall hangs a replica of a map by Lieutenant Henry Roberts, who served with Captain Cook. The map traces the journeys of Cook's three great voyages aboard the *Endeavour* and *Resolution*. The dotted lines seem to cover an impossible amount of distance over all of the world's oceans.

I'm telling you about Cook because his legacy is still in play today. There is a great oil and gas story building in an inlet that bears his name. Cook piloted the *Resolution* there in 1778 while searching for the Northwest Passage. He didn't discover the passage, but he did navigate the Alaskan inlet named for him.

Cook Inlet has been a great source of oil and gas for many years, but the discovery of the giant Prudhoe Bay field shifted attention to the North Slope. Production in Cook Inlet went into decline.

The state of Alaska, in order to entice more investment, is giving companies a 40 percent state refund on drilling and exploration costs, paid in cash. And there are more potential refunds that could cover another 20 percent of costs.

The Cook Inlet is traditionally a risky place to do business. Active volcanoes smolder ominously in the distance. Big tidal swells sweep the inlet, and thick ice can cover it in winter. But the Alaskan incentives make it attractive, and the potential rewards are great. Apache, one of the big oil companies, is gobbling up acreage.

The other interesting thing about Cook Inlet is that most of the producing fields come from exploration done 50 to 60 years ago. The Inlet itself is surprisingly unexplored. Various estimates say Cook Inlet could hold more than 200 million barrels of oil and 13–15 trillion cubic feet of natural gas.

The latter is particularly valuable because Alaska is short of natural gas. While natural gas prices in the lower 48 languish at $4, the price of natural gas in Alaska is north of $6 and hits $10 in the winter. Some fear Alaska could run out of gas.

"They eat what they kill," is how one oilman put it to me. You can't ship natural gas into the inlet just yet. It's a closed market. Alaska needs that gas. The state of Alaska knows it, hence all those goodies. It is a nice opportunity for the oil companies working the inlet.

More than a billion barrels of oil, along with 5 trillion cubic feet of natural gas, have been pumped out of the Cook Inlet area. Oil and gas development in Alaska, as a whole, has been huge. About one-fifth of the domestically produced oil in the United States, for instance, comes from Alaska.

It's sort of ironic, too. When Cook sailed into the inlet, he was looking for the Northwest Passage, a sea lane that cut through the Arctic Ocean and joined the Atlantic and Pacific oceans. In this effort, Cook failed. But as history would prove, the inlet itself became far more valuable for the hidden treasures that lie beneath its frigid waters.

Rocky Mountain Speculation: The Bakken

Isabella Lucy Bird (1831–1904) was an amazing traveler and writer. She traveled throughout Asia. She lived for a time among the Ainu people in northern Japan. Bird made it to Hawaii, where she climbed Mauna Loa. She wandered in Australia and rode horses in Persia. This is a snippet of her life's itinerary. She got around.

In 1873, Bird set off for the Rocky Mountains. Back then, the Rocky Mountain region was an untamed wilderness peopled with hardscrabble pioneers. Bird began her journey in San Francisco. She headed east across Nevada, and then ploughed into the Colorado Territory. Bird set her adventures down in a series of letters to her sister Henrietta. She stitched them together in a book, published in 1879.

Here, she records her vivid descriptions of the landscapes of the Rockies. She writes of the "snow-splotched mountains," the glades and sloping lawns, the elk and the bears. One bear came so close she "heard the grass, crisp with hoar frost, crackle under his feet." She writes of the profound stillness and "cherry-fringed beds of dry streams." And the pines. And the "deep, vast canyons . . . [that] lie in purple gloom."

It's that vastness and beauty, that sense of exploring, that still gives the Rocky Mountains a romantic aura to this day. Today, despite all of our sophisticated toys, the Rocky Mountains remain mysterious in ways of oil and gas.

Oilmen and speculators wonder just how much oil and gas might lie in this region. Some of the hottest exploratory regions in America lie in the Rocky Mountain region, in particular in the so-called Bakken trend.

It's a massive oil reserve that has altered the fortunes of this once-remote area. The Bakken shale could hold more than 4 billion barrels of oil and stretches under North Dakota and Montana (and Canada, but I'm only talking about the U.S. piece here). If that number is correct (it comes from the U.S. Geological Survey), then it would be the biggest oil field discovered in the contiguous United States in more than 40 years.

Plenty of oil is being pumped from Bakken, enough to make any number of investors rich. In 2003, North Dakota produced only 10,000 barrels of oil per day. In 2011, it was up to 400,000.

This makes for a good old-fashioned oil boom in Dakota. You know the labor market is tight when the local McDonald's starts handing out $300 signing bonuses. Workers are coming in from all over, making it tough to find housing. They might sleep in their trucks or pitch tents.

There is a chronic shortage of hotel rooms. I browsed the web to see if I could find a room. I checked the Super 8 Motel—no rooms were available. I checked a few others—no rooms there, either. I used Priceline to search, and there were no rooms available. What is going on here?

Local ranchers are becoming millionaires overnight. This is a boomtown. Or boomtowns. Even the state government is in surplus.

We've always known there was oil there, but the problem was that much of it was inaccessible with current technology. That's changed. The production here is not going to make a dent in the oil market, in which the United States alone consumes more than 7 billion barrels annually, but it's big enough to matter to many ranchers, small companies, and small towns. It's big enough to make North Dakota the fourth-largest oil producer in the United States, behind only Texas, Alaska, and California. Whiting Petroleum's CEO, Jim Volker, calls it "a true game changer."

Just as the call of "Gold!" drew trains of prospectors to the gold rush towns of yore, the call of "Oil!" draws oilmen to small towns in North Dakota. There's a long list of companies working in the Bakken: Continental, Whiting, Marathon, EOG, and others. You can make good money in the Bakken.

Nicholas Sutton thinks so, too. Sutton is the chief behind Resolute Energy (REN:nyse), which I think of as a keeper in the oil and gas arena. He's made his investors a fortune once before.

In 1992, he took HS Resources public at $14 per share. The basic plan was simple, if unoriginal. HS would seek out underinvested oil and gas properties from the giant oil companies. These orphan properties were small change to the big majors like Exxon or Chevron. Picking up these assets was like asking Bill Gates for a quarter.

Then, HS would invest in these properties, too small or old to interest the majors, and get them back in top shape. It worked brilliantly. Sutton built HS into a good-sized oil company. In 2001, Kerr-McGee bought out HS Resources for about $66 per share. Put another way, Sutton started with a $150 million company and sold it for $1.8 billion. Investors who hung in there with Sutton enjoyed returns of nearly 20 percent annually or 354 percent total.

After that gig, Sutton took a break but came back out of retirement to take the helm of Resolute, as chairman and CEO, in 2004. He brought his old team from HS with him: James Piccone, serving as president of the new company; Theodore Gazulis, chief financial officer; and Richard Betz, senior vice president of strategy and planning. And they are looking to do it all over again.

Sutton took a page out of his old playbook. He found some old fields Chevron owned in the southeastern corner of Utah, in an area called the Paradox Basin. The field Sutton wanted was called Aneth and had been discovered in 1956. Sutton picked it up for $86 million in 2004, paying about $5 per barrel of proved reserves. Then he went after some other fields in the same basin, picking up more acreage from Exxon. Again, he paid a cheap price, about $5.85 per barrel of proved reserves.

Now he has a nice, cash-regenerative business. Sutton's Resolute acquired a stake in the Bakken in North Dakota. Sutton commented: "These high-quality assets in North Dakota are oily, large, and highly prospective. While the Bakken shale has been well-known by oil companies for years, technological improvements have only recently unleashed its potential. With this transaction, we are well placed to take full advantage of what we believe is a meaningful opportunity to continue to add to our oil reserves in a relatively low-risk manner."

It's early on the Bakken, but I find the whole thing fascinating. We have a potential major oil boom right here in the United States, and it could be another catalyst for Resolute as it explores that acreage.

Resolute is a tertiary oil recovery player. It injects carbon dioxide (CO_2) into a well to help liquefy the remaining oil and make it easier to extract. It's called "tertiary" because you do this only once other methods have run their course. This is a proven and low-risk technology. Resolute produces oil at a cost of about $25 a barrel.

In any event, the CO_2 angle is timely. As you know, everybody seems to want to cut down on CO_2 emissions. Resolute and its peers, such as Denbury Resources, could be part of that solution. Denbury, for instance, has a project to capture the CO_2 of a Dow Chemical plant, which spews annual emissions equivalent to 27,000 cars.

The government has given money to fund other carbon capture schemes. This one, though, seems economical without government aid. So it boosts U.S. oil supplies, and it helps get rid of the industrial gases that worry Al Gore so much. Maybe that will win it some points with Washington.

Critics pooh-pooh it because it doesn't eliminate CO_2 permanently. The oil extracted is burned at some point. But Denbury maintains more CO_2 is buried underground than taken out.

Either way, Resolute is a fine oil and gas company on its way to much bigger things. It's a low-risk way to own a growing American oil and gas company, with loads of potential run intelligently with a proven company maker.

The Shale Gas Revolution

General Electric is making a big bet on natural gas as a fuel for power generation. It will invest heavily in natural gas turbines and related equipment. The head of GE's energy division said, "There has been a step change in the gas opportunity for power generation that makes it extremely competitive against other forms of power."

That step change is the shale gas revolution. Shale gas is natural gas that lies trapped in rocks and was, for a long time, inaccessible. Then, drilling technology found a way to crack it and get the gas out. Suddenly, we're awash in natural gas, the price has plummeted, and this is where we are today.

It's hard to understate just how revolutionary the whole thing is. Anne-Sophie Corbeau of the International Energy Agency summed it up well. "A few years ago, the United States was ready to import gas," she said. "In 2009, it had become the world's biggest gas producer. This is phenomenal, unbelievable."

It is. America has a huge amount of this energy resource. We will turn to shale gas for energy more and more. It's eating into coal's market share, and recently, it has been taking a bite out of alternative energy.

For example, the construction of new wind farms in the United States will decline next year because of competition from cheap natural gas. So says the largest developer of wind projects in the United States, Iberdrola. The CEO said, "Shale gas makes the production of electricity from other sources not attractive enough."

The effects of shale gas have been revolutionary. Matt Ridley, the respected science writer, put out a report recently titled *The Shale Gas Rock*. It includes a wonderful foreword by Freeman Dyson, the renowned physicist and author. "The most important improvements of the human condition caused by new technologies are often unexpected before they happen and quickly forgotten afterward," Dyson writes.

He relates the story of his grandmother, born around 1850 in Yorkshire. To her, the most important technology to hit working-class homes when she was growing up was wax candles, which replaced tallow candles.

"With wax candles, you could read comfortably at night. With tallow candles, you could not," Dyson writes. "According to my grandmother, wax candles did more than government schools to produce a literate working class. Shale gas is like wax candles." In short, revolutionary.

Shale gas has accumulated some enemies. As Ridley writes, "Shale gas faces a formidable host of enemies in the coal, nuclear, renewable, and environmental industries, all keen, it seems, to strangle it at birth." There are those that say it pollutes drinking water and damages the environment. I could write an entire letter on this subject alone, but instead, I highly recommend Ridley's report to you. It is easy reading and informative.

On this topic, Ridley leaves us a pithy comment worth reproducing here:

All technologies have environmental risks. Press coverage that talks about "toxic," "carcinogenic," and "radioactive" chemicals is meaningless. Vitamin A is toxic. A single cup of coffee contains more known carcinogens than the average American ingests from pesticide residues in a whole year. Bananas are radioactive. The questions that need to be posed are always: how toxic, how carcinogenic, and how radioactive?

In the well-considered opinion of Ridley, endorsed by Dyson, the answer is that shale gas poses no new or special risks. There is more frequent contamination from agricultural runoff or oil spills from the transportation industry or from coal mines, and so on.

These debates often boil down to politics, not economics. If it were otherwise, the United States wouldn't be turning so much of its corn stock into ethanol, but that is another matter.

Still, natural gas enjoys heavy political support of its own. President Barack Obama has endorsed incentives for natural gas-powered vehicles, for instance. As Ridley points out: "Gas-powered vehicles produce almost no particulates, 60 percent less volatile organics, 50 percent less nitrogen oxides and 90 percent less carbon monoxide, which means less smog, ozone, and brown haze."

Natural gas is the place to be and is my favorite energy source in which to invest. I'm not alone in thinking this. I told you about GE. More power companies are replacing coal-fired plants with gas-burning ones. Big Oil is buying up natural gas acreage. Some smaller producers, too, know the value of natural gas acreage. "We are not letting any of our gas acreage go," Floyd Wilson, the CEO of Petrohawk Energy, said recently. "It's going to be solid gold one day."

Another angle into the shale gas story is to focus on the users of natural gas. The chemical industry uses natural gas to make things. "We use natural gas as a source of energy and as a feedstock, like flour is to a bakery," as Cal Dooley, president of the American Chemical Council, put it.

Dooley is excited. He thinks we are on the cusp of a golden age for U.S. chemical producers who use natgas to make things. The United States has lots of cheap natural gas. Many firms are just starting to exploit the opportunities this presents.

Take Sasol. It plans to build the first gas-to-liquids plant in the United States. The site is in Louisiana, and it will cost $10 billion to build. This fascinates me on many levels. First, it's a foreign firm investing in the United States, instead of the more typical: a U.S. firm investing abroad. Second, it's a clear example of a firm explicitly taking advantage of the U.S. natural gas glut.

Sasol will turn cheap American natural gas into diesel fuel and some jet fuel. (Hence, "gas to liquids.") The advantage of Sasol's technology is that it can turn the gas into fuel usable by vehicles without having to mess with the vehicles. To use natural gas, vehicles have to be refitted, and you need special natgas fueling stations. Not with Sasol's technology.

Meanwhile, Dow Chemical plans to open new U.S. ethylene and propylene plants by the end of the decade. This will restart a U.S. ethylene cracker closed in 2009. PotashCorp plans to restart an ammonia plant in Louisiana that it shut down in 2003. Ormet, a maker of aluminum, plants to re-open a plant closed in 2006. There are more.

Shale gas was revolutionary for the United States. It will create many opportunities in the years ahead, from U.S. chemical companies to the people who put together natural gas infrastructure to natural gas producers. Definitely watch and explore it further.

Windfall Profits in American Agriculture

In the United States, one particular industry enjoying windfall profits from exports is agriculture.

In 2009, world trade took a big hit in the wake of the financial crisis. Global exports fell 12 percent. Governments tried to protect their home teams, and a wave of tariffs and other protectionist measures followed. This was what happened during the Great Depression, too when the Smoot-Hawley Tariff Act raised tariffs on more than 900 goods.

As a result, world trade sank by 25 percent during the early years of the Great Depression. But that hasn't happened this time around. In fact, the emerging economies of the world are exporting and importing more than they were before the 2008 crisis.

In the United States, a big winner is agriculture. U.S. farmers produced record exports in 2010. The heat wave frying European crops (in particular,

Russian crops) helped that. But even before the drought, in just the first four months of the year, the United States enjoyed a $4 billion trade surplus in agriculture. For years, the United States has been the world's largest exporter of corn, wheat, and soybeans. It is a leading exporter of many other agricultural goods.

U.S. farmers are cashing in on demand from emerging markets, particularly Asia. China has been trying to build self-sufficiency in food. But it has a long list of hurdles, chiefly a shrinking supply of arable land and water shortages. The median Chinese farm is smaller than one acre. This hinders the economies of scale that come from big farms.

In any event, U.S. farmers are sending more and more goods to the Far East. So, perhaps it is no surprise that first U.S. grain export depot built in 25 years is not on the rim of the Gulf of Mexico, but on the Columbus River in Washington state, about 60 miles from the Pacific Ocean. The new Port of Longview grain terminal will handle 8 million tonnes a year. (The Port of Louisiana is the still the top grain export hub in North America, although California recently passed Louisiana as the top point of departure for U.S. cotton.)

We'll need more depots like the new Port of Longview. American infrastructure has had a hard time keeping up with surging ag exports. Outside of Seattle, for instance, 80 rail cars filled with dried peas sat for three weeks on the train tracks waiting for a ship to unload them.

It's not an isolated example. A soybean exporter in, say, Minnesota, could normally ship 40 tons of beans to Malaysia in 15 to 20 days. With recent bottlenecks, it took 60 days. There are plenty of stories of everything from hazelnuts to soybeans tied up in shipping bottlenecks for weeks.

The United States isn't used to such export strength. The *Wall Street Journal* noted, "America's trading infrastructure grew imbalanced, with a huge capacity to import goods but an attenuated capacity to export them. Loads of grain or corrugated paper leaving the United States took a back seat to the DVDs and toys coming in."

That's the problem. For too long, the focus of the U.S. economy seemed to be overindulged consumers. There were too many stores selling too much junk, too many houses people couldn't afford, and too much debt on all of it. This part of the economy grew to grotesque proportions, stimulated by easy credit.

But underneath it all, there is still the old world of making things. Agriculture is a bright star in the U.S. firmament and an appealing place to invest. The future of American agriculture is bright, indeed, as the FAO makes clear in a recent report, *How to Feed the World in 2050*. This excerpt sums up the investment case:

Even if total demand for food and feed may, indeed, grow more slowly [over the next 40 years], just satisfying the expected food and feed

demand will require a substantial increase of global food production of
70 percent by 2050, involving an additional quantity of nearly 1 billion
tons of cereals and 200 million tons of meat.

In addition to the usual assortment of resource issues such as water, soil, and climate change, there are some topics you wouldn't think of otherwise, such as biodiversity.

To understand the impact of biodiversity, you should know this: The gene pool in plant and animal genetic resources and in the natural ecosystems, which breeders need as options for future selection, is diminishing rapidly. A dozen species of animals provide 90 percent of the animal protein consumed globally, and just four crop species provide half of plant-based calories in the human diet.

Farmers with windfall profits will have more money to expand production. That's more money for things such as seed, tractors, and fertilizers. As long as its export markets remain open, U.S. farmers should do well.

I mentioned the world of making things, and the United States is not a slouch in this department despite common perceptions that "Made in the USA" is becoming extinct.

Still a Nation of Builders

This has always been a nation of builders. Craftsmen. Men and
women for whom straight stitches and clean welds were matters of
personal pride. They made the skyscrapers and the cotton gins. Colt
revolvers. Jeep 4x4s. . . . This was once a country where people
made things. Beautiful things. And so it is again.
                                        —A commercial for the Jeep Grand Cherokee

It's a common lament to say that U.S. manufacturing is in decline. It's received wisdom that the United States doesn't make anything anymore. In truth, there is a lot of stuff made in the United States, which is still a mighty giant in manufacturing.

Turner Investment Partners is a firm out of Berwyn, Pennsylvania. It manages $18 billion. Turner put together the eye-opening report called *U.S. Manufacturing: Still the One.* "If the U.S. manufacturing industry were a national economy," the authors write, "it would be the eighth largest in the world, worth $1.6 trillion." All by itself, the United States is 22 percent of global manufacturing. As an exporter, it ranks third, behind only China and Germany, with an 8 percent market share.

That is a big blow to the idea that the United States doesn't make anything anymore. But how can this be? We all see the same headlines, such as the big failure of U.S. autoworkers. We see the "Made in China" label slapped on nearly everything. We know Japan makes all kinds of electronics that the United States no longer makes. We hear about companies moving plants overseas.

This is where things get more interesting.

Since 1983, manufacturing output in the United States has more than doubled. (This, in inflation-adjusted dollars, by the way, makes the feat all the more impressive.) But it did so with about 26 percent fewer workers. As a result, 50 years ago, about 28 percent of all workers got their paychecks from manufacturing. Today, only 8 percent of the workforce does.

That workforce, though, is productive. It's doing a lot more with less. As Turner reports, "U.S. manufacturing workers . . . are the most productive— 50 percent more productive than workers in the 11 next-best nations."

So it's like the headlines about shark attacks that were common some summers ago. It made it seem as if shark attacks were more common than they were. The public failures of big manufacturers and the headline-grabbing job losses have obscured the real story.

The real story is that the services sector has grown much faster than manufacturing. So when you look at manufacturing's share of the U.S. economy, it has fallen from 28 percent in 1953 to only 12 percent today.

We may weep over the fact that the U.S. economy is so service-driven, but that's not the same as saying that U.S. manufacturing is in decline. The United States is still the world's largest manufacturer.

The nature of that manufacturing base is changing. One way is that the companies populating the forest tend to be smaller. There are fewer giants. "According to the Cato Institute, for every one U.S. manufacturing industry that's suffering a decline in revenue and profits, two U.S. industries, led by small companies, are growing"

The above are just some highlights from Turner's report. My main goal here is to leave you with a different perception of American manufacturers. They are not like dinosaurs on their way to extinction. In fact, some of them are great investments.

One industry I've followed for years is aircraft suppliers, which American companies dominate. This industry has some particular tail winds that make it an attractive place to be for the next several years, starting with fuel costs.

American Aviation Taking Off

Fuel is the largest expense for the airline industry, at 30 percent of operating costs. In addition, the airline industry faces pressures to cut costs. Airlines have cut staffing costs. You can see this in labor costs as a percentage of operating costs. They stand at about a quarter of costs compared with 35 percent in 2001. Airlines have been smarter about pricing and routes, as airfare rates have stayed up.

The big opportunity for the airline industry, though, is to cut into that fuel cost number. The way to do that is with more fuel-efficient aircraft. A new A320, for instance, saves more than 25 percent on fuel costs compared with the older MD-80. The old workhorses of the fleet, such as the 737s an 757s, are lacking in fuel-efficiency.

What's interesting here is that the airline industry has scrimped on investing in new planes. In fact, the world's 50 largest airlines spent only 8 percent of sales on new aircraft in 2011. That is the lowest total in a decade. I'd bet that number climbs in the next few years.

But there is an even more compelling reason to like aircraft suppliers. Actually, there are 33,500 reasons.

Boeing put out its long-term forecast for aircraft for the next two decades. This is a much-watched and commented-on forecast, as Boeing has as good an insight into the backlog of the industry as anyone. Plus, they have a history of being conservative.

Boeing projects that passenger traffic will triple by 2030, and the number of commercial aircraft will double. They estimate the market will need 33,500 new planes. The tab: $4 trillion.

From where is the growth coming? I'm sure you could guess. Randy Tinseth, Boeing's vice president of marketing, explains: "The center of aviation has moved, officially, from Europe and North America to the Asian markets. It's the biggest market today, and it's going to grow at the fastest rate, and unless something unusual happens, it will continue to be the largest market."

Twenty years ago, 72 percent of all air traffic was on carriers from North America or Europe. But the world is moving to a more normal or balanced profile. Today, only 55 percent is. Boeing forecasts that figure will fall to 40 percent by 2030. It's a different world from the one we knew in the twentieth century. It will create new and different opportunity sets for investors.

Boeing's forecast is still a forecast, and it could be wrong, as all such forecasts can be. But if it is wrong in the particulars, I think it will prove directionally accurate. Meaning we're going to need a lot more planes, and that creates a nice tail wind for a certain flock of businesses.

I favor the suppliers over the manufacturers, as some suppliers have better growth prospects and upside potential. I've written about opportunities in aerospace before in my newsletter, highlighting stocks such as Curtiss-Wright (of Wright brothers' fame) and Hexcel and Parker Hannifin. Hexcel may have the best story. It makes honeycombed composite materials that are light, ultrastrong, and fuel-efficient. Boeing and Airbus account for more than half of its sales. The newer plans are heavy in Hexcel materials, and that's helping fuel a bullish story.

In my newsletter portfolio, we've hung onto a half-position in Titanium Metals (TIE:nyse). (We sold the other half for a 107 percent profit.) TIE

	2011	2014	% Increase
Boeing 777	75	100	+33%
Boeing 747	15	24	+60%
Boeing 737	376	484	+29%
Boeing 787	11	117	+964%
Airbus A320	409	454	+11%
Airbus A380	24	28	+17%
Airbus 350	0	21	—

FIGURE 13.4 Aircraft Demand Takes Off
Source: GAMCO Investors, Inc.

earned $1.53 per share at the top of the last cycle in 2006, and the stock topped $30. I see no reason why TIE can't at least match those figures in the next up cycle, especially given the dynamics above. Titanium aircraft are more fuel-efficient. And similar to Hexcel's story, new planes are more titanium-intensive than older planes. I plan to hold long term as the aerospace story unfolds.

In September 2011, I attended the Gabelli seventeenth Annual Aircraft Supplier Conference in Manhattan at the Grand Hyatt by Grand Central Terminal. I make it a point to go to this conference every year since the folks at Gabelli always manage to put on a worthy slate of ideas. And this one was no different, with 15 different companies presenting. (I like Gabelli's shop because of its focus on private market value in determining the attractiveness of an investment, which I share.)

On the commercial aviation side, there was a lot of happy sunshine. Air travel has grown 5 percent per year since 1980, and it is a trend that doesn't look like it is going to slow down anytime soon. Backlogs are at record levels. Figure 13.4 shows projected aircraft deliveries to 2014.

These are cheerful times for those that make the stuff that goes into those planes. It's a story driven by increases in international flights, traffic volume, and, especially, aircraft deliveries outside of North America.

American companies dominate the list of aerospace companies. But there are other wrinkles within aerospace and defense that may do quite well.

Top-Secret America

I was in Manhattan a few days before the tenth anniversary of September 11. There were reminders of the anniversary all over the city. The date inspired a lot of reflection on how America has changed since that horrible day. I don't want to write a treatise on all the ways America has changed in the last decade. But I do want to focus on one important way it has because it ties directly into another powerful (and American-driven) investment theme.

I happened to watch an episode of *Frontline*, called "Top Secret America." It's based on the work of Dana Priest and William Arkin. I admire Priest, who is a legendary reporter at the *Washington Post*. Her expertise is on matters of intelligence and the war on terror.

What Priest uncovered as part of a nearly two-year investigation was a secret America growing up in the wake of September 11. After September 11, America's intelligence, surveillance, and counterterrorism agencies basically got a blank check to fund their efforts. The CIA got a billion dollars right away. So did the NSA. "What we found in the years immediately after September 11 was that the existing agencies grew enormously," Priest says. "They doubled in size, many of them, and new organizations were created as well, big ones."

There was a boom in new agencies geared to fighting this new war. Consider that in 2002, there were 34 new organizations created to work at the top-secret level. In 2003, the government created 39 more; in 2004, 30 more; in 2005, another 35; and more each year since. "Every year," Priest goes on, "more than two dozen, sometimes three dozen, entirely new federal organizations dedicated to counterterrorism [were] being created after September 11."

Moreover, each agency, after its creation, grew and grew. One example is the Office of the Director of National Intelligence. The DNI started as 11 people in the Old Executive Office Building. In short order, it grew to a couple of hundred people and moved to a bigger building. It had two floors in the massive Defense Intelligence Agency building. Still, it grew. "So they moved to some of the priciest real estate in the Washington area," Priest says. "And now they are gigantic, 500,000 square feet, five Wal-Marts stacked on top of each other."

At the conference, the big topic of discussion was defense spending. Everyone is expecting defense-spending cuts. They are inevitable. And this will affect many of the companies at the conference because they have large defense businesses.

However, there is one aspect of defense spending that isn't going to decline. In fact, broader government spending on intelligence, surveillance, and covert warfare is only going to go up. What is going to be cut are the traditional battlefield programs. The big stuff: Tanks. Submarines. No one is going to let the air out of a ballooning secret America. "No one's talking about turning them off," Priest says. "It's not like they've got mobile trailers that they're up in, and then when the floods recede, they're going to take them away."

The rules changed, greasing the skids. The government made it easier to hire contractors to skirt the slow process of hiring more federal workers. When they want to grow quickly, they turn to the private sector. Priest talks about how the big defense contractors, CACI, Lockheed Martin, L-3, and others, saw this boom in intelligence, surveillance, and the like.

The "war on terror" is not one that needs tanks, submarines, and fighter jets. It needs information. It needs people to analyze that information. It needs surveillance equipment. Smart weaponry. Unmanned drones. It's a top-secret America.

Priest talked about how she discovered that nearly a million people have top-secret clearance. That's more than the population of Washington, D.C. There are 1,900 companies and 1,100 federal organizations that work at the top-secret level.

It seems independent of political affiliation. President Obama has shown an affinity for the covert, as David Ignatius reports in a column titled "The Covert Commander in Chief." Obama stepped up the pace of predator drone attacks over Pakistan. He approved the raid on Abbottabad that killed Osama bin Laden. He has favored the covert on many other occasions. "The president appears to be ratcheting up intelligence and paramilitary operations," Ignatius writes, "even as he withdraws uniformed troops from Iraq and Afghanistan."

All of this costs a lot of money.

I am not going to pass judgment on what's happening here. You can decide for yourself. I would encourage you to read Dana Priest's and William Arkin's work. There is a lot out there on the Web, too, in addition to a book, plus the *Frontline* episode.

Some of their work is mind-blowing. If you were to start talking about this stuff at a dinner party, your friends would think you were a conspiracy theorist, but this is real. We're talking about massive nondescript buildings in the Washington area that might be one or two floors up but go 10 stories down. One of the guys on TV said they have shops and restaurants down there "just for them." I'll never look at the Washington suburbs in quite the same way again. What are they are all doing? No one knows for sure.

Anyway, my main focus here is how we can invest intelligently, given the world as it is. And the above mark an unmistakable trend and a big change from the way we used to think of defense and security in a pre-September 11 world. This will have an impact, positive and negative, on a slew of companies.

One of the companies I like is Kratos Defense & Security Solutions (KTOS: NASDAQ), which is the only pure play on national security that I know. The key phrase is C5ISR. That stands for Command, Control, Communications, Computers, Combat Systems, Intelligence, Surveillance, and Reconnaissance. And supporting C5ISR programs is what Kratos does.

Eric DeMarco is the CEO of the company. He spoke at the conference. I could tell DeMarco is the kind of guy who spends a lot of time talking to intelligence personnel. He referred to his own presentation as a "briefing" more than once. And he talked in a no-nonsense and direct manner. It was much like how I imagine a briefing would go in which a CIA guy takes you through a night raid in Afghanistan.

"I'm a firm believer that the world is a dangerous place and will remain a dangerous place," DeMarco began. He's talking his book, as they say, but he's probably right! Listening to him talk was not comforting as he prattled off threats from Iran and North Korea, the emergence of China as a military power, the remilitarization of Russia, and a host of other bad juju.

In a world in which large-scale, conventional platforms are in decline, think the F-22, the Virginia-class submarines, ground combat vehicles, and next-generation aircraft carriers, Kratos focuses on the new, smaller forces of top-secret America. "If you're going to have a smaller force," DeMarco continued, "it's going to have to be better-communicated and smarter." Kratos is all about that.

He then began to lay out the story of this remarkable company. Kratos (pronounced KRAY-tos, from the Greek word for "power" and from the name of the Greek god, son of Styx, who was one of the winged enforcers of Zeus) has over 4,000 employees, many with top-secret security clearances or higher. Most of the work Kratos does takes place on a military base or secure facility. Most of its work is sole source, meaning it is the only contractor on the contract. Kratos has little competition on most of its work.

It's an example of the kind of opportunities top-secret America opens up, for better or for worse. But this next idea might surprise you even more . . . American homes.

American Homes: Buy

Investment ideas are cyclical. They come and go, like fashions or cicadas, obeying their own curious rhythms. In the last few years, rare was the investment thinker who said you should buy a house. Housing was in a bubble that was deflating.

But the investment seasons turn. Today, some smart investors are once again saying you should a buy house. John Paulson was one of them.

You may know him as the man who turned the greatest trade of all time. Betting against the housing market, he netted a cool billion dollars for himself in 2007. One fund he managed rose 590 percent that year. Today, he is one of the richest men in America.

His advice, recently, was different. "If you don't own a home, buy one," Paulson said. "If you own one home, buy another one, and if you own two homes, buy a third and lend your relatives the money to buy a home."

It sounds similar to the advice another investor gave his audience in 1971, at the dawn of another inflationary age. It was Adam Smith (George Goodman) on *The Dick Cavett Show.* Here is a snippet from that conversation:

Smith: *The best investment you can make is a house. That one is easy.*
Cavett: *A house? We were talking about the stock market. Investments. . . .*
Smith: *You asked me the best investment. There are always individual stocks that will go up more, but you don't want to give tips on a television show. For most people, the best investment is a house.*
Cavett: *I already own a house. Now what?*
Smith: *Buy another one.*

It was good advice. In the 1970s, U.S. stocks returned about 5 percent annually, which failed to keep pace with inflation. Still, it was an up-and-down ride. In 1974, the stock market fell 49 percent. Figure 13.5 shows you the average selling prices for existing homes in the 1970s as inflation heated up.

You can see that housing held up well. And think about the effect of a mortgage on 80 percent of that house in 1972. That would mean $6,000 in equity, a sum that went up fivefold in eight years.

Apart from this, you might ponder that it is absurd today to think that anyone can buy an average house for any of these prices, and that, too, is the point. The average price today is $257,500, even after the great collapse in the last few years.

1972	$30,000
1973	$32,000
1974	$35,800
1975	$39,000
1976	$42,200
1977	$47,900
1978	$55,500
1979	$64,200

FIGURE 13.5 Inflation Heats Up: Home Prices Rise
Source: Paper Money by Adam Smith.

"If you have a 7 percent mortgage, and your house is worth half a million dollars," Adam Smith writes, "you may gripe about shoes, lamb chops, and tuition like everybody else, but your heart isn't in it." Your heart won't be in it because you'll be in fine fettle with your house.

You can do a lot better than 7 percent today. For the first time, the rate on a 30-year mortgage slipped below that on a 30-year Treasury bond. You can get a 30-year mortgage at little more than 4 percent today.

Factoring in mortgage rates, housing affordability is back to where it was in September 1996. Then mortgage rates were 8 percent, and the average price of a home was $171,600. As Murray Stahl, the investment strategist at Horizon Asset Management, writes: "One can actually buy a home for a monthly payment that is not many dollars different from the monthly payment one would have needed in September 1996 when rates were significantly higher." Adjusted for inflation, Stahl points out that the payment for an average-priced home today is about 30 percent lower than it was 14 years ago.

The advice of Paulson and Smith starts to make sense, doesn't it?

Essentially, real estate is a way to buy and pay later. And the case for housing extends to other property types, too. Owners of quality real estate are getting deals on mortgages that we are unlikely to see for a generation.

"We think now is one of the best times ever to invest in single-family homes for the long term," writes Aaron Edelheit, CEO of The American Home Real Estate Co. The new investment company recently raised $18 million and owns over 215 homes, mostly in the Southeast.

Why bother? For one thing, housing is cheap. There are many ways to see this. The real estate firm Zillow looked at housing prices compared with income. Price-to-income trends are mostly stable, but exploded upward during the bubble such that prices were more than five times income at the peak in 2005. By Zillow's analysis, most metro areas are far below pre-bubble pricing. Some are whoppers: Las Vegas is 25 percent below the historical trend and Detroit, 35 percent. But many are below trend by 10 percent or more.

"Even more astounding," Edelheit offers, "is to look at home prices in terms of the price of gold. You have to go back to 1979 to get houses this cheap." See Figure 13.6. "And this is based on national home price indexes," Edelheit continues. "If you were to consider that foreclosures, on average, sell for 30–40 percent lower than non-distressed homes, we might be looking at housing prices for foreclosures at the lowest since the 1950s or 1960s."

The individual deals are sometimes fantastic. Jan Brzeski manages Arixa Capital and writes of the values he's found in the Phoenix area. He's found homes selling for half of what they sold for in 1994—yes, 1994!

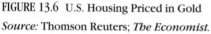

Ounces of gold required to purchase a median-priced new home in the United States

FIGURE 13.6 U.S. Housing Priced in Gold

Source: Thomson Reuters; *The Economist.*

Many houses sell for less than the cost to build them. Yet the population in the area continues to grow, practically guaranteeing a soaking up of such supply over time. Hence, the investment opportunity.

Today, it is easy to get 8 to 12 percent on your investment by renting a home. While many consumers seem unable to muster the financial muscle to buy or own a home, many can rent. Rental markets are busy.

"Property managers we talk with and do business with express to us the surging demand for rental homes," Edelheit reports. "One property manager gets around 50 calls a day inquiring about homes. In our rental portfolio of over 150 homes, only four are vacant." Vacancy rates are low, and rents are rising.

McKinley Capital Partners is another company looking to take advantage of the deals in housing. Backed by Och-Ziff's money, McKinley owns more than 300 homes in the San Francisco Bay Area. It bought these out of foreclosure. But check out the model.

The average purchase price is about $100,000. McKinley puts $10,000–25,000 into the house to improve it. Rental rates deliver an 8–12 percent return on investment. There is upside, too, if McKinley can sell the house down the road for more than it paid out of foreclosure.

There are other outfits doing the same thing in different parts of the country. G8 Capital, Waypoint Real Estate Group, and Carrington Property

Services are all pursuing the buy-rent strategy. The latter hopes to raise funds for a real estate investment trust, which would acquire foreclosed homes.

Housing is still a tangible asset with intrinsic value derived from its usefulness. People have to live somewhere. Different markets offer different opportunities, but there is a lot of room for investors to operate.

"The American Home Real Estate Co. is trying to be a bridge," Edelheit sums up, "between the strong rental demand, excess vacant housing supply, and investor demand for a professionally run single-family housing investment company." Sounds like a good idea to me.

To show you how things might go, I'll end with an analogy put forward by Bill Ackman, founder of Pershing Square Capital Management. He says that single-family rental homes (SFRHs) could become an asset class like timberland.

"For the vast majority of the twentieth century," Ackman says, "timber was never considered an institutional asset class." But led by investors, it did become such a thing, beginning in the 1980s. Timberland REITs and other timberland organizations evolved. By 2008, investors poured about $50 billion into timberland.

As Ackman puts it: "The same features that attracted institutional investors to timber, current yield, inflation protection, portfolio diversification, demand for 'hard assets' and the ability to create long-term tax-deferred gains, also apply to SFRHs."

Acquiring homes out of foreclosure and renting them is tough to play in the stock market, but investing in a housing recovery is much easier. There are title companies, home improvement stores, timber companies, homebuilders, and more to consider.

I want to end this chapter with a uniquely American investment, and one that I am a particular fan of.

Thrifty Deals

I'd like to call these special situations one of the market's best-kept secrets. Though many people still don't understand the basic mechanics, or even know these opportunities exist at all, the truth is that these aren't secrets.

Investing great Peter Lynch wrote two chapters about them in his bestselling book *Beating the Street*. (This is one of the best books about investing out there, by the way, along with *One up on Wall Street*. My well-thumbed hardcovers have made me a lot of money over the years.) Lynch called the idea a "can't-miss proposition (almost)."

And Seth Klarman, another famous and skilled investor, has a chapter about them in his book *Margin of Safety*. Even the measured Klarman, a

master of understatement, calls this special situation "a compelling investment opportunity."

I've been an enthusiast of these things for years. I first wrote about them
in 2005, but the timing wasn't quite right to get in then. Finally, the timing is
right. You would think such opportunities would close with all this coverage. Yet nearly every year, new deals crop up, and the opportunities persist.

I have a few hunches why more people still don't buy these. Part of it is that
they seem boring. Part of it is the payoff doesn't often come right away. Ideally,
you should look at these as three-year holds. (I'll tell you why in a few.) And
part of it is simply that people have prejudices that prevent them from buying.

So what am I talking about? I'm going to tell you, but I want you to keep
reading even if, initially, the idea has no appeal to you. It's important you
understand the full story before you pass judgment.

I'm talking about thrift conversions. A thrift, or a savings and loan, is a
bank. (I used to work for one.) But it is a special kind of bank. It is a bank
owned by its depositors. When a thrift goes public, it's called a "thrift conversion," because the thrift is converting from a company owned by depositors to one owned by public shareholders. This process is what creates the
investment opportunity. Let me give you a simplified example.

Say we have a thrift worth $100. For simplicity's sake, let's just say that
all of its assets are in cash, and it has no liabilities. The thrift decides to convert to a public thrift. So it sells 10 shares at $10 each. It has $200 in cash, and
there are 10 shares outstanding.

But look at it from the investor's point of view. He put $10 in, but he
owns a stock backed by $20 of cash—$200 divided by 10 shares outstanding. Put another way, he owns a bank at 50 percent of book value, or net
worth, per share.

In the real world, the values are not usually as extreme, but the idea is
much a reality. As Klarman writes:

> *The pre-existing net worth of the institution joins the investors' own
> funds, resulting, immediately, in a net worth per share greater than the
> investor's own contribution. In a real sense, investors in a thrift conver-
> sion are buying their own money and getting the pre-existing capital in
> the thrift for free.*

Peter Lynch called it the "hidden-cash-in-the-drawer rebate":

Imagine buying a house and then discovering that the former owners
have cashed your check for the down payment and left the money in an
envelope in a kitchen drawer, along with a note that reads: "Keep this, it
belonged to you in the first place." You've got the house, and it hasn't cost
you a thing. . . . This is the sort of pleasant surprise that awaits investors
who buy shares in any S&L that goes public for the first time.

It's simple. You get a bank at a big discount to book value, a book value that includes a whole bunch of fresh cash.

Most bank stocks over time gravitate toward book value, at least. What often happens to these thrifts is that they get bought out at premiums to book value. According to SNL, a research organization, about 59 percent of the 488 thrifts that have converted since 1982 have been bought out at a premium to book value. In recent years, the pattern is even stronger. Since 1995, 64 percent have been acquired. (I was a banker for 10 years as a corporate lender. One of those years was at a thrift, which then was bought out.)

The multiples paid are good. Most deals are done for 110 percent, even 140 percent, of book value. So, you can see the opportunity. If you pay even 80 percent of book value for a cash-rich thrift, and it trades to just book value, you've got a 25 percent gain, and you've taken little risk. You can do much better. But there are a few points you need to understand.

First, new thrifts have to follow some rules. One is that they can't sell for three years. This is why I said you should look at these investments as three-year holds. Ideally, you want to give the thrift time to ripen and give yourself a shot at maximum gains. (Lynch tells the story of Morris County Savings Bank. It went public at $10.75 per share and sold three years later for $65.)

You don't have to wait three years. But more good things can happen after that first year, and this gets us to our second point.

New thrifts can't buy back stock for at least one year. This is another important date in the life of a thrift, its one-year anniversary. After that, the thrift could use its ample cash to buy back stock at a discount to book value, thereby enriching the remaining shareholders even further.

Consider my simplified example above. If that thrift decided to buy back four shares after one year, what would happen? Let's say the shares trade for $13 per share one year after the conversion. Investors who bought the conversion are all happy, since they made 30 percent. (They paid $10 per share.) So, the thrift wants to buy back four shares, which would cost $52—that's four times $13 per share.

Since it had $200 in cash, it has $148 after the buyback, and there are six shares remaining. Look at what happens to book value per share. The $148 divided by the six remaining shares leaves $24.67 per share in book value.

It's like magic. The shareholders before owned $20 per share in book and own $24.67 per share. The buyback handed them an immediate gain of 23 percent in book value per share. And they still own a cash-rich bank at a big discount to book value. Big upside remains.

So after one year, if the thrift trades for less than book value, this is likely the best use of cash. And many thrifts do implement buybacks. In the last quarter of 2010 alone, five different thrifts announced buybacks of 5–10 percent of their shares.

Finally, one last point: There are no free lunches. Even here. That is to say you have to be careful which thrifts you buy. Some thrifts come with problems and risks you probably don't want to take. Remember the 1980s? Charles Keating in handcuffs? The S&L crisis? Lots of thrifts got in trouble doing all kinds of stupid things. Greedy guys always manage to ruin a good thing. You can easily avoid the problems with a little attention upfront to some key details.

Peter Lynch goes through some of his favorites in his book, and I've relied on his guidance when investing in these things over the years. There is a certain kind of thrift we want to own to increase our odds of success. Lynch calls them the "Jimmy Stewarts."

Surely, you've seen the classic *It's a Wonderful Life*, in which Jimmy Stewart plays the part of a humble banker at an old savings and loan. Lynch wants to find the Jimmy Stewarts. The no-frills, low-cost neighborhood thrifts that make old-fashioned mortgage loans. They don't have splashy advertising. They don't pay to have their names on stadiums. Their branches don't look like Greek temples.

So, the first thing we want to pay attention to is the loan portfolio. We want low-risk loans, like simple, old-fashioned mortgages. We don't want a lot of construction loans or anything that smacks of high finance. We want to look at nonperforming loans (stuff that's gone bad) as a percent of assets. Ideally, we want low numbers, like 2 percent.

Second, we want to look at financial strength. We want lots of equity. This is usually not hard to find with recently converted thrifts because they just went public and have lots of cash. It's common to find ones with equity to assets of 13 percent or 17 percent, or even 20 percent. For perspective, the nation's biggest banks—the JPMorgans and Citis—have ratios of 5 percent or 6 percent. (And that's, surely, overstated, given all the off-balance-sheet stuff. More likely, they have ratios of 1 percent or 2 percent.) This is why they are always getting in trouble. They operate with huge leverage. Thrifts are financially strong.

We want to look at book value. Ideally, we want to buy for less than book value, for all the reasons I went through above.

As Lynch advises, "Pick five S&Ls that fit the Jimmy Stewart profile, invest an equal amount in each of them, and await the favorable returns. One S&L would do better than expected, three OK, and one worse, and the overall result would be superior to having invested in an overpriced Coca-Cola or a Merck."

His comment brings me to a larger point. Taking the long view, making money in the stock market is easy. You buy stocks when they trade far below some standard of historical or absolute valuations, and you sell them when they get well above such bands.

Unfortunately, it is easier said than done because it requires you to buy stocks that most people don't like and that have poor outlooks.

But you get good pricing by standing alone with a thesis that few others share. It is hard on the nerves, but if it were easy, we'd have more Warren Buffetts.

I think such a buy has opened up in a much-hated sector: banks.

The last decade was a rough one for bank stocks. We can see this by looking at the valuation of the sector. The old bit of varnished wisdom on bank stocks was to buy them when they traded at a discount to book and sell them when they got to two times book. That rough guide worked with neat symmetry in the last cycle.

In 1998, bank stocks peaked at 245 percent of book value. They hit bottom in the aftermath of the credit crisis at 89 percent of book value. Today, the median price is just about 100 percent of book value. Say what you will about bank stocks—I can hear the "yes, buts"—the odds look favorable to the upside.

There are many problems with bank stocks these days. An old saying goes, "There are more banks than bankers." The idea is that many of the folks running banks are not bankers in the classic sense. They are gamblers with depositors' money.

You can see that in the number of bank failures in the wake of the 2008 crisis. You also see the bank and thrift index bottoms well before the failures peak. That index will lead the way out. This is consistent with historical experience. In the 1987–1993 commercial real estate debacle, which toppled over many banks, we saw the same pattern. From the bottom, reached early in the wave of bank failures, the index more than doubled over the next three years.

Might we see the same play again? I think we probably will.

There are a number of positive arguments to make for banks. First, most of the trends are going in the right direction. Bank failures are falling. Banks have recapitalized. Most banks have healthy loan loss reserves. If interest rates rise, that should help bank earnings as they charge new higher rates on loans and drag their feet paying depositors.

Plus, the best time to pick bank stocks is after they've all fallen over the waterfall and are bobbing around in the pool at the bottom. A lot of banks did not survive the fall or are shadows of their old selves. This means there is less competition for the well-capitalized banks that remain.

We will see a wave of consolidation in bank stocks. As banks look to grow, an easy way to do that is to buy a smaller institution. The fact that many smaller banks have lots of capital makes them even more attractive. New regulatory costs will make it harder for smaller banks. They will encourage consolidation and create larger banks.

The banks to buy are the small, traditional thrifts that are stuffed with money, as I pointed out. Recently converted thrifts are small banks loaded with cash and, usually, trading at a good discount to book value.

Joe Stillwell of Stillwell Partners has been active in this area. "What we're seeing now is almost too good to be true," he told *Grant's Interest Rate Observer* in 2010. "Clean, overcapitalized thrifts, with less competition than they've seen in years, are coming public at less than one-half of their value to private buyers."

Stillwell outlines what the thrift investor hopes for:

If you, over two, three, four, or five years, take your share count down, so you are then properly capitalized, you've increased your book value, and you've increased your franchise value per share. That's brilliance. And if at the same time . . . you're cutting costs and becoming more efficient, and the parking lot doesn't empty out at 4:59 p.m. every day, you have a chance to be a decent community bank, which, historically, is a 12–15 percent return on equity.

In short, you have a good little business that is sustainable.

So the thesis is as simple as the math. Buy a cash-rich thrift at less than book, hold for three to five years (from its conversion date), and you'll likely get bought at a premium. If not, odds are you'll have made good money as the book value grows and the discount shrinks.

The Best Investments for the Next 50 Years

It's hard to talk about the United States without mentioning one thing: its ability to produce entrepreneurs of exceptional talent. This is not something to underestimate.

Some of the most successful companies of the last half-century had one thing in common: a great entrepreneur/owner behind it. I am certain that the best investments of the next half-century will share this trait. It's simple and intuitive, yet I wonder why more investors don't focus more on it.

I'll use a simple analogy to reveal this idea. Let's say we have two houses. In one, the family that lives there owns it. In the other, there is an absentee owner who rents it out. If you had to guess which house would be in better shape after 10 years, which would you guess?

If you said the former, where the people who lived there owned it, odds are you'd be right. (There are always exceptions.) It's a truism in real estate that owners take better care of property than renters.

The same kind of logic applies in the stock market. When the people running the show are owners, what's known as the owner-operator model, those companies tend to deliver astonishing results over time.

Steve Bregman, a portfolio manager at Horizon Asset Management, recently shared a little experiment. He looked at "the most successful, iconic constituents of the S&P 500 over the past half-century." The impact of OOs was clear.

These include Wal-Mart. "Think how well it did under the aegis of Sam Walton for 20 years," Bregman says. Wal-Mart delivered a return of 20.5 percent annually. But after him, Wal-Mart returned only about 9 percent per year. Then, there is IBM. Under the Watson family, IBM returned 6.6 percent more than the stock market. After the Watsons, only 1.7 percent better than the market. "Good, but not great," Bregman says.

The most recent example of an OO's impact is Apple. Without Steve Jobs for over a decade, Apple turned in a return of 3.1 percent per year worse than the market. With him, 28 percent per year better. For the whole list, give Figure 13.7 a look.

Granted, this is not a scientific experiment, as Bregman notes. (There is scholarly research out there that backs the idea that stocks with owner-CEOs outperform.) But it does show you the importance of that OO.

In only two instances did the company under the OO trail the market. Even then, there is a big qualifier. The table shows that during Jobs I, his first tenure as CEO, Apple trailed the market. But it was only a four-year stretch, which he more than made up for later. And in any event, the table shows results only since the company has been public. If you consider the wealth created by Apple's initial public offering, a different picture emerges. Apple's IPO created more millionaires than any company in history. The original venture capitalists that backed Jobs made billions.

There is another advantage to OO-run companies that Bregman points to. The stocks have a low correlation to the S&P 500. In other words, returns were not as sensitive to the overall market as other stocks. Remember, a correlation of 1 means the stock matched the S&P 500 exactly. The lower the number, the less sensitive the stock to overall market movements.

On average, the OOs had a correlation of only 0.52. By contrast, the average of the largest 50 companies, excluding the OOs, is about 0.70. That is a big difference and meaningful when building a portfolio. The OOs are your stalwarts. They tend not to mirror the broader market.

In any case, this little experiment shows that there is something different about the decision-making process of an OO-run company from that of an ordinary company, and it shows up in returns.

As Bregman points out, there are strategic and tactical advantages to being an OO. You can make decisions that are "at dramatic odds with the mainstream, [whereas] most company managements are highly reactive to investor concerns." OOs focus on the business because they own it. They don't worry about the short-term stock price. Hired-gun CEOs think differently.

For example, the typical company today has accumulated cash, preparing for known risks, waiting for the "all clear" sign before investing. It seems like a good idea, but it's not what creates great piles of wealth. As Bregman puts it, they are "reacting to a crisis that already happened."

Company	Owner-Operator	Start Date	End Date	Tenure (years)	Annualized Return	S&P 500
Apple (I)	Steve Jobs	Dec-80	Jun-85	4	(10.6%)	8.1%
Apple (II)	Steve Jobs	Jan-97	Sep-10	14	34.3%	5.7%
Amazon	Jeff Bezos	May-97	Sep-10	14	40.6%	4.9%
Bed Bath & Beyond	Feinstein/Eisenberg	Jun-92	Sep-10	19	23.0%	8.0%
Dell	Michael Dell	Jun-88	Sep-10	23	24.5%	9.4%
Hewlett-Packard[1]	Hewlett/Packard	Jan-62	Sep-93	32	12.3%	6.1%
IBM[2]	Watson family	Jan-62	Jan-71	9	9.8%	3.2%
Intel[3]	A. Grove/G. Moore	Nov-82	Nov-04	22	20.3%	13.2%
Loews Corp.[4]	Tisch family	Jul-80	Sep-10	31	14.7%	10.9%
Leucadia National	Steinberg/ Cumming	Jun-78	Sep-10	33	24.2%	12.8%
Microsoft	Bill Gates	Mar-86	Jun-08	22	29.2%	10.5%
NIKE	Phil Knight	Dec-80	Sep-10	31	14.5%	10.8%
News Corp.[5]	Rupert Murdoch	May-86	Sep-10	25	6.7%	9.5%
Oracle	Larry Ellison	Mar-86	Sep-10	25	29.5%	9.5%
Polo Ralph Lauren	Ralph Lauren	Jun-97	Sep-10	14	10%	4.5%
Charles Schwab	Charles Schwab	Sep-87	Sep-10	23	23.1%	8.9%
Starbucks (I)	Howard Schultz	Jun-92	Jun-00	8	38.0%	20.0%
Starbucks (II)	Howard Schultz	Jan-08	Sep-10	3	18.1%	(1.1%)
Wal-Mart[6]	Sam Walton	Aug-72	Apr-92	20	20.5%	6.7%
Wynn Resorts	Steve Wynn	Oct-02	Sep-10	8	32.9%	6.8%

[1]Although William Hewlett and David Packard first offered shares to the public in 1957, share price data is only available back to January 1962.

[2]The Watson family has led IBM from the time that Thomas J. Watson became the general manager of Computing Tabulating Recording Corporation (later International Business Machines) in 1914. Watson's eldest son, Thomas Watson Jr., retired from the company in 1971. Although IBM was first listed on the NYSE in 1916, readily available prices begin in January 1962.

[3]Gordon Moore co-founded Intel with Robert Noyce in 1968. The company went public in 1971; however Intel share prices prior to 1982 are not readily available. Note that Andy Grove was Intel's third employee and ran the company until November 2004. It is Grove who is widely considered Intel's key business and strategic leader, and is described as having "participated in founding Intel".

[4]Brothers Preston Robert Tisch and Laurence Tisch began what would come to be Loews Corporation in 1956, and Loews went public in 1959. However, prices are currently only readily available from July 1980.

[5]News Corp was incorporated in Australia in 1979; however, share price data is only available to May 1986.

[6]Wal-Mart was initially traded over-the-counter in 1970. It was listed on the NYSE in 1972, which is when readily available share price data begins.

FIGURE 13.7 The Triumph of Owner Operators

Source: Horizon Kinetics, LLC.

By contrast, look at the OOs. OOs accumulated cash before the downturn. So rather than continuing "to husband cash, they have been investing it assertively for the last two years."

Take AutoNation, an example from Bregman's own portfolio. In 2011, there were 13 percent fewer dealerships than there were in 2008, which sounds scary. Yet AutoNation repurchased 17 percent of its shares during this rough period. The stock hit 52-week highs, and that investment paid off handsomely.

So, that's the case for OOs in a nutshell. It doesn't mean there aren't great investments without OOs, but OOs do tip the odds in your favor. I prefer to invest in owner-operators. The United States has produced a fair number of capable OOs, and I expect it will continue to do so.

I think there are many opportunities in the United States of America, more than I can touch on here. For all my globe-trotting in overseas markets, the great bulk of my portfolio is still in companies that call America home. They may have attractive businesses overseas and play well on international trends, but they are still headquartered in New York, or Dallas, or Garfield Heights, Ohio, or Littleton, Colorado.

For investors, America is still a land of many opportunities.

Five Key Takeaways

- America is rich in natural resources. I touched on phosphate, coal, oil, and gas. Check out Stonegate Agricom, Cline Mining, and Resolute Energy as representative examples of the kinds of investments that I like in these areas. And don't forget natural gas. Matt Ridley's shale gas report is worth reading. Check it out here: www.thegwpf .org/images/stories/gwpf-reports/Shale-Gas_4_May_11.pdf.
- America still has plenty of manufacturing muscle. American aircraft suppliers are one such area of strength.
- Top-secret America is another big U.S. trend: increased spending on intelligence, surveillance, and covert capabilities. Check out Kratos Defense & Security Solutions for a pure play on national security.
- American homes are cheap, and smart money is increasingly looking to U.S. housing as an investment. (You can learn more about Edelheit's company by contacting him at info@americanhome company.com. Note: There is a $100,000 minimum investment, and it's open to accredited investors only.)
- Thrift conversions are a uniquely American opportunity. You can find recently converted thrifts by checking out SNL's Thrift Investor (www.snl.com).

CHAPTER 14

An Investor's Guide to the World Right Side Up

W e both reached for the check. "No, no, I invited you," I said. "I'll pay." Then my guest made an offer I couldn't refuse.

"Come on, we're in markets. Let's flip for it."

Well, how could I resist that? Everyone in markets, from the careful investor to highflying speculator, learns to live with chance, and even to relish it. It's part of the thrill of markets (and life); you just never know how things might play out.

So, we flipped. I called heads. Heads it was. And Frank Holmes paid for dinner.

Frank is the CEO and chief investment officer of U.S. Global Investors, which is a mutual fund company with a slate of award-winning funds. We met him earlier in the book on our Colombia jaunt, and my meeting with him serves as a nice capstone to our journey.

We met at Cookshop in Chelsea, Manhattan, a restaurant that favors seasonally available and locally sourced ingredients prepared simply. (We had excellent split-roasted chicken, cooked over a wood fire. Worth a visit if you are in the area.) We had a great conversation that covered seemingly everything.

One of the things we talked about was S-curves, which is kind of the house salad at U.S. Global. Holmes explained what this macro scenario is and why his firm relentlessly seeks them out. Take a look at Figure 14.1, which shows you a generic curve. The main thing here is to invest in the middle part of the curve, when growth accelerates.

It's a simple idea, which is part of its appeal. And there are many historical examples, in population growth, oil consumption, and demand for cars, among many other things. It's loosely based on an idea by economist Simon

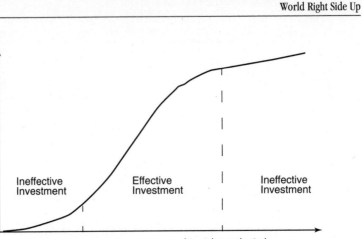

FIGURE 14.1 What to Look For: An S-Curve

Source: US Global Investors.

Kuznets, who found long cycles (around 20 years) of boom times around an increase in infrastructure spending.

One historical example is the U.S. interstate highway system in the 1950s. "This system of interstate highways consumed 55 percent of the world's commodities," Frank said. It led to a great flourishing of businesses that had no reason to exist before. Motels, gas stations, and restaurants spread across the great highways of America. It reduced travel times between cities. For example, travel time between:

- Seattle and Portland declined by nearly 25 percent.
- Cleveland and New York City declined by a third.
- Atlanta and Birmingham declined by nearly 40 percent.
- Chicago and Minneapolis declined by nearly 25 percent.

It created a more mobile society and had a profound effect on businesses. Think about what it meant for truckers, retailers, and managing inventories. "We try to take a look at this model, look at emerging countries, and go back and forth in history trying to identify where they are on this S-curve," Frank said.

What's driving the big S-curves of today's economy? Population growth is one thing. It took over a century for world population to move from 1 billion to 2 billion (from roughly 1805 to 1927), but only 40 years to go from 3 billion to 6 billion (from 1960 to 2000). So looking at Figure 14.2, you can see this giant S-curve we've been through, and you can reflect on the dramatic changes that took place in the steep part of that curve.

"What's significant here is that in the 1970s, the world's population was half of what it is today," Frank pointed out. "China and India had no global

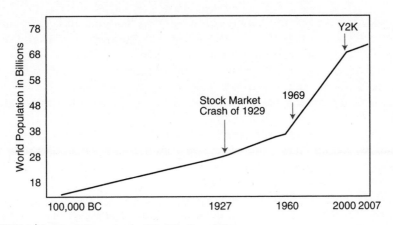

FIGURE 14.2 The S-Curve in the World's Population
Source: US Global Investors.

footprints then." Russia was behind the Iron Curtain. Today, they are embracing an infrastructure build-out that will be as dramatic in effects as the interstate highway system was for the United States.

Following that S-curve, you will find we're in the middle of similar curves today in the demand for these items:

- Cars
- Electricity
- Steel
- Oil

Frank made some interesting points about cars. In developing markets, most people pay for cars with cash. "Loyalty for car buyers in the United States and Europe is not to the car buyers," Frank said, "but to who will give them the money, because over 90 percent of all cars have a note against them. But in Africa . . . it is a cash trade." That leaves them less sensitive to global financial markets. So, in 2008, when the world was falling apart, Nigeria actually had positive growth. So did Mozambique. These were predominantly cash economies.

Another way to get at the S-curve model is to think of water. It can be a solid, liquid, or gas. There is a temperature at which dramatic things happen. "The same thing happens with demographics, consumption or GDP per capita," Frank maintained. There is a certain point at which dramatic changes take place and put you on the steeply sloped part of the S-curve.

Governmental policy drives a lot in this analysis, and Frank mentioned it often. Government is a precursor to change. "China has gone from a communist country to a socialist country to slowly moving toward capitalism," he said. The S-curve in China began with Deng Xiaoping and the opening up of China. The largest real estate transfer in the world was when China gave citizens plots of land. "This was very significant," Frank notes, "even though these leases are for 40 to 60 years, because it's a transfer of wealth, which the Chinese are able to borrow against, sell, and trade."

Greater freedoms led to the creation of a rising middle class. Today, China has the second-largest number of billionaires in the world. "These are not oligarchs, like in Russia" Frank pointed out. "These are people that are basically getting Pizza Huts." They are entrepreneurs, starting businesses and growing them. "What happens when you get 60 million people making $100,000 a year? What does it change?"

It changes a lot. It means a lot of people want air conditioners, cars, and homes. It means a lot more coal, steel, and metals. The power of TV and the Internet helps fuel this desire. "Everyone in the world wants what we have. They can see it. And they want that dream. They are willing to work 60, 70 hours a week to get that," Frank explained. "They are not out picketing on Wall Street."

So, how does this tie back into making money in markets around the world?

U.S. Global starts with a comparison between the E-7 and G-7 countries (essentially, the big emerging markets versus the big developed markets). The E-7 countries have half the world's population, but only 20 percent of the world's output. The G-7 is the opposite. Take a look Figure 14.3.

E7	Pop. (million)*	Nominal GDP (bn USD) 2010*	G7	Pop. (million)*	Nominal GDP (bn USD) 2010*
China	1,330	5,879	United States	310	14,582
India	1,173	1,729	Japan	127	5,498
Indonesia	243	707	Germany	82	3,310
Brazil	201	2,088	France	65	2,560
Pakistan	184	175	UK	62	2,246
Russia	139	1,480	Italy	61	2,051
Mexico	112	1,040	Canada	34	1,574
Total	3,382	13,098	Total	741	31,821
	49% of world total	21% of world total		11% of world total	50% of world total

*As of December 2010.

FIGURE 14.3 Catching Up: E-7 versus G-7

Source: U.S. Global Investors.

Frank looks for certain things, like a favorable tax policy or an infra-structure spending plan. "We create a relative valuation model to see where shifts are happening around the world," he said. With this view, U.S. Global can plot other countries and compare them to the G-7 and E-7 framework, so he remains in the most favorable situations.

Many interesting insights come from such work. For instance, Frank's plotted out the infrastructure spending plans of the E-7. It's a huge amount of money, some $6 trillion over the next three years alone—that will fuel commodity demand. He mentioned China's high-speed rail as something that "will change everything." Again, the highway analogy comes to mind. The rail system will span 24,000 miles and link up 240 cities and 700 million people. Think of all the trade that will unlock, just as with the U.S. highway system, only on a much bigger scale.

The final proof for these things is, as they say, in the eating. In searching for S-curves, Frank and his team have uncovered many gems to put up the kind of performance numbers they have. U.S. Global Investors was an early investor in the new Colombia, for instance. It seeded Pacific Rubiales at 25 cents per share. Today, it's C$22 per share and has been as high as C$35 per share.

Finding gems like that makes it all worth it. You only have to get rich once. If you had put $10,000 with Frank's Global Resources Fund in 2000, you'd have nearly $60,000 today. And that was during a rough decade for stocks. (If you had put the $10,000 in the S&P 500, you'd have about $11,000 today.) This goes to show you—if you can get past the noise and paralyzing fear, there are plenty of opportunities out there in all kinds of markets.

Another Way to Invest in S-Curves

You can invest in any of U.S. Global's award-winning funds and let them look for the S-curves for you. You can invest in U.S. Global itself, which trades on the NASDAQ under the symbol GROW.

GROW is a money manager. The usual rule of thumb for money manag-ers is to pay no more than 3 percent of assets under management (AUM) plus tangible book value. It is generally hard to lose money with money managers if you follow this rule, unless the manager just flames out.

As I write, GROW's tangible book value is $2.67 per share. As of Sep-tember 30, its fiscal year-end, GROW managed $2.6 billion. So if you do the math, you get an upper bound around $8 per share. You can easily update these calculations anytime.

Insiders own 15 percent of the stock. Overwhelmingly, this is Frank's stake. He's been a steady buyer of the stock on the open market over the last few years, too. In 2011, he bought over $250,000 worth of stock at a range of prices, paying as much as $10 per share. But he was a buyer all last year and in 2009 (as far back as I have records), paying as much as $14 per share. So he's vested in making this work. I love investing in situations like this, in which you have a smart, capable chief who is a big owner as well.

The trends are good at GROW, too. In 2011 (fiscal year ended September), AUM was up 11 percent, revenues were up 20 percent, and earnings per share were up 46 percent. And I like the dividend, which comes to 24 cents annually as I write.

GROW has a stable of funds with good track records and top rankings. Lipper ranked the World Precious Metals Fund at number four and the Gold and Precious Metals Fund at number nine. Lipper names GROW's Global Resources Fund number one by total return over the last 10 years in a category of 30 such funds. Overall, GROW has won 29 Lipper awards since 2000.

I tell you all of this because these rankings are important in growing that AUM figure over time. Moreover, AUM, either by winning new clients or by continued good results, drives the fees GROW earns and, in turn, those earnings per share. I am confident that GROW's product line will continue to deliver the goods. About 70 percent of GROW's AUM is from retail investors and the rest from institutional clients. Good funds are important in attracting both.

GROW's focus on emerging markets and commodities is appealing, as I think there are lots of opportunities here. The market hit these areas hard in the downturn, but the long-term opportunities remain. They simply got cheaper.

In his annual letter, Frank reflects on the wide market swings we've seen. "I've lived through many market cycles," he writes, "and have learned that there are always opportunities in global markets." He goes on:

Global markets present tremendous opportunities to those able to sort out what's meaningful from the background noise. . . . We believe actions should be shaped by knowledge, beliefs, and values, not emotions. When investors understand volatility, they can manage market movements better and make better decisions. They can steer their financial ships with confidence, rather than sitting powerless and being pushed around by the market's powerful tides.

I share these views. The United States Trust Co. of New York used to run an advertisement with the tag line "The toughest time to invest is always now." It's a rare instance of truth in advertising. There are always bad things happening, and if there aren't bad things happening, there are always people warning that bad things are about to happen.

It's frustrating and annoying when you are holding stocks that are getting thrashed, but this is how opportunities are born. If the market were always coolly rational and evenhanded in weighing stock prices, it would be a more difficult market to make any money in. The market, thankfully, makes lots of mistakes.

U.S. Global Investors is a good buy. You get paid nearly 4 percent for holding a cash-rich, debt-free money manager with a proven record. We have all the incentives lined up, as Frank Holmes owns a large stake in the business. As opportunities open up in the far corners of the world, we can be sure Frank will be among the first ones to find them.

Envoi

Investment ideas and observations may seem to have the shelf life of a carton of milk, but the book you hold in your hands is timeless. Sure, over the next couple of years, some of the specific analysis will be overcome by events and become out of date.

But as this process continues, the book becomes more of a historical record and a reference. Frankly, I wish there were more books like this one, written by investors about different places, themes, and eras. It would be wonderful if I could pick up a book written by a fellow investor on India in 1980 and another in 1960 and yet another in 1940. It would be great to compare notes, to see what investors thought then, and how trends played out. I'd be fascinated to see if certain themes persisted—if, say, investors fingered hotels as a great investment opportunity in 1940, 1960, and in 1980. That would make you question the validity of the idea and ask why it seems to persist.

I've dreamed of a treasure-trove of like-minded investor travelogues from South Africa, Colombia, Brazil, or China. Wouldn't it have been instructive to get a report from someone in Australia just as it opened up the great veins of iron ore and other goodies to China? Or to wander beside an investor picking his way through Southeast Asia in the early 1950s before things got ugly? Or to read an investor's view of Argentina in the 1920s when it was among the richest economies in the world? Those would make for absorbing reading. They would inform our present-day efforts immensely.

Alas, such a library does not exist. There are books here and there. Jim Rogers has a pair, including the classic *Investment Biker*. And Mark Mobius has contributed with *Passport to Profits*. There are some others, but believe me, the library is thin, indeed.

Most investors don't think it a great loss, but most investors have a way of discounting the past or ignoring it completely. This is a big mistake. I hope I've shown the ways in which past experiences (history) intertwine with and inform present-day investment opportunities. It's a great field of study, without much competition.

Maybe this will change as the world turns right side up. In the past, the Western markets were so far ahead of everyone else that no one else really mattered, and many markets around the world remained closed. You couldn't write an investment book on opportunities in the Soviet Union in 1980. Those markets were behind the Iron Curtain. Around the world, in a similar fashion, many markets were simply off-limits.

That has changed. Investors' perspectives will have to change. Perhaps this book will sit on the shelves of some investors in the year 2020 as a reference book and inspiration for their own globe-trotting. Maybe they'll be happy readers who have profited from the advice within. I'd like to think so.

Well, we've come to the end of our journey. We've covered an awful lot of ground in the previous pages. For me, the adventure continues. There are new markets to explore and new opportunities to dig up. Older markets change and become new again. I'll keep writing, thinking, traveling, and asking questions. It's a never-ending pursuit that I encourage you to join. Besides making a little money and learning about the world, it is a lot of fun.

Final Takeaways

- Check out U.S. Global Investors. Their website's wealth of information will help you find out more on how to invest in its excellent funds as they search the world for S-curves. The website is www.usfunds.com.
- You can invest in U.S. Global Investors itself. The ticker is GROW. As I write, it is a debt-free, cash-rich gem with a proven insider, and it evens pays a dividend.
- Enjoy the hunt. I hope to you meet out there on the trail someday!

About the Author

Chris Mayer worked for a decade as a corporate banker before founding the newsletter *Capital & Crisis* in 2004, and later *Mayer's Special Situations*. His one-of-a-kind research goes out to over 20,000 readers worldwide. You'll find Chris as a regular columnist at *The Daily Reckoning* and oft-quoted at *MarketWatch*. He's been a guest on *Forbes on Fox*, CNN Radio, CNBC, and other TV and radio programs. He travels the world looking for the absolute best deals, and shows his readers how to get in (and out) of the market's most attractive investments. In 2008, he published his first book, *Invest Like a Dealmaker: Secrets from a Former Banking Insider*.

Index